Alpine Gardening

by the same author

★

THE PROPAGATION OF ALPINES
ALPINES WITHOUT A GARDEN
RUSSIAN COMFREY

★

(with E. H. Haywood)
RAPID TOMATO RIPENING

To Frances

The splendid autumn flowering Gentian—*G. sino-ornata*
(*From the* Botanical Magazine *by courtesy of the Royal Horticultural Society*)

ALPINE GARDENING

by

LAWRENCE D. HILLS

FABER AND FABER
24 Russell Square
London

First published in mcmlv
by Faber and Faber Limited
24 Russell Square London W.C.1
Printed in Great Britain by
R. MacLehose and Company Limited
The University Press Glasgow

To

MY MOTHER

Who has a garden now

Contents

PREFACE   *page* 11

1. THE ALPINE BANK   13

2. THE ALPINE BORDER   24

3. THE DRY WALL   61

4. ALPINE PATHS AND ALPINE LAWNS   89

5. THE SMALL ROCK GARDEN   106

6. ALPINE SOILS   138

7. ALPINES PLANT BY PLANT   147

8. PROPAGATING ALPINES   278

   APPENDIX   311

   INDEX   335

5

Illustrations

Gentiana sino-ornata   *frontispiece*

1. The Alpine Bank with massed Helianthemums   *facing page* 16
2. Polygonum vacciniifolium   17
3. Oenothera missouriensis   32
4. Iberis sempervirens Little Gem   33
5. An Alpine Border of Ericas   96
6. Campanula carpatica White Star   97
7. Fritillaria Meleagris   112
8. Hypsela longiflora and Selliera radicans   113
9. Narcissus cyclamineus   128
10. Mazus reptans   128
11. Narcissus bulbocodium   129
12. Nierembergia rivularis   129
13. An example of good Dry Wall planting   144
14. Convolvulus mauritanicus   145
15. Campanula Poscharskyana   160
16. Helianthemums as Wall Plants   161
17. Acaena microphylla   176
18. Polygala Chamaebuxus rubra   177
19. A Natural outcrop in the Welsh mountains   192
20. A small rock garden in Cheddar stone   193
21. An outcrop garden in Sandstone   193
22. A Chelsea Flower Show Water Garden   208
23. Primula Florindae   209
24. Ramonda Myconi   209
25. Campanula garganica   240
26. Erodium macradenum   241
27. Gentiana lagodechiana   256
28. Leontopodium alpinum (Edelweiss)   256
29. Silene Schafta   257
30. Saxifrage Burseriana cuttings   288
31. The Kabschia System of plunging   289
32. Conifer cuttings with and without Hormones   304
33. Ramonda leaf cuttings inserted   305
34. Rooted and unrooted Ramonda leaf cuttings   308

7

Figures in the Text

1. Alpine Border for a small garden   *page* 25
2. Plan of a large Alpine Border   26
3. A Dry Wall to hold a high bank   69
4. An outcrop in the Cheddar Gorge   107
5. The principles of Rock garden building   114
6. Diagram of a water garden   123
7. *Androsace sarmentosa* with runners   155
8. *Antirrhinum Asarina* seed pods   157
9. Stem-rooting Aubrieta cutting   164
10. Flowering size *Cyclamen neapolitanum* corm   180
11. Stem-rooting Dianthus cutting   185
12. Pre-flowering cutting of *Gentiana sino-ornata*   198
13. Rooted cutting of *Gentiana Macaulayi*   199
14. Dividing *Iris pumila*   213
15. Branch of Lithospermum showing cutting   219
16. Inserted cutting of *Lithospermum* Heavenly Blue   220
17. *Morisia hypogaea* lifted for propagation   224
18. Root cuttings of Morisia   224
19. Pan of Morisia root cuttings   225
20. Morisia cutting, two months' growth   226
21. *Primula denticulata* lifted for propagation   243
22. *Primula denticulata* root cutting   245
23. A division of *Selliera radicans*   260
24. *Sisyrinchium bellum* seed vessels   264
25. Pot plant of *Viola arenaria rosea*   273
26. Ripening Viola seed pod   274
27. Box cutting frame   281
28. Concrete cutting frame   282
29. Helianthemum cutting with bud   283
30. Helianthemum branch showing cuttings   284
31. 'Making' a Helianthemum cutting   285
32. The cutting inserted   287
33. Helianthemum cutting ready to pot   288
34. Lithospermum cutting rooted with Hortomone   289

Figures in the Text

35. Lithospermum cutting without Hortomone   290
36. *Armeria caespitosa* cuttings   292
37. Hand action in making small cuttings   292
38. A 'stripping' cutting of *Linum alpinum*   294
39. Kabschia Saxifrage cutting   294
40. Kabschia Saxifrage cutting inserted   295
41. Summer germinating weeds   299
42. Summer germinating weeds   299
43. Dying flower of *Gentiana Farreri*   307
44. Pod of *Gentiana Farreri* after stripping   308

Preface

Alpine gardening is simply gardening with Alpines, the small and brilliant plants from the mountains of the world that can be chosen to flower at almost any time of year except the depths of winter. The rock garden is only one of the many ways in which they can bring colour and ever-changing interest even to the smallest and most cat- and soot-infested town garden on the worst and coldest soil.

Most amateur gardeners know only five or six alpines. This book is concerned with the easiest, hardiest and most rewarding six hundred with the widest range of garden uses; in the miniature herbaceous border, the alpine bank, the alpine path or lawn, the dry wall and finally the rock and water garden where wise choice and skill can reduce the weed problem so greatly that they are no more trouble than herbaceous plants or shrubs.

In the Preface to *Alpines Without a Garden*, I mentioned this book as a companion volume dealing with rock gardens from doormat size upwards and these are covered fully from the viewpoint of the pan gardener who finds (as I have) that at last he has the joy of expanding to hearthrug area and more. The great rock gardens that take a whole-time gardener to keep them weeded are passing like the sailing ships, but there is no reason why the little rock gardens that an amateur can build in a weekend should not be as well made and successful as any masterpiece of the expert landscape gardener. It is a matter of knowing your rock and knowing your plants and the main purpose of this book is to introduce my many small and growing friends to those whose horizon is limited by Aubrieta, Arabis, blue Veronica, one Sedum, a mossy Saxifrage and that silver-grey weed, the Cerastium.

This is not therefore a book for the expert who finds his pleasure in growing ever more difficult species in pans in an alpine house, relishing their difficulty rather as others enjoy solving *The Times* crossword puzzle. Nor is it a complete book on alpines for if I described as fully as I did the simple and hardy plants with which I dealt (all the 2,500 species) in my *The Propagation of Alpines*, this would take about five books the size of this one, and there are many more still that I do not know.

Preface

This is purely a gardener's book about how to know, grow and use alpines in the many ways that I have found successful in my twenty years with these captivating little plants. Therefore, though the *R.H.S. Gardening Dictionary* (1951 edition) has been taken as the standard authority on plant names, this is not an authoritative reference work on this aspect. One of the problems of the amateur (even greater for the nurseryman) is the changing of the botanical names under which all species are known, for few have popular names in English. I have used in every case the names in widest common use, for my purpose is not to debate with scholars but to help gardeners to know more alpines and to grow them successfully. Those who miss a well-known plant because they happen to know it by a newer (or older) name should look first in the index where as many as possible of these alternative names will be found.

Readers of *Alpines without A Garden* will not find all the small species for miniature gardens in these pages, but except for a few that are mentioned as part hardy, like Crassula sarcocaulis, all the other miniature species can be grown as well in the open. Use both books, and rejoice that you can grow more and different alpines now that you can expand beyond window sill space.

Once again my first thanks must go to my enthusiastic voluntary typist, Miss P. M. Lyall and to Mr. H. G. Lyall for his extensive notes on the Primulas which he grows with such great skill. My gratitude is also due to Mr. G. H. Preston of Kew for helpful advice and photographic facilities, to Miss Whitely of the Lindley Library and Mr. Alan Hinshelwood for assistance in many problems, and finally to Mr. Peter Marter who read the book in MSS. I wish also to thank the Editors of the *R.H.S. Journal* and Curtis's *Botanical Magazine* for the use of the frontispiece and Mr. G. G. Whitelegg for Plate 22. It was on his nursery, when I was twenty-two, that I first grew alpines and I have grown them ever since. I like them, and that is really why I have written this book.

LAWRENCE D. HILLS

BARNET, *April* 1953
BRAINTREE, *December* 1954

I

The Alpine Bank

The rock garden is an attempt to reproduce a natural rock formation in the garden, landscape painting with plants and stone in colours that change through the year from the first Saxifrage to the last Gentian. However well or badly we build, we are modelling our work on nature, even though our plants come from the mountains of the whole world and our jutting outcrop of Cheddar stone is set in Essex clay. It is, however, a man-made convention with some rules that are as fixed as the laws of perspective, a form of art as unnatural as drawing animals on cave walls. Men do it because it gives them pleasure, we like to look at things in bloom, and how we use them in our gardens is a matter of taste, our taste; the only failures are if the result fails to please, like a bad painting (usually because too much has been attempted in a small space or because we have mixed our conventions), or the plants die.

There is no law that says 'if you want to grow alpines you must have rock' any more than there is one that Geraniums must be grown with Lobelia. Very many of them grow better without any conventional rock garden, especially those which are not naturally found on small outcrops in high hills, and they often develop new good qualities and garden uses when they are used away from the 'rockery'.

The Alpine Bank

When you look at an alpine bank at any time during the summer but especially in June, July or August, distantly from a bedroom window or at close range, it makes you wonder why rocks were ever introduced into the garden at all. Rock has its very valuable use in providing a natural setting and conditions for small species, but the alpine bank is a garden feature as colourful as, though for a far longer season than, an Iris garden or a costly Rhododendron bed. It is an example of changing the convention to use 'colours' which are never seen to the best advantage, to paint a different sort of picture altogether.

13

The Alpine Bank

The alpine bank is simply Helianthemums or Sun Roses planted in bulk on a slope that may be as steep as a railway cutting, about 45° (a square halved cornerways) or as gentle as one in four. Other plants may be included, but the main blaze of colour comes from the race which has been most scorned and crippled by the rock garden. No-one who has grown only the old double red Mrs. Earle, or any single Sun Rose, rather despised because it swamps treasured species, has any idea of how glorious these cheap, common, drought-resisting and cold-despising plants are when given their heads and allowed to riot in what is far nearer their natural conditions than even the best-built outcrop of the most expensive stone.

The majority of the fifty or more varieties in cultivation (see Chapter 7 for a full descriptive list) have single flowers, varying from the size of a shilling to that of half a crown, in reds, crimsons, pinks, flames, yellows, oranges, even browns, in every possible combination of self-colour and contrasting centre, and every shade between. There are about ten double varieties, but no blues or any related colours like violet or mauve; the colours are all pure and clear. They start flowering often in May, with stragglers, blaze through the summer and produce stray blooms often as late as October. One bush will not do this, but with a full range and a great number of individual plants, the display must be seen to be believed.

The best alpine bank I have ever seen was on three sides of a tennis court cut into a hill side, the back was over fifteen feet high, solid Helianthemums, their colours contrasting, and their evergreen foliage ranging from grey white to dark green, still improving on a bare bank of mainly hungry subsoil even in winter. The best I ever owned was about thirty feet long, rising to a thorn hedge, about four feet high sloping to two feet at the far end, with a maximum slope of about one in two. It replaced a weedy grass bank of nettles and horseradish and was, with roughly twenty varieties, the finest display of anything in that garden; it made one forget all the achievement of a bed of rare Gentians, and look forward to Helianthemum time.

You can plant small ones, on the bank of soil at the bottom of the lawn, which is going to look like a long grave however you build it if there is no room to come forward and break the rigid line, beside the drive-in to the garage where the subsoil has been heaped against the wall or (as I did) slanting beside a lawn so that the distorted line of the perspective gives an impression of far greater distance than there is in a small garden.

You can make them large, always providing that they are not steeper than the natural triangle slope of soil at rest, using ladders to plant on a grand scale, for the many bare and hungry banks that there are in gardens where each house sits on a flat foundation, going like a staircase step by step up 'Hillview Road' to 'Fairview Heights', and the result on any soil other than absolutely naked chalk rock, is just as good.

The alpine bank is not a rock garden set on edge for those who cannot afford good limestone, with the weed problem multiplied because it is all plants, or the herbaceous border tilted sharply with weeding, lifting, splitting and staking all to be done in addition to the normal work on the flat. Both these penalties would be gladly accepted by those who had really seen one in glowing health, especially where a large proportion of the garden was this sort of awkward waste space.

It uses the very qualities that make the Helianthemum a bad rock garden plant. The mass of foliage which crushes the small Campanula or Dianthus meets in a solid floor below which annual weeds struggle to germinate. If the preliminary weeding is done well, the work of keeping the alpine bank clean dwindles, new seeds are not brought to the surface, as it need never be dug, and it stays planted and permanent for an average of four years; after this some plants will die out, but replacements are so easily raised that this is no worry. The majority keep on spreading, apart from any self-sown seedlings.

The time spent in weeding and care is a fraction of that of the normal rock garden, and though the number of plants required is large, even the man who does not think ahead but buys by the hundred at a reduction from any nursery for such cheap and easy plants, the cost is relatively low. Compared with a dry wall to hold a bank of the same height in bought stone, or a rock garden with individual pieces large enough to cut out the effect of a flight of steps, plants are cheaper than rock, mainly because of the great increase in transport charges.

Where one has only concrete lumps, brick burrs, flints or other horrors available and any rock garden is going to look as unnatural as a load of hardcore shot down a hillside, you cannot make a natural rock garden. Therefore it is better to make a good alpine bank which is not modelled on a rock formation but is meant to give formal pleasure to the eye like an avenue of flowering cherries or a clipped yew hedge, than the sort of mess that Reginald Farrar called 'A Devil's Lapful'.

The limitation is that the bank must be in full sun or have sun for a considerable part of the day. Helianthemums will not thrive in shade, and without their full colour range, soil-retaining roots, and leaves that stay on and shield the earth from winter rain washing, the other suitable plants cannot do the job. In shade you must find other ways out, some

15

through alpine gardening, but where you have got a bank that is suitable, rejoice as if you had moved to a house in whose garden Azaleas grew like weeds.

Making the Alpine Bank

The small bank, or one at an angle that allows easy standing, is simple to plant and weed, but where one gets much over four or five feet, and there is not a lawn or path above on which to lie and reach down to cover the upper part, permanent steps are needed. There is no need to climb up often, but it must be possible to reach any part of the surface with safety.

It is no use fitting in large rocks on the surface or even sinking them a little way in the ground: the moving thrust of your weight as you stretch to weed, take cuttings or replace will work it loose. Use something like old kerbstones, broken concrete fence posts, or stout wood well creosoted like the top of a gate post, tunnel out a hole at an angle pointing down into the bank and ram it in hard so only about six inches stick out. Then your weight is trying to lift the whole bank, and you have a permanent method of moving about, though the stones will be hidden by the foliage.

An ordinary pair of steps is little use for it is made to stand beside something upright like a wall; reaching sideways from steps standing at the foot of a bank is awkward and dangerous if you fall with bad luck, and if you lean them against the bank your feet slip, because the steps slope the wrong way. A ladder is best, but to give more than toe hold on the rungs as it lies flat against the bank, it wants stout wooden blocks about two and a half inches thick screwed or nailed to the underside, with a board across to stop them sinking in, very much like the sort of fixture needed on a ladder used for painting a big greenhouse. On the large alpine bank mentioned earlier, a pair of iron 'feet' with a kind of bracket had been made by a blacksmith, to bolt on through holes in the ladder sides whenever it was needed. This applies, of course, only where the bank is on the same scale as a Chelsea Flower Show gold-medal-winning rock garden.

The best time to make an alpine bank is in the spring, February, March or April, and the first and most important job is clearing the perennial weeds. Where the bank is poor subsoil there will be very few, but these should come out, because as fertility builds up they will increase. These weeds are convolvulus, dock, thistle (all kinds), dandelion, nettle (the big one with yellow roots like steel wire for strength), couch grass (twitch, scutch or whatever its local name may be), and any other unpleasant variants you may have, like the celandine with roots like a

1. The Alpine Bank in full glory of massed Helianthemums. There are about two dozen varieties ranging from pale yellow to crimson in this part of the author's Bank at Wells, Somerset. With Alpine Phlox for early colour the display continues from April to the Autumn, with less weeding than any herbaceous border, and no staking

2. *Polygonum vacciniifolium* is an ideal Alpine Bank plant for a poor soil and full sun. Its thicket of pale pink spires in late autumn extends the display still further, and its evergreen, weed-suppressing foliage makes it valuable on the rock garden. Photographed at Kew in October

collection of little milk bottles that scatter at a touch. Distinguishing these weeds is important, because they cannot be grown with alpines, and the more that come out at the start the less trouble in the future. Ignorance of the difference between perennial weeds which should go straight to the bonfire, because even their smallest root fragments will grow, and annual weeds which will decay without trouble, is the main reason why the expensive modern jobbing gardener is such a bad bargain.

The same care in digging out these persistent roots should be used even where it is possible, with a low bank of poor soil, to spread a layer of better stuff over the surface, for they will only come through and rejoice in the richer food.

All the plants to be grown on the alpine bank are those which thrive in poor soil, but they are not natural colonisers of acid subsoil, therefore the treatment varies. If the soil is good enough to grow chickweed, grounsel, fathen and the normal weeds of a good vegetable garden, then no manuring or extra humus is required; the routine is simply to get out the weeds, level off the surface of slope, and plant. If it is growing colts-foot, with large rounded leaves, grey white on the undersides, rosebay willowherb (*Lythrum salicifolium*, the bombed site weed) or Oxford Ragwort, which has yellow daisy flowers and much cut lacy leaves, it is subsoil or near it in poverty.

In this case, if the angle of slope permits real digging, put in leaf-mould, hop manure, or compost and scatter about 2 oz. to the square yard of a complete fertiliser before you dig. Weigh 2 oz. and see how much it looks, then judge bulk by handfuls. Another bad soil is the fine black type almost like soot of the town garden, which has been manured only by cats for the fifty years since good farm land or market garden went under bricks and mortar. Treat this as subsoil, but replace the general fertiliser with 2 oz. of nitro-chalk, or slaked lime; the main trouble with this sort of soil is the constant locking up of lime by the sulphur washed down out of the smoke.

It would seem to the modern gardener that some sort of chemical would weed a bank like this, attacking in the summer and leaving it to wash clean by the spring. The problem is that most of the weedkiller will run down to the bottom and unless the bank rises from a wide path or a court yard, both draining well away from the garden, the result is disaster below. Sodium chlorate is impossible, but a 2-4-D based selective killer as used for lawns is safe above a lawn, though this will not kill couch grass and causes convolvulus only slight annoyance.

Where a bank is covered with towering nettles they should be cut in

B

June with scythe or hook and 2-4-D at double lawn strength put on twice at intervals of a fortnight. This reduces them by the following spring to a state in which they can be forked out as remnants, not a hopeless struggle like wrestling with several tons of buried hoop iron. The need is for something to go on as a dusting powder or fine spray that will kill convolvulus by contact. If this is invented, apply on a very still day in accordance with the maker's instructions and rejoice at a real marvel of science.

Tecane and several other new preparations kill couch grass, but always the problem is the washings and the difficulty of getting the solution to soak into the side of a slope. For practical purposes, unless the bank is absolutely so weedy as to be undiggable, it is best just to dig and pick out with perseverance, especially as the poorer the soil the fewer the weeds and a subsoil bank which is the worst to dig will have least. The better soil at a shallower angle is far less trouble.

Planting the Alpine Bank

For subsoil slopes and banks that are too steep for normal digging, where one can get out the weeds and level back the soil with a whack of the spade to hold it till it firms, deep hole planting is the best system. Take out tunnels about a foot deep with a trowel, pointing downwards at the opposite angle to the slope, about nine or ten inches apart in a horizontal row. Then fill up the holes for a bit over half their depths with a mixture of leafmould, or horticultural peat if you have none, as a greatly inferior substitute, and bone meal. It wants to work out at about a tablespoonful of bone meal a hole mixed in with the dead leaves. In place of bone meal rather less of a general fertiliser can be used, but bone meal lasts longer.

The pot plants, either bought or home raised, should be standing ready in water, they want to go in really well soaked. Put them in the hole and ram back the removed soil round them, using the reversed trowel or an old spade handle with the shaft cut off about six inches long and rounded, not pointed like a cabbage-planting dibber. They should go in so that the lower side of the pot-shaped soil ball is about half an inch below soil level at the bottom lip of the hole. This rammed soil wants to make a shallow cup round each plant, about an inch deep; its function is to serve as a bit of a rain trap, it will fill in naturally, but during the first few months it will be a great help, because though it is possible to water plants on a steep slope, unless the hollow is there most of the water merely washes the soil away and does no good.

Plant your next row staggered so each plant comes about nine inches down and between the first ones, and continue down on this principle. Incidentally, someone to pass up plants and leafmould is a great asset.

This sounds a very great deal of trouble, but it is only needed for the sort of subsoil slope that is either an eyesore or an expensive walling job. The plants are in permanently and their moisture-retaining food store is deep below the reach of surface rooting weeds. They are growing at an advantage over the normal weeds of the bank, if the few really persistent deep-rooting ones are removed and with this type of site there is no convolvulus, nettle or couch grass problem. Where the slope permits normal digging in of humus, no more than for making any other sort of bed, or the soil is any normal garden type, there is only need to take out the holes to about six inches, using no leafmould, and planting at the same spacing, with the same water-holding hollows, which are always a help with sideways planting.

Plants for the Alpine Bank

This rate of planting, roughly one dozen to the square yard, sounds expensive, but plants are replacing rock, and the need is to secure a quick cover with a good web of roots to prevent the soil washing down the bank to any great extent. The spacing may be increased on more gentle slopes and on richer soils, but with subsoil and the normal dry and awkward position, even a ten inch spacing means that the plants meet in a solid mass by the autumn of the first year.

The cost is reduced for those who think ahead, from July to the following April for those who have existing Helianthemum plants to supply cuttings, or from the spring of one year to the spring of the next where one starts with none at all. Buy in ones or threes in as many varieties as possible, plant anywhere in full sun, beside a path in a kitchen garden or on any spare ground, let the raw material or stock plants flower and then from July to September take cuttings intensively. Even if only a few cloches are available one can multiply by between 12 and 50 for each plant, according to how large they were to start with and the separate habits of each (Ben Lui and Ben Ledi always make fewest). The full routine is given in Chapter 8, but with plants so easy failure is almost impossible, even for complete beginners. The cost of a bought Helianthemum is mainly its share of its colleagues that grew too big for their pots and were thrown away—no nurseryman dare increase his stock as intensively as the amateur who is, in effect, growing from easy cuttings the 'rock' to hold his bank and turn it from an eyesore to an asset to any garden.

This method has the great advantage that before the plants go permanently on the bank one sees exactly what the colours are. If the varieties are true to name you can plant contrasting colours with the aid of the list on page 204 but if your taste is for toning colours or you have really decided views on what exact shade goes with which, it is a real advantage to see them all together before you do the main job.

Broad drifts are best, a dozen of a kind or even half a dozen, rather than a stamp collection style dotting of individual plants; but it is not advisable to attempt a formal pattern, they will spread out of it, some grow faster than others and they will never produce straight lines. The arrangement is a matter of taste: some people like a random scattering, and a complete mixture including kinds that have lost their labels from a nursery is often cheap, but it will usually have a large proportion of the commoner single yellows. It is the flames, salmons and dark reds that are the most needed to secure a really representative display.

The selection of further species is limited by the conditions. The more you plant of other things which are less suited to the alpine bank, the fewer you can have of Helianthemums which really enjoy it. As an example, Hypericums of the stronger species can be planted but their yellow is only for a shorter portion of the period during which every yellow Helianthemum is shouting with the same colour. The common blue Veronica (*V. rupestris* or *V. prostrata*) provides another colour, but not in generous measure, and they swamp it with their growth.

An essential race for the bottom of the bank are, however, the alpine Phloxes, the hybrids of *P. subulata*, with gorsey evergreen mats of foliage lying about four inches thick. These make an excellent 'lower storey' and they flower in April and May in a softer and paler range of colour. A single or double staggered row, a foot apart and if it is a lawn below, a foot from the edge, with plenty of the powerful new deep red *P. Temiscaming* and the pale violet G. F. Wilson, is very well worth adding.

Their foliage has another asset. The bottom of the bank is always the richest soil, and there will always be some washing down. This collects in the turf-like foliage and if anything improves them, for unlike Aubrieta they make adventitious or above-ground roots, so any soil among the foliage merely acts as a top dressing. They, therefore, act as a 'long stop' as well as extending the flowering season.

The alpine Phloxes are as easy to increase as Helianthemums but they do not make so many cuttings from first year plants. An old clump, however, will provide plenty, and by filling one with leafmould or fine light soil about July, just working in down in between the branches, in the early spring it can be lifted, split up and planted direct. These natural layerings do not go ahead as fast as young pot plants, but with deep, firm planting and some watering they will take hold and spread.

At the top of the bank, above the Helianthemums, several other species can find a home, Aubrieta, the stronger Sedums, *S. acre* our native Stonecrop, *S. rupestre* and *S. spurium* and two good ground holders, *Ajuga reptans* and *Polygonum vacciniifolium*. The last named is really good, and it flowers late, with small pink spires in August and September. It is possible to include Campanulas such as *C. Portenschlagiana* and *C. Poscharskyana*, but they will in time get swamped by the Helianthemums, which suit the position so much better than any other race and flower so long and in such a colour range that the best effect is always from these alone, and alpine Phloxes at the bottom.

The alpine bank is not a home for all the easiest alpines, it cannot give the long season succession from February to November of a large selection of species like the rock garden, neither can it excite the envy of the alpine expert. It is designed for two jobs, to hold up a steep slope without rock, and to give a great sheet of summer colour. It does both well. Modify it by planting many other shrubs and species and one or other of these objectives will suffer.

Upkeep of the Alpine Bank

During the first months after planting the bank will require weeding; it is possible to hoe it where the slope is steep enough to stand, but on a subsoil bank there is no need to worry about grass unless this is couch. The need is to prevent the first flush of weed germination overwhelming the plants at the start, and to get out any remaining fragments of the perennial species while they are still small. After that it is merely a case of pulling out any which struggle through the carpet, before they spread. Chickweed, as an example, on a bank of soil good enough to grow it, will need tearing up in armfuls perhaps three times the first year if not destroyed early as seedlings, but after the Helianthemums are solid there is no more trouble with it.

Unlike the normal bed or border, the alpine bank is never dug and therefore, apart from any blown seeds, there are no more to germinate once the full strangling effect is secured. Those who believe in what is now the 'orthodox no-digging theory' can of course mulch the surface with compost, but if this is badly made it merely adds more weed seeds. Good compost or leafmould worked down between the plants is an asset as a moisture holder and a soil enricher, the thick woven branches will stop it rolling down or blowing off, but except on subsoil so poor that the Helianthemums will not grow vigorously, it is unnecessary, though an improvement if they seem to be merely struggling.

The main operation after the bank is established is the annual trim. Helianthemums appreciate being cut back hard, otherwise the more powerful will become long trails of bare wood, and slow down in flower display and growth speed. They should therefore be clipped back with shears either in the spring, about March, or in July or at the end of August. The idea is always to keep a complete cover on the bank, and a cut at the end of July gives plenty of time to grow solid again before the winter, and usually produces a second flower display in the autumn. It also supplies ample cuttings for increase; those who begin with a small bank and extend it as enthusiasm feeds on success, can raise a level batch this way instead of taking a few here and there.

Spring cutting is also good, but it should always be done when the plants are growing well—it is an advantage to the plant as the sap moves more easily up new wood than through the 'hardened arteries' of thick old stems. The timing depends on the claims of other jobs, but it should not be left later than September, as they must have time to get growing again; better wait till the spring than do it too late. The second summer the stronger varieties will always want cutting back hard, the 'Queens' which are large-flowered and semi-prostrate and the old single pink *Rhodanthe carneum* need it most, but never be afraid of the shears, a struggling and weak specimen (relatively) is greatly improved by a clip that extends to its neighbours. When they all start level often the weakling will pull ahead and catch up, it is the old and effective principle of pruning bush roses by the Bible ('To him that hath shall be given, from he that hath not shall be taken away').

As plants are trimmed back, either all together or in batches, it is a good opportunity to clean out any suppressed weeds, and secure self-sown seedlings, which are worth potting to grow on until they flower, but as all Helianthemums commonly grown are hybrids, they may no more resemble their parents than kittens fathered by a stray. There is always a chance of something personally attractive provided one has the strength of mind to throw away the duds. Cuttings are so easy that there is no other advantage in finding seedlings.

A spring survey after the third year will reveal that some bushes have died. In some cases their neighbours will fill the gap, in others replacements should go in on the same principle as in a Kentish chestnut coppice. Those who cut the hop poles in a leased woodland are bound to replace any that are rotten in every yearly square that is felled, and so a coppice lasts through century after century. As raising young plants is so simple this is no disadvantage, and one never has to replant completely; the average four year life in full health can be doubled in the case of individuals which are growing happily in the right place, as they are on the alpine bank.

The Alpine Bank

2

The Alpine Border

The problem of the average front garden is that the picture is so rigidly framed by fences that landscape gardening on this scale is more like heraldry as Chaucer knew it; a small bright picture that is personal to the owner which is his achievement and his pride. The path to the front door, the way round so that the windows can be cleaned and the back entrance, which may be a six foot wide drive-in to the garage, are as fixed as the quarterings on a shield.

Consider the front border along the low wall that parts the garden from the pavement. It is usually about a foot wide, and so are most of the available beds, and they can be made no wider without abolishing the lawn, and even if the paths are not cast concrete, they cannot be altered because they are needed. The front border can be planted with annuals or bedding plants such as dwarf Dahlias, but except for a permanent *Lonicera nitida* hedge into which those who pass will tuck their empty cigarette packets, there is no perennial solution. One front garden is like another because the limitations are the same.

The herbaceous border with plants chosen to flower in a long succession, planted so that there is no large gap at any season in its length and rising in a bank of bloom from Thrift and other low growing subjects in front to Delphiniums at the back, needs width. To do it justice you need at least four feet from front to back, and though it can be fitted in with the back towards either side fence, with the narrow beds compelled by a rigid frame of paths it is often no more possible than a tennis court.

It is here that the alpine border is of most value. Its plants are as brilliant, on a miniature scale, as those of the herbaceous border, but they are so small that there is room for sufficient kinds to keep up a display from March to November in a bed which is only wide enough for one Michaelmas Daisy tightly staked and leaning across the path. The principles of planting are the same, except that there is less need to study

24

height, six inch high species do not block the view of three inchers because one looks down at the border; but it is a garden feature, very much more attractive than many, which is perfectly suited to the smallest space. On a large scale it is less effective, but for widths up to two feet and for any length it combines the qualities of a one-sixth or one-twelfth scale herbaceous border, and a rock garden.

ALPINE BORDER FOR A SMALL FRONT GARDEN IN FULL SUN.
ON ANY SOIL.

FIG. 1. Key. (1) *Frankenia thymifolia*. (2) *Campanula pusilla*. (3) *Potentilla verna nana*. (4) *Dianthus Mars*. (5) *Gentiana lagodechiana*. (6) *Iris lacustris*. (7) *Saxifraga oppositifolia splendens*. (8) *Erica carnea Eileen Porter*. (9) *Oenothera pumila*. (10) *Phlox amoena*. (11) *Rosa Oakington Ruby*. (12) *Delphinium sinense*. (13) *Linum salsoloides nanum*. (14) *Aethionema Warley Rose*. (15) *Morisia hypogaea*. (16) *Erodium chamaedroides roseum*. (17) *Campanula pulloides*. (18) *Serratula Shawii*. (19) *Gypsophila cerastioides*. (20) *Achillea Lewisii*. (21) *Thymus Serpyllum major*. Bulbs below the carpeters: (A) *Chinodoxa sardensis*. (B) *Eranthis hyemalis*. (C) *Iris reticulata*. (D) *Narcissus nanus*. Other plants may, of course, be used; this is merely to show the principles of herbaceous border planning, considering height, colour and flowering seasons in relation to each other, worked out in miniature with alpines.

It can be used with the straight lines and regular curves of the formal gardening tradition, of round beds of Roses, bird baths and sun dials, or with the curves, irregular shapes and winding paths of the informal garden into which the rock garden fits. Where the site is flat and space is strictly limited so that all that can be built is a high steep mound which is going to look like a pudding turned out on a plate however well the rocks are placed, the alpine border is going to be far more fitting than a rock garden.

Because it is on a level it escapes the plant-destroying drought of the badly made rock garden. Gentians as an example grow far better in this sort of border than on a pile of rocks, and though some species, notably those which dislike winter damp cannot be used, the range of plants for full sun is roughly three-quarters of those that suit the small rock garden. It has also the advantage that because the requirements of alpines differ so widely, it can be planted with shade-loving or damp-loving species in greater variety than is possible with the normal herbaceous border using traditional plants.

The Alpine Border

The alpine border may sound a complete heresy to the orthodox gardener or alpine expert but it is a method of enjoying the beauty of alpines without using rock and it differs *only* from the alpine house in growing easier plants in a way that is both cheap and possible in very many more gardens. Though alpine borders are very rare because few people other than rock garden enthusiasts know the very real beauty of the species that can be grown, they are common in the nursery trade.

The nurseryman, especially if he has a landscape department, has a rock garden for show, but where he wishes to grow a large number of healthy specimens to provide cuttings, seed and good clumps to divide, he plants an alpine border. Weeding is easier, one can even hoe, especially with a swan-neck hoe on a foot long handle, one can get about between the plants more comfortably, and there is no need for him to lock up capital in rock, when a piece of good Westmorland stone with a square foot of face may have cost him ten shillings.

It is not, however, a 'poor man's rock garden', it is another way of growing alpines no less worthy of attention and very effective on a flat site or in a small garden.

LARGE ALPINE BORDER, DOUBLE SIDED,
NORMAL SOIL, FULL SUN.

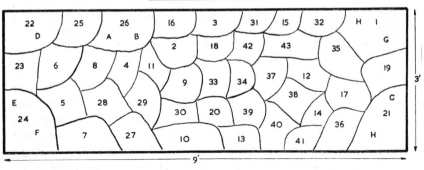

FIG. 2. In this larger border the plants used in the first plan appear under the numbers and the bulbs under the letters in the key to Fig. 1. The following are additions: (22) *Hypsela longiflora*. (23) *Mazus Pumilio*. (24) *Selliera radicans*. (25) *Claytonia australasica*. (26) *Gentiana Macaulayi*. (27) *Gentiana saxosa*. (28) *Polygala Chamaebuxus purpurea*. (29) *Primula rosea grandiflora*. (30) *Ajuga Brockbankii*. (31) *Armeria caespitosa*. (32) *Polygala calcarea*. (33) *Solidago brachystachys*. (34) *Penstemon heterophyllus*. (35) *Hypericum reptans*. (36) *Phlox Lilac Queen*. (37) *Delphinium nudicaule*. (38) *Rosa pumila*. (39) *Geranium lancastriense*. (40) *Dianthus parnassicus*. (41) *Inula acaulis*. (42) *Penstemon rupicola*. (43) *Umbilicus oppositifolius*. Extra bulbs: (E) *Crocus Tomasinianus*. (F) *Crocus pulchellus*. (G) *Anemone blanda atrocaerulea*. (H) *Triteleia uniflora*. Note that all the "extra leafmould" plants are kept at one end.

26

The Alpine Border

Making the Alpine Border

The main requirement of alpines in the garden is the right soil for the right kind, and good soil is very much cheaper than rock. The sort of town garden which its owner bewails will grow nothing can be made to grow good alpines easily, for though one cannot replace the whole top spit of the large herbaceous border, a small alpine bed is easy.

Dig out the soil so that you have a trench a foot deep, the whole size of the border, put back about four inches of rough drainage material in the bottom and fill in with John Innes Seed Compost. For a border a foot wide and nine feet long you will need about two hundredweight. This soil is a good general alpine mixture, with a reasonable supply of humus and plenty of sharp gritty sand in it. It will have been sterilised by steam so that any weed seeds or roots will have been cooked like rice or potatoes, and therefore the plants have a long start on anything which may blow in. The reason why alpine pans and troughs grow better plants than those on a town rock garden is simply because the pan gardener has to buy his soil. In larger quantities it is not only far easier to obtain, it is cheaper in proportion, and very much better value than horse manure in London.

Where your soil is really horrible, sift out the broken glass, cinders and stones and use them for drainage, the remaining poor, humus-starved, soot-like mixture that has been manured only by cats for twenty years, can be used to build up somewhere else in the garden. With better soils the pile can be sifted, especially to pick out the perennial weed roots, and used to mix in with other ingredients to bring it to a better alpine mixture. Soils are dealt with fully in Chapter 6, including the recipes for the several types of alpine mixture.

On a heavy clay there is usually no difference in treatment; what the alpines need is good gritty stuff for the full root depth, not just a little leafmould dug in on the surface. If it is the sort of very greasy clay which is going to make a hidden pond from the trampling on the bottom of the trench, dig an outlet drain to a lower level, or rejoice in your good fortune and have a wet corner for the plants that delight in this sort of place. On a clay or clayish soil the bottom of the hole should always be dug over before the drainage material is put in to destroy the puddling effect of treading.

If the bed is made up with good soil so that this one factor is right, the problem is then one of choosing the plants that fit the situation. There are plenty of plants for full sun, a large number for full sun and drought, including the Sedums which will thrive up to the foot of a privet hedge, plenty for semi-shade and some real beauties for shade and damp; dry shade is the only awkward position. Therefore, choose your site if possible so that it gets full sun or morning and afternoon sun only, even if you have to remove some tree branches in gardens where shutting out the neighbours has shut you in.

Where the soil is not a difficult one, but a good light loam, it is possible to avoid beginning with a hole the size of your border, merely digging in leafmould and some grit to improve the drainage, but it should be remembered that alpines are not swiftly growing plants taking a great bulk of nutriment, and a well-manured vegetable garden will grow them too fast and sappy. It is easy in a good garden to be too rich, and as the soil supply in the prepared bed lasts year after year without renewal, it is always best to start with a properly made up border.

Another advantage of the trench is the ease of supplying the soil requirements of the different groups, but though one can have lime lovers at one end and normal soil at the other, real lime haters, a class of plants that includes *Gentiana sino-ornata*, cannot share a bed. Those which merely like additional leafmould can fit in with any soil, merely needing an area filled in with their particular choice.

Planting and Care of the Alpine Border

The alpine border can be planted at almost any time of year because most alpines are grown in pots and can be put in with no more root disturbance than bedding Geraniums, but the best seasons are September, October and November and February, March and April, missing both the dead of winter and the heat of summer. Each one should be well soaked before planting and should go in with the soil ball just below the surface; take a hole out with a trowel, put in your plant, without breaking up the soil ball round the roots, and ram back the soil firmly round it. Firm planting of anything is important, and alpines need it, especially *Gentiana acaulis*, the lovely Swiss spring flowering species, and one should always remember that most alpines are accustomed to being walked on by goats and other creatures. There is no natural equivalent to the patting and fussing of those who do not use the trowel handle as a rammer. The soil must be firmly in contact with the roots as they circle the shape of the pot.

The spacing apart varies: some species are going to need only six square inches, others are going to spread, and though the lists at the end of this chapter are restricted to relatively small plants for this sort of border, it is advisable to look up each one in Chapter 7 so that you know exactly what it is going to do. As a very rough estimate, for a border of small plants only, it should work out at one to every eight square inches. The plants are very much more accessible than on a rock garden, the roots are not out of reach and it is possible during either of the planting seasons to move any that are growing too fast for their neighbours.

After they are planted water them in well. Whenever you water an alpine border, or anything else, give it a good soak or none. Standing at a distance with your thumb on a hose that will not quite reach may leave the surface wet, but it does no real good. The water wants to soak down about two inches: dig up a corner and see how it is going, then add several canfuls more, using the rose and giving a real good drench. It will then rain all night, but this will do no harm, and after this only in exceptional drought will the border need any watering at all.

After watering it is a custom among some gardeners to cover the levelled-off surface of the border with limestone or granite chippings—the grade used for chicken grit, washed free from dust under a tap, is the most easily available in small quantities. The object is not to give the impression of rock, but to stop the rain splashing soil on the low blooms. The carpeters and mat-forming plants protect their flowers with their own foliage, but some species, such as Gentians and the Kabschia Saxifrages, do get rather dirty faces. Another advantage is that the chipping surface seems to discourage the dainty rakings of the cats. In general it should be said that the smaller the plant the more it needs chipping up. The chips have the disadvantage that they are rather hard on the fingers when one is weeding and many successful alpine borders have been made without them.

There are very many possible planting schemes and the only broad principle that covers them is the idea of keeping something in bloom over as long a season as possible. One very good plan for those with little space is to have flat patches in the border covered with carpeters beneath which are planted spring flowering bulbs and autumn flowering Crocus, not the giant Colchicum with its poisonous leaves, but the miniature species that are small copies of the familiar purple companion of the Snowdrop. The carpeters are summer flowering and the bulbs naturalise happily beneath them, giving three periods in bloom for the same small area.

In places, towards the centre is best, the taller species are planted, ideally those with a long flowering season such as *Aethionema Warley Rose*, the miniature Roses, *Penstemon Roezlii* and certain Dianthus hybrids. The rise to nine inches or a foot is effective in a narrow border, but few alpines are tall and slender, though the relatively tiny Delphinium species can be used for those who wish to copy a full-sized herbaceous border. The effect is of a series of low domes or bushes, and the horizontal spread of foliage reduces the weed problem as well as removing any need for staking.

The planting plans in this chapter (Figs. 1 and 2) are intended as guides to what can be done, and they can also be used as schemes for the small rock garden, with spreading to allow for rock. There is, of course, nothing to prevent those who wish adding low rocks to the alpine border, ideally choosing flat wide pieces that act as stepping stones, especially on one that is too wide to reach the middle portions in comfort, but the plants will hide the rock quite rapidly. Species which trail and are at their best where they can ramp powerfully down a slope, those which prefer a crevice and genuinely need root contact with stone, as well as any which dislike winter damp, including the more robust Androsaces, should all be excluded.

The object of the map is to show where each species is to be found when you wish to propagate it, to look it up for any purpose, or to talk or even boast about it. It is useful at first while you are learning the 'faces' of your alpines, but after even a single summer there will be many that need no labels; you know them and their differences stand out as sharply as those of a cauliflower and a brussels sprout. This type of plan, even drawn very badly, is extremely useful as a map of the border because it removes the very real problem of labelling. With twenty or thirty species, each with a relatively long name, a large wooden label for each is going to give the effect of a graveyard, or a 'Treasure Hunt' at a fête on the vicarage lawn, at least until the plants grow up and hide them. The ideal labels are the permanent lead type with embossed letters, which can be bent over so they are flat on the ground and can be read by looking down at them. They are however expensive, though a complete set to last a lifetime is no more costly than a large plaster goblin or a crew of cast concrete rabbits. The small plastic labels that can be used over and over again are excellent for seed pans or batches of cuttings, but they do not hold the ground well in the open and are inclined to work loose and blow away. There are metal labels with a flat oval plate to be read downwards, and a stem that thrusts into the ground, written on with a special waterproof ink, and the larger plastic type thrust well home in the soil, but the cheapest is still the old-fashioned wooden one.

Do not buy them ready painted, the paint is inclined to come off, bringing the writing with it when they are exposed to rain and sun for a long time. Tip your bundle or boxful (for choice five or six inches long and thicker than the cheap kind split from the wood that makes the outer 'plys' of three-ply) into a pan or baking dish with Cuprinol or other wood preservative, not creosote, and leave them to soak for twenty-four hours, turning and stirring occasionally. Then spread them to dry before storing for use as required. Buy a tube of 'flake white' oil colour paint as used for oil paintings, squeeze a little on a rag, wipe it on thinly and write the name on with a gardening pencil. The pencil writes a waterproof name, the still-wet paint closes over it a little as well as making it show up, and the wood preservative gives your label about two years' life without rotting off at ground level. The idea of the oil colour tube is useful because only a very small quantity of paint is required, the cap can be screwed on and it will neither upset nor form a hard skin, and it can be used to the last squeeze without mess or trouble.

A border of this type requires weeding, but as it should not be dug every autumn there is less than for a bed of herbaceous plants. Though there is a certain amount of cutting and removing dead flower stems, and pruning back plants which are over-running their neighbours, it is a labour-saving garden feature compared with the bedding plant and forgetmenot with bulbs, routine of so many small front gardens. Alpines very largely look after themselves, provided the selection is restricted to those which are relatively easy in the right soil and situation. Slug baiting with metaldyhyde, and destruction of ants with gammexane or paradichlorbenzine (they are immune to D.D.T.), and derris for any greenfly are normal garden routine if these pests attack. Few alpines have any of the special and complex viruses and diseases of the vegetable garden.

The Primula Corner for Wet Shade

The garden which falls towards one of its boundaries so that a part is always damp and even swampy has the advantage of a natural Primula corner. This can range in dampness from the sort of bed that grows Polyanthus well to a degree of sogginess that produces rushes as well as moss on the lawn. The lesser degree of dampness is often found on new estates where concrete roads are laid with no reference to old land drains, and something forgotten for five hundred years may give you the opportunity to enjoy a really striking garden feature where normal plants struggle and die.

The large Primulas which delight in this sort of place are among the most striking of the many treasures from the Far East in our gardens, and though they are usually regarded as 'rock plants' they are far too big for most rock gardens. They are usually planted by the side of a cemented pool, but unless they are where they get the overflow they do not thrive. Their needs are plenty of moisture, if they are in full sun, which is inclined to fade the flowers of the deep red varieties, or they can make do with less water if they are in shade. Because the Candelabra group, which is the most striking, go up as high as three feet in whorl on whorl of florets in May and June, the best position is one with shelter from strong winds to save the trouble and difficulty of staking.

They are without question the most splendid plants that can be grown in the shade, and as their thick stems are sparrow-proof, unlike those of the familiar Wanda type Primula, they are highly suited for town gardens. Their leaves die off in winter and because they are below ground through the worst period for smoke and smog, they have a great advantage over other plants in London. They are described in detail on pages 244, as they are very little known to most town gardeners. In many country houses of fame they are to be found rioting beside ponds and streams, or planted in moist and open woodland, but because of their association with this sort of site, few people consider them for small gardens. By selection of species it is possible to have something in bloom in the Primula corner from March to early August, and the addition of the giant Cowslip types, makes scent an attraction as well as the wide range of colour available.

The naturally damp corner is easy, and again it depends on what the soil is like and the weeds that are there. If it is a shocking poor town garden soil with a thriving crop of docks, the best policy is to dig it out over the whole area in the same way as an alpine border, but going rather deeper to make sure of getting out the roots and not using the soil which came out because it will be full of dock seeds. John Innes Seed or Potting Compost, which is rather richer, is very good stuff for Primulas.

Where the site is heavy wet cold clay, the same procedure is adopted but one need only go down about nine inches; on this sort of soil where the docks will be large and almost impossible to dig out, a selective weedkiller should be used during the early summer and planting be carried out the following spring. If the soil is reasonably good, and not troubled with perennial weeds, it should be single trenched with plenty of leafmould dug in, and grit if the soil is a clay. Primulas take more feeding than most alpines, and good compost and leafmould are both of great value for them. Double trenching should be strictly in accordance with the diagrams in gardening books because Primulas do not like lifeless subsoil to grow in; dig so that the top spit stays at the top, and as long as it has some humus in it, they will grow well. Hop manure can be

3. *Oenothera missouriensis*, the powerful trailing Evening Primrose, needs full sun and plenty of room: it is wasted swamping less rampant species and hiding expensive rock. The Alpine Bank displays its four-inch diameter flowers from June to October to the best advantage

4. *Iberis sempervirens*, Little Gem, the small perennial Candytuft, is a tough and evergreen shrub about four inches high. In May and June it adds dazzling white to the flame, yellow, pink, and crimson variations and combinations of the Helianthemums, and it is sturdy enough to compete with them

used and even very old rotten sawdust, but this wants to be so decayed that it is very dark brown, almost black, but leafmould, horticultural peat and compost are best, not manure, because what is required is the moisture-retaining power, free passage for the roots in the case of a clay, and slowly available plant foods released as required.

On the naturally damp site, which should never be raised as a bed because it can soon get too dry if it is built up, there is no more difficulty in growing these Primulas than Polyanthus, and even if it is only moderately damp in summer one can manage the hybrids of *P. japonica* but the drier they are grown, the smaller the flower spikes. There are many Primulas which will grow well under drier conditions, notably the Primrose type, but for the full and splendid glory of the best of them, you need a damp place.

This can be contrived even in the most unlikely gardens far more easily than making a lily pool or a concrete path. Consider first the levels of the garden and where the water goes when it rains. Many front gardens simply run it straight out across the pavement, others have paths that drain into a grating that gets choked with leaves, and frequently there is a shed with a line of drip-worn holes in the path beside it where the rain wastes itself in making the inside damp. The need is to contrive a method of sending a larger share of run-off water to the dry part of the garden, and if the proposed bed is dry because it is at the highest point, one can solve the problem with a hose.

The usual cause of preventable dryness is a sandy soil that lets the water away too quickly, and the remedy for this is the 'semi-pond' or artificial wet corner. First dig out your bed eighteen inches to two feet deep in an irregular shape if you are making an informal feature, which is the most effective—a simple rough crescent or whatever fits into the sheltered space available, or a square one if you are trying something like a Primula herbaceous border. The diameter wants to be a foot larger all round than you want the completed bed to be, exactly as though you were making a pond.

Then mix up a batch of cement, four or five parts of sand to one of cement, or three parts sand and one of fine central-heating furnace ashes to one cement. The last mixture makes 'temporary cement', it sets hard but it is easy to smash out with a cold chisel, so that you have not built something that is going to be a problem in future garden alterations.

Begin with a ring of shovelfuls of cement round your hole, and set the first course of concrete lumps, brick burrs, clinkers or anything in the way of hard rubbish you have. Before they go in place, water them; cement will only stick to a surface that is wet. You are not building a solid wall, all that is needed is a very leaky pond which will hold the water from draining away longer than your soil would by nature, and the whole thing is going to be completely buried, so it does not matter how it looks. Empty bottles are good, fitted in with the bottom pointing to the inside of the hole where two rounded lumps do not meet well, tins naturally rust and should not be used, but otherwise it is an opportunity to get rid of the unsightly material which so many people feel that they ought to 'make a rockery to use up'.

There are two main principles of construction: always wet your stone before putting on the cement and avoid having the joins one above the other; any brick wall provides an example of the method of bonding. If the material available most easily is old bricks, make a wall one brick thick using half bricks for the headers, or whole bricks with their length sticking out behind the wall into the soil, there is no need to use the house-building system of two bricks lengthways and one crossways. When the wall has been built up to the lowest ground level, leave it to set for about three days and then fill in the soil behind it.

An alternative is to build the wall first, sloping it slightly backwards so that the upper courses come further back than the bottom ones, putting back the soil and ramming it firmly behind as you go. Then water the face of the wall, taking care to get the water well in the cracks, and fill in the gaps with cement, spreading it out well with a trowel over the surface. This uses rather less cement but is not so strong, but cement may well be the only bought item. On a sandy soil the bottom of the hole will usually provide sand that is of too poor quality, because it contains some clay, for a builder, but quite good enough for this job.

The bottom of the hole should be about 90 per cent covered; you need to leave gaps here and there in case you find yourself with a better pond than you have ever made, because you do not want one. A very good material for the bottom is broken glass; some gardens have a real store of this, plus broken bottles and central-heating furnace clinker. Throw it on the bottom, spread so it is about two inches thick and spread the cement on top after watering to make it stick. The difference between bottom and sides is that it has not to support itself so smaller stuff and more awkward bits can be used; a two-inch layer of cement could be used but one may as well tip in all the worst rubbish and get it out of the way.

When it has had three days to set, run the hose in it, not only to see if it drains properly—it ought to leak itself empty in about twenty-four hours, and one can bash another hole or two in the bottom or fill some up—but to wash out any free lime, which Primulas on the whole dislike.

Then cover the bottom with a drainage layer of stones or hard rubbish, to prevent the soil packing solid in the exit holes. Fill in with soil, either John Innes or a made-up Primula mixture with plenty of humus in it, treading it firm, and then plant the Primulas.

The planting principles are the same as for an alpine border, but as they have a greater height range, from about six inches up to three feet, it is far more important to put the tall ones at the back. After planting, water well on the standard routine for the high level bed. Take the hose up to the bed and simply leave it trickling all night, or through the day, a twelve hour slow soak. This will be needed at most once a week in summer, and so that the soil is not washed away where the hose is set each time, two or three pockets of pebbles on the surface should be made at the sides among the leaves to take the trickle.

In a really impossible shady but sheltered place, a good Primula corner is worth the trouble, and if it is dry because of a privet hedge or robbing tree roots, the wall will keep most of the roots out. As the drainage is from the bottom it does not mean a wet patch round it, and as it is only used where the subsoil is sandy and the water gets away fast, there is no risk of soil sourness, if the bed is not dry. There is no need to use the hose; in some summers the restricted drainage keeps it damp enough, and in winter when the Primulas are dormant the normal supply is always sufficient.

Hose pipe is relatively expensive and dragging one the length of the garden is unattractive as a regular job, so that it is helpful to put in a permanent pipe leading up to the corner. The cheapest is common steel water piping, which screws together with collars and red lead or motor gasket jointing compound, to caulk it. Buried underground about a foot along a bed or path with the lower end finished off with an elbow and a short length of pipe tapped to take a screw-on hose connection, this makes a permanent irrigator. A section of hose with a screw socket on each end enables the outside tap to be connected when normal watering in the garden is done for the day. It is essential to be able to unscrew the elbow at the lower end (collars that take a spanner should be used here) so that the water can be drained out of the pipe in winter because of the risk of a freeze up, and to bear in mind that the limit of pressure is below the level of the cistern in your roof. Water will flow uphill, with the pressure of the mains behind it, and with the same plumbing ingenuity that many people will spend making a fountain one can conquer dry shade and make Primulas grow in an 'impossible' place. They are worth it.

Before you try this method get in touch with your local council water-department. This device counts as a lawn sprinkler, and regulations differ: some councils insist that a garden hose supply must be used with a rose and held in the hand and want you to fit a meter if you have anything like this. Meters mean a heavy charge for fitting plus 2s. per 1,000 gallons (London 1954), but stress the fact that you will only need it on for short periods in hot weather, and your borough engineer will be co-operative, especially if he has grown these Primulas himself.

Where the Primula border is not above the level of the water supply harnessing rainfall is very effective and far less trouble. I once made a good Primula corner of this type in a dry, chalky garden in the Chilterns by using the collection area of the roof of a small bungalow. A trench was dug from beside the down pipe from the gutter to about six inches below the top of the wall round the corner, it was roughly eight inches wide and a foot deep, with a fall of about one in thirty. It was filled with broken crockery etc. etc., except for a covering of rammed top soil, and it worked perfectly. The spout of the down pipe was turned round so that it flowed into a brick-sided hole with the crockery drain at the bottom, and the rain water trickled quietly along it to the Primulas. It was necessary to turn the spout back to its normal grating in winter as neither the drain nor the bog could cope with a real flood at that season.

The same sort of trench, with agricultural field drain pipes (ask a builders' merchant), just laid along the bottom in contact with each other, bricks on edge at the sides with pieces of tile laid across the tops, will lead water anywhere you want it downhill and go on doing it safely buried for years. A rubble drain, however, blocks with mud unless the water is clear, as from a roof. The sources of supply can be a grating at a path corner where water collects, or anywhere that rain water is running to waste on the surface. The best supply is from a shed roof, and the drain can either take the down pipe from the gutter or the overflow from the water butt, or from a ground gutter. This is most neatly made with concrete trowelled smooth into a long trough where the drips are now splashing on the path, or a piece of old iron guttering may be fixed up to take it, the last is very effective along behind the shed where the rain water is soaking in to rot the wood of the fence. So long as an underground drain of this type has a fall all the way, it can turn sharp corners, but an 'all path route' is advised, to avoid difficulties when digging.

These complications are *only* for those with utterly dry gardens on sandy soil, or where dry shade must be used; they are given at length not because they are essential to Primula growing, only one in a hundred gardeners need consider them, but because that one gardener is very often the most determined of all to grow Primulas. Those with heavy clay or anywhere damp and shady, anywhere Polyanthus are growing well in shade, can go ahead without any difficulty and trust to the moisture-retaining power of leafmould or other humus and an occasional good watering during a dry spell to grow these beautiful and on the whole neglected plants really well.

According to some authorities, these wet Primulas hate lime, and it is true that they often fail in really chalky gardens. They do not like lime, but they are not lime haters like some Gentians or Rhododendrons, and it is summer drought that usually finishes them in the sort of sunny glaring white garden where Flowering Cherries are a picture and Aubrieta thrive. With a Primula corner of the type described, plus shade and shelter from winds, they will grow well, but in soil nearer standard leafy mixture. If they suffer when drought can be ruled out as the cause, then use Epsom salts as recommended for lime-hating Gentians on page 200, as a means of reducing the lime in the soil on the same principle as that of a water softener. It will not work for Gentians on chalk, but it is effective at Primula level of intolerance.

Plants for the Alpine Border

The lists that follow are for guidance in border planning. The first covers approximately 200 species and varieties for almost any soil. These are plants for the standard alpine mixture, with extra ground chalk or other lime for those marked 'limy' and additional leafmould for those with 'leafy' after their colour description. Provided there was sufficient moisture and the soil was replaced as recommended earlier, this collection could be grown in a garden which was almost solid chalk, or on the coldest and most unpleasant clay.

The flowering seasons are approximate and vary with the weather and climate; in Cornwall as an example many species flower earlier than in Yorkshire, and individual plants seem to have considerable personal choice in the matter. They are an average, and show the period when flowering can be expected. It is a custom among gardening writers to sprinkle lists of this nature with indicator letters to save space, but to avoid continual reference to a key to find out what abbreviations like 'N.A.T.O.' or 'B.B.C.' mean when applied to plants, in these lists one only is used, an asterisk (*) which shows that the plant with this sign against its first name will grow in semi-shade.

Colour too is approximate, as it is not possible to give a really good description in a small space. The word 'Pink' means a number of shades (it is not used here in its hunting sense) as an example, and those who use these lists for quick reference should always turn up their selected plants in Chapter 7 for a full account of each.

The remaining lists are of alpines for a lime-free soil, and next there is a list of plants for the Primula border or wet corner, and finally one of those suitable for shade. To some degree the lists can overlap, most of the 'leafy' subjects from the first one can go in with the species that hate lime, and many semi-shade plants (which are marked with an asterisk throughout) will take shade to some degree. They should always be looked up before they are rearranged, as these lists are purely a broad and rough classification, so that it can be decided whether or not they will fit your conditions. The purpose of these lists is to help in planning, so that heights, flowering seasons and colours can be seen at once, and the limitations of soil and amount of sunlight considered. If the soil conditions are right there is no need to make any distinction between a country garden and one in a town, 'full sun' in Hampstead grows the same plants as in Hampshire—there are differences but not large ones.

The number of varieties is purely a matter of taste, and though these lists are limited to plants of comparatively small size so that a large selection can be grown in a small space, it is as effective, as an example, to fill a bed solid with Helianthemums or Phloxes, or (on the right soil) have one large mass of *Lithospermum* Heavenly Blue if you prefer one splash of really heavenly blue during its flowering season. Trailing plants from the wall plant lists in the next chapter are not so effective; they need height to trail from and very many of them dislike lying flat on the ground. A solid mass of carpeters with bulbs is effective, and this, with the many additional species that are more powerful than those selected in the lists for the alpine border, is dealt with in Chapter 4 as the alpine lawn.

On a lime-free soil, that is one where Azaleas and Rhododendrons will grow without difficulty, there are two special planting schemes available. A Gentian bed, with a flowering season from April to November, could be planted, or an Erica border. This is an Erica garden using small varieties only, and, starting with the early flowering *Erica carnea* one can have it in bloom almost the whole year round. On a normal soil one can grow the spring and summer flowering Gentians, not the autumn glories like *G. sino-ornata*, and though the small varieties of *Erica carnea* give a display in winter and early spring either with or without lime, one cannot grow the species of heather that bloom in summer.

There are plenty of other planting systems; it is simply a question of

38

selecting those that you like from the species that like your soil and situation. It is possible to grow lime haters in a raised bed of suitable soil, watering only after stirring in Epsom salts to precipitate the lime (hardness) in the mains supply, but it is both simpler and more certain of success to grow really well the plants that will do so easily.

LIST OF ALPINES FOR THE ALPINE BORDER IN FULL SUN AND PART SHADE

An asterisk (*) indicates suitable for semi-shade

Approx. height (inches)		Flowering period									
		Feb.	Mar.	Apr.	May	June	July	Aug.	Sep.	Oct.	Nov.
4 — 6	Achillea Lewisii. Creamy yellow					————	————	————			
4 — 6	Aethionema Warley Rose. Pink				————	————	————	————			
3 — 6	Ajuga Brockbankii. Blue				————	————					
4 — 6	Alyssum spinosum. White					————	————				
4 — 6	,, ,, roseum. Pale pink					————	————				
1 — 2	Androsace sempervivoides. Pink				————	————					
4 — 6	Aquilegia discolor. Blue and white				————	————					
4 — 6	,, pyrenaica. Blue, yellow centre				————	————					
2 — 3	Arabis carduchorum. White		————	————							
1 — 2	Arenaria purpurascens. Pale lilac					————	————				
1 — 2	Armeria caespitosa. Shell pink. Limy				————	————	————				
1 — 2	Campanula arvatica. Violet. Limy					————	————				
2 — 4	,, fenestrellata. Blue and white. Limy						————				
2 — 4	,, garganica. Blue. Limy						————				
2 — 3	,, haylodgensis fl. pl. Blue double. Limy						————				
2 — 3	,, pulla. Violet. Limy						————				

40

Approx. height (inches)		Flowering period										
		Feb.	Mar.	Apr.	May	June	July	Aug.	Sep.	Oct.	Nov.
3 — 6	Campanula pulloides. Violet. Limy						———	———			
3 — 4	„ pusilla. Blue. Limy					———	———	———			
3 — 4	„ pusilla alba. White. Limy					———	———	———			
3 — 4	„ Tymonsii. Pale blue. Limy						———	———			
3 — 4	„ Waldsteiniana. Violet. Limy						———	———			
2 — 3	*Centaurium scilloides. Pink						———	———			
2 — 3	Cyclamen coum. Pink. Leafy	———	———								
2 — 3	„ album. White. Leafy	———	———								
3 — 4	„ europaeum. Pink. Leafy						———	———	———		
3 — 4	„ neapolitanum. Pale pink. Leafy							———	———	———	
3 — 4	„ album. White. Leafy							———	———	———	
4 — 6	„ repandum. Crimson. Leafy			———	———						
8 — 12	Delphinium nudicaule. Pale scarlet					———	———				
8 — 12	„ sinense. Blue					———	———				
1 — 2	Dianthus alpinus. Pink. Limy					———	———				
2 — 4	„ Boydii. Pink. Limy					———	———				
4 — 6	„ caesius. Pink. Limy				———	———					

41

Flowering period

Approx. height (inches)		Feb.	Mar.	Apr.	May	June	July	Aug.	Sep.	Oct.	Nov.
2 — 3	Dianthus caesius Little Jock. Pink double. Limy				—	—					
3 — 4	,, Crossways. Cerise. Leafy					—	—	—			
3 — 4	,, Elf. Crimson. Leafy					—	—	—			
1 — 2	,, Freynii. Pink. Limy					—	—				
2 — 3	,, haematocalyx. Purple red. Limy				—	—					
3 — 4	,, Jupiter. Salmon. Leafy				—	—	—				
2 — 3	,, Mars. Crimson double. Leafy				—	—	—				
1 — 2	,, microlepis. Pink. Limy				—	—					
4 — 6 *	,, Napoleon III. Crimson double. Leafy					—	—	—			
1 — 2	,, parnassicus. Pink						—	—			
6 — 8 *	,, Spark. Crimson. Leafy					—	—	—			
6 — 9	Erica carnea. Pink. Peaty	—	—							—	—
6 — 9	,, Cecilia M. Beale. White. Peaty		—	—							—
6 — 9	,, Eileen Porter. Carmine. Peaty		—	—							—
6 — 9	,, Queen of Spain. Pink. Peaty		—	—							
6 — 9	,, Vivellii. Nearest crimson. Peaty		—	—							
1 — 2	Erodium chamaedroides roseum. Pink				—	—	—	—	—		

Approx. height (inches)		Flowering period									
		Feb.	Mar.	Apr.	May	June	July	Aug.	Sep.	Oct.	Nov.
3 — 4	*Gentiana acaulis. Blue	●————————●									
3 — 4	* „ angustifolia. Blue				●————————————●						
4 — 6	* „ Clusii. Blue			●———●							
4 — 6	* „ dinarica. Blue			●————●							
3 — 4	* „ lagodechiana. Blue						●———●				
4 — 6	* „ Macaulayi. Blue. Leafy						●————●				
1 — 2	* „ saxosa. White. Leafy						●——————●				
8 — 12	* „ septemfida. Blue						●———●				
1 — 2	* „ verna. Blue			●————●							
2 — 3	Geranium lancastriense. Pink					●——————————●					
4 — 6	Hypericum sanguineum nummularium. Yellow					●——————●					
2 — 3	„ reptans. Yellow					●————●					
4 — 5	Iberis sempervirens Little Gem. White				●————●						
2 — 3	„ saxatilis. White		●————●								
2 — 3	„ taurica. White		●————●								
1 — 2	Inula acaulis. Yellow			●————●							
6 — 8	Iris Chamaeiris. Yellow			●————●							

Flowering period table

Approx. height (inches)		Feb.	Mar.	Apr.	May	June	July	Aug.	Sep.	Oct.	Nov.
7 — 9	*Iris cristata. Blue and gold. Leafy				———						
3 — 4	* ,, lacustris. Blue and gold. Leafy							———	———		
3 — 4	,, mellita. Smoky red			———							
2 — 3	,, minuta. Yellow	———	———	———							
5 — 6	,, pumila atroviolacea. Purple		———	———							
5 — 6	,, lutea. Yellow	———	———	———							
6 — 8	Jasminium Parkeri. Yellow					———					
2 — 3	Linaria alpina. Violet and orange					———	———	———	———		
2 — 3	,, ,, rosea. Pink and orange					———	———	———	———		
2 — 3	,, faucicola. Violet					———	———	———			
1 — 2	,, globosa rosea. Pink			———	———	———	———				
8 — 12	Linum arboreum. Yellow					———	———	———	———		
6 — 9	,, flavum. Yellow					———	———	———	———		
2 — 3	,, salsoloides nanum. White. Limy			———							
6 — 8	Lithospermum graminifolium. Blue. Limy			———	———	———	———				
8 — 9	,, intermedium. Deep blue. Limy			———	———	———	———	———			
½ — 1	Morisia hypogaea. Yellow	———	———	———	———	———	———				

44

Flowering period table:

Approx. height (inches)		Flowering period
8 — 9	Oenothera pumila. Yellow	May–Sep.
3 — 4	Penstemon confertus. Creamy yellow	May–Aug.
10 — 18	„ heterophyllus. Blue	June–Aug.
4 — 6	„ rupicola. Coral red	May–July
8 — 12	„ Scouleri. Lilac	May–Aug.
2 — 3	„ Weald Beacon. Coral red	May–July
3 — 4	*Phlox amoena rosea. Deep pink	May–June
4 — 6	* „ bifida. White	May–June
2 — 3	„ Douglasii Beauty of Ronsdorf. Pink	May–June
2 — 3	„ „ Boothman's Variety. Lavender	May–June
2 — 3	„ „ Eva. Pink, deeper eye	May–June
2 — 3	„ „ Lilac Queen. Lilac	May–July
3 — 4	„ „ Rose Queen. Pink	May–July
3 — 4	* „ procumbens. Pink	May–June
4 — 6	* „ stolonifera. Pink	Apr.–June
6 — 8	* „ „ Blue Ridge. Blue	May–June
1 — 2	Polygala calcarea. Blue. Limy	May–June

Months columns: Feb. Mar. Apr. May June July Aug. Sep. Oct. Nov.

45

Flowering period

Approx. height (inches)		Feb.	Mar.	Apr.	May	June	July	Aug.	Sep.	Oct.	Nov.
4 — 6	*Polygala Chamaebuxus. Cream and yellow. Leafy				—	—	—				
4 — 6	* ,, purpurea. Purple and yellow. Leafy				—	—	—				
6 — 12	Primula capitata. Violet purple						—	—	—		
1½ — 2	* ,, Clarkei. Pink. Leafy			—	—						
4 — 6	* ,, farinosa. Purple to pink. Leafy			—	—	—					
3 — 4	* ,, frondosa. Pale purple. Leafy			—	—						
8 — 12	* ,, involucrata. White. Leafy			—	—						
3 — 4	,, pubescens. Deep pink. Limy				—	—					
3 — 4	,, ,, Faldonside. Crimson. Limy				—	—					
3 — 4	,, ,, Mrs. J. H. Wilson. Violet. Limy				—	—					
3 — 4	,, ,, The General. Terra-cotta. Limy				—	—					
6 — 8	* ,, rosea grandiflora. Pink. Leafy			—	—						
8 — 12	Rhododendron ferrugineum. Carmine					—	—				
4 — 6	Rosa gallica Little Dot. Double white				—	—	—	—	—		
4 — 6	,, Maid Marion. Double Red				—	—	—	—	—		
6 — 8	,, Oakington Ruby. Double crimson				—	—	—	—	—		
4 — 6	,, Peon. Single crimson				—	—	—	—	—		

46

Approx. height (inches)		Flowering period									
		Feb.	Mar.	Apr.	May	June	July	Aug.	Sep.	Oct.	Nov.
6 — 8	Rosa pumila. Double pink				—	—	—	—	—		
3 — 4	„ Rouletti. Semi-double pink				—	—	—	—	—		
2 — 3	Saxifraga Aizoon baldensis. White. Limy					—					
1 — 2 *	„ Burseriana Gloria. White. Limy		—	—							
1 — 2 *	„ „ His Majesty. Pale pink. Limy		—	—							
1 — 2 *	„ „ sulphurea. Pale yellow. Limy		—	—							
1 — 2 *	„ Irvingii. Pale pink. Limy		—	—							
½ — 1 *	„ oppositifolia. Rose purple. Leafy		—	—							
½ — 1 *	„ „ coccinea. Crimson. Leafy		—	—							
½ — 1 *	„ „ latina. Pink. Leafy		—	—							
½ — 1 *	„ „ splendens. Red purple. Leafy		—	—							
2 — 3 *	„ Primulaize. Salmon			—							
2 — 3	Sedum kamtschaticum. Yellow. Limy and dry						—	—			
2 — 3	„ spathulifolium. Yellow. Limy and dry						—				
2 — 3	„ spurium. Pink. Limy and dry						—				
2 — 3	„ „ splendens. Red. Limy and dry							—	—		
2 — 3	„ „ Schorbuser Blut. Crimson. Limy and dry							—	—		

47

Approx. height (inches)		Flowering period									
		Feb.	Mar.	Apr.	May	June	July	Aug.	Sep.	Oct.	Nov.
4 — 6	Serratula Shawii. Crimson								—		
8 — 9	Sisyrinchium angustifolium. Violet blue					—	—	—			
4 — 6	,, bellum. Violet blue					—	—	—			
8 — 12	,, Bermudianum. Blue and yellow					—	—	—			
6 — 8	Solidago brachystachys. Yellow							—			
4 — 6	Thymus carnosus. Lilac					—	—				
4 — 6	,, nitidus. Lilac					—	—				
4 — 6	Umbilicus oppositifolius. Yellow				—	—					
2 — 3	Veronica Allionii. Blue					—	—				
3 — 4	,, Bonarota. Blue				—	—	—				
4 — 6	,, lutea. Yellow				—	—	—				
4 — 6	,, pyroliformis. Leafy. Pale blue						—				
3 — 4	,, satureioides. Dark blue				—	—	—				
4 — 6	,, saxatilis. Blue						—				
4 — 6	,, spicata nana. Violet					—	—				
1 — 2	*Viola saxatilis aetolica. Yellow			—	—	—	—				
1 — 2	* ,, arenaria rosea. Deep pink. Leafy				—	—					

48

Approx. height (inches)		Flowering period								
		Feb.	Mar.	Apr.	May	June	July	Aug.	Sep.	Oct.	Nov.
4—6	*Viola biflora. Yellow. Leafy					———					
1—2	,, cornuta minor. Lavender			———————————							
2—3	,, elegantula. Rose pink			———————							
1—2	* ,, hederacea. Violet and white. Leafy					———————————					
4—6	Wahlenbergia dalmatica. Violet blue. Limy						———				
2—4	,, dinarica. Violet blue. Limy						———				
4—6	,, graminifolia. Lavender. Limy							———			
1—2	,, pumilio. Lavender					———					
1—2	,, serpyllifolia major. Deep violet. Limy										

BULBS FOR PLANTING UNDER CARPETERS, FOR SUN OR SEMI-SHADE

Approx. height (inches)		Flowering period								
		Feb.	Mar.	Apr.	May	June	July	Aug.	Sep.	Oct.	Nov.
3—4	*Anemone blanda. Blue	———									
3—4	* ,, atrocaerulea. Dark blue	———									
3—4	* ,, rosea. Pink	———									
3—4	Chinodoxa sardensis. Blue		—								
1½—2	Crocus Balansae. Orange	—									
2—3	,, Fleischeri. White		—								
2—3	,, longiflorus. Violet blue										—

Approx. height (inches)		Flowering period									
		Feb.	Mar.	Apr.	May	June	July	Aug.	Sep.	Oct.	Nov.
1½ — 2	Crocus medius. Deep purple									—	—
2 — 3	,, ochroleucus. White									—	—
2 — 3	,, pulchellus. Lavender								—		
2 — 3	,, susianus. Yellow	—	—								
2 — 3	,, Tomasinianus. Pale blue	—	—								
2 — 3	,, ,, Whitwell Purple. Purple	—	—								
3 — 4	,, zonatus Kotschyanus. Lavender blue							—			
2 — 3	Eranthis hyemalis (Aconite). Yellow	—	—								
8 — 12	*Fritillaria Meleagris. Various colours			—							
3 — 4	Galanthus byzantinus. White	—									
9 — 12	Iris reticulata. Violet blue	—	—								
9 — 12	,, ,, Hercules. Purple, orange splash	—	—								
9 — 12	,, ,, J. S. Dijt. Red purple	—	—								
3 — 4	Muscari azureum. Blue		—								
5 — 6	Narcissus Bulbocodium. Yellow		—								
6 — 8	,, ,, citrinus. Pale yellow		—								
6 — 8	,, ,, cyclamineus. Yellow		—								

Approx. height (inches)		Flowering period									
		Feb.	Mar.	Apr.	May	June	July	Aug.	Sep.	Oct.	Nov.
3 — 4	Narcissus juncifolius. Yellow			—							
4 — 6	,, nanus. Yellow		—	—							
4 — 6	*Sternbergia lutea. Yellow. Leafy								—	—	
4 — 6	Triteleia uniflora. Pale blue			—	—						
4 — 6	,, ,, violacea. Deeper blue			—	—						
6 — 8	Tulipa praestans var. Tubergen. Scarlet			—							
3 — 4	,, tarda. Yellow and white			—							

CARPETERS FOR BULB COVER IN THE ALPINE BORDER, SUN OR SEMI-SHADE. ALL UNDER ONE INCH HIGH

	Flowering period									
	Feb.	Mar.	Apr.	May	June	July	Aug.	Sep.	Oct.	Nov.
*Claytonia australasica. White. Leafy										
Frankenia thymifolia. Pink. Limy					—	—				
Gypsophila cerastioides. White. Limy										
*Hypsela longiflora. White and crimson. Leafy						—				
*Mazus Pumilio. Lilac, yellow centre. Leafy						—				
Nierembergia rivularis. White										
Potentilla verna nana. Yellow			—	—	—					
Sedum dasyphyllum. White. Limy, dry					—	—				
,, hispanicum. Pale pink. Limy, dry					—	—				

51

Approx. height (inches)		Flowering period										
		Feb.	Mar.	Apr.	May	June	July	Aug.	Sep.	Oct.	Nov.
	Sedum lydium. White. Limy, dry						——	——			
	,, sexangulare. Yellow. Limy, dry						——	——			
	*Selliera radicans. White. Leafy							——			
	Thymus Serpyllum major. Crimson										

There are many more carpeters, these are merely a few for this particular purpose. Others of more robust growth will be found in the list at the end of Chapter 4.

LIST OF LIME HATERS FOR SUN OR SEMI-SHADE

Approx. height (inches)		Flowering period										
		Feb.	Mar.	Apr.	May	June	July	Aug.	Sep.	Oct.	Nov.
6 — 8	Azalea roseaflorum fl. pl. Salmon red				——						
9 — 12	Erica ciliaris Mrs. C. H. Gill. Nearest red						——	——	——	——	
3 — 6	,, cinerea coccinea. Crimson						——	——	——		
4 — 6	,, ,, pygmaea. Pink						——	——			
9 — 12	,, ,, P. S. Patrick. Purple						——	——	——	——	
8 — 9	,, hybrida Dawn. Pink					——	——	——	——	——	
4 — 6	,, Gwen. Pink										
8 — 9	,, vulgaris J. H. Hamilton. Double pink							——	——		
2 — 3	,, minima. Purple							——	——		
1 — 2	,, nana compacta. Purple							——	——		
3 — 4	,, Sister Anne. Pink							——	——		

Approx. height (inches)		Flowering period									
		Feb.	Mar.	Apr.	May	June	July	Aug.	Sep.	Oct.	Nov.
2 — 3	*Gentiana hexaphylla. Pale blue						—	—			
4 — 6	" * sino-ornata. Royal blue							—	—		
3 — 4	" * Veitchiorum. Indigo blue					—	—				
4 — 6	Lithospermum diffusum Heavenly Blue. Blue					—	—	—			
8 — 12	Polygala paucifolia. Rose purple				—						
3 — 4	" Vayredae. Pink and yellow				—						
4 — 6	Rhododendron campylogynum. Purple					—					
3 — 4	" imperator. Pink				—						
6 — 8	" keleticum. Purple					—					
1 — 2	" radicans. Pale red purple			—							
8 — 9	Sisyrinchium Douglasii. Red purple	—									
8 — 9	" " album. White		—								
8 — 9	" filifolium. White				—						

LIST OF PLANTS FOR THE DAMP CORNER IN SHADE OR SEMI-SHADE
All Primula soil

Approx. height (inches)		Flowering period									
8 — 9	Dodecatheon alpinum. Deep magenta pink				—						
9 — 12	" Hendersonii. Lilac				—						
9 — 12	" integrifolium. Carmine (varies)				—						

53

Approx. height (inches)		Flowering period									
		Feb.	Mar.	Apr.	May	June	July	Aug.	Sep.	Oct.	Nov.
12—18	Dodecatheon Jeffreyi. Deep rose pink (varies)				—	—					
12—18	„ latilobum. Pink, yellow eye				—	—					
18—24	„ Meadia. Pale pink (varies)				—	—					
10—12	Iris Forrestii. Yellow				—	—					
8—9	„ ruthenica. Violet blue				—	—					
6—8	Mimulus Bee's Dazzler. Scarlet					—	—	—	—		
6—8	„ Chelsea Pensioner. Crimson					—	—	—	—		
4—6	„ Dainty. Yellow					—	—	—	—		
3—4	„ Plymtree. Pink					—	—	—	—		
6—8	„ Prince Bismark. Cherry red					—	—	—	—		
2—3	„ Whitecroft Scarlet. Scarlet					—	—	—	—		
6—8	Ourisia coccinea. Scarlet					—	—				
12—15	Primula alpicola. Sulphur yellow				—	—					
12—15	„ violacea. Reddish violet				—	—					
12—18	„ Asthore. Mixed, pastel shades				—	—					
8—12	„ aurantiaca. Orange				—	—					
18—24	„ Beesiana. Deep lilac				—	—					

Approx. height (inches)		Feb.	Mar.	Apr.	May	June	July	Aug.	Sep.	Oct.	Nov.
						Flowering period					
24 — 30	Primula Bulleyana. Orange					│					
6 — 9	,, denticulata. Lilac		│	│							
6 — 9	,, ,, alba. White		│	│							
6 — 9	,, ,, Ascot Red. Mixed, near reds		│	│	│						
6 — 9	,, ,, Hay's variety. Violet		│	│							
24 — 36	,, Florindae. Yellow						│	│	│		
24 — 30	,, helodoxa. Yellow					│	│				
18 — 24	,, japonica. Crimson (varies)				│	│					
18 — 24	,, Millers Crimson. Crimson				│	│					
18 — 24	,, Postford White. White				│	│					
24 — 36	,, pulverulenta. Magenta				│	│					
24 — 36	,, Bartley Strain. Shell pink				│	│					
24 — 36	,, Red Hugh. Fiery red				│	│	│				
12 — 18	,, secundiflora. Violet purple					│	│				
18 — 24	,, sikkimensis. Yellow					│	│				
12 — 18	,, Waltoni. Magenta crimson				│	│	│				
24 — 30	,, Wilsoni. Red purple				│	│					

55

LIST OF PLANTS FOR THE ALPINE BORDER IN SHADE

Including semi-shade species that will take shade with humus, and powerful plants for dry shade

Approx. height (inches)		Flowering period									
		Feb.	Mar.	Apr.	May	June	July	Aug.	Sep.	Oct.	Nov.
4 — 6	Ajuga reptans. Blue. Strong, dry shade				—	—					
3 — 4	Anemone blanda. Blue. Bulb		—	—							
3 — 4	,, ,, atrocaerulea. Dark blue. Bulb		—	—							
3 — 4	,, ,, rosea. Pink. Bulb		—	—							
6 — 9	Astilbe chinensis pumila. Deep pink. Leafy					—	—				
3 — 4	,, glaberrima saxatilis. Pink. Leafy					—	—				
4 — 6	,, simplicifolia. Pale pink. Leafy					—	—				
1	Claytonia australasica. White. Carpeter. Leafy										
1 — 2	Cotula squalida. Foliage only. Strong, dry shade										
2 — 3	Cyclamen coum. Pink. Leafy	—	—								
2 — 3	,, ,, album. White. Leafy	—	—								
3 — 4	,, europaeum. Pink. Leafy							—			
3 — 4	,, neapolitanum. Pale pink. Leafy								—	—	
3 — 4	,, ,, album. White. Leafy								—	—	
4 — 6	,, repandum. Crimson. Leafy		—	—							
8 — 9	Dodecatheon alpinum. Deep magenta pink. Leafy				—	—					

56

Approx. height (inches)		Flowering period										
		Feb.	Mar.	Apr.	May	June	July	Aug.	Sep.	Oct.	Nov.
9—12	Dodecatheon Hendersonii. Lilac. Leafy				—	—					
9—12	„ integrifolium. Carmine (varies). Leafy			—	—	—					
12—18	„ Jeffreyi. Deep rose pink (varies). Leafy				—	—					
12—18	„ latilobum. Pink, yellow eye. Leafy			—	—	—					
18—24	„ Meadia. Pale pink (varies). Leafy			—	—	—					
2—3	Eranthis hyemalis. Yellow. Bulb	—									
4—6	Erythronium californicum. Yellow and cream. Bulb		—	—							
4—6	„ Dens-canis. Mixed. Bulb		—	—							
4—6	„ revolutum Johnsonii. Pink. Bulb		—	—							
4—6	„ Watsonii. White. Bulb		—	—							
3—4	Hutchinsia alpina. White. Carpeter. Strong				—	—					
1	Linaria aequitriloba. Lavender. Carpeter					—	—	—	—		
1	„ hepaticifolia. Pale pink. Carpeter					—	—	—	—		
1—2	Mazus Pumilio. Lavender. Carpeter. Leafy						—	—			
1—2	„ reptans. Lilac and yellow. Carpeter. Leafy						—	—			
6—9	Omphalodes cappadocica. Blue					—	—	—			
6—9	„ verna. Blue	—	—	—	—						

57

Approx. height (inches)		Feb.	Mar.	Apr.	May	June	July	Aug.	Sep.	Oct.	Nov.
						Flowering period					
6 — 9	Ourisia coccinea. Scarlet. Leafy					—	—				
6 — 8	Polygonum affine. Pink. Strong							—	—		
6 — 9	Primula denticulata. Lilac		—								
6 — 9	,, alba. White		—								
6 — 9	,, ,, Ascot Red. Mixed, near reds		—								
6 — 9	,, ,, Hay's variety. Violet		—								
4 — 6	Juliana Altaica grandiflora. Pink		—								
4 — 6	,, Betty Green. Almost scarlet		—								
4 — 6	,, David Green. Crimson, yellow eye		—								
4 — 6	,, E. R. Janes. Orange-yellow		—								
4 — 6	,, Garryarde Guinevere. Lavender pink		—								
4 — 6	,, Lady Greer. Cream yellow		—								
4 — 6	,, Mrs. J. H. Wilson. Lavender		—								
4 — 6	,, Romeo. Violet		—								
4 — 6	,, Wanda. Magenta crimson		—								
4 — 6	,, (double) Bonaccord Lavender		—								
4 — 6	,, ,, purity. White		—								

58

Approx. height (inches)		Flowering period									
		Feb.	Mar.	Apr.	May	June	July	Aug.	Sep.	Oct.	Nov.
4 — 6	Primula Juliana (double) Marie Crouse. Royal purple		—	—							
4 — 6	,, ,, Our Pat. Nearest to blue		—	—							
4 — 6	,, ,, Quaker Bonnet. Lilac		—	—							
4 — 6	,, ,, Red Paddy. Crimson		—	—							
3 — 4	Saxifraga hypnoides James Brenner. White		—	—	—						
3 — 4	,, ,, Kingii. White			—	—						
3 — 4	,, ,, Peter Pan. Red			—	—						
3 — 4	,, ,, Pixie. Deep red			—	—						
3 — 4	,, ,, Stormonth's Variety. Crimson			—	—						
4 — 6	,, moschata Carnival. Deep pink			—	—						
4 — 6	,, ,, General Joffre. Crimson			—	—						
4 — 6	,, ,, Mrs. Piper. Pink			—	—						
4 — 6	,, ,, Pompadour. Carmine red			—	—						
4 — 6	,, ,, Sir Douglas Haig. Crimson			—	—						
4 — 6	,, ,, Triumph. Almost scarlet			—	—						
4 — 6	,, umbrosa var. primuloides. Pale pink				—						
1 — 2	Selliera radicans. White. Carpeter. Leafy						—	—	—	—	

Approx. height (inches)		Flowering period
		Feb. *Mar.* *Apr.* *May* *June* *July* *Aug.* *Sep.* *Oct.* *Nov.*
3 — 4	Waldsteinia fragarioides. Yellow	——
3 — 4	,, trifolia. Yellow	——

3

The Dry Wall

The horticultural dry wall is entirely different to the Cotswold, Yorkshire or Lake District 'stone hedge'. Its purpose is not to use up stone that litters a hill pasture in making a cattle-proof barrier but to retain soil and grow plants. The builder's 'rustic wall' of flat slabs cemented edge to edge, usually in a pair, with a space full of soil between for planting only along the top is in another class; the dry wall of the garden uses rammed soil instead of cement and, up to about seven feet high, is a gardening operation to build.

It is in effect an alpine border on edge, with the same long flowering season, and the same range of species which do well in shade, but in almost vertical wasted space. The slope in front of the house will take an alpine bank, but the back of the platform cut out of the hillside, facing the rearward windows, in shade or semi-shade is more suited to the wall for there are few good species for this situation with soil-holding roots. In full sun it has the advantage of greater steepness, a two foot high wall need only slope back four inches, one seven feet high about one foot nine, and where a drive-in or a path must come close to the foot of the slope, a dry wall is the best and most colourful solution.

Its plants are chosen for different qualities. They are trailing rather than upright and selected for their preference for growing edgeways. On the dry wall a great many species which dislike winter damp, such as the hairy-leaved Androsaces and the Onosmas, are far happier than on the rock garden, and, under conditions of drought, sun and semi-starvation, very many flower far better than they do planted on the flat.

The dry wall is a formal garden feature, it is not trying to look like part of nature. It goes with straight lines, stone steps, paving and clipped hedges, and therefore there is no need to build it with weathered and waterworn rock. The only disadvantage of using broken pavement slabs is that they are too thin, and of flints, their relatively small size and curly awkward shapes. The best walling stone is flat on one or both

61

surfaces, sandstones which break flat with a square face are ideal, so are old kerbstones, or even lumps of old brickwork, overburnt bricks or brick burrs. Broken concrete too is good, so long as the pieces are not too rounded to fit together—the more rectangular the material the stronger and firmer the wall.

Good rock garden stone, weathered stuff, is collected on the hills of Britain from formations very much like a natural rock garden; it has to be hauled down by tractor and trailer and put on rail for usually a considerable journey. Dry wall stone is far more common. Kentish rag (grey), Bargate sandstone (light brown), Somerset (cream) are trade names, whatever is available locally, and sufficiently fine grained and hard not to flake to pieces in frost, and will make a good wall. This choice of local stone is not because it is natural to your neighbourhood, but because it is going to be cheaper with the shorter journey by road direct.

The best source is your local builder, who may know of an old stone wall coming down, and though you cannot rely on his idea of the sort of material that makes a good rock garden you can for walling. He will know the local stone, and which will break up in frost and which will not. The best effect is from using stone of one colour, not dazzling white but brown or grey for choice, because it goes better with foliage and flowers, but there is nothing to prevent one using a mixture; it looks far better than on a rock garden. Those who wish to use up stone that is in the way, even flints or marble fragments, can employ it better in a dry wall, even if they make a raised bed with it against a garden wall (heap it above the damp course of a house and you may have trouble), than in a rock garden.

When you buy stone it is as well to allow an average of one ton to thirty square feet of wall face, and to remember that a ton at a time in a four-ton lorry is going to cost nearly four times as much for cartage as four tons at once in one trip, even if the pile does block up the paths.

Building and planting the Dry Wall

A dry wall is best planted as it is built. Its cement is soil and the plants are built in to the vertical and horizontal joints as it goes up layer by layer; their roots can run back into the soil behind, unlike those planted in 'pockets' in a cemented wall. The best time to build is in the autumn, for choice in October and November for then one can plant all the Aubrieta and several other division subjects, especially Sedums, as mere strands of unrooted branches. A bunch of four or five mature trailing stems of Aubrieta, about a foot long, with the growing tips held together in a clump against the face, will root easily at this season in the very thin sandwich filling of soil at a horizontal joint, and will flower modestly the first year before making a better and longer-lived clump than they will in many other situations.

Because the spring glory of the Aubrieta can be secured so easily by this method, using no pots or frame space, autumn is the best time; the spring from February to April needs rooted divisions of Aubrieta, or pot stuff and this is less easy to supply in the quantity required on a big wall. A number of other plants can be sandwiched in either in the spring or autumn from cuttings rooted in the open ground in early summer (see Chapter 7 for a full account), including Helianthemums, *Veronica rupestris*, alpine Phloxes (from layerings) and that lovely late summer ramper *Polygonum vacciniifolium*. This method of planting is easy and effective, even though replacements can only be put in when rebuilding.

The dry wall holds up a steep bank in two ways: firstly on the principle of preventing small falls of soil growing into large ones, as the thin brick lining of a tunnel holds thousands of tons of earth above it, and secondly because it slopes backwards, so that the bottom stones come further forward than those at the top. Because it is on this slant, some of the thrust is transferred downwards. A cemented house wall is upright, but nothing is pushing behind it. A dry wall should never be straight upright and must lean back to take the thrust in the same way as the slightly sloped-back brick retaining walls in such positions as the mouths of railway tunnels or the high steep sides of the entrances to London stations where back gardens end far above the carriage windows.

The low dry wall from one to two feet high has little need to worry about soil thrust, but there are other reasons that make this backward slope or 'batter' essential. Apart from the water that soaks down behind the wall, which varies with the type of soil, the only water supply is the rain that drives against it. The slight ledge of stones set so that they underlap each other a bit, never overlap, collects some of this rain and runs it back along the slanting rock into the soil seam. You also need firmness of construction even on a small scale because the bed above may need digging and standing on to weed. Therefore, though you can do without batter up to two feet high, it is best to allow the standard backward slope of two to three inches in every foot of height.

The first operation in facing a slope with a dry wall is usually to trench back the face from the foot to allow the bottom stones to be placed. This has the advantage of providing a supply of soil to mix up to nearer an alpine mixture to be rammed in place behind the courses. The wall is frequently at a much steeper angle than the existing bank and therefore one has a triangle of space to fill in behind it, and soil may be needed in considerable quantity, so it is as well to work out the position of the wall so that it will provide a good quantity from this trenching. Perennial weeds should be removed, though any roots will be shut in by the stone; any near a join may struggle through, especially convolvulus, and they are hard to get out when the wall is up. Tree roots should be sawn off well away from the wall; if they can crook an elbow against the back, as they grow they can push it over; sawn off, they merely produce fibrous roots which compete with the plants for food and moisture, but not enough to bother about.

Along the line of the wall, a shallow trench should be dug, perhaps an inch deep on the outer side and four on the inner, about eighteen inches wide, narrower if the wall is up to two feet high and built of small stone. The object of the sloping floor is to start your batter and to give a surface for your wall to push on. As a wall needs to be straight, a line should be used to cut out the trench so that the faces of the stone are in line along the front edge.

Then set your first stones, the largest and flattest on both top and bottom that you have, the higher the wall the more this matters; it is a good principle but for a low wall it can be less strict. They should sit firm and level; if they have bulges below, dig out a hole to take it, and make small piles of soil under the hollows; you should be able to stand on them without their rocking. Then ram the soil down behind them, holding them in place with your foot so they do not move outwards. Two rammers will be found very useful, one short one, like those used for firming pot Chrysanthemums, about eight inches long, cut from an old spade handle with a flat end to ram with and the top either rounded off to fit your hand, or made from the handle part of the shaft. This punches the soil hard into the joints and small spaces. Thumping the stones down firm and ramming the back soil is the task of the second tool, a stout post about three feet long or more with the upper part rounded for easy gripping. A navvy's rammer, with a shaft like a broomstick and a heavy iron head is ideal, but it is quite easy to rig up something for a job you only do once.

Another gadget worth using is a 'batter gauge', especially for the higher walls. This can be a stout flat piece of wood, with a string and a weight on the end, such as a large iron nut, which is thrust over the wall a foot out, when the wall is four feet high. If the weight hangs against the bottom then the batter is right, and so on up. Instead of this rough garden version of the bricklayer's plump bob, one can use a straight piece of timber, say 2 in. × 1 in., and as long as the wall is to be tall, and nail short lengths to the wider surface at foot or six inch intervals, overlapping by the amount the wall should have sloped back in that distance. It is easy to correct a fault in the batter by whacking the protruding stone in with the large rammer, so long as one does not get too far ahead and have too much to alter, which is why it is best to check as you go.

Before the next course is put in place, about an inch of soil should be spread and levelled over the upper surface of the firmed bottom layer. Then set your next course stones in place, taking care that the vertical joints do not come over each other like a brick wall. As your stones are going to be all shapes and sizes, this is not always possible—one large one may reach up two courses high in some places—but it is the guiding rule, because the holding power of the stones is by friction on each other as well as their own weight. The smaller and lighter the pieces the more vertical joints in line with each other should be avoided.

The first foot of the wall is often left unplanted, because the plants above will trail down over the blank space. In a low wall, where there is not much planting area, clump-forming plants, such as Thrifts, Hypericums, or in shade, mossy Saxifrages, can go in below the second course. This is the main difference between planting a wall and a rock garden, or alpine bank or border: the stronger the trailer the higher up it should be planted. Aubrieta wants a clear foot or eighteen inches below it, but in the next course above, a clump plant which will grow up and out and only down to a limited extent can go in to use the room. As a general rule the plant proportion is roughly one to every eighteen inch square. Because of the dry conditions and ample sun, invasive species are less rampant on the wall, but any strangling is usually on plants below, not at the sides where trailers are concerned. The lists at the end of this chapter are classified into trailers and clumpers on this account. The general aim of planting, to secure a full colour range over the longest possible season, in full sun, semi-shade or shade, by using a large number of different species instead of a few which fill the space and leave a gap when they are over, is the same here as in all alpine gardening.

Where a horizontal joint is being planted with divisions or rooted stuff from cuttings, the soil layer should be spread in two halves, the roots or unrooted stems laid back to reach into the soil behind, with the small quantity of foliage lapping over the outer edge of the lower rock so that it will sit neatly against the face, then more soil is added and the next stone set firmly on top. Some of these horizontal plantings may die out, but as they cost only time and not much of that, this is not an important consideration, and one can afford to be lavish with them.

The pot plants and those bought as pot stuff go in the vertical joints. If the soil ball is well filled with roots, it is possible to squash them a bit,

E   65

but not to the extent that is needed horizontally. Get them about an inch back from the face, with a soil covering on the rock below, and squeeze the next rock up to them so that the round soil ball becomes oval. Then fill in the rest of the space above and behind them with firm soil; they will have to draw their water from that which seeps along the soil below and that behind them and there must be a root run to the rammed earth behind. It is no good making a stone, brick or concrete-lined cavity, packing it full of soil and expecting plants to grow edgeways in it. The idea of placing the pot-grown plants so that they are a bit further in than the face of the stones is to provide a bit of catchment from rain driving against the face of the wall, in the same way as on the alpine bank.

All plants should stand in water to get thoroughly wet before they go in, as they need a starting stock, and the stone is apt to suck up moisture when it is dry, which is one of the reasons why the summer is a bad planting time. Divisions too appreciate dipping, though it is as well to avoid washing more soil than can be avoided off the open ground stuff or rooted divisions. When you are unwrapping the plants before standing them in water, be sure and get out any weeds in the soil ball. As most of the surface is going to be stone, and strong-growing perennial plants the rest, there should be no weeding on the wall garden, but some nurserymen can sell you trouble, or you may have grown it yourself. Look to see if there are any thick white thistle or dandelion roots, yellow dock fangs, or the claw-tipped interlacing fingers of couch grass matted round the soil ball. It is easy to pull or cut off a weed at surface level, slice off the root where it leaves through the drainage hole, and send the plant still with the thistle that has already half-strangled it ready to try its luck in the dry wall. These roots are utterly distinct from those of alpines, and as they usually grow against the sides of the soil ball they can be picked off easily before planting.

Never in any circumstances put in an alpine anywhere still wrapped in paper, or in a cardboard pot. The roots may grow through the wet material, but paper and cardboard are concentrated cellulose which will rot by bacterial action that takes nitrogen from the soil in competition with the new feeding roots of the plant. Compost, leafmould and peat are past the nitrogen-grabbing stage of decay but wet newspaper can rob newly planted alpines so severely that they may not recover.

As the wall rises, planting and fitting in the stones layer by layer, a new aspect must be considered. The relatively narrow blocks, perhaps eight inches to a foot long, three inches high and four deep, are held to each other by friction and their own weight—the soil in the joints only

The Dry Wall

holds them together very slightly indeed, its main use is to grow plants. 'Tie-stones' to hold the wall in to the soil are needed above two feet high and are useful for added strength even at lesser heights.

These are long pieces set so that their length goes back into the bank and their short height and width is on the face. As a general principle they should be between four and six feet apart and a foot above each other, but spaced irregularly on a staggered pattern as the building of the wall decides. Some of the push of the soil trying to get back to a thirty-eight degree natural slope (a heap of loose earth or sand ten feet in diameter will be four feet high, and the sides of the cone will be at this angle), is directly downwards behind the wall. The tie-stones take this thrust and transfer it into an attempt to lift the whole weight of the wall, or push it into the ground, exactly the sort of force that it is made to stand. In addition they have a friction grip on the soil round them and add greatly to the strength of the wall.

They mean that more stone is required; the thirty square feet to the ton includes a normal quantity of them, but when you are building anything with stone there will be an accumulation of ugly and awkward pieces that refuse to fit in nicely, and these can be used up as tie-stones. Triangular fragments, those with a protruding tongue or a difficult bulge, can have the best face on the front of the wall, and the rest, on rammed soil below it so they sit at the correct angle for their whole length and hold the wall against falling forward.

The wall that needs the most ties is one built of flints. These are awkward to set in regular courses because they are so curved that they will not lie flat and firm. Long flints used as tie-stones every four feet and in every other layer will hold firm into rammed soil, and with the smaller and rounder lumps fitted so that they lock each other as far as possible the flint wall will stay up without cement. As the garden where flints are used is usually one where the need is to get them out of the way, there is no need to stint, but they should be no closer than two feet apart; they need the rammed soil round them to hold on. With flints it is best to come round a corner in a curve, about a quarter of a circle six or eight feet in diameter, because it is difficult to make a right angle with such short pieces.

The top of the wall is best finished with larger stones, and the flatter ones. Though as the wall goes up the smaller stone is used higher as a general principle, the topmost ones are the most likely to be knocked off, and therefore bigger stuff, acting as frequent flat tie-stones, is the best finish. Between them plants should go in, both to cascade over the top or to sit as neat domes in the vertical joints, and, especially if there is a border behind the wall, keep the digging fork away from the back, as both plant roots and the firmness of the stones can be damaged by disturbance. One can finish by turfing up to the line of the larger stones, and filling in with alpines, if there is a lawn above, but not a narrow bed for annuals or Dahlias, for apart from the root competition of greedier plants, you do not want anything that requires frequent digging.

Building the Larger Wall

Anyone can build a three foot wall and have it firm and blazing with the long display that finishes with Zauschneria in November. When you get higher still, a few more problems arise which are still within the ability of a gardener to solve. The most important is drainage, which comes in where the bank cuts across a line of field drains, a layer of sand or gravel, has a slope above it down which water flows in quantity in wet weather, or is on heavy clay.

The last is far the most common, and because you are going to ram the soil behind the wall, even though this has been lightened by the addition of sand, coarse grit and peat or leafmould, it will have some of the effect of the rammed clay puddling that is still keeping some derelict canals watertight after a hundred and fifty years. A brick or concrete wall will have lines of drainpipes showing in the face, as it lets no water through and if they were not there, the water behind would push it over on some soils. A dry wall is not solid; water can get through at every joint and usually there is so little that it merely forms the water supply of the plants, but where one is making a high wall against a clay bank it must be considered.

The usual countermeasure is to take out the bottom trench rather wider and deeper and fill it with gravel or other drainage material such as broken clinker. On clay this will not act as a soak away, and either a drain like those used to bring water to the damp corner is put in to lead it away, or gaps between the lower stones are connected with the drainage material behind. This is usually sufficient, it needs to be possible for water to soak away slowly from behind the wall in case any accumulates.

Where there is a gravel seam about half-way down, drainage material should be lead up to it in cores at intervals to lead the seepage to the drainage layer. Another system is to build normally to the layer, then have a seam of drainage material leading to gaps in the face of the wall. If there are cut land drains in the slope, and modern earth-moving machinery can disregard these utterly, it is best to buy some more of these agricultural field drains, and lead them straight through the soil to discharge through the wall. Hard tennis courts are frequently well drained below and it is a sound principle that any pipe you meet is there to carry water and should be extended through the wall or down and under. Surface water from a slope should be treated in the same way: see where it wants to go and get it there quickly in a pipe or drain.

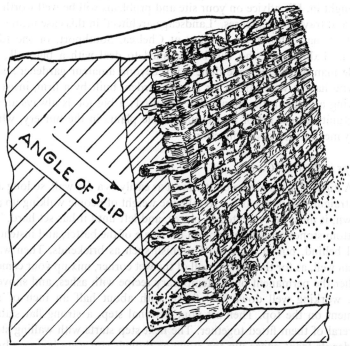

FIG. 3. A Dry Wall, no plants shown.

These water problems are rare, but they can bring the wall down with a run, and good attention to drainage solves them permanently. A Primula garden at the foot of the wall, restricting the planting of the wall itself to ferns and damp lovers, including Mimulus, is a very lovely solution in extreme cases.

It is important when you are going high to keep the batter accurate and ample. If you start off with three inches in the foot and finish with two, it not only looks bad but the change means a source of weakness. It is better to use four inches to the foot and make sure than have the wall come down, for a stone faced 45° slope will hold on the most shifting sand, and if you have to rebuild after a disaster, always take the batter back further if you can—you were probably too steep the first time.

Above seven feet the problems of thrust and stone-handling begin to get difficult. One can build a dinghy with book-read directions and amateur carpenter's skill but a full-sized tea clipper brings in too many problems with no small scale answers. If one has the stone and the time (or labour) to build a very high wall, it is height not length that brings difficulties; an architect or a genuine landscape architect should be brought in. His advice on your site and problems will be well worth his fee and travelling expenses. 'Landscape architect' in this case means the sort of man who shows gardens at Chelsea, Southport, or the Ideal Home Exhibition, who will be qualified to deal with a big wall; the little man will never have done a job beyond amateur gardener's size. If you have a wall garden, or a rock garden, built by a firm, insist on having a voice in the plants that are used; a big job is always an opportunity to get rid of all the unsaleable plants in the nursery, which may mean a very poor collection.

Steps in the Wall Garden

A flight of steps can be built almost as easily as a dry wall, so long as it is straight, but as it has got to take the weight of people walking up and down, it must be cemented in places, and left until it has set hard. The bottom stones are set flat, not on the angle of the batter, and instead of soil behind, put in more hard rubbish such as brickends. Then water them well, as for the sunken wall of the wet corner, mix up your cement, either the permanent or the temporary recipe with ashes, and shovel it on, working well down and finish with about half an inch of stiff cement on the top. Then set your actional step, a strong flat slab or several of them fitted together. The next step starts with walling stone under its front edge; dip the stone as though you were laying a brick and cement it down, rough stuff at the back, more cement and so on all the way. The sides are perfectly simple dry walling and if the flight is straight and facing the sun, both sides will be excellent for growing plants. When you are turning the corner of a wall, use long stones, so that they can lock into each other like the dovetailing on a well-made modern wooden box, or a brick wall.

If you have plenty of large flat stones, which can hold themselves from rocking and resist pushing in to the soil with the weight of someone treading, the steps can be made with only rammed earth below, but with small fragments they must be cemented. The width of the steps should be at least fifteen inches and their rise about six for comfort. Curved steps can be made but are considerably more difficult, because each must taper off to a triangle like an opening fan, and one needs a good deal of room to get the height into the quarter circle. The awkward bits of the step slabs can hide under the dry wall at the sides and the next

The Dry Wall

step above. They should only be attempted by those who are prepared to spend plenty of time and who enjoy pottering; the temporary cement is useful here as it enables the first attempt to be cleared away easily if it looks too awful.

Building a dry wall on a curve is fairly simple. Drive in a peg with a piece of string, half the diameter of the circle whose segment or half you wish to make, tied to it, and have another peg tied at the free end, then scratch the mark with the point of the second peg at the end of the stretched string. This is the standard 'gardener's compass' once used for marking out round beds and for planting the regular circles of carpet bedding plants. Building is normal; one goes ahead with the straight rocks set like the edges of a twelve-sided threepenny bit, and a post can be substituted for the peg, with a string lengthened by retying as you go up so that the batter can follow the same curve to the top. This is for the sort of curve you would use for steps, or a rounded corner, with the pivot peg set *inside* the wall, the slower curve for a path can be built without thinking of it, in fact the garden line is recommended at the start of a straight wall because it is so easy to get into a curve without meaning to.

A straight line is always the shortest distance between two points, and curves and elaborations always take up more stone, as well as looking fussy in a small garden. Many pictures are attractive at first sight, but annoying to live with, and in general the less elaborate the layout scheme, the more permanently successful it is.

Care and Upkeep of the Dry Wall

The first item of upkeep is to water the face of the wall thoroughly, especially for the benefit of the direct planted stuff; if building is done in a dry autumn it may be necessary to do this three or four times, but usually the rain comes and takes over. Use a rosed can and aim at damping the stone thoroughly as well as the plants, it does not matter if a great deal runs off, it does give the plants a moist atmosphere round the leaves and some runs into the crevices.

Apart from this there is nothing to do other than trimming back Aubrieta, Helianthemums and a few other species that need it, and the removal of any stray weeds that appear in the soil seams. As time goes on, some plants will die out, with age or because something above them has grown down and crowded them to death. In the second case, if the invader is colourful and doing well, he can be left in possession, but attention to cutting back usually prevents this trouble.

The vertical joint plants can be replaced by taking the remains out with a narrow trowel, reaching well back, pouring in water with the

71

The Dry Wall

spout of a can (with correct batter enough should go in to give them a start), then replacing with another pot plant, and new soil well firmed back with the small rammer. Horizontal joints can only be planted by taking down part of the wall and rebuilding, a job that needs slightly more care than the first building, but easier in a way because anyone who builds even six feet of wall two feet high knows far more about it at the finish of the job than when he (or she) began.

A casual system that is often effective for those who are lazy or pushed for time, is direct sowing. A number of species (see the list at the end of the chapter), can be sown in March or April direct into the soil seams and crevices. Large-seeded subjects, especially *Antirrhinum Asarina*, can be put in by making a jab with a small dibber and inserting the seed with a little soil packed back on top of it. One can sprinkle seed along a ledge with a thin fillet of soil on it, or even toss seed against the face on chance some will find a hold and grow.

Only a fraction of the seeds sown by this method survive, but those which do triumph by this method, always used by Nature for alpine sowing, are often surprisingly successful. Tough but impermanent things like *Linaria alpina* are good and will grow well in the most unlikely places. Those who can save their own seeds, from the easier Campanulas especially, will find it well worth trying, but it is only recommended where seed can be used with Nature's generosity; when one has only a pinch in the packet corner, more reliable methods are needed. Still, it does save time, and an old envelope full of 'Campanula?' or 'Aubrieta Doubtful' may as well have a chance rather than be thrown away.

The highest mortality is in builders' walls, made with thin stone of crazy-paving type cemented edge to edge. The only merit of these is that a ton can cover 135 square feet of surface, leaving gaps in places for planting and a narrow strip along the top. The only water they get is from the top between the two halves, and the space usually has been filled with poor soil and builders' rubbish which is very difficult to get out. If possible take out the soil, put some better stuff in, and plant with drought-resisting wall plants.

It is possible to make a double-sided dry wall to divide one part of the garden from the other, but it should be at least three feet across the top and must come out at the base for the batter on both sides if it is to hold plants. This means that a six foot high wall will be about five feet wide at the base, which is going to look very clumsy. A hedge or a brick or stone wall built with cement, going straight up and planted for wall fruit or climbers on its sunny side is more suitable. Low walls round raised beds are not subject to this disadvantage, but it should be re-

72

membered that the bed will always be drier than most of the garden, an advantage where one is growing things that need to be dry in summer, like the Oncocyclis Irises. The dry wall well built does a very good job in the garden but like every other garden feature, it should not be made to do things for which it is not designed.

Plants for the Dry Wall

The first list is for wall plants in full sun, or sun for part of the day, one can use either, and though the sunnier the better, most of the species listed are sufficiently tough to stand less than an all day blaze in summer. The second deals with species for shade, real shade, and it will be noted that some plants are on both lists: the reason is that species like *Campanula Portenschlagiana* will double in the role of shade plant like an old actor who can do anything but double Hamlet and the First Gravedigger. Many alpine border plants are listed also as they are equally good on the dry wall.

In addition to heights (on the flat) in inches, which are misleading with wall plants because a clump of Aubrieta may be only four inches high, but it can be three feet long downwards, 'C' has been added for Clump-forming plants, those which spread in a dome against the face of the stonework, they can be quite large, and 'T' for Trailing. It is not possible to condense how far they trail in a list which is merely intended to be a rough classification to help in planning a wall, this varies with the soil, sun, and general health; it may be a foot, it may be four feet in a season, *Arenaria montana* can do either, but reference to Chapter 7 will give a guide to the growth speed and size of the individual species.

It will be seen that May and June are the easiest months to fill, and one can plan a wall simply for that period, but if one is going to run on through the summer and into the autumn there must be room for the later and less well-known plants that flower after the Aubrieta.

There is no list of lime haters. This is because very few wall plants are from peaty or leafy soil, and those which need conditions near that of a shaded wood do not thrive edgeways. Therefore though it would be possible to make a sandstone wall on lime-free soil, starring *Lithospermum* Heavenly Blue, you still could not plant it with woodland Gentians, it would get too dry. Those who want a wall on this soil would do better to add some lime and grow the plants that like this dry sunny position. Though many of the species are lime lovers, the standard alpine soil does them all, extra can be added, and leafmould put in for plants that do better with it, but the general principle is to make up on mixture with lime for the whole job. Aubrietas and Campanulas will need extra lime on a lime-free soil. There was a case of a lady who lived on the edge of Dartmoor giving up alpines as 'too difficult', her Aubrieta always faded to a poor washy colour and died, and her Sedums struggled and dwindled; she took a great deal of persuading to plant all the lovely lime haters which suited her soil and not a dry wall, but a bank of Ericas.

Two further lists follow, one of species to plant as open ground cutting and rooted and unrooted divisions, and the other of species for direct sowing.

LIST OF ALPINES FOR THE DRY WALL IN SUN AND SEMI-SHADE

C=clump-forming plants ; T=trailing plants

Height (inches) Habit		Flowering period
		Feb. Mar. Apr. May June July Aug. Sep. Oct. Nov.
4—6.C	Achillea Clavenae. White	June—Aug.
4—6.C	,, Kellereri. White	June—Aug.
4—6.C	,, Lewisii. Creamy yellow	June—Aug.
4—6.T	,, tomentosa. Golden yellow	June—Aug.
4—5.C	,, umbellata. White	June—Aug.
4—6.C	Aethionema coridifolium. Pink	May—Aug.
8—12.C	,, grandiflorum. Pale pink	May—Aug.
4—6.C	,, iberideum. White	Apr.—June
6—8.C	,, pulchellum. Pale pink	May—Aug.
6—8.C	,, Warley Rose. Deep pink	May—Aug.
8—9.T	Alyssum saxatile. Yellow	Apr.—May
3—4.T	Androsace lanuginosa. Lilac, yellow eye	July—Sep.
3—4.T	,, ,, var. Leichtlinii. Pink	July—Sep.
3—4.T	,, sarmentosa. Pink	May
3—4.T	,, ,, Chumbyi. Deeper pink	May
3—4.T	,, ,, Watkinsii. Deep pink, red eye	May

75

Height (inches) Habit		Flowering period									
		Feb.	Mar.	Apr.	May	June	July	Aug.	Sep.	Oct.	Nov.
3 — 4.T	Anthyllis montana. Dark crimson. Limy					——	——	——	——		
3 — 4.T	,, Vulneraria. Yellow. Limy				—						
3 — 4.T	,, ,, var. Dillenii. Crimson. Limy				—						
4 — 6.T	Antirrhinum Asarina. Pale yellow					——	——	——			
8 — 9.T	Arabis albida. White		——	——	——	——					
6 — 8.T	,, aubrietioides. Pale pink		——	——	——	——					
6 — 8.T	Arenaria montana. White				——	——					
8 — 9.C	Armeria corsica. Brick red				——	——					
8 — 9.C	,, maritima. Pink				——	——					
8 — 9.C	,, Vindictive. Deep pink				——	——					
4 — 6.T	Aubrieta. Limy. All the hybrids including:		——	——	——	——					
4 — 6.T	,, Barkers Double. Dark red		——	——	——	——					
4 — 6.T	,, Blue King. Nearest a blue		——	——	——	——					
4 — 6.T	,, Carnival. Violet purple		——	——	——	——					
4 — 6.T	,, Dawn. Deep pink (semi-double)		——	——	——	——					
4 — 6.T	,, Gloriosa. Clearest pink		——	——	——	——					
4 — 6.T	,, Godstone. Violet purple		——	——	——	——					

Height (inches) Habit		Flowering period									
		Feb.	Mar.	Apr.	May	June	July	Aug.	Sep.	Oct.	Nov.
4 — 6.T	Aubrieta Gurgedyke. Violet purple		———	———	———	———					
4 — 6.T	,, Henslow Purple. Red purple		———	———	———	———					
4 — 6.T	,, Magnificent. Red		———	———	———	———					
4 — 6.T	,, Rosea splendens. Deepest pink		———	———	———	———					
4 — 6.T	,, Russell's Crimson. Crimson		———	———	———	———					
4 — 6.T	,, Vindictive. Dark red		———	———	———	———					
3 — 4.T	Calamintha alpina. Dark or pale violet (varies)					———	———	———			
8 — 9.C	Campanula carpatica. Violet, lavender blue, white. Limy					———	———	———			
2 — 3.C	,, fenestrellata. Blue and white. Limy					———	———				
3 — 4.C	,, garganica. Blue. Limy					———	———				
4 — 6.T	,, isophylla. Pale violet blue. Limy					———	———	———	———		
4 — 6.T	,, ,, alba. White. Limy					———	———	———	———		
3 — 4.T	,, Portenschlagiana. Violet. Limy					———	———	———			
12 — 15.T	,, Poscharskyana. Lavender. Limy				———	———	———	———	———	———	
8 — 12.C	Ceratostigma plumbaginoides. Clear blue						———	———	———	———	
4 — 6.T	Convolvulus mauritanicus. Deep lilac blue					———	———	———	———	———	
5 — 6.C	Dianthus caesius. Rose pink					———	———				

Height (inches) Habit		Feb.	Mar.	Apr.	May	June	July	Aug.	Sep.	Oct.	Nov.
						Flowering period					
3 — 4.C	Dianthus caesius Little Jock. Pink (double)					───	───				
4 — 6.C	„ deltoides. Deep pink					───	───	───			
4 — 6.C	„ „ Bowles variety. Crimson					───	───	───			
4 — 6.C	„ hybrid. Crossways. Cerise			───	───	───	───	───	───		
3 — 4.C	„ „ Elf. Crimson. Leafy			───	───	───	───	───	───		
6 — 8.C	„ „ Highland Frazer. Deep pink					───	───				
6 — 8.C	„ „ Queen. Crimson					───	───				
3 — 4.C	„ „ Jupiter. Salmon. Leafy (double)				───	───	───	───	───		
3 — 4.C	„ „ Mars. Crimson. Leafy (double)				───	───	───	───	───		
4 — 6.C	„ „ Napoleon III. Crimson. Leafy (semi-double)					───	───	───	───		
6 — 8.C	„ „ Spark. Crimson. Leafy				───	───	───	───	───		
4 — 6.T	Erodium absinthoides. Lilac pink				───	───	───	───	───		
4 — 6.C	„ „ amanum. White				───	───	───	───	───		
4 — 6.C	„ cheilanthifolium. Pink				───	───	───	───	───		
3 — 4.C	„ chrysanthum. Yellow				───	───	───	───	───		
4 — 6.C	„ macradenum. Magenta pink			───	───	───	───	───	───		
6 — 8.C	„ Merstham Pink. Deep pink				───	───	───	───	───		

Height (inches) Habit			Flowering period									
		Feb.	Mar.	Apr.	May	June	July	Aug.	Sep.	Oct.	Nov.
4 — 6.C	Erodium supracanum. Pink					————————					
6 — 8.T	Geranium sanguineum. Magenta red						————				
2 — 3.T	„ „ lancastriense. Clear pale pink						——				
4 — 6.T	Geranium Wallichianum. Blue							————————			
2 — 3.T	Gypsophila fratensis. Pale pink. Limy						——				
4 — 6.T	„ repens. White. Limy						————				
4 — 6.T	„ repens rosea. Pale pink. Limy						————				
8 — 9.T	„ Rosey Veil. Pale pink							————————			
6 — 9.C	Helianthemums. All varieties, including the following mainly prostrate species, which 'trail' for a short distance.										
6 — 9.C	Helianthemum Amy Baring. Orange. Prostrate					————————					
6 — 9.C	„ Apricot. Apricot orange. Prostrate					————————					
6 — 9.C	„ Ben Dearg. Flame red. Clump					————————					
6 — 9.C	„ Ben Heckla. Brick red. Prostrate					————————					
6 — 9.C	„ Ben Hope. Rose pink. Clump					————————					
6 — 9.C	„ Ben Nevis. Yellow, orange eye. Prostrate					————————					
6 — 8.C	„ Golden Queen. Yellow. Prostrate					————————					
6 — 8.C	„ Mrs. Clay. Orange bronze. Clump					————————					

Height (inches) Habit		Flowering period									
		Feb.	Mar.	Apr.	May	June	July	Aug.	Sep.	Oct.	Nov.
6 — 8.C	Helianthemum Rose Queen. Pink. Prostrate					———	———	———			
6 — 8.C	,, Salmon Queen. Salmon. Prostrate					———	———	———			
3 — 4.T	Hippocrepis comosa. Yellow. Limy					———	———	———	———		
3 — 4.T	,, E. R. Janes. Lemon yellow. Limy					———	———	———	———		
2 — 3.C	Hypericum anagalloides. Orange (varies)					———	———	———	———		
8 — 12.C	,, olympicum. Golden yellow					———	———				
8 — 12.C	,, citrinum. Pale yellow					———	———	———	———		
4 — 6.C	,, polyphyllum. Yellow					———	———	———	———		
4 — 6.T	,, rhodopeum. Yellow					———	———	———	———		
8 — 9.C	Iberis gibraltarica. Lilac			———	———						
6 — 8.C	,, sempervirens. White				———	———					
2 — 3.C	Linaria alpina. Violet and orange					———	———	———	———	———	
2 — 3.C	,, rosea. Pink and orange					———	———	———	———	———	
3 — 4.C	,, faucicola. Violet					———	———	———	———	———	
4 — 6.C	Linum alpinum. Blue. Limy				———	———	———	———	———	———	
8 — 9.C	Lithospermum graminifolium. Blue					———	———				
8 — 9.C	,, intermedium. Indigo blue					———	———				

Height (inches) Habit		Feb.	Mar.	Apr.	May	June	July	Aug.	Sep.	Oct.	Nov.
						Flowering period					
9—12.C	Nepeta Mussinii. Lavender					——	——	——	——	——	
8—9.C	Oenothera missourensis. Yellow				——	——	——	——	——	——	
8—9.C	“ pumila. Yellow				——	——	——	——	——	——	
4—6.T	“ riparia. Yellow				——	——	——	——			
8—9.C	Onosma albo-roseum. Pink				——	——					
6—8.C	“ echioides. Yellow				——	——					
9—12.C	“ tauricum. Yellow				——	——					
18—12.C	Penstemon heterophyllus. Blue					——	——	——			
3—4.T	Phlox Douglasii Lilac Queen. Lilac				——	——					
2—4.T	“ rosea. Pale pink				——	——					
4—6.T	“ procumbens. Deep pink. Leafy				——	——					
3—4.T	“ subulata Apple Blossom. Pale pink				——	——					
4—6.C	“ Betty. Near salmon			——	——						
3—4.T	“ Brightness. Pink			——	——	——					
3—4.T	“ Eventide. Pale lilac			——	——						
3—4.T	“ Fairy. Lilac, dark eye			——	——	——					
4—6.T	“ G. F. Wilson. Pale violet			——	——	——					

F

81

Height (inches) Habit	Plant	Feb.	Mar.	Apr.	May	June	July	Aug.	Sep.	Oct.	Nov.
4—6.T	Phlox subulata Margery. Deep pink			———	———	———					
3—4.T	,, May Snow. White			———	———						
3—4.T	,, Moerheimii. Pink, deeper eye			———	———	———					
3—4.T	,, Nelsoni. White			———	———	———					
3—4.T	,, Sampson. Deep pink, dark eye			———	———	———					
4—6.T	,, Temiscaming. Almost crimson			———	———	———					
2—3.T	Polygonum vacciniifolium. Pink							———	———	———	
2—3.C	Potentilla alba. White. Limy			———	———						
6—9.T	,, fragiformis. Yellow				———	———					
8—12.C	,, hybrid. Gibson's Scarlet. Scarlet					———	———	———	———		
8—12.C	,, ,, Hamlet. Dark red (double)					———	———	———	———		
8—12.C	,, ,, Monsieur Rouillard. Crimson, orange blotch					———	———	———	———		
8—12.C	,, ,, William Rollinson. Orange (double)					———	———	———	———		
8—12.C	,, ,, Yellow Queen. Golden yellow					———	———	———	———		
6—8.T	,, nepalensis. Crimson					———	———	———	———	———	
8—12.T	,, ,, Miss Willmott. Rosy pink					———	———	———	———	———	
8—12.T	,, ,, Roxana. Orange scarlet					———	———	———	———	———	

Flowering period

82

Flowering period

Height (inches) Habit		Feb.	Mar.	Apr.	May	June	July	Aug.	Sep.	Oct.	Nov.
8—12.C	Potentilla rupestris. White					———	———	———	———		
4—6.T	„ Tonguei. Apricot, crimson eye					———	———	———	———		
3—4.C	Pterocephalus perennis Parnassi. Pale pink. Limy					———	———				
3—4.C	Ramonda Myconi. Lavender. Semi-shade					———					
4—6.T	Saponaria ocymoides. Pale pink				———	———	———				
4—6.T	„ „ alba. White				———	———	———				
4—6.T	„ „ splendens. Deeper pink				———	———					
6—8.C	Saxifraga Aizoon. Creamy white. Limy				———	———					
6—8.C	„ „ lutea. Pale yellow. Limy				———	———	———				
6—8.C	„ „ rosea. Pale pink. Limy				———	———					
8—12.C	„ Cotyledon caterhamensis. Pink. Limy				———	———					
8—12.C	„ lingulata. White. Limy				———	———					
4—6.C	Sedum kamtschaticum. Orange						———	———	———		
6—9.T	„ rupestre. Yellow					———	———				
2—3.C	„ spathulifolium. Yellow						———	———	———		
4—6.T	„ spurium. Pale pink					———					
4—6.T	„ splendens. Purple red						———	———	———		

Height (inches) Habit		Feb.	Mar.	Apr.	May	June	July	Aug.	Sep.	Oct.	Nov.
								Flowering period			
4 — 6.T	Sedum spurium Schorbuser Blut. Crimson							—	—		
6 — 8.C	Solidago brachystachys. Yellow						—	—	—		
2 — 3.T	Thymus Doefleri. Pink					—	—				
2 — 3.T	,, lanuginosus. Pink					—	—	—			
2 — 3.T	,, floribundus. Pink					—	—	—			
2 — 3.T	,, Serpyllum major. Crimson					—	—				
4 — 6.C	Umbilicus oppositifolius. Yellow				—	—					
2 — 3.T	Veronica armena. Sky blue					—	—	—			
2 — 3.T	,, pectinata. Pale blue				—	—					
2 — 3.T	,, rosea. Pale pink				—	—					
3 — 4.T	,, rupestris. Blue				—	—					
3 — 4.T	,, rosea. Pale pink				—	—					
2 — 3.T	,, Mrs. Holt. Pink				—	—					
9 — 12.C	Zauschneria californica. Scarlet					—	—	—	—		

LIST OF WALL PLANTS FOR SHADE

| 4 — 6.T | Ajuga reptans. Blue | | | | — | | | | | | |
| 3 — 4.C | Asplenium Trichomanes. Fern. Wet or dry | | | | | | | | | | |

Height (inches) Habit		Flowering period									
		Feb.	Mar.	Apr.	May	June	July	Aug.	Sep.	Oct.	Nov.
4—6.C	Blechnum Spicant. Fern. Wet or dry										
3—4.T	Campanula Portenschlagiana. Violet							───			
3—4.T	„ pulloides. Deep violet							────────			
3—4.C	Ceterach officinarum. Fern. Wet or dry										
4—6.C	Corydalis lutea. Yellow				──						
1—2.T	Hutchinsia alpina. White				────						
1—2.T	Linaria Cymbalaria. Lavender					──────		──			
6—8.C	Mimulus Bee's Dazzler. Scarlet. Damp only					────────────					
6—8.C	„ Chelsea Pensioner. Crimson. Damp only						────────				
4—6.C	„ Dainty. Yellow. Damp only						────────				
3—4.C	„ Plymtree. Pink. Damp only						────────				
6—8.C	„ Prince Bismark. Cherry red. Damp only						────────────				
2—3.C	„ Whitecroft Scarlet. Scarlet. Driest										
6—8.C	Omphalodes cappadocica. Bright blue. Leafy				──						
6—8.C	„ verna. Blue. Leafy			────────							
6—8.C	„ alba. White. Leafy			────────							
6—8.C	Polygonum affine. Pink								────────		

85

Height (inches) Habit		Flowering period									
		Feb.	Mar.	Apr.	May	June	July	Aug.	Sep.	Oct.	Nov.
4—6.C	Primula Altaica grandiflora. Pink		—	—							
4—6.C	„ Betty Green. Scarlet (nearest)		—	—							
4—6.C	— David Green. Crimson		—	—							
4—6.C	„ E. R. Janes. Orange pink		—	—							
4—6.C	„ Romeo. Parma violet		—	—							
4—6.C	„ Snow Queen. White		—	—							
4—6.C	„ Wanda. Magenta red		—	—							
3—4.C	Ramonda Myconi. Lavender and yellow				—	—					
3—4.C	„ „ alba. White				—	—					
3—4.C	„ „ rosea. Pink				—	—					
3—4.C	„ Nathaliae. Lavender blue				—	—					
2—3.C	Saxifraga Elizabethae. Yellow		—	—							
2—3.C	„ hypnoides Kingii. White				—	—					
2—3.C	„ „ Peter Pan. Red				—	—					
4—6.C	„ moschata General Joffre. Crimson			—	—						
4—6.C	„ „ Mrs. Piper. Pink			—	—						
4—6.C	„ „ Pompadour. Carmine red			—	—						

Height (inches) Habit		Flowering period									
		Feb.	Mar.	Apr.	May	June	July	Aug.	Sep.	Oct.	Nov.
4 — 6.C	Saxifraga moschata Sir Douglas Haig. Crimson				—						
4 — 6.C	" Triumph. Almost scarlet				—						
3 — 4.C	" umbrosa var. primuloides. Pale pink				—						
3 — 4.T	Waldsteinia fragarioides. Yellow				—						

The Dry Wall

The following plants are suitable for use in the horizontal soil seams as roots or unrooted divisions or rooted cuttings from the open ground. Some are from each of the previous lists.

Arabis albida. Unrooted stems. Autumn only.

Arabis aubrietioides. Unrooted strands. Autumn only.

Armeria corsica. Unrooted divisions.

Armeria maritima. Unrooted divisions.

Aubrieta. Unrooted stems, autumn only.

Dianthus caesius. Rooted divisions. Autumn.

Dianthus hybrids, other than the Allwoodii alpinus group. Divisions.

Helianthemums. Rooted open ground cuttings.

Omphalodes cappadocica. Rooted divisions.

Omphalodes verna. Rooted divisions.

Phlox Douglasii hybrids. Rooted layers.

Phlox subulata hybrids. Rooted layers.

Polygonum vacciniifolium. Rooted open ground cuttings.

Primula hybrids ('Wanda' division). Rooted divisions. Autumn.

Saxifraga Encrusted varieties. Rooted divisions. Autumn.

Saxifraga hypnoides hybrids. Rooted divisions or unrooted stems. Autumn.

Saxifraga moschata hybrids. Unrooted stems. Autumn.

Saxifraga umbrosa var. primuloides. Rooted divisions.

Sedum. All species. Rooted divisions or unrooted stems.

Veronica rupestris. All vars. Rooted open ground cuttings.

The following plants are suitable for direct sowing, all in the spring. In every case they are species from which seed is available in quantity, and it could also be regarded as a list of the easiest subjects of all from seed.

Alyssum saxatile.

Antirrhinum Asarina. Large seed, insert with dibber.

Aubrieta. Mixed.   *Corydalis lutea.* Insert with dibber.

Campanula carpatica. Mixed.   *Campanula fenestrellata.*

Campanula garganica.   *Dianthus.* Mixed.

Helianthemums. Mixed, insert with dibber.

Hippocrepis comosa. Insert with dibber.

Linaria alpina.   *Linaria alpina rosea.*

Linaria faucicola.   *Lychnis Lagascae.*

Others may be added, if seed is available in really generous quantities, from the wall plants listed. It cannot be recommended as a seed-raising method except where there is more seed available than time; it merely increases the number of self-sown seedlings in the wall. Those sown by the plants themselves always do very well.

4

Alpine Paths and Alpine Lawns

The well-raked gravel drive began when nothing travelled fast enough to throw up a window-smashing stone or churn out ruts with braking or acceleration, and both are usually approximately in the same places every day for a car. Gravel gives a non-slip surface for horses and crunching carriage wheels; concrete is permanent, frost-proof and weed-free, ideal both for the motorist and an age when the glory of the garden does not easily include men to dig out the weeds with broken dinner knives.

Because concrete is the best surface where tyre wear and car weight must be considered there is no reason why we should allow it to cramp our gardens into rigid frames, lined with imitation 'cracks' to look like crazy paving, or (as in America) mixed with dye and cast into patterns. Dyed concrete is a 'hate' of all who agree with Francis Bacon in his *Essay on Gardens* (1597) that 'as for designs in divers coloured earths, I have seen better things in tarts'. The concrete path is useful where there is going to be heavy traffic, wheelbarrows in quantity, or frequent passing of a garden tractor, as in a kitchen garden. With lesser wear one can use the alpine path. This is a path in which the 'weeds' are those you have chosen for flowering qualities, adding to the display area in a small garden, and saving labour in a large one.

The Alpine Path

Consider first a straight gravel path going down beside two beds, each with a foot wide grass border, needing not only mowing, but edging with long-handled shears. If you need a path wide enough for two people to walk abreast and wish to keep the gravel clean with weedkiller, you can save on labour, especially your own (unless you like mowing and edging), by replacing the grass with a low dry wall each side. Planted only to within six inches of the bottom, and with care to avoid foliage splashing, you can both use weedkiller and grow plants.

89

Alpine Paths and Alpine Lawns

A modern weedkiller is better than the old sodium chlorate, which can soak up the stone and may cause trouble, but be careful with any weed-killer if your drainings flow to a Primula corner.

If your path has to take wheelbarrows but only occasional two-abreast walking, all that you really need is a relatively narrow strip of hard surface down the centre, and something only moderately hard at the sides, to take the legs of the barrow when it is standing on the path for weeding the borders or a rest. On a weedy path one can see exactly where the wear comes: small trodden weeds in the middle, lusty growth at the sides.

Lay a foot wide belt of paving down the middle, fill up the cambered sides with soil and plant with carpeters, selected for the sun or shade of the position, and capable of standing up to treading, and you have the alpine path. Where no barrows need run, the paving can be restricted to 'stepping stones' with gaps between, with the same solid carpet of tough plants that can compete successfully with our native weeds. Those weeds that do become established are more easily removed than from between gravel, and the display of the carpeters in their several seasons makes this flowering path a garden feature where many species normally shunned as invasive stranglers can find a useful home.

The centre of a gravel path is usually firm, and there is no need to dig it up; the preliminary stage should be a good treatment with weed-killer during the autumn, before spring construction. Though it can be made at dry wall building time, Aubrieta is not used, and here the saving season for those who have a stock of the plants concerned, all of which are easy division subjects, is February, March and April. Exactly as with Helianthemums, those who make up their minds one spring, buy and plant on spare ground and propagate intensively, can cut the cost of planting to a fraction.

The cost of paving depends on its thickness, very largely because of the weight; you can as an example cover fifteen square yards of path with a ton of inch to inch and a half thick york stone, two and a half to three inches will only cover eight square yards, either 45 feet or 24 feet of continuous narrow alpine path. Thick stone bedded in sand will hold firm in large pieces, thin stuff in small fragments needs concrete below if it is going to hold under barrow wheeling, unlike so much of the crazy paving of the 1930's which can be a permanent irritation as it dips and sinks.

Mix your concrete either as the temporary type with ashes or normal four sand, one cement; or three gravel, one sand, one cement. Water the hard surface of the path centre and shovel out sufficient to make a layer about an inch and a half thick at the highest part, in the centre if the path is cambered. Then wet the under surface of the stone, which should be clean and free from soil or old cement, and set it in place. You are not trying to make an 'amusing' jig-saw puzzle of triangles (if you have got unbroken flags it is all to the good), you are laying a formal straight path, and the job is to make them sit firm and level. A line should run along each side so your edges are straight, and if you have a curve it can be marked out with the 'gardener's compass'. Each slab wants to fit against its neighbour, with a thin seam of cement between: squeeze them up against each other so it comes out like toothpaste and scrape off the surplus with the trowel.

Essential tools are a spirit level, and a four foot length of planed square 2 × 1 in. timber as a straight edge. Set this with the inch wide side on the laid paving, put the level on the upper side, and check your level every yard, both longways and from corner to corner. If a stone is too high you can push it down, if too low, pull it up and add more cement spread over the whole surface of its bed. It is easier to press down than to add more, so it is a good plan to bed in enough cement to allow for some squeezing every time. As the path is going to stay in place for a number of years, and badly set stones can not only trip those who walk, but work loose under a loaded barrow as it drops from a high stone to a low one, it is worth taking the trouble to lay them well.

The main source of cheap paving is broken flags from city pavements; the grey artificial stone is the least expensive (50s.-60s. a ton apart from cartage, about ten square yards coverage) but this will never get mossy; the older york stone which is browner, and more kindly fine grained sandstone runs thinner and goes further, up to fifteen square yards at 80s.-90s. The larger the piece the better for this sort of job, but even then, especially if one comes round a bend when a number of long triangles are needed, there is going to be a good deal of fitting in and cementing up the cracks. If a gap is more than an inch across, fit a piece of stone in it to level, it will be stronger than temporary cement.

All this trowel work is going to mean cement smears on the upper surface; these will dry white and harsh, and may leave permanent roughness. Therefore have a can of water handy and wash off the surface of the path, using a broom and scrubbing the stone dead clean every few yards. The most important detail in garden cement work is washing tools. If you let it set hard this job can ruin your barrow, your trowel, your shovel and your watering can with caked hard lumps, and therefore a bucket of water for dipping and washing is a constant need. Unless you can make a solid surface of boards, mix on the path behind you so that you have a firm surface and one that will not be harmed. Many a front lawn in the 1930's was turfed on top of where cement had been mixed, leaving a solid floor with only a skin of soil for the roots—the poor patch which shows up in dry weather.

If your path has to take barrows, a small garden tractor or a motor mower, even a large hand mower, it is worth considering slopes instead of any steps you may have. Steps mean a stout plank with a block the height of the rise to bring anything with wheels up them sharply. This is a heavy piece of garden furniture, and if two steps are involved, it needs a strut below it. With a sharp corner at the bottom and perhaps another step down through a narrow, knuckle-barking door at the bottom, steps may be worth avoiding. Steps are easier walking but worse wheeling, and when paths are concerned the traffic determines the solution.

A slope of one in twenty-four is not too steep for both easy walking and wheeling. A paved path of any type can be laid in cement on a slope, using a different straight edge. Mark off a line from one end in a long angle, coming in to half an inch at the other, plane it up, or saw it accurately, so that when the spirit level on the top inch wide side reads as level, the path is sloping one and a half inches in its four foot length, which gives you the angle you need. At the sides you will probably need dry walling, low and easy to build, taking, as it is two long triangles, only slightly more stone than one two feet high and eighteen feet long.

As you come down, if you have started with a gravel path and have decided to scrap the steps, you will have to pick-axe or fork up the path and this means that you must build as though you were doing an alpine path on new soil. Dig down roughly another four inches, so four or five inches of concrete goes under instead of one and a half, but firm your soil below by ramming. To save concrete and give greater firmness, broken bricks, etc. can be rammed down along the line of the path. Digging out a gravel path for its whole width is hard work, but it will have to be done once only; the question is whether the saving of the awkwardness of the steps is worth it. The answer varies with the garden.

At this stage the alpine path is a narrow strip of hard, firm concrete, surfaced with paving and laid by working from the sides. It needs at least a fortnight to set, and if it is done in very early spring, it can be protected from frost by covering it with old sacks. It should fit your barrow, either definitely with the legs each side of it, or definitely with them on it and an inch to spare each side; one that takes about a quarter an inch of each leg if it is dead central is going to be the bane of every journey. No-one should start concreting until they have taken all

92

factors into consideration, though temporary cement does allow one to change one's mind at the cost of labour. As a job like this may stretch over several weekends, always finish with the last stone bedded and overlapping a rough surface of concrete. Stop when the bed is ready for a stone, and you cannot put the next in place; a thin skin of cement on top will not hold it, apart from the fact that the level will be out. When you start again, damp the old surface to make the new concrete stick to it. If you are not using broken bricks below the concrete on a new path, you will need to peg rough boards along each side as retainers or 'shuttering', because the weight of the paving will squeeze it out; with the shallower layer on hard gravel this is unnecessary.

Planting the Alpine Path

It is not necessary to dig up the path at the sides, portions should be forked up here and there to allow soakage for draining. Then fill in at the sides with soil, treading it firm, so that the surface is level with the paving. The luxury way of filling is with sterilised John Innes, but though this gives a long start on the weeds, there should be no dandelion roots in the path below, and individual attention with weed-killer is well repaid before you start; it is really rather too good for the job. The need is for soil that is entirely free from perennial weed roots, and with as few weed seeds as possible. Normal garden soil sterilised as directed in Chapter 6, with some leafmould, is all you need.

Planting distances depend on how quick you want cover, and a good average distance is between eight inches and a foot each way, getting them in firmly, even running a roller over them in the case of such species as Thyme, Acaena, and *Cotula squalida*, (the best weed strangler for the shady path). Again one plants in drifts, so that each species can do its best with competition only at the frontiers. The Thymes are the only plants that offer a colour range in varieties that have the same growth speed and tastes.

Where a central paved barrow track is not required, it is very much easier to convert a gravel path bit by bit, introducing carpeters and letting them spread. Thymes, *Frankenia thymifolia*, Acaenas and *Hutchinsia alpina* are 'weeds' for sun, *Arenaria balearica*, *Cotula squalida* and Mazus for shade, and though they cannot compete with the swift native species for rich soil, such as chickweed, it does not take much to turn the balance in their favour on a path. The poorer the downland or the sheep-cropped hill pasture, the more Thyme will be found among the grass, and with some removal of struggling native species, the 'weeds' of our choice will take over. We are not exchanging native weeds for worse pests, the species used do not seed on any scale and though they spread it is easy enough to destroy them not only by weed-killer, but by hoeing off at the time when our climate is hardest on them.

Fork up the path surface at the sides of the central strip for walking, and work in some sterilised soil or leafmould in the case of species that like it, then plant as for the sides of the paved alpine path, firming the surface. If preliminary weed-killer treatment has got rid of dandelions, the carpeters should get growing with very little trouble and spread of their own accord. Begin with a trial area, to see how they like the situation and how you like the effect of a flowering path. The main drawback is that, once the alpines are in, the path must be weeded by hand; there is no weed-killer that will destroy grass only, and the weaker alpines will always go under first whatever chemical is used.

A path of solid alpines can include stepping stones, on the lines of those which landscape gardeners in the 1930's used in lawns as informal pathways to dodge the wear on grass where regular crossings of a lawn were likely. These stones are rarely used today: they gave trouble with mowing, which alpines evade, because the species used grow as a carpet by natural habit, instead of striving to become a hayfield. Stepping stones should be large, roughly a foot square in area, but they cannot be set straight on the soil because though they support our weight by spreading it like snow shoes, when they are trodden on at the edges, they dig in. Either use flat pieces three inches or more thick, and seat them level on well-rammed soil, or dig down six inches and seat them in concrete; the set concrete hidden below a good flat chunk of york stone or sandstone is acting as a thicker rock but far more cheaply, though less strongly, than the solid strip below a path to take greater wear and weight.

Paving, Crazy or Square

Paving is the ideal terrace top and when it is planted there is no need to use carpeters only, those which spread in domes are equally effective and widen the range. The terrace is not designed for through traffic, it is the carpeted floor of the drawing room, rather than the well-used passage to the kitchen with the pattern worn off the linoleum.

Thick squared paving is a formal feature that is usually inherited; today, apart from carriage, real york stone cut to fit can cost 30s. a square yard. As it is rectangular the gaps are small, and the planting space is a series of long slots, which in course of time accumulate enough dust to give foothold to weeds, and where these can get a tap root down below the level of the sand in which the paving is bedded they can grow to heroic size. Strong weed-killer applied along the crack is the only way; there are weed-killer injectors for thistles and others with thick roots that are impossible to get out short of lifting the paving and digging three or four feet after them.

Empty living space can only be kept bare by constant effort, and it is possible to grow plants in these narrow cracks, and where they grow there is no room for weeds, provided these plants are perennial and strong enough to compete. The easiest way to establish them is by direct sowing, and here the conditions are much easier than on the dry wall because each slab is a catchment surface, running water off at its edges. There is wastage, but provided one is prepared to wait and make several trials, a great many plants can be established easily.

First sweep some sifted and sterilised soil into the cracks; so little is needed that it is worth avoiding beginning with well-sown weeds in garden soil that may be full of dormant seeds. Then sow on the surface, cover with a little more soil and firm it in place. Water with a rosed can and leave the thin sown seeds to live or die as they choose. Because some good soil has been added any blown or scattered weed seeds will germinate well, but the alpines will have a head start on them. Weeding may well be required later in the year, and some thinning where there has been a very thick germination, and it is as well to wait until weeds can be identified. A thick crop of Hypericums, of which all the easy species are excellent, in paving will look very like a flood of some fierce weed, but if you have sown in areas and not mixed your seed you can tell the alpines by the fact that the individual seedlings are all alike, the weeds will be single and varied. Like direct wall sowing, it is not a method of raising rare species safely, but a good way of using your surplus of easily saved seed.

The other system for this type of paving is the direct planting of tough division subjects, carpeters which will take treading, so that casual wear will not harm them even though they have spread on the surface of the stone. Dome-forming plants are not suitable for treading, and therefore they should be kept away from the line of the journey from french windows to steps or any other place where walking may be direct and frequent.

Sweep in some soil, and then tuck down rooted fragments with a dibber as men once caulked the seams of wooden ships, then firm some more soil on to them and water well. It is a slow job, like weeding, and a really good sponge rubber cushion to kneel on is an advantage. By this method all the small Sedums can be established easily; their flowering season may be brief, but even if all they have to grow in is the soil in the crack they will thrive. Usually this paving is laid on a sand layer, and

Alpine Paths and Alpine Lawns

though plants in this are often moderately starved, Sedums are all the better for it. Thymes also are excellent and *Frankenia thymifolia* flourishes.

In shade with shelter and where the paving is inclined to grow moss from damp, *Mimulus* Whitecroft Scarlet is beautiful, even though in cold districts it may have to be re-sown each year. Plymtree and Dainty are both good but the best effect is from low plants; where anything really nice like *Hypsela longiflora* can be established to seam the paving with white and crimson (plenty of fine leafmould is needed in the starting soil, about half this and half good loam), the result is charming. Division subjects of this type, bought and planted in March or April (the best time for both direct sowing and fragment planting), can be split up from pot stuff. It is possible to stand cloches over a new-planted seam, but unless glass is placed at the ends and supported with sticks it does not act as a portable frame but a draught tunnel. To give the new divisions a start, especially at a time of cold drying winds, it is better to place brown paper over them, weighed down with stones so that it ridges up above the plants and gives some warmth and humidity during the first two or three days. The really easy things need no assistance beyond watering until they are started, and it is for these that the method and position are best suited.

Laying crazy paving in concrete is the same operation as the strip for the centre of the alpine path: take out your soil six or eight inches deep, tread firm, pile in hardcore which is any hard stony rubbish, or a gravel or clinker layer, and then go straight ahead with your jig-saw puzzle of fragments. There are, however, two important differences.

Firstly, you are not laying a narrow strip which will only have a small catchment area, you are putting a solid surface down which will catch rain, and in many tropical islands such as the Bahamas, a concreted space the size of a terraced garden in a lavish house in Surrey, provides the water supply for a village. An inch of rain means roughly 100 tons on an acre, over four gallons a square yard, and though the lawn or a bed will take this and soak it away, a large terrace is going to get rid of it over the edges in quite a considerable stream. Therefore, when you put down a sizable area of paving, consider the water.

It is easy, by using a less sharply sloped 'straight-edge', to give your paving a fall of one in fifty or one in a hundred which will hardly show, so that it will run off to a gravel or tile-filled surface drain through which it can escape or be led where it is wanted. If a dry wall is topped by a large area of paving, core drains of gravel or clay field drains should lead it down and out through the face or at the bottom. Small areas, ten

96

5. The *Erica* Bed is a type of Alpine Border suitable for a limefree or low lime soil. The principle is to plant a range of species and hybrids of this race selected so that one or more are in flower at every season of the year. This photograph, taken in August, shows *Erica vagans* in the centre and a mass of *E. carnea* varieties in the foreground ready to take over in the Autumn and flower round until late Spring. An established bed needs very little weeding

6. *Campanula carpatica* White Star is an eight inch high 'Canterbury Bell' of the Alpine Border, where *Pentstemon hetrophyllus* is a towering Delphinium. Plant it towards the back, and always raise the named Campanulas from cuttings or division; seed means mongrels without the flower shape, colour, or habit of the parents

square yards or so, do not matter, but it is as well to remember that absolutely level paving runs the water off on all sides (except in a high wind) and paving with low spots is going to mean that all through the winter these will be pools at intervals and this may destroy plants.

The second detail is the planting holes. Just as in the dry wall, it must be possible for the plants to get down into soil, and therefore it is necessary as one builds to leave spaces. Fill in a core of soil in the gravel layer, fit in a triangle of small pieces of wood to hold the cement away and then bed the stone round. Plant when the paving is set, and it is better to have a few good spaces into which one can reach with a narrow-bladed trowel, than a great many. Paving in concrete is weed-proof and firm, the more spaces one has the more room for weeds, and though one can clean paving with weed-killer this means destruction of the plants. A triangle roughly three inches at the sides can be planted and dug fairly clean of weeds if need be; inches and half inches in quantity may mean as much work as a gravel path.

Thicker paving, laid in sand, about two and a half to three inch stone bedded in four inches of sand on firmed soil, is easier to plant. The stones settle themselves in and if they are fairly large fragments, do not rock. As one plants, soil can be added where it is likely to be needed in the sand layer below the crevices. The disadvantage of this paving is that there are many more joints to weed than with squared. Dust and washings can build up soil and the weeds get away. Where it is well laid it can be treated as squared paving and planted by direct sowing and division. For thin, cheap paving, concrete below gives the firmest and most weed-free result; those who wish to lay in sand should use the largest pieces they can get and thump and pack them home well. If the wear is only walking they will stand up to it without much rocking.

The Alpine Lawn

This is essentially a flowering lawn that needs no mowing and is an ideal home for naturalised bulbs. Though it can be planted with tough species, it cannot provide playing space for a family and it can either be an extension of the rock garden on the flat, or a formal feature like an alpine border.

As an example of where it can be fitted in most effectively in a small front garden, consider a short straight drive-in to a garage. In some houses this leads up to a concreted area sloped to the middle with a drain for washing, but the actional drive-in is two strips with a space in the middle. The strips need at least six inches of packed gravel and eight of concrete and want to be a foot or eighteen inches wide, in trenches with boards on edge at the sides for the last three inches if you lay them yourself. They also need a surface ribbed crossways by thumping a stout plank across the width of the strip, both to get it well packed and make it reasonably non-skid.

Usually this is part of the builder's job, and the space in between, frequently a home for rubbish, is turfed. This can be dug up exactly in the same way as an alpine border, filled in with sterilised John Innes Compost, and planted with carpeters with small spring and autumn flowering bulbs below. The total height of the species concerned is not more than four inches in the case of the bulbs, and the car goes over them without damage. If the car is left standing on the drive-in for hours it will do no harm; days are another matter, and if the space must be used for washing down, the drainage complete with oil will be even tougher on the alpines than on the grass. The space in the middle of the drive with which this chapter began took the hammering of the hooves; now there is no wear, except at the sides, and the track of the tyres is determined by gate width and the garage door, usually within quite narrow limits.

The alpine lawn can replace small and awkward patches of turf, but it cannot do the same landscape gardening job as grass. Mown grass since the days when Drake bowled at Plymouth Hoe on a scythe-mown green (lawn mowers were invented in 1831, but pony-drawn, the first hand one was shown at the 1851 exhibition by Messrs. Shanks), is a relief to the eye. It is the wall of the picture gallery of our garden, it is not meant to flower, which is why no-one has ever suggested an 'all daisy' lawn, even though this hardy native is very long flowering. Its mowing is mechanised, we can weed it selectively as though it were a grain crop, and it makes a valuable contribution to the compost heap.

An alpine lawn is a separate garden feature, long flowering when bulbs are included, and needing little attention. The use of sterilised soil for the top four inches and digging out the soil below to make sure of removing all perennial weed roots is even more important than with the border; it reduces weeding to a minimum and when complete cover has been secured it is only going to mean an occasional clean-up for blown weed seeds that germinate. It may be necessary to prune back some of the plants that are encroaching on the others, but by avoiding the use of species that differ too widely in growth speed, this is not often necessary.

Worms do no harm, though their casts can be broken up with flicks of a birch broom, and merely act as a top dressing. There is a great deal of difference between a free worm feeding on decayed vegetable matter and soil bacteria, and one circling hungrily inside the 'Iron

Curtain' of a small pot containing a treasured plant. Leaves should be swept off the alpine lawn, but no attempt should be made to remove the foliage of bulbs until this dries off by nature; it has to complete its task of storing sunlight and minerals for the bulbs the following year.

One of the best planting systems is the Thyme Lawn, popularised by Mrs. V. Sackville-West. This is suitable for poor soil, very limy soil, in fact almost any soil but solid peat. It is composed of varieties of *Thymus Serpyllum*, all of which have roughly the same growth speed but range in colour from crimson through many shades of pink to white. Non-flowering species can be used in shade purely to act as weed-suppressing ground cover and moisture conservation for the spring and autumn flowering bulbs beneath. Under deciduous trees, the early bulbs can flower in the spring sunlight, leaving a tough shade-tolerant species to fill in the space and keep down the struggling weeds. Spacing is the same; eight inches to a foot apart, as in the path.

The carpeting plants have suffered from always being used in crazy paving which is not the best place to see them in their beauty. The alpine path, which is paving that is three-quarters plants with stone reduced to a minimum, and the alpine lawn with no stone at all, use all their qualities to the best advantage. These two garden features can be fancifully described as 'Concertos for Carpeters', garden music in which a neglected instrument is given a chance to show what can be done. The alpine bank is a Helianthemum solo accompanied on the alpine Phloxes, but the rock garden itself is a full Symphony.

Plants for the Alpine Path and Alpine Lawn

To save duplication, the carpeters are all listed together because, except for differences in growth speed, they are suitable for paths, lawns and paving. As their height is measured in fractions of an inch, 'habit' replaces height. Here 'Q' means quick-growing, 'M' a moderate speed, and 'S' slow. The alpine path takes the fastest growing, but one can make an alpine lawn out of any class provided one keeps the 'Q's as an example together; planted with 'S' species they will strangle them far more easily than weeds.

The bulbs to plant below the alpine lawn are listed in Chapter 2, and therefore they are not repeated. All the carpeters are suitable for tucking into paving but some need more care than others, the Arenarias, Frankenia, and Stachys.

The second list is of plants that are really easy for direct sowing in paving. In the crazy or other path where there are plantable pockets, other species can be added. These need to be tough, because they may get over-watered in winter and because their main function is to replace weeds with something stronger. They must also be clump plants, not trailers, because even though one can avoid treading on them, a trailing branch when stepped on is between the hammer of the shoe and the anvil of the stone. A third short list has been added of plants that are especially good in this sort of position.

With paving it is advisable to use all three methods to increase the range of species, carpeters alone mean a preponderance of white and pale colours, apart from Thymes. A few good hardy carpeters in bright yellow, blue or crimson, shade-tolerant if possible, would be very much more valuable to alpine gardeners than still more difficult plants from the edge of the snow line for the fussed and favoured pan under glass. Perhaps there are more lusty rampant creatures awaiting the plant hunter down on the windy islands of the far South or forgotten on the mountains of the world. A hundred and fifty years ago we looked only for Orchids and warm greenhouse plants, now the 'House Plants' of America and Scandinavia; today we need no-trouble plants for small gardens, and they may be waiting for us as rare weeds among the grass in New Zealand, just as our own Wild Thyme, which is the best of carpeters, struggles in Sussex turf.

LIST OF CARPETERS FOR ALPINE PATHS AND LAWNS

Q = quick-growing; M = moderate; S = slow

Habit		Flowering period									
		Feb.	Mar.	Apr.	May	June	July	Aug.	Sep.	Oct.	Nov.
Q.	Acaena Buchananii. Red seed heads. Sun, shade					—	—	—	—		
Q.	,, inermis. Khaki leaves. Sun, shade					—	—	—	—		
Q.	,, microphylla. Sun, shade					—	—	—			
Q.	Arenaria balearica. White. Shade				—						
Q.	,, caespitosa. White. Sun, shade					—	—				
Q.	,, aurea. Golden foliage. White. Sun, shade					—	—				
M.	Campanula pusilla. Blue. Limy. Sun, semi-shade					—	—	—	—		
M.	,, alba. White. Limy. Sun, semi-shade					—	—	—			
M.	Claytonia australasica. White. Leafy. Semi-shade, shade					—	—	—	—		
Q.	Cotula squalida. Foliage only. Sun, shade										
M.	Frankenia thymifolia. Shell pink. Sun						—				
S.	Gypsophila cerastioides. White. Limy. Sun					—	—				
Q.	Hutchinsia alpina. White. Semi-shade, shade				—						
S.	Hypsela longiflora. Crimson and white. Leafy. Sun, semi-shade					—	—	—	—		
M.	Linaria aequitriloba. Lavender. Semi-shade, shade					—	—	—	—		
M.	,, hepaticifolia. Pink. Semi-shade, shade					—	—	—	—		

101

Habit		Flowering period									
		Feb.	Mar.	Apr.	May	June	July	Aug.	Sep.	Oct.	Nov.
M.	Mazus Pumilio. Lilac (mostly). Leafy. Semi-shade, shade						—	—			
Q.	reptans. Lilac. Leafy. Sun, shade						—	—			
M.	Nierembergia rivularis. White. Sun						—	—			
Q.	Sedum album murale. Red foliage. Pink. Sun					—					
M.	dasyphyllum. Grey foliage. White. Sun					—	—				
M.	hispanicum minus. Golden foliage. Pale pink. Sun					—	—				
M.	lydium. Green foliage. White. Sun					—	—				
Q.	sexangulare. Yellow. Sun					—					
M.	Selliera radicans. White. Leafy. Sun, semi-shade					—	—	—	—		
M.	Stachys corsica. Creamy white. Leafy. Semi-shade					—	—	—			
M.	Thymus nummularius. Pale red purple. Sun					—	—				
M.	Serpyllum. Pale crimson. Sun					—	—	—			
M.	albus. White. Sun					—	—	—			
M.	Annie Hall. Pale pink. Sun					—	—	—			
M.	aureus. Yellow foliage. Lilac. Sun					—	—	—			
M.	carmineus. Deep pink. Sun					—	—	—			
M.	coccineus. Crimson. Sun					—	—	—			

Habit / Approx. height (inches)		Feb.	Mar.	Apr.	May	June	July	Aug.	Sep.	Oct.	Nov.
M.	Thymus Serpyllum major. Strong foliage. Crimson. Sun					━	━	━			
M.	„ Pink Chintz. Pink, slightly salmon. Sun					━	━	━			
Q.	Veronica repens. Pale blue. Semi-shade				━	━					

LIST OF CLUMP PLANTS TO SOW DIRECT IN PAVING

Approx. height (inches)		Feb.	Mar.	Apr.	May	June	July	Aug.	Sep.	Oct.	Nov.
2—3	Anthyllis montana. Crimson. Limy. Sun				━	━					
2—3	„ Vulneraria. Yellow. Limy. Sun				━	━	━				
2—3	„ „ var. Dillenii. Crimson. Limy. Sun				━	━	━				
6—9	Armeria corsica. Brick red. Sun				━	━					
6—8	„ maritima. Pink. Sun				━	━					
2—3	Campanula fenestrellata. Blue and white. Sun					━	━				
3—4	„ garganica. Pale blue. Sun					━	━				
4—6	Dianthus caesius. Pink. Sun				━	━					
2—3	Erinus alpinus. Lilac purple. Sun, shade			━	━						
2—3	„ albus. White. Sun, shade			━	━						
2—3	„ Dr. Hanele. Carmine red. Sun, shade			━	━						
2—3	„ Mrs. Charles Boyle. Pink. Sun, shade			━	━						

Flowering period

Approx. height (inches)		Flowering period										
		Feb.	Mar.	Apr.	May	June	July	Aug.	Sep.	Oct.	Nov.
3—4	Hippocrepis comosa. Yellow. Sun					—	—	—			
3—4	„ „ E. R. Janes. Pale yellow. Sun					—	—	—			
6—8	Hypericum olympicum. Yellow. Sun						—	—			
6—8	„ „ citrinum. Pale yellow. Sun						—	—			
4—6	„ „ polyphyllum. Yellow. Sun						—	—			
2—3	Linaria alpina. Violet and orange. Sun				—	—	—	—	—		
2—3	„ „ rosea. Pink and orange. Sun				—	—	—	—	—		
2—3	„ „ faucicola. Violet. Sun				—	—	—	—	—		
2—3	Mimulus Whitecroft Scarlet. Scarlet. Semi-shade, shade				—	—	—	—	—		
	(All Mimulus hybrids, but from seed they are mixed)										
6—9	Oenothera pumila. Yellow. Sun										
3—4	Pterocephalus perennis Parnassi. Pink. Sun						—	—			
3—4	Viola arenaria rosea. Pink. Sun, semi-shade				—						

Other species can be tried when seed is available, selected from the clump-formers in the wall plants list or those for the alpine border.

LIST OF PLANTS FOR POCKETS IN PAVING

Approx. height (inches)		Flowering period										
4—6	Achillea Lewisii. Creamy yellow. Sun					—	—	—			
2—3	Campanula haylodgensis fl. pl. Blue. Limy. Sun						—	—			

Flowering period — approximate flowering periods shown against months: *Feb. Mar. Apr. May June July Aug. Sep. Oct. Nov.*

Approx. height (inches)	Plant
2—3	Campanula pulla. Deep violet. Limy. Sun
3—4	Dianthus caesius Little Jock. Pink. Limy. Sun
1—2	Erodium chamaedroides roseum. Pink. Sun, semi-shade
2—3	Geranium sanguineum lancastriense. Pink. Sun
2—3	Gypsophila fratensis. Pale pink. Limy. Sun
2—3	Linum salsoloides nanum. White. Limy. Sun
6—8	Lithospermum graminifolium. Blue. Limy. Sun
8—9	,, intermedium. Deep blue. Limy. Sun
2—3	Phlox Douglasii hybrids, all vars. Planted as rooted layers
2—3	Potentilla alba. White. Sun
1	,, verna nana. Yellow. Sun
2—3	Saxifraga Elizabethae. Yellow. Limy. Sun, semi-shade
3—4	,, hypnoides, all hybrids. Semi-shade
4—6	,, moschata, all vars. Semi-shade, shade
3—4	Sedum spurium Schorbuser Blut. Crimson. Sun

All Sedums listed as wall plants will grow in paving and can be established from tucked-in divisions.

105

5

The Small Rock Garden

In the Alps, the English Lake District, or the Cheddar Gorge one can see natural rock gardens with all the mistakes, except perhaps the 'shark's tooth pool'—surrounded with triangular fragments of paving stuck in the cement—of the amateur. The overhang of a quarry falls and there is the straight line of the 'dog's grave' type; a landslide leaves a tumbled pile of rock, the strata lying in every direction, some propped up like fingers pointing to the sky and all sloping downwards at the natural angle of slope. The only invariable difference between nature's handiwork and man's is that you never find a mountain made of perhaps five sorts of material, limestone, flint, sandstone, brick and marble, though some volcanic formations can build in perfectly appalling taste. Yet in these same hills there are corners to which one can almost supply the nameboard of the landscape architect, so often has the type of formation that appeals to an artist in rock been used by him on the rock garden bank at Chelsea.

The first type of natural rock 'formation' has one other point in common with a bad rock garden, it grows only a few of the very toughest plants. Rock piled haphazard like coals in a cellar does not grow a range of species, and though a man could fill his garden with a great slope of slithering fragments from a slate quarry, and have a perfect reproduction of a very nasty bit of climbing he has known as a mountaineer, it fails the test of so many pictures: 'It is not a thing one can live with, all very well in an Art Gallery for those who like this modern stuff, but think of seeing it every morning at breakfast.'

The well built rock garden shares one important quality with the mountain scenery that is its basic model, the outcrop or water-worn stream bed where the quieter influences of erosion, and the decay first of mosses and lichens, then of generations of plants, have built up soil; on both the corner of the hills that is the best hunting ground for the plant collector, and on its reproduction in our gardens, plants grow in the

106

greatest profusion. We are 'painting' the type of formation in which the biggest range of alpines grow in nature, and the conventions of rock garden construction are, generally speaking, controlled by the plants themselves.

In a garden we have not room for the broad effects of nature, a great slope of Rhododendrons carpeting the ground or a cliff where the in-

FIG. 4. An Outcrop in the Cheddar Gorge.

habitants of the expert's alpine pans cling in mighty and unreachable clumps, we must concentrate and give a rather exaggerated picture, because of the limitations of its frame in our gardens. Because the British mountain flora is comparatively poor, we use those species from all over the world which have developed or possess the quality of growing and flowering at low levels in our gardens, and in their separate seasons give duration to the living 'canvas'.

There are people who consider that a rock garden is out of place where there is no natural rock formation, they object strongly to 'A great mass of stone in the middle of the lawn'. If a rock garden looks as though it had been dragged in by the ears, then the site has been badly selected, if it looks like a pile of stone, then it has been badly built, but every man rules his own garden. Beauty is in the prejudice of the beholder, and as a garden of any kind is as unnatural as any other human art, there is no need to consider anything but your own taste.

The Small Rock Garden

The Choice of a Site

The rock garden is informal, that is, it is part of the wild garden and is in the opposite tradition to the formal layout of straight lines, paths and paving. Therefore it looks best away from these features, but this is rarely possible in the small garden where there is no room to lead the eye from one picture to another or take the viewer through the tall door in the yew hedge to a different landscape altogether. The most we can do is to bear in mind that sundials, square pools, plaster goblins and standard roses in neat round beds in the lawn are in a different pattern of gardening to an outcrop of rock, and look best apart.

Though these points should be considered in choosing the site, they make no difference to the success of the plants, and if we wish to have a rock garden where the landscape traditions built up in more spacious days forbid, then we might as well build a good one, for one that is badly made will look no more in keeping.

Trees are a real limitation; they provide dry shade in summer, and drip in winter, the very reverse of the clear light of the high hills and frozen snow, the normal moisture-free covering of most alpines during their resting period. Therefore if you have trees, then the rock garden must go somewhere else. Shade from buildings giving morning or afternoon sun only is not without winter drip, but the robbing roots nullify any watering and may thrust up suckers which are worse than any weeds and the dead leaves must be removed each autumn. The only shade that is normally experienced by alpines is that of rocks; the trees they grow among are small and stunted, like the Conifers suitable for the rock garden. The garden wall and your house may provide a site where you can grow the restricted range of alpines that enjoy or tolerate shade. If you have trees in quantity and like them, do not try to grow alpines, but make a different sort of garden for the many species, especially dwarf shrubs and such glade plants as *Meconopsis Baileyi*, that suit your conditions.

Then if possible you need a natural slope or fall in the ground. This is not necessarily because the rock garden will look more natural, but so that there will be some water soaking in from the back. Consider the frequent amateur choice of the conical heap of soil removed when digging a pool. This is going to be steep and as dry as a double-sided dry wall; the rain falls only on its very small area, and runs off again. This is entirely apart from the fact that it is extremely difficult to make it look like anything other than a conical heap of soil removed when digging a pool.

The Small Rock Garden

Though it is not a recognised principle of landscape gardening, the idea of making a rock garden to 'use up' something seems a sure recipe for failure, and formal ways of utilising soil and surplus stone are always the most successful, when the surplus arises from something you have dug on a flat surface.

It is possible to use a flat site, for a ravine garden, dug down as a winding valley, with the soil spread or gently rising towards it, like the rock garden at Kew, or one can come up gently to a smaller outcrop from the edge of a lawn. In the completely flat small garden with its layout determined by essential paths, the best effect is secured by using the alpine lawn, path or border, and the dry wall or alpine bank for the long straight pile of earth. Good stone these days is expensive and it is best employed where it will give the perfect effect. So long as the site is sunny and not too dry in summer, however, one can make one's own rules, though the next owner of your garden may well consider your creation a horror.

Rock and its Strata Line

The ideal rock for almost any rock garden is limestone. The hard limestones of Westmorland, Somerset and several other areas is the traditional rock garden material of the landscape gardener, simply because it is good. It does not flake with frost, it weathers well, its markings are a sure guide to its placing, plant roots are fond of it, in nature they would run back as far as twenty feet into its crevices to gather moisture and finally, its quiet grey is an ideal contrast with the colours of alpines.

This stone is exposed on the surface in natural 'rock gardens' when the dip of the strata is slanting in the reverse direction to the slope of the hillside, or where a stream has bared the rock into a gulley. Always the greatest accumulation of the soil in which plants grow, made of rock fragments and decayed humus, is where the rock slopes backwards. The bare rock face which points down the slope is washed clean by the rain and its contribution of fragments collects in a more favourable site lower down, the one which is your model.

The rock outcrop is solid; we see the weathered nose of the formation jutting out of the hillside, which may in Britain be accumulated peat or even a normal loam through which the strata thrusts by some freak of geology (mountain limestone is the remains of sea creatures' shells, sea lilies and even corals which have been subjected to great pressure; it was formed long before the coal measures). The rock garden is not solid, we merely use the imported stone to reproduce the parts that show, to exert the same effect on the plants as these weathered surface rocks of the outcrop have in nature, and to make our picture.

Because we are reproducing solid rock with fragments on the surface, all the stones must follow the same 'dip' or 'strata line', which gives the essential unity that makes all the difference between the high standard of the Chelsea or Southport Flower Show garden, and a pile of haphazard fragments. Apart from appearances, there are two direct advantages. The upper surface of a rock set as in Fig. 5 runs the rain backwards into the slope, and holds any soil that washes on to it, exactly as in nature. Reverse the slope and it runs the rain off like the roof of a house, and this difference is one of the reasons why well built rock gardens grow better plants.

In nature, strata do all kinds of things under pressure and shock, they can curve and bend and alter directions suddenly, but not on the scale of a small garden. The faces of the rock in your garden should line up with each other according to the dip of the strata, which can be in two directions—you are working with a series of slanting lines, as shown in Fig. 4. Regular curves are not used by nature with rock that breaks square, like limestone. Rounded shapes are worn by running water, and on the upper surfaces of the exposed rock by rain.

Limestone, in the formations on which the rock garden is modelled, weathers in two ways. On the face, that is, the sides and fronts of the portion protruding from the hillside, the rain drives and trickles, the lichens and the mosses grow and the softer parts are slowly worn away, in layers, because the rock was laid down in layers (or 'strata'), some harder than each other. This face is usually darker than the top, even black in places but more often dark grey, and it frequently has long fissures or deep cracks running along the line of the layers. It is lining up these layers that gives the effect of a natural formation. The right way for these lines to run is horizontally or at a dip either in one or two slants. Stand the rocks so they point upright and it shrieks to those who build well like a first attempt on a violin to a musician.

The upper surface of the rock wears differently, it pits and rounds with the rain, which collects in its hollows into which eroded fragments wash, and in which first moss and then plants which need only a small quantity of soil will grow—on the rock garden small Sedums, and Sempervivums, with encrusted Saxifrages in the larger holes. The underside of the rock and the back, which have been split from the underlying formation by the quarry men, are unweathered, and these are the surfaces which are buried.

In short, every piece of rock must be set the way up that it 'grew',

110

with the top that has the rain rounding and pitting upwards, and the weathered faces crossed horizontally by the lines of the strata at the front and sides. Put the strata edgeways, and the rain-worn top facing to the front and it will look almost as odd as a concrete rabbit set with its pedestal in the air.

Water-worn limestone has the upper surface rounded where the softer portions have been eroded, often into long deep grooves, the face may be cut into a series of tongues and large hollows may have been worn by falling water or fragments swirling round in an eddy. The strata at the face and sides may be just the same as outcrop stone, or it may have been acted on by water, but when it is set in the rock garden, remember always that water flows downhill. Do not build up a crag with flat water-worn slabs, their channels pointing to the sky or to the front; streams do not flow vertically or edgeways.

Water-worn stone, even used without a water garden, should go to the bottom of the ravine, and the hollows should point in the same direction either flat, or with a slight fall one way or the other, which is simply how water flows. Their hollows may be filled with soil and planted, like a dry stream bed, they can be used as stepping stones in the alpine lawn and a very good, almost flat rock garden can be made with them, but always consider how they were made and where they were found in nature. If you do not wish to model on nature, you can do just as well with cheaper, harsher, unweathered stone in a dry wall, using it formally; the worst effect is always from a hybrid that misses both objectives.

There are many types of sandstone, but some are unsuitable for rock garden making. These are usually recent formations which split up with frost and crumble; you need a fine grained sandstone which has had considerable pressure on it in the geological past, one that is not going to revert to sand and small flakes.

These stones were laid down in fairly quiet water, the upper surfaces are often ripple-marked with wavelets when the world was much younger, and their strata are not strongly marked, though they can be seen, and they rarely jut steeply out of a hillside, they lie more level. The same principles apply: the stone breaks roughly square, a solid rock formation keeps the same dip all the way through, and the strata follow the same line. The great ravine garden at Kew, now one of the best rock gardens open to the public all through the year, was formerly a glaring example of bad rock setting. Its rebuilding began just before the war, and part is re-done each winter, but as it was started with no dip in the strata, they have to continue it, which gives a rather step-like effect.

The sandstone rock garden is not modelled on the lane or railway-cutting side, nor does it copy the disused quarry or the cliff eroded fantastically by blown sand in a desert country; in the English garden it is either the outcrop that has had the soil washed from it because it slopes in the reverse direction to the lie of the ground, or the water-carved ravine.

If possible it should be used in fairly large pieces, to reduce the effect of small steps coming down a slope, and as it is more widely distributed than mountain limestone there is a considerable chance that carriage will be less and bring down the cost; it is therefore highly suitable for the ravine garden which is the type that uses the most rock.

There are of course many other rocks, including granite and marble, but these are less appreciated by plants, and their colour is inclined to glare; the rock garden needs grey, or the brown sandstone, and though it is possible to build with other stone, using the same guiding principles, it is far less easy to secure a good result. If one is going to spend money for stone, Westmorland Limestone is about £6 a ton in the London area plus delivery from the nearest goods depot (1953 price); the best should be bought. Unsuitable rock is just as heavy and far less pleasant to live with.

The price of stone is about three times its cost in 1939. Cheddar stone in London is about 15s. a ton cheaper, and both come down in cost nearer the quarries. Both types and sandstones weigh 160 lb. per cubic foot, and to visualise how much exactly a ton is going to be, think of the ordinary large, square type biscuit tin; a rock that size is half a hundredweight, forty of those, very roughly. They will not all be near cubes, and if you have any choice you want to choose those with the most weathered outer face, so that you have less to bury. The old principle was that two-thirds of every rock should be under ground, but with care a very much higher proportion can be brought into the picture. The bigger the rock garden, the larger the pieces needed to give a good effect; on a small garden scale, biscuit tin size means easy lifting, and a ton goes a long way. You are building for plants, not trying to produce the boldest effect.

If you fetch rock from the yard of the supplier, take some strong sacks with you to avoid grazing the weathering with raw scars, wrap each rock in a protecting coat, but remember the weight if you lift them out of the car in the sack that provides an easy handle, but may be rotten. The advice of the manager of a famous London supplier is worth quoting for take-away rock buyers:

'There is always plenty of room in the back of the car, and more in the spare-wheel compartment, but a cubic foot of rock, even in small bits,

7. *Fritillaria Meleagris* is the rare British Snake's-head Fritillary, but a cheap and easy bulb, flowering in April and May, ideal naturalized under carpeters which give a second crop of bloom in summer off the same ground. The photograph is *F. Meleagris alba*, but the original species, in a variety of wine-purple shades, is even more charming

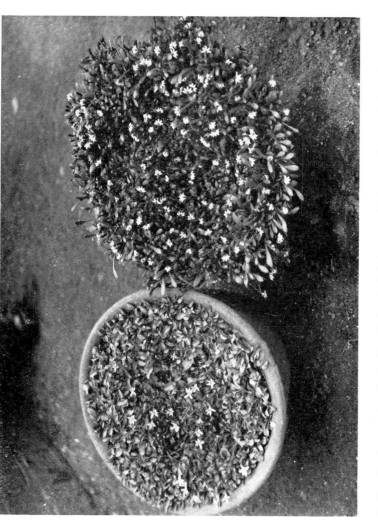

8. Two lovely carpeters for leafy soil. On the left (nearest the boot toe) *Hypsela longiflora*, white and crimson flowers with three petals on one side, two on the other. On the right, *Selliera radicans*, with five petals all on one side of the bloom, so they look like tiny white-gloved hands. Gardeners differ from botanists in considering that these are two distinct plants

weighs about fourteen stone. You can easily put as much as five extra people in the back, all dead weight and your springs aren't made for it. One good bump and towing to a garage, plus repairs, and you have spent far more than the cost of hiring our lorry which is built for the job.'

The small, local haulage contractor can run you up to choose and come back with the load; his springs are designed for dead weight, yours are not.

Building the Outcrop Rock Garden

A natural rock outcrop can be a vertical cliff, a steep crag of solid stone, but there are two reasons why this type is not a suitable subject for the gardener. Firstly, the natural crag will hold only a very few species, and these are specialised cliff dwellers. Secondly, the quantity of rock required to hold the thrust of soil would be too great for most small garden owners, the great outcrops of the big professional builder need sheer-legs, tackles and rollers to swing them in place. The dry wall is designed for this situation, the rock garden as we can build it ourselves is entirely unsuitable.

Consider first the most common site of all. This is the straight bank halfway down the garden where the level drops four or five feet to the lower lawn. We have considered the formal ways of dealing with it, which are simple, but we are determined to have a rock garden which will look like a natural outcrop. At the higher level the garden is formal, so there is no incongruity or mixture of styles visible from above. Go down the path or steps to the lawn and here is another picture, the mountain scenery we have painted in stone and plants.

If we keep the straight edge of the lawn, five feet away from the crest of our four foot drop to give the 38°, it is still going to look like a straight bank with rocks on it, and provided we use the rock construction principles that are determined by plant needs we can grow alpines successfully, but will not have a natural outcrop effect. For this we want room to come forward in places, to build sheer crags on a small scale, to cut back into the slope in bays, and to follow the line of our strata until all the effect of stepping stones is lost. Because we want this effect with as little rock as possible, we need plenty of room in front, coming forward to alpine lawn levels, with small rocks still following the strata lines at the cost of making our lawn edge an irregular shape. If we consider mowing convenience we can finish the lawn in a line drawn further back, but the best parting between lawn and rock garden is a winding path on which to walk for weeding, and close range appreciation.

The Small Rock Garden

The first stage of construction is always thorough digging to remove perennial weed roots, these are even worse built in under a rock garden than behind the dry wall. Therefore treat your slope just as you would for a dry wall, and if there are cut drains or a gravel layer that is likely to give trouble, use the measures advised in Chapter 3. If your slope is already a gentle one, then you will want to dig out the top eight inches or so, to make up into alpine soil and give room to work; if the slope is sharper than you need, as it will be if you have pulled down an existing dry wall, or a bad steep rock garden, then you will want to buy or mix a very great deal more to ram in place behind your stone and provide a more gradual average slope. The fortunate gardener is the one who has a bad rock garden in good stone to pull down; he can get all the weeds that curse it out in one determined attack, and have enough stone to build a better one twice the size.

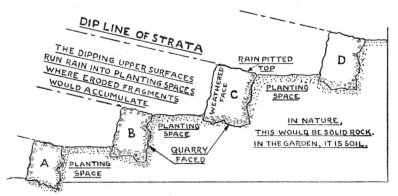

Fig. 5. The Principles of Rock Garden Building.

The best way to build a rock garden is from the top downwards. The rocks are not bonded into each other course by course, the soil below is at rest in most places, and the important stage is always placing the main rocks which are going to determine the stratum line and getting them just right. Choose two good ones, with plenty of 'face' for your biggest crag, the weather-resisting tough nose of the outcrop, dig out the soil where they are going to stand, or bank it up and tread it firm, and try them in place so they meet in a 'V' or 'L' with the joint at the front or side to be planted as a crevice.

They have only one way up, the way they 'grew', but the number of slants they can take is considerable, and it is best to give plenty of time to getting them just right; try them all ways, stepping back on to the lawn and having a look and propping them up with stones underneath,

114

tilting them back with a brick as a prop. A Chelsea rock garden, which takes about a fortnight to build, is 'conducted' by the builder from the path, three or four men struggling with the first giant rocks for perhaps two days, moving them an inch this way and an inch that, in obedience to Stokowski-like waves of the hands, and then taking the half-ton lumps away and trying two more. When the landscape gardener, the builder and the owner are all one person, it is easier, and so are half-hundredweight rocks quicker to handle.

When your first rocks are set to your satisfaction, tilting slightly back with the dip of your strata, fill in the soil behind and ram it firmly, holding them in place with your knee or a boot and ramming well into the crevices, so that there are no air spaces. If the top of the crag is higher than the bank, then slope the soil down to its level gently. If the position you choose is well forward on the slope, it is a good plan to build up a core of bricks or rough stone below so that the weight of the rock is not on soft soil but something solid.

This principle is used by the men who build many hundreds of table rock gardens at flower shows each year, using stout wooden boxes to stand them on and peat to fill in between; the small rock garden is on the same scale and uses the same methods. The lower part of your rock should be below ground level, perhaps a couple of inches or an inch when you fill in below, but like the nurseryman who has brought perhaps nine good fragments in his car trailer, you aim at hiding as little as possible of good weathered face.

The next rocks below your crag have their upper surfaces lined up with its bottom, and slant back at the same angle, but they come very much further forward. They aim to look like the nose of another part of the same solid formation, their top strata laid down at the same time as the bottom one of the rocks above, but behind them is packed soil, a foot or two of backward-sloping planting room. This is not a 'pocket' as it is often called, it is perhaps a foot of alpine soil on top of solid earth and here a good drift of something can be put in afterwards; a rock garden is rarely planted as you build.

There should be no attempt at spacing your rock regularly over the surface. Concentrate on a good outcrop, using plenty, then between there is room for slopes of alpine soil, in which smaller rocks show as though they were part of it. A long lump, say three inches broad with a face varying from two inches at one end to four at the other, perhaps a foot long, does not make up much of your ton, but fitted in on the surface it gives very good value, especially if it is among low carpeters where it will not be hidden.

Where you come down sharply, you need big rocks; come down gently and smaller ones can be used, because though your angle is generally one at which soil rests, there is some thrust where your rocks are at roughly dry wall angle of steepness and you need weight to hold it. The thrust that counts is from the depth of soil behind, so that behind an eight inch high rock is far less than behind one that towers eighteen. The low ones with some surface area are always best to stand on, so plant the hollows in the tops of the big tall rocks, and leave the others for weeding footholds.

The bank will come down in 'steps', but especially if you have a double slant on your strata, this is not obtrusive, and the layers will be irregular as the rock would have broken in nature. The planting room is mainly exactly where it would be naturally, where the soil had built up behind the slanting rocks. The exception is the slopes. These are what are often called 'screes', the trickle of weathered-off chips of rock that flow like water down the valleys of the outcrop. It is usually the custom to surface them with a layer of limestone or granite chippings and below this a mixture of soil and chips, in which many small species find their best home, as they grow in this sort of situation by nature. The mixture will be found in the next chapter.

By bringing your high points forward from the straight line of the bank, setting some right back as bays, and coming well forward at low levels, you can break up the whole formal impression of the straight division of your garden. It will occupy as much space as a good wide herbaceous border, and flower for a rather longer season. Make the largest planting areas at the bottom; in nature there would be more soil here anyway, and this is going to be the least dry part, so that you have here a good Gentian home, and there is nothing like good Gentians against grey stone.

If you have too little rock to do all you want, do not dot the pieces here and there. Concentrate in fewer outcrops, then use larger planting slopes, with the effect more of an alpine bank, but using less powerful plants, and stick to your strata line, using the rocks where they show most among the smaller species.

The Outcrop on a Flat Site

Where you are determined to build a rock garden, and have a pile of soil available, the task is to make your outcrop avoid the sort of mound that cries out for a small and pathetic headstone. Therefore you should spread your soil into a long slope, with perhaps three crags, at long intervals, coming up say six inches on the lowest above an alpine lawn, taking the fairly shallow strata dip back to within three inches of ground level, come up again perhaps a foot, and then go back to a further foot starting perhaps six inches from ground level. Follow these through so that their dip meets ground level at one side and comes high at the other. Keep your planting low and do not attempt bold crags—low on the ground they are going to look like tank traps; what you are attempting to create is the sort of shallow rock formation that might outcrop in a fairly flat situation. If you have got a huge mound of earth, you can treat it as the first type of outcrop, by breaking the line and coming well forward on the side that is most suitable, and building a formal dry wall to hold the back, but an artificial mound is always best used artificially, that is in purely formal gardening.

A pile of hungry subsoil is far better distributed where it can be dug and manured in the vegetable garden, or used as filling at the back of a dry wall, than for alpines.

The outcrop garden is the ideal first attempt; it is effective in all sizes from that of a hearthrug upwards but the smaller the site the simpler should be the scheme. The more features you attempt in a small area, the more fiddling it looks, for your model is a full scale 'unabridged extract' from mountain scenery, you are not making a miniature garden in a trough or pan for close range viewing on a windowsill or pedestal. Therefore the glass pool with goldfish painted on the underside, the miniature bridge and figures to give a false scale, are completely out of keeping. The Japanese garden is rigidly formal, and in a separate tradition altogether.

The most common failing of the amateur rockery is too much stone, and a few good rocks placed with care, plus well-selected plants on suitable soil, give a far better effect than a massive random pile stuck into a mound of earth, even though lack of space prevents the separation of formal straight lines and the informal outcrop.

The Water-Carved Outcrop and the Pool Garden

This is the type of garden commonly built on a large scale show exhibit, adding the splash and sparkle of falling water to the picture. It is based on the many places in our hills where a spring or stream has cut into the overlying soil or peat and exposed the rock below. After a night's rain many small highland towns are noisy with the little burns that have woken up as the water comes down the mountains.

There is no need to use water in this type of garden, one's picture can be the rocky surround of the spring and the dry stream bed with alpines growing in the soil washed between the rocks; and those who feel that mountain scenery in their district is 'unnatural' have only to consider the many streams that begin in sandstone country where water cuts through to the underlying rock. This type can be large or small: one with a total area of two square yards looks fussy, an irregular 6 ft. × 6 ft. against a bank is a comfortable size, but where water is used more room is needed for a good effect.

The general principles of construction are the same, but the stratum line is always flatter. Consider the fact that water always takes the easy road and though there are falls that have cut through against a dipping stratum in the opposite direction to the slope, they more usually come down a steplike formation of almost level rocks. Plate 21 shows one of this type. Where a stream does come down forward-dipping strata it is rarely a suitable model. The landscape gardener is using a small electric circulating pump and he wants as much flashing waterfall as he can get. A genuine stream gets very little value for water—the one on the side of the Ben like a silver wire in the distance is more like a large tap full on when you get up to it, and its bed is swept clean. When dry it can be bare as an upended pig trough with the same sort of channel. No pump suitable for a small garden can provide the curves of deep folding water like the muscles of a strong man where a mountain stream in flood is coming down the shortest way in a narrow bed of smooth worn rock.

Cut into your bank for this sort of garden, do not build up forward. Set your big rocks to line up as the back and sides of a ravine; this is not an outcrop but a 'cut in', where the stream has taken out the soil to bed rock, your 'V' is the other way round. The bottom should if possible have flat water-worn stone set right way up and round in the centre, definite sides, and planting room between this and the 'cliffs' which go up fairly steeply with ledge-like planting spaces that go down behind them. Bring down the floor of the widening ravine in stages, keeping the idea of a central bed of worn rock and flat spaces at the sides flooded when the stream is high, and holding soil in their breaks and hollows. Without water you are not coming down in stages to provide falls, though each drop in level uses suitable stone for them, you merely do not want your cliffs at the sides too high and steep because of the rock they will need, a slab three feet high is going over the cubic foot by a long way. Wherever the water would be running constantly you want solid stone, planted in its hollows; the big planting areas come in the ledges, and away from the stream bed.

With sandstone you build on sandstone principles which fit this construction very well: not much dip and come down in irregular steps. Fern planting is very effective in this sort of garden, especially well into the 'V',

118

the ferns listed have no objections to lime so they can go well on any rock.

This type of garden is very effective cut into a shrub-covered bank, and where rock is cheap, as in a sandstone district, the proportion of planting space can be reduced, but where one is using nearer solid rock, big blocks on each other with planting areas like those in a dry wall, obviously one builds from the bottom. It can also be made part of the normal outcrop, complete with water-worn stone in the mouth of the ravine.

Water in the Rock Garden

It is not possible to make a water garden by using the supply from the mains, partly because the average flow is only about two gallons a minute, which makes a most unsatisfactory fall, but mainly because the regulations are deliberately (and rightly) designed to prevent gardeners keeping a tap constantly running all the summer. The water authority will insist on a meter for which (London 1954) an installation charge of £10 is made, and the supply itself costs 2s. 6d. 1,000 gallons. The first cost is more than buying a circulating pump with motor, and the second more expensive than the current to run it. Apart from this, there is the problem of disposing of the water run to waste.

Using the same water over and over again like a stage army still needs both an overflow and an inlet from the mains; the pool system is filled slowly with the hose, and this can be used to balance up evaporation and any leakage, which does not infringe any regulations as it is a normal garden use. At the edge of the lowest pool there will need to be a soak-away (an ideal site for a Primula bog), because the rocks that have been set like a stream channel and the pools themselves will catch a considerable quantity of rain, especially in winter, and a summer thunderstorm will always set the falls dribbling on their own accord.

In a few rare cases it is possible to dig a channel from an existing stream, but a sluice gate set in concrete will be required, and the eroding force of the water, the mud it will carry and its flood risk make a builder essential for this work. A better solution that is possible in some very lucky gardens, where a stream or river with a considerable flow is available, is a hydraulic ram. This is an automatic pump run by the flow of the stream which drives a relatively small quantity of water to a considerable height so the flood risk does not arise, and though the first cost is as much as a pump, it costs nothing to run. I once saw one which had kept working unattended in a lovely rock garden right through the war; the brambles and weeds of four years' neglect were hiding the rocks, but the Primulas towered and the ferns grew by the still-splashing falls. The device is used to supply water from streams on many farms and country houses, and the makers should be consulted if there is any chance that one can be used.

The normal garden solution is a ¼ h.p. pump, which is cheaper to instal than many people imagine. Its fitting, because it requires a buried watertight brick compartment above the level of the lowest pool, and an underground cable from the mains, is a job for a contractor approved by the electricity authority. In no circumstances should the amateur tamper with a 240 volt current when moist soil is concerned; this kind of outdoor job cannot be fixed up with cheap flex like a reading lamp, for apart from the risk of severe shocks, leakages from bad workmanship can mean incredible electricity bills. The procedure is to approach your electricity authority and they will know the nearest contractor who can do a good job, which will come very much cheaper than anything you can rig up yourself.

The rock garden illustrated in Plate 22 is running on ¼ h.p., which is the best size; smaller than this means a dribbling fall if you take it high, and larger types cost very much more. They are silent and need very little attention for they consist of a centrifugal pump directly driven by a small electric motor, with no valves or gearing. Once in place with a moveable rock fitted over them, or a small manhole in a path, opening for switching on and off or occasional attention, they are no trouble. If you are going to use water in the rock garden, it is worth doing the job well at the start, for secondhand makeshifts are always more expensive in the end. This type of pump is mass produced and designed for the rock garden to lift a bulk of water a short distance; you are not paying for power or refinements that you do not need.

This size pumps about 30 gallons a minute, nearly five cubic feet of water, which gives a really good fall, no trickling or dribbling but something worth looking at, and runs for four hours for the cost of a one-bar electric fire on for an hour (one unit). Though the theoretical height the pump on this much power should lift is between twelve and fifteen feet, this depends on the way it is fitted. At the bottom you must have a strainer on the inlet to keep out dead leaves etc., and a valve so you can shut the water out when the system is drained in winter to prevent burst pipes. These are supplied by the pump makers and are concealed under an overhanging rock, but the resistance takes three feet off the height you can pump. You lose head as follows: a foot for each ten feet of pipe and for each rounded elbow, two feet for a right angled elbow and six inches for a rounded bend.

This is with galvanised iron piping two inches internal diameter; with one and a half inch pipe the loss is four times as great, and the flow would go down to twenty gallons a minute or less. Therefore, use the larger size piping and if the pump can be placed so that there are no sharp corners you lose less power, in other words get more and higher waterfalls for the same money. The diagram of a water garden in Fig. 6 is of one with six feet of total fall, which is well within the power of the pump with the layout in the plan; the pools could easily be much longer but sharp corners in the pipe at top and bottom would take as much power as would push the water twenty feet further along the straight. A hydraulic engineer at Chelsea Flower Show can see at once which garden has used the best pipe layout; the pumps are the same size, and those who have skimped on good piping have the smallest waterfalls.

The point is stressed because the gardener's part in the fitting is one of arguing with the contractor, who may have got the wrong-sized pipe in stock or the wrong fittings. Use the pump maker's fittings and a minimum size of two inch pipe; one and a half will suit a $\frac{1}{8}$ h.p. motor and pump, but even then the larger pipe gives a better flow. If the contractor is a builder it is worth going in to the question of using earthenware drainpipes, cemented at the joints. These come cheaper and as you can use three inch size which gives an even easier flow, and there is no risk of any rust, they justify the extra labour cost of using them.

Though the pump makers supply all the fittings, and metal pipes screw together quickly and simply, cutting the pipes and putting on screwthreads needs special tools, and with a pipe bending machine it is often possible to put the water exactly where you want it in one long slow curve. Your part is to say what you want, and though you can even get the pools made by the builder, keep him away from the rockwork. There never was a builder who could make anything other than a stiff and unnatural horror out of a rock garden; his is a different skill and you want him to do his part well and leave the rest to you. Beware of the small man with a lot of one inch piping in his hands offering it cheaply; he may convince you, but he cannot alter the laws of hydraulics, which were thoroughly understood by the men who made the pump which should give you summer after summer of silent and troubleless service.

Building the Waterfall Rock Garden

Dig out first the 'V' or 'L' of your ravine, either straight into the bank or at an angle to it, and then the pool at the head, either in the nick of the 'V' or the angle of the 'L', below the sheer drop of the crag. The excavation wants to be about eight inches wider and longer than you need it, and in shaping it you should avoid sharp angles as these are a common source of cracks. See that the sides are all firm earth; ramming is a good idea with soft places; then spread a three inch layer of concrete over the whole area (three parts gravel, one sand, one Portland cement), mixed about as thick as stiff porridge; shape it to your pool sides and bottom, and leave it about two days to set. Then damp the surface and face it with a mixture of three parts sand to one cement, trowelled on in a layer about half an inch thick. You should finish this stage with a series of long shaped pools along the course of your stream, and one large one at the bottom, which is the only one really suitable for water-lilies.

When the coating cement is dry, rock placing round the pools begins. The important rocks are those over which the water flows. Use either one of the necessary height, or, as the falling water will hide the surface, one less good, but capped with a flat water-worn piece, with a straight edge. Long experience with show rock gardens has proved that a straight sharp edge and a slight overlap, about quarter an inch, at the lip produces the most waterfall for the pump size; it is quite easy with a notch in the rock to produce something no more attractive than a bath wastepipe in full gush, so choose the pieces carefully (see Fig. 6). The lower rock wants to overlap the bottom pool end slightly, and to prevent leakage and settling as the water trickles round and under it, secure this rock with cement, damping it first, and even firmly seating bricks below it to which it is secured with more cement. Try it first on soil, and be sure you have it right before it sets, as these cemented rocks cannot be moved afterwards. Then seat the lip rock on the top, followed by the side rocks also in cement, and go on round the pool, hiding the hard outline of the concrete with flat, overlapping rocks, slightly thinner than the two side pieces.

In places, where the strata would put them, have large rocks overlapping, but all the rock work wants to follow the natural formation; the stream has cut through solid rock, the water-worn rock in its course must not follow a separate or random direction like a flagged or crazy paving path. Though rock can be let in at a lower level, by making your concrete lower at that point (it must be well set first to take the weight of the rock), this is not advisable, because the join of rock and concrete often means leaks.

These overlapping rocks have a utilitarian value. Fish in small pools suffer greatly from the sun, and can get shade under them, also thrushes will, in shallow water, behave just like kingfishers or herons. They come on the rock garden for snail-cracking stones, see a fish flapping as it is carried over the lip of the fall, snatch it, and then search the pool. Cats will do exactly the same, and the bright goldfish is the most frequent sufferer. The overlap provides a refuge, though one always loses some unlucky fish.

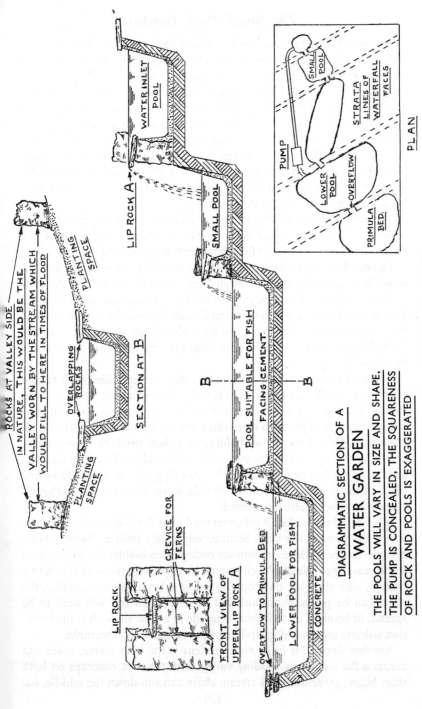

ROCKS AT VALLEY SIDE
IN NATURE, THIS WOULD BE THE
VALLEY WORN BY THE STREAM WHICH
WOULD FILL TO HERE IN TIMES OF FLOOD

OVERLAPPING
PLANTING ROCKS
SPACE

PLANTING
SPACE

SECTION AT B

WATER INLET
POOL

LIP ROCK A

SMALL POOL

POOL SUITABLE FOR FISH
FACING CEMENT

B——B

LIP ROCK

FRONT VIEW OF
UPPER LIP ROCK A

CREVICE FOR
FERNS

CONCRETE

PRIMULA BED

LOWER POOL FOR FISH

OVERFLOW TO PRIMULA BED

SMALL
POOL

PUMP

LOWER
POOL

OVERFLOW

PRIMULA
BED

STRATA
LINES OF
WATERFALL
FACES

PLAN

DIAGRAMMATIC SECTION OF A
WATER GARDEN
THE POOLS WILL VARY IN SIZE AND SHAPE,
THE PUMP IS CONCEALED, THE SQUARENESS
OF ROCK AND POOLS IS EXAGGERATED

FIG. 6. Diagram of a Water Garden.

The pipe from the lower pool can feed back the water in two ways. Either it is hidden under one of the overlapping stones of the upper pool or a separate pool out of sight is made behind the highest outcrop, so that your system starts with a fall into the first one, the usual flower show system. The pipe is then above the level of the water, and pumping into a small reservoir pond which is lead over between rocks and over a lip like all the others. A two-foot fall here is most effective and as this situation is usually quite sheltered, it is a good place for Mimulus and hardy Calceolarias, not to mention ferns in plenty, as these love to be splashed. A high inlet avoids any chance of water siphoning back into the pipe, in winter a danger from freezing.

The other portions of the stream sides will be no damper than the rest of the rock garden; beyond the concrete the ground will dry unless you have leaks, and it is near the falls that damp-lovers should go.

The overlapping rocks are not safe for standing, your weight has too much leverage and you may smash them or break the hold of the concrete, so planting should be in gum boots, or before the water is let in. The rest of the building follows normal methods, only the stratum line has been determined by the rocks you have already set in cement, and this should be followed, to produce an effect the very reverse of the 'shark's tooth pool'.

The soakaway or overflow should be dug out and filled with rubble over quite a wide area, say four feet square and about as deep, even though the upper part is to be a Primula bog, because you will probably run the hose through more often and the rain catching goes on all the winter. On a heavy water-holding clay there needs to be some provision for getting the surplus away; on a dry sandy soil the Primulas and the soaking will cope with very little extra digging. There should be one place in the concrete, or one whole side, lower than the rest so that all spare water goes where it is needed.

It is possible to make an informal pool on a flat site, a rock garden in which the pond is the main feature, very rarely built at flower shows because as one of the most famous rock garden builders in Britain said some years ago, 'We don't sell water'. If this is dug out so that it is in a hollow, with the rock outcropping round it on a flat stratum line, the effect can be perfectly natural, but the excavated soil will need to be spread, or brought up to it from one side in a slow slope. It is the imitation volcano crater or slag-tip-like pile that becomes unbearable.

Another device for large rock gardens is the long ravine, taken out across a flat site like a winding valley, with the rock outcrops on both sides below garden level. A stream chain can run down the middle, but the only viewpoint is from the centre, therefore a path is needed all the way. This needs more rock than an outcrop, and is difficult to make on a small scale, though where an existing path falls between two high banks it can be very effective.

Though it is not the purpose of this book to deal with water plants or fish, the pools can take any species suitable for the outdoor pond, the swift circulation of the water, with plenty of aeration from the falls, enables fish which do not like really stagnant streams to thrive. Those who do not wish to use the rather gaudy goldfish can do very well with minnows. These are not sticklebacks, but a round-nosed sturdy creature without spines and with a line of dark markings along the sides like the gun ports of a frigate (Nelson's period, not modern). They run up to four inches long, seven inches is a record, and though they tolerate still water, they delight in waterfalls and will jump on summer evenings like trout, taking any flies that fall in, in the same way. Their advantages are that they will eat any midge or gnat larvae (these breed in any fishless pond), they do not attack other fish, are extremely hardy and are perfectly at home in a restricted space; pools holding as little as five gallons have kept them for years. They can be obtained cheaply from aquarium dealers (their scientific name is *Phoxinus phoxinus*), or from small boys. In this case one should insist on the right species; sticklebacks, three, seven and twenty-eight spined, are all called 'minnows' by the modern child in the 'fishing with jam jar' age group, and these are less efficient larvae cleaners and, though small, will destroy young goldfish. Gudgeon, bleak and the stone loach are all good small pool plus waterfall fish, British natives, and though protectively coloured inclined to play at the surface, so you see something of them. The loach is a bottom feeder, but rushes about wildly in thundery weather. Brown trout are unsuitable, not because of the confined space but because their jumping is not to scale, yearlings can leap high in the air and are found dead on the sides in the morning. (I learnt this when I was a boy from bitter experience with a dozen bought out of pocket money.)

Before any fish or plants go in, the pool system should be filled and emptied at least three times during the first fortnight, to wash out the poisons in the cement, the upper pools being cleared by siphoning. The cautions on washing off cement quickly apply even more strongly in the rock garden; nothing looks worse than hard white smears on the carefully set faces. In calculating how much material you need for a job, it is important to consider the shrinkage of the concrete. Gravel is sold by the cubic yard; this is enough to cover twelve square yards of concrete three inches thick; the sand and cement will be taken up by shrinkage.

Cement is sold by weight, usually in stout paper bags, and you will need roughly 8 lb. for every square foot of three inch concrete, and about 4 lb. for each square foot of facing.

Planting the Rock Garden

Rock garden planting is very much the same as in the alpine border, but a greater range of species is available. The large garden can take the dry wall species, with crevice planting for those that go edgeways, and the alpine lawn and border plants come in as well. The lists at the end of this chapter are restricted to the additional varieties, for the scree, for crevice planting, the upper surfaces of rocks, and beside water.

The ruling principle is that small rock gardens must grow small species if anything like a range of colour and flowering seasons is to be secured; with plenty of room one can grow all types, but keep them away from each other. The bane of rock gardens is weeding, and therefore as far as possible digging of any kind should be avoided. By top dressing with leafmould or sterilised soil, scattering bonemeal below thriving clumps and attention to cutting, weeding can be greatly reduced because complete ground cover between rocks means less space for them. A healthy Lithospermum or Polygonum should not be disturbed; it is keeping down weeds and any plants it may be encroaching on should be moved.

The crags and higher portions will be the driest, and therefore the plants for these should be chosen with this in mind, but as the slope is gradual and the rocks act as rain traps, there should be little drought trouble.

The best rock garden planting time is the spring, the most suitable division season, but as it is not planted during building one can spread the work over a long period, doing the construction in the autumn but avoiding frosty weather for concrete and planting by degrees.

The alpine specialist will miss many favourites from the lists that follow; the main consideration is hardiness on the normal rock garden, and though further species can be added by using cloches to provide winter protection from rain, the need is to provide a selection of plants which will give little trouble on the modern rock garden. The enthusiasm which will grow with success will soon range further than the mere five hundred odd species described in this book.

All small and slow growing cushion-like species can go on the scree slopes; those in the following list are those which must have this position. Very many wall plants are ideal in crevices, and here too direct seeding can be used for suitable plants.

LIST OF ADDITIONAL ALPINES FOR THE ROCK GARDEN. Other lists all apply

Approx. height (inches)		Flowering period									
		Feb.	Mar.	Apr.	May	June	July	Aug.	Sep.	Oct.	Nov.
3 — 4	Androsace carnea var. Halleri. Pink. Scree		—								
2 — 3	Asperula suberosa. Pink. Scree			—	—	—					
3 — 4	Calceolaria biflora. Yellow. Waterside, shelter					—	—				
2 — 3	,, tenella. Yellow. Waterside, shade and shelter					—	—	—			
	Conifers. Foliage only. Lower slopes										
2 — 3	Draba Aizoon. Yellow. Scree		—								
1 — 2	,, Dedeana. White. Scree			—							
2 — 3	,, sibirica. Yellow. Scree			—	—						
3 — 4	Geranium subcaulescens. Rose pink. Scree					—	—	—	—		
4 — 6	Helianthemum Tuberaria. Yellow. Waterside					—	—				
6 — 8	Leontopodium alpinum. Grey. Crevice					—	—				
1 — 2	Petrocallis pyrenaica. Lavender. Scree			—	—						
2 — 3	Saponaria Boissieri. Pink. Scree				—	—					
1 — 2	Saxifraga Faldonside. Yellow. Scree	—	—	—							
12 — 15	,, longifolia, varieties. White. Crevice				—						
	Sempervivums. Mainly foliage. Crevice and rock hollows										

127

The Small Rock Garden

This short list is of species that really need rock or look best only on the rock garden. As a help in planning and ordering when all are nothing but names, the following list of essential alpines for the small rock garden is included. They are for full sun, flower well and are easy and hardy if their not very exacting tastes are considered. Other men might choose other lists; these plants are my oldest friends on the rock garden, and they are intended as a collection for the amateur. Because they are for the small rock garden, strong-growing species have been excluded unless they are really good and worth the room.

9. *Narcissus cyclamineus*, with a slender trumpet and back petals folded upwards like those of a cyclamen, grows about five inches high and flowers in March and April. It likes leafy soil and sun, but needs summer moisture

10. *Mazus reptans* is a carpeter that likes leafy soil, with foliage that shades the ground in a moisture-saving mulch and keeps the rain-splashed mud off the miniature Daffodil. It flowers from June to August, lilac with orange spots, when the bulbs are dormant below the carpet

11. *Narcissus Bulbocodium*, the 'Hoop petticoat Narcissus' is a six inch miniature for the Alpine Border. It flowers at Daffodil time in March and April and is fond of a leafy soil in a sunny place, not desperately dry in Summer

12. *Nierembergia rivularis*, with large white cup flowers from June to August also likes leafmould and a sunny place. With bulbs below and foliage above to shade the soil, the carpeter and the Narcissus co-operate and give two flower crops from the same small area

ESSENTIAL ALPINES FOR THE SMALL ROCK GARDEN

Flowering period

	Feb.	Mar.	Apr.	May	June	July	Aug.	Sep.	Oct.	Nov.
Aethionema Warley Rose				●————————●						
Ajuga Brockbankii				●——●						
Androsace sempervivoides			●——●							
Aquilegia pyrenaica				●——●						
Arenaria purpurascens				●——●						
Armeria caespitosa			●————————————●							
Asperula suberosa				●————●						
Campanula arvatica					●————————●					
" fenestrellata						●●				
" glomerata acaulis					●————————●					
" pulla					●————————●					
" pusilla					●————————●					
Cyclamen neapolitanum							●————●			
" " album								●●		
Dianthus alpinus					●————●					
" haematocalyx				●————————————————●						
" Jupiter					●——————————●					

129

Flowering period

	Feb.	Mar.	Apr.	May	June	July	Aug.	Sep.	Oct.	Nov.
Dianthus Mars										
„ parnassicus					———					
Erinus alpinus, all varieties				———————						
Erodium chamaedroides roseum				———————————————						
„ Merstham Pink				———————————						
Frankenia thymifolia					———————					
Gentiana angustifolia			———————							
„ lagodechiana					———————————					
„ Macaulayi						———				
„ saxosa						———————				
Geranium sanguineum lancastriense					———————					
Gypsophila cerastioides					———————					
Helianthemum alpestre serpyllifolium					———————					
„ Ben Dearg					———————					
Hypericum nummularium						———				
Hypsela longiflora					———————					
Iberis saxatilis		———								

Flowering period

	Feb.	Mar.	Apr.	May	June	July	Aug.	Sep.	Oct.	Nov.
Iberis taurica				———	———					
Iris lacustris				———	———	———	———	———		
„ mellita				———	———					
Inula acaulis			———							
Linaria alpina				———	———	———	———	———		
„ globosa rosea				———	———	———	———			
Linum salsoloides nanum				———	———	———	———	———		
Lithospermum graminifolium					———	———				
Mimulus Whitecroft Scarlet					———	———	———	———		
Morisia hypogaea			———	———						
Oenothera pumila					———	———	———	———		
Penstemon rupicola				———	———					
Petrocallis pyrenaica				———	———					
Phlox amoena				———	———					
„ bifida				———	———	———				
„ Douglasii Boothman's Variety				———						
„ Eva				———	———					

					Flowering period					
	Feb.	Mar.	Apr.	May	June	July	Aug.	Sep.	Oct.	Nov.
Phlox Douglasii Lilac Queen				●──						
,, subulata Brightness				●──						
,, ,, May Snow				──●──						
,, ,, Sampson				──●──						
,, ,, Temiscaming				──●──						
Polygala calcarea				●──						
,, Chamaebuxus				●────────●						
,, ,, purpurea				●────────●						
Potentilla verna nana			●────────●							
Primula capitata Mooreana					●──●					
,, Clarkei				●──						
,, pubescens Faldonside				●──●						
,, ,, Mrs. J. H. Wilson				●──●						
,, rosea grandiflora			●──●							
Ramonda Myconi				●──────────●						
,, ,, rosea				●──────────●						
Rhododendron ferrugineum					●──●					

	Feb.	Mar.	Apr.	May	June	July	Aug.	Sep.	Oct.	Nov.
					Flowering period					
Rosa Oakington Ruby				────	────	────	────	────	────	
,, pumila				────	────	────	────	────	────	────
Saxifraga Aizoon baldensis					──					
,, Burseriana (all varieties)		────	────							
,, Elizabethae		────	────							
,, Faldonside		────	────							
,, Irvingii		────	────							
,, oppositifolia (all varieties)		────	────							
,, Primulaize				────	────					
Sedum dasyphyllum					────	────				
,, hispanicum minus					────	────				
,, kamtschaticum						────	────	────		
,, lydium					────	────	────			
,, spurium Schorbuser Blut.					────	────	────	────		
Selliera radicans										
Sempervivum arachnoideum (foliage, flowers rare)										
,, tectorum (foliage, flowers rare)										

	Flowering period									
	Feb.	Mar.	Apr.	May	June	July	Aug.	Sep.	Oct.	Nov.
Serratula Shawii								■	■	
Silene Schafta								■	■	
Solidago brachystachys							■	■		
Thymus Serpyllum albus					■	■	■			
" " carmineus					■	■	■			
" " coccineus					■	■	■			
" " major					■	■	■			
Umbilicus oppositifolius				■	■					
Veronica armena					■	■	■			
" pyroliformis					■	■				
" rupestris Mrs. Holt										
" saxatilis				■						
Viola cornuta minor				■	■	■	■	■		
" rothamgensis				■	■	■	■	■		
Wahlenbergia dinarica						■	■			
" pumilio					■	■				
" serpyllifolia major				■	■					

134

Flowering period

	Feb.	Mar.	Apr.	May	June	July	Aug.	Sep.	Oct.	Nov.
Zauschneria californica								———	——	—

ADDITIONAL PLANTS FOR WATERSIDE

	Feb.	Mar.	Apr.	May	June	July	Aug.	Sep.	Oct.	Nov.
Calceolaria biflora					——	——	—			
„ tenella					——	——	—			
Corydalis lutea (crevices)				—	——	—				
Dodecatheon (all species)				—	——					
Ferns (all hardy varieties) (crevices)										
Helianthemum Tuberaria					—	——				
Iris ruthenica										
Mimulus (all varieties)					——	——	——	——		
Ourisia coccinea					——	—				
Primula denticulata (vars.)			—	——						
Sisyrinchium bellum (a 'rush replica')							——			

ADDITIONAL PLANTS FOR THE NON-LIMY GARDEN

	Feb.	Mar.	Apr.	May	June	July	Aug.	Sep.	Oct.	Nov.
Azalea roseaflorum				—	——					
Gentiana hexaphylla						——	—			
„ sino-ornata								——	——	

135

	Flowering period									
	Feb.	Mar.	Apr.	May	June	July	Aug.	Sept.	Oct.	Nov.
Gentiana Veitchiorum						———				
Lithospermum Heavenly Blue				——						

136

The Small Rock Garden

These lists are simply selections of plants I like and consider the best value in their type. A few like Ramonda need a shaded crevice. A few are included because they serve a special purpose, the Sisyrinchiums are good imitation rushes by the stream side, where they are beyond the concrete, the others in that list like a bit of splashing, the big Primulas need more moisture and room, *P. denticulata* and its varieties will do wet and dry. The lime haters are just those which give the most pleasure and advantage to the fortunate garden. As in the other categories, there is already a full list of them earlier and the selection of bulbs on pages 49–51 adds further early and late species to go under the carpeters which are included in the first list of a hundred plants.

Not all the plants listed here are widely cultivated; some may need long searching in the catalogues of alpine specialists, but all are worth the hunting, and most should be obtainable from any good alpine nurseryman.

6

Alpine Soils

An alpine soil is one in which alpines will grow in the garden; it is not necessarily the same as that in which they would grow by nature. To help them overcome the problems of growing where nature never intended, we get the soil as near as we can to their needs in these circumstances. Growing good alpines is very much more a matter of having the right soil for the right plant than of anything else, and there must be the plant foods which they need in the form in which they can take them, otherwise they will grow soft and sappy and will be neither long-lived nor free-flowering.

An average alpine soil should be gritty, with sharp sand like the rock fragments normally in their diet, contain humus to hold moisture and provide plant foods, and some good loam to give further food and a certain ability to stick together when rammed. The mixture must vary: some species need more humus or more loam, a number very much more grit and a greater number still more lime.

The modern gardener does not use the complicated soil recipes of the past. The work of the John Innes Horticultural Institution on soils for pot plants has revealed that only two basic mixtures are necessary: a potting soil, known as 'John Innes Potting Compost' which is seven parts of steam-sterilised loam, three of horticultural peat, and two of sharp sand; and a seed-raising mixture, 'John Innes Seed Compost', composed of two parts loam, one peat and one sand. To these are added measured quantities of superphosphate and chalk for the seed mixture, which are necessary because the loam has been sterilised, or in the case of the potting soil a general fertiliser called 'John Innes Base', which includes superphosphate to make it a bit richer. In this book the term 'Soil' is used for these, not 'Compost', to avoid confusion with the equally well-known Indore and other composts which are vegetable wastes rotted down with an organic nitrogen source.

These mixtures are described, with a full account of the sterilisation

138

process, in *Seed and Potting Composts* by W. J. C. Lawrence and J. Newell (Allen & Unwin 5s.); but they were not designed for alpines, they were devised to suit plants with a narrower range of tastes, and to be absolutely standard. Today most nurserymen use them with success but when applied to alpines they are rather like electric light plugs, if they fit anything unusual it is a matter of luck. For this reason, many alpine specialists, including those at Kew, ignore the invention and go on in the old way.

The John Innes Seed Soil is, by coincidence, a good general alpine mixture, and it is today the easiest soil to buy for those who must buy soil, which is a great deal cheaper than either rock or manure. The gritty sand recommended for making this soil is ideal for alpines, and neither this nor the peat can contain any weed seeds. The loam is sterilised by steam, which cooks both seeds and any root fragments like grains of rice and potatoes, so where it is used the only weeds one has to contend with are those that blow in. The mixture is used for raising alpine seeds and the general run of pot-grown alpines by most commercial growers, because of the saving in the cost of weeding.

Unfortunately, though it was meant to be dead standard, the loam varies in quality, and so does the efficiency of the steaming process. It is not a standard product like a packet of soap powder; only the recipe was invented by the John Innes Institution, and they have often considered taking legal action against firms who sell below standard soil. Therefore it should be bought only from reputable nurserymen and sundriesmen, who will send it by goods train anywhere and deliver larger quantities by road. In small quantities it is sold by the bushel, weighing 72 lb. when dry, and this is enough to fill a window box three feet long, nine inches wide and six inches deep, or roughly fifteen ordinary eight inch seed pans. The 1953 cost in the London area for this quantity was between 3s. and 5s.

On the rock garden, or under the alpine lawn, you will need about a six-inch deep surface layer, and a bag containing one hundredweight, which is the larger scale unit, is enough to cover four square feet to this depth. To save carriage, and because other ingredients are needed in different proportions, it is best to buy only the loam ready sterilised, but the complete mixture removes any need for sifting and mixing and removes the problem of the garden where 'Nothing grows, I have such fearful soil' so far as the small-scale alpine border or garden goes.

If you are going to buy loam, or soil, it saves weeding if you buy it sterilised, or rather gives the plants a long start on the weeds. The large-

Alpine Soils

scale steam plant used is very efficient, and the cost is not excessive unless one is a long distance from the supplier, but though the destruction of spores and resting forms of diseases and pests is important to the commercial grower who raises tomatoes in a greenhouse crop after crop, year after year, the only gain to the alpine gardener is this weedseed destruction. Normal garden soil with additions is just as good, and many alpine growers use unsterilised soil even for seed pans, where the advantage of cutting out the competition with slower germinating seeds is considerable.

The question is, what is a 'normal garden soil'?

The only soil which can play no part in an alpine mixture is a raw hungry subsoil, and, with assistance, some species will grow even in that. The ordinary black light soil, stony or otherwise, of a great many town gardens, which grows vegetables if it is repeatedly manured, and does most herbaceous plants moderately well, is quite good, with modifications. It is not a clay, it is not a loam, it has merely been a garden a very long time.

Sift the top eight inches, the soil you take off the rock garden site, or dig out of the alpine border through about a three-eighths inch mesh sieve. This is not only to break it fine and make it easy to work in between the layers of a dry wall, but to make sure that any weed roots are got out before you build them in to give trouble. Throw the stones, broken glass, etc. into the drainage layer, the weed roots should be burnt or composted if you are a good compost maker. To three parts of this soil by bulk (soil recipes need not be exact—judge by eye, bucketful or barrowload) add one part of good loam, two parts of leafmould, sifted only to break up the lumps and allow sticks and stones to be picked out, and one part of sharp sand. Add next a 48 (3½-inch) pot of bone meal to the barrowload and another of ground chalk or limestone flour to the pile, then mix it. Shovel it first one way and then the other so the whole lot is thoroughly mixed; the lime may make the outsides of the lumps look like white, but there is very little there really: this is not a lime-lovers' mixture, but a general, ordinary alpine soil.

The '48 pot to the barrowload' is a traditional gardener's measure; within horticultural limits of accuracy it has worked very well for perhaps two hundred years but modern metal, rubber-tyred barrows are usually smaller than the stout beechwood vehicle of the 1900's. Think of the biscuit tins holding roughly a third of a bushel each; it ought to work out at roughly half an ounce of each to a biscuit tin full. The reason why so much is needed is because a town garden soil is usually very poor on lime, and both this and the bone meal stay in the soil and

140

keep on releasing their value for a long time. Artificial fertilisers are too quick for alpines.

This basic mixture needs altering to suit the sort of soil that your garden is on. If it is the top layer of loam, which is part sand, part clay on top of solid chalk, cut out the extra loam and the lime, and take your soil only six inches or even four deep. On a heavy clay, the sort that bakes in summer but grows rose trees well, leave out the loam and add an extra half a part of really gritty sand. On the sort of poor sand that grows pine trees and nothing much else, double the loam. The object is to make roughly the same sort of mixture, not too rich, with plenty of grit and humus and slowly available plant foods. Your unaided soil will probably grow a great many alpines easily, all the tough ones, but it is worth taking the trouble to grow more, even buying ingredients at a cost that is less than most of the gardening gadgets which are used once and then left to rust, rather than blaming your garden for not suiting plants from the mountains of the world.

When you are mixing your own unsterilised soil, buy unsterilised loam—a few less weeds will not make all that difference, you will have some to pull out anyway. Take them when they first come up as seedlings if you have a bad crop; a short-handled hoe is the best tool and with a small rock garden the area to cover is not great—you would do as much for onions. This is one of the reasons why compost is rarely used for alpines; well-made it is too rich, badly made it produces the worst possible crop of weeds. The main difficulty in rock garden weeding is the fear of pulling up plants; the remedy is to know your plants by sight.

Before the separate mixtures to suit different classes of alpines are considered, it is well to take each of these ingredients separately, beginning with the loam, sterilised or otherwise. This is the top spit from under pasture land which grass roots and bacterial action have made darker, richer and more crumby than the soil below, and the dead grass roots should still be in it, making it what is known as 'fibrous loam'. In the past it was the custom in private gardens to stack turf grass side downwards in a high square pile to rot for a year and provide a store of this ingredient when it was needed, and those who have an opportunity to dig the top surface from grassland, or can buy any near, as an example from where a house is being built, should seize the opportunity. Turf for this purpose is dug out in lumps about four inches thick, not sold in thin rolls as for a lawn.

The humus for alpine soil is best supplied as leafmould, and it is possible to make this better and cheaper than you can buy it; its cost is only time and thinking ahead. Every autumn stack your leaves to make leafmould. Though oak or beech is the best, any deciduous tree except the London plane (with the peeling bark) will have rotted enough to be used in the second spring, after fifteen months, and be really excellent by the third. At Kew very large stacks are made and hoarded, vintage leafmould, matured ten or even twenty years in the stack is excellent, and the modern gardener who burns his leaves and buys inferior substitutes has only himself to blame for a starved, dry soil.

In the small garden the best system is to drive in four stout posts and surround them with three foot high wire netting stapled on; this prevents the wind blowing the leaves about. Stack them in and tread them down, with no sticks or other rubbish. The rotting is slow and does not produce the weed-seed destroying heat of the good compost heap. Then leave them; the netting can be removed when they have settled firm. They need no turning, no addition of anything, only time to decay. Leafmould can be bought, but this is usually dug by the lorryload out of woodland, complete with sticks, roots, stones, and often the seeds of many weeds—the reason for its disfavour today. Stack leafmould is greatly superior, it is low nitrogen, high potash and high phosphate, and though its feed value for vegetables is not high, it is excellent for providing slowly available nutriment for alpines, herbaceous plants and shrubs, and giving moisture-holding power on sand or opening up the solid clay for root penetration and easier digging. It is worth making an arrangement with those who sweep up the leaves of street trees, provided one can avoid plane tree planted portions, to secure some good loads for the humus-starved town garden.

Horticultural peat is mainly decayed water plants; it is sold compressed in bales, which should be broken up and watered well before use. It does not provide anything like the nutriment of leafmould, and is valuable only in improving the mechanical condition of the soil. Apart from this, it must be bought and anything which can be made easily and better in your own garden can well save money for other items.

Some peat is needed for certain alpines, notably dwarf Rhododendrons, Ericas and other species which naturally grow in peaty soil. This is not chemically neutral, but acid, it is not fluffy like sedge peat, but fibrous, powdery, and contains roots, often of bracken, which should be removed in the sifting. Relatively little is required and it is worth buying as 'Rhododendron peat' if it cannot be bought as the peat blocks used for burning, these can be broken up and sifted as a very good cheap supply for species that need it, but not as a substitute for leafmould.

On very poor soils, as an additional food supply for established strong-growing alpines, especially lime haters, municipal compost can be used. This is a dried and ground compost made from dustbin refuse and sewage sludge by some far-sighted corporations, notably Dumfries and Leatherhead, supplied very reasonably in bags by goods train any-where. Because the heating of the heaps is accurately controlled (they go up to 200° F.), all weed seeds are destroyed (and of course any harm-ful bacteria) and it is without smell of any kind. It is a standard product, unlike an amateur heap, and added as one extra part to a very poor town-soil-based alpine mixture, or one without loam made with a clay which is not fertile, it improves the food value greatly. For vegetables and general garden use it is both cheaper than town-bought manure and better value than any other preparation sold to supply both plant foods and humus.

Older books on alpines stress the importance of adding mortar rubble to soil for plants that like lime. This was perfectly correct when they were written, but the changeover from the old-fashioned lime mortar which weathered to calcium carbonate and sand, to modern Portland cement which makes a better and more lasting wall, but remains a hard and complicated mass of hydrated double silicates of alumina and calcium silicate, is now almost complete. Modern mortar rubble does not give slowly available calcium even if it is smashed with a hammer, and the easily crushed plaster rubble is mainly calcium sulphate which is not readily available either.

Therefore use ground chalk or ground limestone or the limestone flour which is sold to go in pig or poultry food, if only a little is required. Slaked lime normally used in gardens is less effective; it is very fine and washes out too fast; both the other types are coarser and last longer in the soil.

The sand wants to be the type that makes good mortar, if possible coarse sharp fragments, from quarter of an inch long downwards; its job is not to provide food but drainage and as on a heavy clay you will need a quantity, it is worth remembering that the sharpness is not strictly essential, road grit will do very well. Fine sand is wanted for seed soils and cutting frames, alpine soil needs it fairly coarse.

The bone meal is the most lasting and slow organic plant feed, and it can be used for all alpines without fear of soft growth from overfeeding. Never use anything stronger in the way of artificial fertilisers or organic manures; the total growth of a rampant Aubrieta is nothing in a season compared with potatoes followed by spring cabbage, and they do not need the feed, even on the scale necessary to supply a tall Delphinium for its summer height. The stress on feeding in this chapter is merely because the soil needs to start with a stock when you build, and then it runs on its capital and natural income for year after year.

It is easy to convert the general alpine soil to a lime-lovers mixture for good Campanula, Gypsophila and Aubrieta growing: merely double the lime, and if the soil has been based on one from a chalky garden it will need none anyway. The lime-haters mixture needs a separate basic recipe, two parts leafmould, one part acid peat, one part sand and one of good loam, plus the 48 pot of bone meal. A richer leafy mixture meant for woodland plants such as *Lithospermum* Heavenly Blue, needs three of leafmould, two of loam, and one of sand.

In both mixtures there is some loam, to provide more plant food, and where this is very limy, it can be replaced with half a part of municipal or other good compost. Lime haters in gardens often suffer from starvation after some years, if a lime-free loam can be bought, it is much better. This is supplied by some alpine specialists, and it is better to buy enough to cover one-fifth of your Gentian bed area, than to keep buying fresh plants; it will last almost indefinitely with the top dressings recommended for individual species.

It is possible to buy an outfit with full directions to test soil or bought loam cheaply and simply; if it is neutral or acid it will do Gentians, strongly alkaline means too much lime; stick to the plants you can grow. The gardener's test is, 'Will Azaleas grow easily?' If they do then you can grow the whole range of alpines, adding lime for the lime lovers, and if you are on a peaty or poor sandy soil with peat, importing loam. Because it is just the people who cannot grow any class of plant who always prefer it to the wide range that enjoy their soil, an account is given under 'Gentians' in the next chapter on how to grow the thin-leaved woodland species and other lime haters in defiance of anything short of solid chalk. For more normal soils, lime-haters' mixture will grow them.

Plants that need a gritty soil, the scree mixture, are satisfied with either normal alpine soil, lime-lovers' soil, or lime-haters' soil with an equal quantity of lime-stone chippings or in the last case (very few species need it, none of those described in this book) granite chippings, fine broken flower-pot or pounded slate. These last two types of grit are useful, because very many small alpines are fond of them; the miniature Androsaces do best with equal parts of smashed slate and lime-stone chippings with their good alpine mixture, and *Armeria caespitosa* and *Petrocallis pyrenaica* both like broken crocks. This mixture is purely a surface coating, say four inches; below lies alpine soil, and if they need more nourishment they have only to send down for it, but otherwise it is very near their natural diet.

13. An example of good wall planting from Kew. The white, June and July flowering *Gypsophila repens* is a strong and trailing species and is therefore planted high to hang down. *Zauschneria californica* below, with slender scarlet trumpets in September and October, thrusts up, so must go in a lower layer of the wall

14. *Convolvulus mauritanicus* dies back to a woody rootstock in winter. On the rock garden this may rot, but edgeways in the dry wall, nearer its natural home, it is fully hardy. Plant it high so that its ramping trailing branches can display their lilac-blue flowers from June to October with almost Aubrieta splendour

Alpine Soils

These mixtures assume that, like most gardeners, one is making up the soil from unsterilised ingredients. If, however, one starts with John Innes Seed Compost, a known recipe, containing the sterilised loam, one still retains weed-seed freedom because none of the additional ingredients to alter this to the required mixture will contain any. John Innes Seed Compost is half loam, quarter peat and quarter sand, therefore to convert it to a lime-haters' mixture add another quarter of its bulk of sand to get that levelled up, then another quarter of acid peat and three-quarters of whole bulk before you start, of leafmould, to bring up the humus. You do not know how limy the loam was, and some ground chalk will have been added to each bushel to balance the extra acidity from the sterilising, but the real acid peat will probably take care of this.

These soil recipes are all approximate; most of the time one does not need a full-scale mixture either way. Very many plants just like some extra lime or rather more leafmould dug in round when they are planted, and this is mentioned under each species in the next chapter. As an example, three parts John Innes and one part roughly extra leafmould will do all the carpeters that like this sort of rather leafier mixture but are not lime-haters at all.

There are now electric soil sterilisers on the market which will heat about a bushel at a time, and when one is doing the loam only they are quite efficient, though the soil wants to be as dry as possible first—the more cold water one has to raise to 180° F. the more units they use. Never sterilise peat or leafmould mixed with loam or ready-mixed soil of any type, this produces toxic substances highly dangerous to plants; do the loam only, as this is where the weed seeds are. Wait till it cools, say 48 hours to be sure, then mix in one and a half ounces of superphosphate to each bushel of loam.

The process first destroys all the soil bacteria, then when they come back, with ample food in the bacterial nitrogen released by the bodies of those destroyed, they simply swarm; the superphosphate is to give sufficient phosphorus to stop them robbing the stock in the loam. This bacterial boom releases a great deal of food when the slump comes; it is excellent for young tomato plants, but alpines do not appreciate it so much, therefore if possible leave your soil under cover in a heap for at least three weeks, so things can get back to normal. The soil is then mixed in the usual way.

Do not sterilise the normal garden soil; this is going to contain some humus, perhaps even a quantity of lime, it can therefore behave like ready-mixed soil and give trouble. There are several methods of

Alpine Soils

sterilising soil by heat, described in *Seed and Potting Composts*, but as they need a soil steriliser which is always a relatively big job of brickwork and metal, it is not worth attempting on the scale that alpines need. It is far simpler to buy any loam you require for seed mixtures or to make up soil, and simpler still to go ahead, just as Reginald Farrar did, and the staff at Kew do now, and mix your good loam, leafmould, sand and other ingredients in the traditional way.

The secret of growing alpines is to make your soil to fit the plant, and to spend knowledge and trouble on considering the needs of those which have fads. If you do not want to consider soils and just wish to use a standard mixture, determined by what your garden starts with, then choose those that suit what you have got; there are plenty to fit your garden. It is essential, however, to bring whatever you have got to somewhere near an alpine mixture, rather more gritty and with some humus in it, instead of the hungry town garden soil or the heavy clay. Even on those unaided soils, you can still grow the tougher species. Helianthemums are almost unkillable, and others will be found in the following chapter, but do not blame the plants if other species fail, blame yourself for not taking the trouble to provide the soil they need.

7

Alpines Plant by Plant

The following series of accounts of alpine species is not in any way a complete encyclopaedia of all that can be or have been grown on the rock garden, or in any other part of the garden. No alpine house species are included, and as the number of alpines in cultivation increases mainly by the addition of more in this last category, it may strike the expert as being rather old-fashioned. This is not, however, a book for those who gain pleasure by growing more difficult species as a trial of skill, it is for those who wish to garden with alpines, and is restricted to plants which will grow well and flower well provided their requirements are considered in the way of soil, situation and growing methods.

Because it is not possible to give full accounts of all possible species for this purpose in the space available, the alpines are restricted first by ruling out all which are not hardy, next those which do not give real value in flower display for their space, and finally, with reluctance, those which are likely to be extremely expensive. There is another reason for exclusion, a personal one: I do not know all the alpines in cultivation by direct experience, only somewhere near fifteen hundred of them; my list has been selected of those I have grown and propagated, some species by the thousand, and I therefore prefer to write of the most suitable six hundred of the plants which are my friends.

The names under which they are described are those under which they will be found listed in most alpine catalogues, because the need is to enable amateur gardeners to buy from nurserymen. After some, further names are given under which they may be found, often with the note 'correctly' or 'now' in front of them. This means that the species concerned is described under the name in the *Dictionary of Gardening* published by the Royal Horticultural Society at 10 guineas (1951 edition), which has been taken as the standard authority for nomenclature. The amateur should regard these as the married names of actresses or authoresses given in brackets in a newspaper after the familiar one under which everyone knows her. These and further names will be found in the index, to avoid those who take a plunge on something new and resounding from finding that they already have it.

Alpines cannot be grown under popular names, for most of them have none and the number of species involved is too great. The fishmonger has only about a dozen species on his slab (the skate is two, his tail appears separately as 'rock eel'), and though the ichthyologist alters the Large Dog Fish from *Scyllium stellare* to *Scyliorhinus stellaris*, he can still keep selling it as 'Rock Salmon'. These botanical names are here to stay, and once we are used to them they are as easy to use as 'Delphinium', 'Buddleia', or 'Antirrhinum', all of which have become part of garden English because they have been unchanged for so long.

These names, derived from Latin, Greek and even Sanskrit and Persian, often tell us something of interest or value in identification concerning the plant, and therefore Appendix I has been added from my *Propagation of Alpines* (Faber & Faber, 25s.). This gives the principles of name construction, why some specific (or second, the 'Christian' name as it were) have capital letters and some not, why some end one way and some another, and a dictionary of specific names common among alpines, with their pronunciation. It is by that very fine botanical scholar and taxonomist Mr. W. T. Stearn, who is in no way responsible for my views on nomenclature, which are purely those of a gardener, writing for other gardeners.

Acaena. New Zealand Burr

The Acaenas are tough carpeters for sun or shade, on any soil, solid chalk or the poorest sand, drought-tolerant and very hardy. They are ideal paving and alpine path plants because they will stand up to more treading on than anything else. The stems root to the ground at the joints, and spread so powerfully that they should never be planted on the rock garden, except in a problem corner. They produce a turf about half an inch high which needs no mowing, and with small bulbs underplanted are effective as an alpine lawn on their own or with something equally tough.

The best of the tribe is *A. microphylla*, which has bronzy green leaves, tiny and more solid on the general plan of those of a strawberry, and though the flowers are inconspicuous, the seed heads from June to September are like small chestnut burrs covered with long dark red spines, which make a good colour contrast. The drier and poorer the soil the more seed heads there are, but in the shade the display is greatly reduced. There are two other kinds, *A. Buchananii* with silver grey foliage, and *A. inermis* which has almost khaki leaves. In a quiet way they are attractive, despite the need to dig them up when they spread too far. Increase is easy, simply replant the fragments where they are wanted at any time through the summer; though they keep their foliage through the winter they do not transplant well then, and this is the time to get rid of them if necessary.

The seed does not ripen in this country. It is designed to catch in the fur of animals and the introduction of sheep into New Zealand has spread them widely; there they have been found useful on aerodromes, as they stand up to tyre wear better than grass in a dry season.

Achillea. Rock Milfoil

The Achilleas are strong-growing plants with furry foliage, and on the small rock garden they are apt to spend the summer spreading over other plants, and the winter quietly dying. The best is *A. Lewisii* (correctly A. 'King Edward'). This grows as a carpet of rather greyish ferny leaves, with creamy yellow flowers in small flat clusters on four to six inch stems from June to August, sometimes starting earlier and finishing later. It is in effect a miniature and greatly glorified version of the common Milfoil, a weed found in lawns. The golden yellow flowered *A. tomentosa* has rather larger dark green foliage, and its heads are more like the 'plates' of the well-known border species, with the same useful 'after the Aubrieta' flowering season.

There are several white-flowered species with grey foliage, including *A. Clavenae*, *A. Kellereri* and *A. umbellata*, small relations of the cut flower hybrid 'The Pearl' though very distant ones, all flowering roughly over the same period.

On the small rock garden the Achilleas need full sun, and are best with a lime-lovers' mixture to starve them into brilliance and small size. They are good in rock clefts and edgeways positions, and stand up to a great deal of drought, but in better soil, on the flat and damp, they run to stem and leaf. On the wall garden and dry bank they are at their best. Increase is easiest from divisions in spring; rooted fragments can be pulled off and planted in the open ground for replanting later where they are needed, or soft cuttings of all species are easily rooted in the sand frame in August.

Aethionema. Warley Rose, Rock Candytuft

Aethionema Warley Rose is the most essential rock plant for every garden. It is a small bush with wiry stems and closely set grey leaves rather like those of a small Sedum but slender, little blunt spines that stay on all the year. From May to August it flowers with clear pink heads like miniature Hydrangeas, about the diameter of a sixpence, in generous quantities. An established clump can be a foot across or more and six inches high; a real sight which confounds the ignorance of those who say the rock garden needs annuals for summer colour.

It is fully hardy and likes a limy soil, but this can be supplied as a lime-lovers' mixture or as chalk in the normal alpine soil, and full sun. The plant is very long lived, but after three years or so it is inclined to get straggly, so should be cut back to the main stems in April to allow young wood to develop; it will flower later that season but will be neater and more vigorous. A scattering of bone meal in spring, lightly forked in, is appreciated by established plants.

The plant is a sterile hybrid that appeared in the famous garden at Warley owned by Miss Ellen Willmott, who was perhaps the sensible 'Aunt' of rock gardening, just as Reginald Farrar was its 'Father'. It therefore sets no seed but is increased by soft cuttings taken from the base of the flower stems, about ¾ inch long and inserted in the sand frame, from June to September; but select those which have no flower bud, a growing point is needed. They should be potted when rooted in normal alpine soil and grown on in a cold frame, pinching back at intervals to make bushy plants for late spring planting the following year.

This plant is one of the few alpines to have a popular name; ask any nursery for 'Warley Rose' and they know exactly what you mean, the best good all round rock plant for small garden and large.

Though Warley Rose is as good in the dry wall as it is on the rock garden, there are a number of other Aethionemas which are larger, and excellent where there is more room to spare. The race comes from the dry mountain slopes of the Mediterranean and does best with plenty of sun. Planted edgeways on the dry wall they live longer and more happily than they will on any rock garden.

The best of these is the Rock Candytuft, or *Aethionema grandiflorum*, which grows a foot high, thrusting up stout branches from a woody main root stock from June to August, and carrying large pale pink flowerheads an inch or more across on the same Hydrangea pattern as those of Warley Rose but much bigger and stronger. The stems should be cut back after flowering unless it is desired to save seed, because the plant flowers longer and grows more strongly if the work of seed ripening is avoided. It needs full sun and lime like Warley Rose, and in the wall garden it is a good halfway-down plant; unlike Aubrieta it does not want room below to trail but space above or its flower stems will hide plants in the next 'storey'. The leaves are the same blunt grey spines as Warley Rose but thicker and stronger.

It is usually raised from seed sown in March or April, potted and grown in a cold frame for September planting, but it can be grown easily from soft cuttings taken in July and August. This is an advantage, because there is a mystery about this plant.

William Robinson writing in 1870 describes its flower colour as 'purple', and so do the collectors who first saw it in North Persia, Hohenacker in 1843, and Haussknecht who sent back the first seed in 1857. Even as late as 1914 it was described as 'rosy purple', and evidently its colour varies at home, but by constant raising from seed only the pale pink has survived. If your Rock Candytuft seedling suddenly inherits its remote ancestors' flower colour, propagate from cuttings and treasure it; in twenty years it may make your garden as famous as Miss Willmott's.

There used to be a great many Aethionemas in cultivation, about twenty altogether, including *A. cordatum* and *A. moricandianum* which were yellow flowered, but we have today only a few, including *A. cordifolium* which is a smaller version of the Rock Candytuft with greyer foliage; *A. iberideum* which is clear white, with the advantage of flowering from March to June, and *A. pulchellum* which is nearer Warley Rose, but pale pink and about 8 in. high. This one too is rumoured to have a deep pink form lost in its past.

Anyone with a chalky garden and plenty of dry wall space could have a great deal of fun searching for lost Aethionemas in seed from various sources; the more the merrier, they are easy to raise and even the also-ran seedlings are good wall plants. A number of the less common species are annuals or do not live long, but *A. grandiflorum*, like Warley Rose, is very lasting; there was a 15 year old plant at Six Hills Nurseries in the 1930's, two feet across each way. We could do with more good strong colours in tough long flowering alpines for everyone; we cannot all go plant collecting but these plants offer a good hunting ground for the amateur in the unexplored mountains among the genes and chromosomes for the qualities that are locked in their heredity.

Ajuga. Creeping Bugle

These are plants many people have without knowing the name. The common ones are forms of our native *A. reptans*, with rather deeply veined long oval leaves about two inches long, either variegated green and white or metallic bronzy and coppery colours, set on stout creeping

stems that root to the ground at the joints. The flowers in May and June
are short spikes of florets rather like those of a dead-nettle (it is a
member of the same order, *Labiatae*) but blue. It is an easy plant, not
very brilliant but very tough, thriving in dry places and poor soil where
it flowers best, but with advantages on the awkward corner, especially
where early bulbs can be planted below its evergreen foliage which prevents their low flowers from becoming rain splashed. Under these circumstances, not on the rock garden, it is useful as it is capable of
fighting with a number of lesser weeds and winning.

There is, however, another species that is a good alpine, *A. Brockbankii*. This is very much smaller with bright pale green leaves and
larger heads of flowers; the slender, long lower lipped 'Antirrhinum
pattern' florets of the order, but clear sky blue, one of the best blues in
the whole tribe. It needs full sun and normal alpine soil and keeps to
itself, forming a small patch of foliage with rather more stem which does
not root into the ground, though the total height including flower spikes is
about six inches. It is surprisingly rare, but worth searching for, as its
Gentian blue in May and June is charming. It is correctly *A. genevensis var. Brockbankii*.

The common species can simply be dug up and planted where they are
wanted; in the spring, or in the autumn when one is planting bulbs, but
A. Brockbankii needs increasing from soft cuttings of the stems produced after flowering in July and August, rooting in the sand frame and
wintering in pots in the cold frame for spring planting in its permanent
home.

Alyssum. Gold Dust

There is one Alyssum that is almost as well known as the little white
annual one that rivals Lobelia for edging. This is *A. saxatile*, a big powerful plant that develops woody stems as much as half an inch thick, and
has large grey green leaves in bunches. It flowers like fury in May and
June and provides the best bright golden yellow to go with deep violet
or dark red or lavender Aubrieta in the wall garden. It is too strongly
growing and its foliage too floppy to be worth its room on the small rock
garden, so keep it strictly to where it can use vertical space beside the
paths where it will live longest and flower the best.

When an Alyssum has grown old and woody, it pays to cut it back
after flowering until only the main stem, which can be as thick as a
baby's wrist, is left and it will make new growth and take on a new lease
of life. Both this plant and the pale yellow *A. saxatile citrinum* are so
easy from seed, sown in the spring or in July when the pods from one's

own plants are light brown and splitting ready for collection, that there is no need to keep plants when they are past their best. About four years is their normal span, but a good plant in a wall can be left for as long as it will thrive.

The species for the small rock garden are first *A. serpyllifolium*, with flat crawling stems edged with small oval grey leaves, white on the undersides, and miniature yellow flower heads in June or July. This will not swamp other plants and is a creeping shrub that does well trailing over a rock, needing sun and normal soil with plenty of lime, just like its big relation which it in no way resembles.

Then there are two bush Alyssums, *A. spinosum* and *A. spinosum roseum;* the last is quite a good rose pink, the other white, and they grow as neat domes about six inches high with a good flower display in June and July. The spines are not fierce like those of a cactus, and both plants are attractive in a quiet way but not very exciting. These are rare in their pure form because they cross and the result of the seedling is a washy half-and-half form. They will root with difficulty from soft cuttings after flowering in August, but a hormone makes them much easier (see Chapter 9). *A. serpyllifolium* comes true from seed, sown in April and wintered in a cold frame for spring planting, or it can be rooted easily from summer cuttings. *Ptilotriohum* is the new first name of the two *A. spinosum* species.

Androsace. Rock Jasmine

This popular name (as usual) is applied to one species only, *A. lanuginosa*, which is a very good easy wall plant or for a place on the sunny rock garden. It makes a mat of trailing stems with small silky-haired grey green leaves shaped like those of a willow, and about an inch long. These root like strawberry runners from the joints, so increase is easy, though the tips with about three leaf pairs on the stem root readily in sand at any time in the summer.

Its flowers are generous in quantity and look like small heads of Verbena, lilac with a yellow eye. The more common variety, *A. lanuginosa var. Leichtlinii*, has white or pale pink flowers and its yellow eye changes to red when it has been open some time. The flowering season is from June until October, and its foliage stays on all the winter. This is the disadvantage of the Androsaces in this group: they have hairy leaves and we give them a wet winter instead of a dry one with all the water frozen solid, so they are easy to lose from damp. This Himalayan species and its variety will come through the winter safely on the normal rock garden, but it is happier planted in a cleft between two rocks than on the flat. It is, however, much more effective and safer in the dry wall, with the other Androsaces in the rosette group.

These include *A. sarmentosa* (or *A. primuloides*) with pink flower heads, *A. sarmentosa Watkinsii* which is deep pink with a red eye, and *A. sarmentosa Chumbyi* which is smaller and a midway colour. There are a number of intermediate forms, and most nurseries have them very mixed, so it is a case of seeing them in flower in May and June before buying a new one. All are built on the same plan, a rosette of grey green leaves covered with soft hair, from which will spring further rosettes on runners, like a strawberry, that root when they reach the ground. The flowers are Verbena-like heads on stems about four inches long, thin and wiry because their job is to tremble and toss the seeds as far as possible in the winds of the high mountains.

On the wall garden there is no need to worry about protecting them with panes of glass in winter, which always blow off on a cold January night when it is raining copiously. They are hardy edgeways and tender flat, and it is hoped that the wall garden will bring them back to popularity, as the race nearly died out in Britain during the 1939-46 war. The runner rooting is not essential, in fact if dry conditions and stone to lie against prevent it, the flower display is better and they trail quite happily in an Aubrieta-like mass. Their needs are simple, normal alpine soil with lime in plenty and full sun, though *A. lanuginosa* adds to its lead as the best of the lot by tolerating morning or afternoon sun only.

Increase of the rosette varieties, when they have not found a soil-filled joint to root in, is easy. Cut off the runners with as much of the thin brown stem as possible and pot firmly in sandy soil, like Aubrieta but in July or August, and keep them through the winter in a frame, watering with care. In the depth of the winter if they get very dry and flag, stand them in a tin to soak, so as not to wet the foliage. It is easier still to plant one's wall by dividing rooted pieces in September or October, using a good trail of stem and root running back into the soil behind, with the rosettes sitting cosily against the face of the stone.

There is a species which is a very good tough little alpine for the small rock garden, *A. sempervivoides*, or 'resembling a houseleek', which it does to some extent, as its leaves have no hairs on them at all. This one makes very small rosettes, about half an inch across, which keep in a tight dome that extends slowly from the edges with short-stemmed runners. When its generous crop of little Verbena heads, the colour of the rose Else Poulsen, is in full glory in April and May, the plant is about as tall as an upright match. A clump as large as a saucer is a real picture, on a 'wrong end of a telescope' scale.

It needs somewhere on the lower slopes of the rock garden where it will not be baked up in the summer, in gritty limy soil in company with other small species such as the Kabschia Saxifrages and *Petrocallis pyrenaica*. The best method of increase is by digging up rooted runners in July, potting and growing on for spring planting. They are no trouble in the cold frame, but as the plant increases in size so slowly, greed in propagation should be avoided. It is rare not because it is difficult, but because it is slow. If you can save seed sow in July in a pan on the grit system, and do not pot until the seedlings are as big as sixpences.

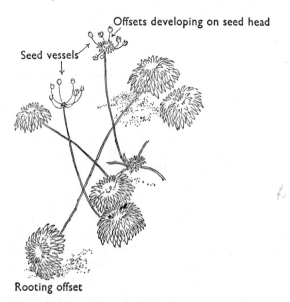

Offsets developing on seed head

Seed vessels

Rooting offset

FIG. 7. *Androsace sarmentosa*, with runners.

Those who wish to try more difficult Androsaces for this position should begin with *A. carnea var. Halleri*, which is also a colony of slow-growing rosettes but with longer and narrower leaves, rather like those of *Armeria caespitosa*; these are dark green and closely clustered, with small heads of up to nine florets in April and May. These can be as much as the diameter of a sixpence across, and the relatively large flower head is carried on a stem from two to even four inches high. There are several smaller varieties of *A. carnea*, but this is the toughest of the high mountain species, the others border on alpine house plants. It is the mild wet winters that finish them in our climate.

Both species are very fond of pounded slate in the soil round their roots; very little is needed and it is easy to smash, and this should be added to the potting soil, say standard limy mixture three parts to one slate, as they need a richer soil than the scree when they are being grown on in pots before planting. *Androsace carnea var. Halleri* is better raised from seed than from division; both are increased in the same way.

Anthyllis. Kidney Vetch. Lady's Fingers

The best of this race of pea tribe wall plants is *A. montana* from the Swiss Alps. It has large, dark crimson clover-like flowers from June to September, contrasting well with silver-grey leaves on short branching stems. It is a powerful mat-former on the rock garden, and both flowers and flourishes best on the sunny wall in full sun with plenty of lime, and it is ideal for chalky soil. The one best we have in cultivation is perhaps the variety *A. montana rubra*, because it is a much better and richer colour than the usual forms seen wild today.

We have two native species, *A. Vulneraria* with long narrow leaves not cut out at the edges, and yellow flowers the size and shape of those on a gorse but in cluster heads; and *A. Vulneraria var. Dillenii*, with crimson clusters. Both flower in May and June, and need starving with plenty of lime on a dry wall to do their best, which is well worth seeing.

Increase *A. montana* from soft cuttings in the sand frame, taking them with at least an inch of stem, more if possible, and use a hormone as they are not too easy to root. They will make plants by the following spring from non-flowering wood cuttings inserted in June or July. The other two are easy from seed sown when it is ripe, or in the spring. It is easy to raise, but be careful digging the plants out of the seed box or pan; all pea tribe plants hate having their main tap root broken when they are young, so use a handfork or a table fork, and don't snatch and hurry over it.

Antirrhinum Asarina. Creeping Snapdragon

This species from Spain is very far from the bedding Antirrhinum. It has ivy shaped leaves, rather furry, and trailing stems that are perfectly appropriate hanging down a sunny dry wall. Its flowers are the size and shape of those of a border Antirrhinum, but carried singly, not in a spike, cream yellow with a bright yellow mouth. On rich soil these are hidden by the leaves, but on limy poor soil with plenty of sun it is an Antirrhinum that trails like an Aubrieta and flowers from June to September.

Increase is easy from seed. The capsules are almost as big as hazel nuts, and the seeds large and black. They can be sown in August to produce plants to go out about April, or one can sow them direct. This is very useful when something has died low on the wall, and you do not want to rebuild the section. Just poke a hole with a dibber or skewer and sow your seeds direct in the soil layer, two to a hole going in about an inch. If you have saved your own you can afford to be generous, and if the job is done about March you will have them in flower the same year.

Green vessels, unready

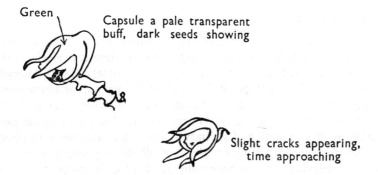

Green

Capsule a pale transparent buff, dark seeds showing

Slight cracks appearing, time approaching

Fig. 8. *Antirrhinum Asarina* seed vessels, the calyx is still green when the seeds are ripe.

There is reputed to be a pink variety, and if this appears, propagate only from soft cuttings taken from the rips of the shoots at any time during the summer. This plant does not cross with the border Antirrhinums because it has 18 chromosomes and they have 16. This warning is to save other enthusiasts from trying fruitlessly for four years, as I did, to pull off a cross with *A. nanum* Flame or Dazzler. The 'Rock Hybrids' advertised are all crosses with *A. glutinosum*, a rather dingy miniature with cream flowers; their colours are dull and they are neither perennial nor attractive.

157

Aquilegia pyrenaica. Miniature Columbine

This plant, one of the few of its race that is not more suited for the herbaceous border or, at the other end of the scale, a pan in the alpine house surrounded with a minefield of slug bait, is a really nice little creature for the small rock garden. It grows between four and six inches high when it is in flower in May and June; little blue Columbine flowers with yellow centres, and the foliage is a neat clump of the familiar leaves.

Give it normal or poor and limy soil, and full sun, but do not forget to mark where it is because it goes completely dormant in winter, and it is frequently dug up and thrown away by mistake. Seed is set and it should be saved and sown in July or August, but leave it in the pan until it wakes up in the spring, when it should be potted ready for planting about May. It is quite safe to let it flower the first year if it will, and it often does, but later than normal, doing better the next season when it is established. Another small and pleasant species is *A. discolor*, which is blue and white, also about six inches high and just as easy.

Arabis. White Rocket

The ordinary *A. albida*, one of our few national rock plants, is suited only to the wall garden with plenty of room. Here it is glorious, the best early white of all; it flowers from March to June, and with Aubrieta and Alyssum is part of the spring glory of the dry wall or sunny bank. Like Aubrieta it is a good plan to cut it back after flowering, and with poor soil and full sun it does its very best. It is very easy to increase, either by direct planting of six inch to a foot long cuttings with plenty of old stem; direct potting or, easiest of all, direct planting in the wall garden, delaying your cut back until October for this purpose. It roots best by these rough and ready methods in September or October, but there is little in it. There are several pink forms, and of these the best is *A. rubella* which is not quite so vigorous but very nearly so, with a deeper and better colour than *A. aubrietioides*, though with the Aubrieta colours to choose from, both are cast into the shade. Grow it with Henslow Purple or Magnificent for a good contrast.

For the rock garden there are several smaller species. Of these *A. blepharophylla* is the best, with neat rosettes of dark green leaves that sit closely together in a clump, and flower heads on four to six inch stems of a good deep pink rather on the magenta side (the order *Cruciferae* always avoids clear blues, salmon and scarlet) but sturdy and in generous quantity from April to June. It can be raised from seed sown in August

158

(if you can save your own) or in the spring, and is quite easy but is re-puted to vary. It can be increased by division in September, or from cuttings of the rosettes with at least an inch of stem if you can get it, inserted in the sand frame in July and August. It needs the same soil as the larger species, and full sun.

Another good small rock garden species is *A. carduchorum*, with smaller rosettes still; it looks more like a small Androsace, and grows only about three inches high, with flowers like *A. albida* but on a greatly reduced scale, in April and May. It is easily increased by division and is quite an attractive little plant.

Arenaria. Sandworts

The Arenarias are a varied collection, and the least attractive of them are often described as Saginas and Minuartias, just as some people are described as actresses or commission agents in a police court.

The true Sandwort is *A. caespitosa*, alias *Sagina glabra* correctly *Minuartia verna caespitosa*. It grows a close flat turf as a strong carpeter which is thickly covered, or sparsely in shade, with small starry white flowers in May and June. It grows well in any ordinary soil in any place that is not too sun-baked; good turf for the alpine path and for bulb cover, but do not put it in the alpine lawn or it will spread and strangle. If there is any trouble getting it to grow really well, mix leafmould in the top soil, and in John Innes Seed Compost it thrives. It has the great ad-vantage that it will flourish in considerable shade. It has a golden foliaged relation, *A. caespitosa aurea*, which is more straggly and in-vasive but less easy; it is strangling today and dying slowly tomorrow. These two are reputed to smell of violets when in flower and are quite good in the right place, which is not on the small rock garden.

There is another Sandwort with even smaller leaves and the same almost stemless white flowers in April and May, *A. balearica*. This plant needs shade and moisture and is ideal for the shaded path, where it covers the ground like duckweed. When it is growing well it grows so fast that it once covered a forgotten hand fork like a spade under snow, according to a gardener who hates it.

Arenaria montana is entirely different; it has small pointed leaves on trailing red barked stems, with large white flowers, as big as halfpennies, in real profusion in May and June. It is a very strong and easy plant for the wall garden, and needs planting near the top with nothing below it, because it wants two to three feet to trail down. It can be cut back after flowering to reduce its area, but as it flowers also on the old wood it is worth letting it run for three years if there is room. Any soil, plenty of sun, and keep it off the rock garden. Cuttings are rather hard to root, so it is best raised from seed which comes true and should be sown in March or April for autumn or spring planting.

The most pleasant member of this piratical tribe is *A. purpurascens*. This grows as a very neat clump of pointed dark green leaves set closely together in fours, with small star-like pale lilac flowers on two inch stems in May and June. It is a nice hardy little species for the smallest rock garden, and likes morning or afternoon sun only, and where it will not be too dry in summer, like one of the smaller Saxifrages for which it is a good companion. It is not fussy about soil, but prefers a gritty one with some lime and leafmould. It is best increased by division in spring but will root easily from cuttings in summer, or can be raised from seed sown in March.

Armeria. Thrifts

Armeria caespitosa, the Dwarf Thrift from Spain, is one of the best all round alpines for the small rock garden. It is as hardy as any other Thrift, in full sun and in the gritty limy soil that suits the small Dianthus and Campanulas that are its favourite companions, for it is very easily swamped by larger species. The flowering season is officially May, June and July, but the individual plant seems to have wide discretion whether it will have a real burst in the season, or spread it out from April to August.

It grows as a colony of small dark green hedgehogs of foliage about an inch high, and with age six inches across, and the miniature Thrift flowers are rather bigger across than a sixpence, clear shell pink in colour and now carried on stems about an inch long. The original plants were stemless, but seed raising in Britain has crossed with the border Thrifts. Seed is set freely and is fluffy stuff which should be gathered as soon as it will come loose from the head, and sown in pans either in early summer or the spring. It wants to stay in the pans, which should be grit covered, until it has at least three hedgehogs of foliage before potting. A holiday in Spain should secure some of the original for anyone, and a watch should be kept for a dark red form that is rumoured. It grows on walls by the roadsides and is not common, so take seed only, there are no snags on bringing this home.

It can also be propagated by careful division in September or April, or cuttings of single rosettes in June and July inserted in exactly the same way as Saxifrage cuttings in a pan. Elderly plants appreciate sifted leafy limy soil worked down between the rosettes so they can root into it; the best treatment for a plant that starts going bare in the middle, and

15. *Campanula Poscharskyana* is the most lusty of the trailing Campanulas. It is best in full sun on a dry wall with poor soil and plenty of lime and then its sprays of large, star-like, lavender-blue flowers are not fewer because of the demands of rampant foliage

16. Helianthemums make good wall plants; the compact, clump-forming *Ben Dearg* illustrated is not quite so good as the trailing varieties, but this September photograph shows the advantage of timely trimming back. Above is *Antirrhinum Asarina*, the trailing species, only the tips of its yellow florets show

the preliminary treatment for one that is to be divided, as the stems root into the new soil and the new roots get away fast.

Armeria corsica is an alpine border and dry wall plant. It has grassy foliage, more slender and a paler green than that of the border Thrift, but with the same type of flowers on nine inch stems in May and June. These are what is described as salmon red or brick red, and it is worth growing for its unusual colour; it is tough, easy and can be increased by division or cuttings with old brown mature wood at the base in July or August.

The common Thrift, *A. maritima* and its varieties, of which *A. Vindictive* is the best and nearest a red, are also good wall plants for those who like a neat bulge of dark green cushion on the face of the stone, and a May and June flower cluster. Tear up your big plants in October or early spring, lay a lump on the soil at a joint with the brown old stem reaching back to the rammed earth behind, put on some more soil as a covering and set on the next big stone, so that the leaves sit close against the outer face of the rock. Our native Sea Pink can take a great deal of rough treatment, and on the dry wall it is as happy as it is in 'Districts Rockall' for there are some splendid clumps in the cliffs of this sea-swept rock, and it therefore has the distinction of being the first British wild flower you meet when flying the Atlantic from America.

Asperula suberosa

This very small but attractive species comes from the dry mountains of Greece and, like the Greeks, it is much tougher than many people imagine. It has small grey leaves on slender branches, very slender and hairy, and fragile pale pink trumpets in May, June and July, and it will spread in time to an eight inch disc of foliage, and come through the winter with the greatest good temper year after year. Its height is between two and three inches and although it can be treasured and fussed over in an alpine house, it is perfectly hardy outside.

The plant needs a gritty soil and prefers a rather limy one; small Dianthus conditions are ideal, but it prefers a dry place. It is a good crevice plant on the rock garden, but although it will grow in the dry wall it is rather lost because it is so small. It can be increased by small soft cuttings about three-quarters of an inch long in the sand frame in July or August or, much easier, dig it up in September, split and pot firmly in gritty limy soil. Do this just as though it were an Aubrieta, using old stems with some root if available, and a small bunch of young foliage sitting on top of the soil. Winter it in a cold frame and it will be ready to plant by April. This new discovery (1945) was the result of a nurseryman's mistake that came off, and the result should be not only more people growing this nice little plant, but having some to give away.

Astilbe

There are three miniature Spiraeas or Astilbes for the small rock garden, which are very nice plants for a moist place and in shade. They need a leafy soil, just about the sort of mixture needed for Lithospermum or a lime-hating Gentian. *A. simplicifolia* has pale green leaves low on the ground, rather like those of ivy but more slender, and in June and July it flowers with feathery Meadowsweet clusters on six inch stems, pale pink in colour and quite charming. Its colleague, *A. chinensis pumila*, has smaller, more deeply divided foliage and tighter, deeper pink spikes, some being almost red, and it is a perfect scale model of the greenhouse Spiraea, running up to nine inches when well established. The smallest species, with three-inch spires, is *A. glaberrima saxatilis*. This has tiny crinkly leaves and will form a low mat on the ground; it is slow growing, rare and worth finding, though no more difficult than the others.

All three plants die down completely in winter, and should be marked to avoid careless forking. They are increased most easily by division of the clumps in April when they are just coming through, and direct replanting. They can be raised from seed, but it is dust fine and rather difficult. Use the gritty system and sow in early spring, and do not pot until there is plenty of foliage showing. When seed does come up you get simply thousands, but very often it doesn't.

Aubrieta. Rock Cress (very rarely used)

The Aubrietas are the only really National rock plant; everyone has got them and with good reason. From April to June they give a really good blaze of colour, and the only people who cannot grow them well are those with peaty or entirely lime-free soils. Here extra lime is needed, and the lime-lovers mixture should be used. In the town garden with a great deal of smoke in the air, slaked lime and bone meal in equal parts forked round the clumps every autumn will keep them fed.

They are very good wall plants, a good perennial edging for the front of the herbaceous border, and fine subjects for the larger rock garden for holding down the weeds and making a blaze of colour, but not as neighbours for anything tiny and special. On the small rock garden one has the choice of one good clump of Aubrieta, or about nine different species flowering at different seasons, and whether one has an 'Aubrieta time' when the rock garden is a real sight and then dull periods, is a matter of choice.

After the first mass flowering, especially where space is limited, cut back the clumps with shears or scissors, and there will be a second display in late summer. On the rock garden or dry wall this is not necessary every year, but where the branches trail further than a foot to eighteen inches, the health of the plant suffers, apart from the untidiness. Regular trimming, shortening the branches to about six inches, or less in the case of weaker specimens, in summer or autumn is one of the secrets of good Aubrieta growing.

Propagation is very easy in October and November, but not at other times of the year; in fact it is this ease that makes these months best for dry wall construction. Do not give a summer trim the year you want to increase your stock, but cut back when you are building to secure as many branches with eight inches to a foot of grey barked old stem as possible. Unlike most alpines, Aubrieta roots badly from soft green summer cuttings, it wants a minimum of three inches of old wood to make good roots. For the wall garden these can be planted direct, but where they are needed for transplanting two other methods should be used.

The first is the nurseryman's way. Gather three or four branches into a bunch with the heads together, one will do if you are short of stock, coil the stems down inside a 60 size pot with a little soil in the bottom, and simply pot them firmly in standard alpine soil. They should spend the winter in a cold frame or cold greenhouse, and as they will grow quite a bit with the protection, they can be planted on the rock garden about April. Water well before knocking out of the pots as they will not have much root. A good nurseryman keeps them in the pot until the following autumn, but if they have not to be sent away by post, they are quite all right with the shorter period.

The other system is in open ground trenches; putting them in during October, treading them firm so the tips sit along the ground like a row of little cabbages, and just keeping them weed free till the following September, when they are dug up with as much soil as possible and re-planted where they are required. Cut them back about June so that they make stockier plants, as they will be strong enough by then to benefit. It is also possible to use four-inch-long cuttings in the sand frame; in-serted in October for potting in the spring, this is a very good winter use for the propagating frame that normally does nothing in the winter.

The old clumps can be divided and used in the wall garden or rock garden in October, but the divisions are not usually so strong as starting fresh with young cuttings. Aubrieta can be raised from seed sown in March, but these will always be mostly pale lavender blue, the colour of the original wild *A. deltoidea*. Good seedlings may occur, but these are unlikely to be better than the existing varieties, the lucky chances of generations of nurserymen. The seedlings are pricked out when they have got four true leaves and potted for autumn planting.

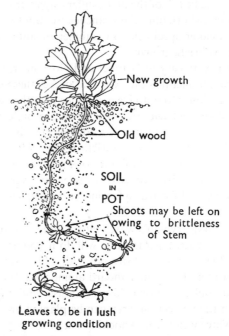

FIG. 9. Stem-rooting division of Aubrieta, pot not shown.

There are many named varieties, of which Blue King is the nearest to a pale blue; Carnival, Gurgedyke and Godstone are the best purples, and Vindictive, Magnificent and Russell's Crimson the best reds. Blue Aubrieta has always got violet in it and the reds are never crimson; the nearest to a clear pink is the old *Gloriosa*; *rosea splendens* is nearer a rose pink, and Henslow Purple is a colour on its own, a red purple not a violet one. There are now a number of doubles, or rather semi-doubles, with larger flowers and an extra ring of petals. Barkers Double is a very good dark red, and Dawn a good rose pink, and both are such strong colours that even those who object to double flowers on the rock garden should grow them.

Labelling is essential; once the flowers are out of bloom the plants are hard to tell apart, so though the ideal policy is to choose the colours you like and increase them year by year, it is easy without labels to find that what you have done is to produce thriving plants of the washy colour you never cared for, when they flower in the spring.

Azalea roseaflorum fl. pl. (also known as *Azalea balsaminiflora*)

This best of all alpine shrubs for the small garden is now officially a Rhododendron, *R. indicum var. balsaminaeflorum.* If you have a chalky garden do not waste your money, but if you grow Azaleas and Rhododendrons, or your neighbours do, have a try with this lime-hating species.

It is always compact and low growing, and even a ten-year-old specimen will only be about eight inches high, as it grows outwards rather than upwards and in May and June is covered with the most lovely double salmon red flowers, almost the exact colour of a Gloire de Dijon rose. When grown with *Lithospermum* Heavenly Blue, which needs exactly the same sort of soil, the leafy and peaty mixture mentioned at the beginning of this chapter, the two make the most perfect and striking colour contrast that can be contrived on the rock garden.

Plant it low as it does not like to get too dry; in full sun, or with morning or afternoon sun only, and nip off the dead blooms as they go over. It needs no pruning other than removing dead or straggling branches, and it appreciates some bone meal in the spring. It drops its pointed pale green leaves in winter, so do not imagine that your plant has died the first autumn.

Propagation is from soft cuttings in July and August, but it is a slow job, and is dealt with in Chapter 8.

Bulbs

There are a great number of hardy bulbs suitable for the rock garden and for naturalising under carpeters in alpine lawns or paths. Those who like them and wish to try still more are advised to study the catalogue of a specialist firm, bearing in mind that the cheapest of any species will always be the easiest, and the most glowing account does not always mean the best for beginners. There is space only for a general selection of varieties that are hardy, thrive well when naturalised, and are easily obtainable, usually at a price well below the cost of ordinary Tulips, Daffodils and Hyacinths, which are all too large and gaudy for the alpine gardener.

The most essential group is the spring and autumn flowering Crocuses, the flowering months of these and all the following bulbs being given in the table on page 49. Though one can use the ordinary hybrid varieties, the original wild species are smaller and more charming. *C. susianus* with very wide open golden cups, striped with brown; *C. Balansae*, orange with very small and slender leaves; *C. Tomasinianus*, clear sapphire blue; *C. Tomasinianus* Whitwell Purple, a red purple, and *C. Fleischeri*, white with a scarlet pistil in the middle, all make a fine beginner's collection for spring flowering at normal crocus time. The autumn display begins with *C. zonatus Kotschyanus* (now *C. Kotschyanus*) with wide open lavender blue flowers and white pistils, that waits until the spring to put up its leaves which die down, having stored the food for next year's display. In October and November there are *C. medius*, two inches high with rich violet cups; *C. ochroleucus*, white cups, yellow centred; *C. longiflorus*, long narrow cups violet blue with scarlet stigmas, and *C. pulchellus*, lavender with a golden throat. These last four have ordinary Crocus leaves and habits; they look like Crocuses that have missed the bus, and the only reason why few people enjoy colour from the Crocus corner twice a year is that these want to be planted in the spring, at Gladioli time, because they are in full flower at the normal planting season.

The miniature Daffodils are next in importance, and there are now a number of new hybrids between four and eight inches high which are excellent, but less suited to the rock garden; bulbs do not grow high in the mountains and unless they are very small, look out of place. The most rock garden worthy is *N. minimus* (correctly *N. asturiensis*), which likes a gritty leafy soil and full sun, and is two to three inches high, a perfect miniature trumpet Daffodil, pale yellow and flowering in April. For the alpine lawn and path stronger species are more suited which, like Crocuses, enjoy the John Innes Seed Compost that keeps down the weeds *Narcissus nanus* is a larger *minimus* up to six inches high; *N. Bulbocodium* is the 'hoop petticoat' Daffodil with small pointed outer petals and a large inner trumpet, sulphur yellow; *N. juncifolius* has very narrow grassy leaves and small golden trumpets, and *N. cyclamineus* has its outer petals turned back like those of a Cyclamen, dancing on nodding stems about eight inches high. All flower in March and April, and under the alpine lawn's fairy turf, they naturalise as well as varieties five times as big in the rough grass of the orchard. Those who wish to specialise are advised to read *Daffodils for Amateurs* by M. J. Jefferson-Brown (Faber & Faber, 6s. 6d.), and to note that 'Daffodil' is simply the English popular name for Narcissus; there are enough name muddles without keeping alive distinctions which were exploded in the seventeenth century.

The small Tulips for naturalising on the rock garden are best restricted to two really hardy and striking species, as so many of the
original wild ones are floppy and dingy to eyes accustomed to the glory
of the Darwins in the border. These are *T. praestans var. Tubergen*
which is about five inches high with from three to five blooms on a stem,
and tiny pointed Tulip heads of a vivid orange scarlet in May; and *T.
tarda* (formerly *T. dasystemon*) which is also branching, and with little
yellow flowers in April. Both are easy and really worth looking at, even
in competition with the trick which is scorned by experts as 'unfair to
species', of planting the 'Van Thol' varieties, the earliest of the forced
Tulips sold by florists, under the alpine lawn. These, when not forced,
come on about April, and in their full Tulip range of colour are most
attractive for those who do not mind their large flower size; but more
expensive.

Iris reticulata and its hybrids give a real variety of colour as miniature
Spanish Iris for the alpine border lawn or path. They grow between
nine and twelve inches high, which is on the tall side, but in February
and March they are so welcome that this can be forgiven. The original
species is a deep violet blue; *I. reticulata Krelagei* is red purple; *I.
reticulata Hercules* purple with an orange blotch, and *I. reticulata
J. S. Dijt*, the new Dutch variety, is both nearest to a real red and sweetly
scented as well. Like all Iris, they like lime, and extra chalk or ground
limestone should be added where they are planted.

Then there are the very ordinary small bulbs that are usually rather
lost in the border, but come into their own with a carpet of alpines to
keep the soil from splashing on their little faces with the rain. *Chinodoxa
sardensis* with sprays of sky blue flower; *Muscari azureum*, the little
blue grape Hyacinth; *Eranthis hyemalis*, the Winter Aconite, with its
bronze green collared buttercups, and of course Snowdrops, not for-
getting the uncommon autumn flowering species, *Galanthus byzantinus* which grows about four inches high and flowers in November,
with green streaks on its larger versions of the familiar hanging
'drops'.

Though the Anemones for the rock garden are usually sold as plants,
it is often possible to buy their tubers as dry bulbs cheaply. The best all
round species, for sun, semi-shade or even shade, is *Anemone blanda*,
which has low, rather ferny foliage which dies down completely after
the flowers in March and April are over. These are many-petalled
'daisies' about two inches across, powder blue in the species, dark blue
in the lovely variety *A. blanda atrocaerulea*, and of course white for *A.
blanda alba*. The height in flower is between four and six inches, and if

167

they are left undisturbed under carpeters they increase and multiply, often coming up from self-sown seedlings. This easy, cheap and very cheerful species is lost in a lawn and unsuitable for massing before bedding plants; it is happiest as an alpine gardener's 'bulb'. *Anemone apennina* has rather smaller flowers, but prefers semi-shade or shade, otherwise it is the same plant for practical purposes, and *A. nemorosa* (the British 'Wooden Enemy' of childhood in the country) is best in full shade, its variety Blue Bonnet is a good deep blue, and *Allenii* and *Robinsoniana* are the best lavenders. There are many other Anemones; their main trouble on the small rock garden or alpine border is a mass of foliage after flowering, which rules out the splendid *A. Pulsatilla* with rich purple cup flowers, a plant for sun and lime. The glaring scarlet *A. fulgens* is not fully hardy and is best left to those in mild places by the sea.

The longest-flowering bulb of them all, with starry pale blue flowers on six inch stems and narrow grassy foliage, is *Triteleia uniflora.* The display keeps going from April to October, a modest succession rather than a sudden burst, and the only reason this bulb has not won a real place in amateur affections is because of its constant name changes; the correct name is now *Brodiaea uniflora*, and it has been *Milla uniflora* after a long spell as a *Triteleia*. There is a slightly deeper blue species, whose foliage smells slightly of garlic, *T. uniflora caerulea* (or *T. uniflora violacea*) which may shortly become *Ipheion uniflorum*. If they have a disadvantage it is that they seed themselves, but they are long flowering, hardy and easy on any soil in full sun or semi-shade, despite the need to look them up under several names if the nurseryman has tried to be up-to-date.

Sternbergia lutea is reputed to be the Lily of the Field that toiled not, neither did it spin but outshone Solomon in all his glory. In flower it is a giant golden yellow Crocus, with a flower up to two and a half inches long that appears in September or October, sometimes two from a bulb. In the spring the leaves appear, broad ribbons that are between six inches and a foot long, dying down during the summer when they have fed the large bulb. It prefers a dry and sunny place, it is good under Sedum carpeters, and is best left undisturbed for a long time. It may take a year to become established, but once it is at home, it is a splendid and unusual bulb. It is not easy to increase, most are collected wild, but it is reasonably cheap to buy.

Last of all there are two lovely races for shade and leafmould, for where the path goes under the trees or the edges of the Azalea or Rhododendron bed; they do not hate lime, they just grow by nature on the edges of woodland and like the soil. Standard leafy soil grows them well.

The Erythroniums, or Dog's Tooth Violets, have turned-back petals on their star-like flowers, and pointed oval leaves. The easiest is *E. Dens-canis* from Southern Europe, with brown marked leaves and six petalled stars on six inch stems, usually sold mixed in purple, lavender, lilac and pink variations, though named separate colours are available. There are many American species of which *E. revolutum Johnsonii*, which is a good rose pink, and its variety *E. revolutum Watsonii* which is white, are the easiest. *E. californicum*, yellow with cream markings, is nearly as good. All flower in March and April and grow roughly six inches high.

The best Fritillaria for this sort of situation is our native *F. Meleagris*, which has grassy foliage and hanging bell flowers of varied colours, mainly wine purples mottled with white and heavily veined and mottled. This flowers in April and May and grows from nine inches to a foot high. There are many other Fritillarias, but they prefer to be in a place where they are sunbaked after flowering; most are more suited to the pans of the specialist, and none are so fitted for British gardens as our own wild flower.

This bulb is now very rare except in favoured districts, but as it is raised easily by nurserymen and sold so cheaply, there is no possible justification for anyone gathering any.

As a general rule when planting these bulbs (spring and summer flowering in the autumn, September and October; and autumn flowering in the spring), plant as deep as the bulb is tall or wide, whichever is the greater; three-quarters of an inch deep for a Crocus corm, not a quarter because it is flat; and about an inch for a *Narcissus nanus* which is roughly that high as the bulb. Depth is measured from soil surface to the place at which the shoot will appear. The exception is the last group; the Erythroniums want to be about four inches down and the *Fritillaria Meleagris* three or two. These two want to be cool, and the other kinds want warmed soil near the surface. They can, however, move themselves up or down in the soil quite a way; ordinary Bluebells can sink themselves as much as a foot, but how they do it is not certain, and like so much of plant growth, it is a mystery that is rarely studied.

Generally speaking, all these bulbs are increased by division of the offsets, the small bulbs round the parents which can be removed if the clump has to be dug up. The larger ones are then replanted and the small stuff put in somewhere out of the way on good soil, plenty of loam and leafmould, in shallow trenches somewhere sunny, to grow larger.

With Tulips the flowers should be pinched off as they are open, to grow larger bulbs; that is why a tour of the Lincolnshire bulb fields rarely includes sales of cut bloom. A Tulip flower takes a great deal out of the bulb, but Daffodils and Iris and the species do not mind, and can both flower and increase in size.

Very many bulbs of this type will set seed, and *Triteleia uniflora*, *Tulipa tarda* and the Erythroniums are well worth raising in this way; the other small species are so cheap that there is little need to bother. Sow during the summer as soon as it is ripe, in deep boxes, kipper box type not seed trays, with plenty of drainage in the bottom and leafy soil; keep on a dry shelf during the winter, and plant out the small bulbs in the spring as for offsets.

In most cases, however, all that one needs to do with these small bulbs is to leave them alone. Let their foliage stay on to do its work of fixing the energy from the sunlight to build up the food store in the bulb, and they will grow up year after year. Remove it only when it is dead and brown, NEVER tie your miniature Daffodils into tiny knots.

Calamintha alpina

This is a good wall plant but of sufficiently moderate growth to find a home on the small rock garden. It produces short spires of the typical Mint tribe (*Labiatae*), long-lipped Snapdragons from June to the end of August, from a mat of small oval dark green leaves on brown barked slender branches, usually about four inches high when in flower. It will spread to as much as a foot across, and does best in full sun in normal or poor soil.

Today it is usually raised from seed sown in March, pricked out and then potted for autumn planting, but this seems to have resulted in the loss of the best form. Modern plants are usually pale lavender in colour, but the original was dark violet, the colour of hectograph ink. In any event, it is a useful late summer flowering species, but the lost dark form is worth looking for, either among seedlings or in Switzerland, where it was originally collected and where good colour forms may still exist. If these are recovered, propagate from cuttings of the young wood in April or May, it does not root so well after flowering, in the normal sand frame.

There are two other species, *C. grandiflora* and *C. suaveolens*, both of which are rather dingy herbaceous plants and not worth growing. *C. alpina* is the beauty of the tribe, and it has aromatic foliage with a scent that is not quite Mint and not quite Thyme, which has been used as a flavour for certain exotic drinks.

Alpines Plant by Plant

Calceolaria

The Calceolarias for the pool rock garden have little in common with the hybrids used for bedding, or the fleshy monsters with flowers like well stuffed purses beloved by thrips and the gardener who cherishes a greenhouse. None are plants for the cold or bitterly exposed garden, they are on the borderline of hardiness so far as this book is concerned and included because they are so good by the waterside, in clefts and crevices.

The easiest is perhaps *C. biflora*, which has the merit of setting a great deal of seed, suitable for sowing in February or March in the cold frame or greenhouse, to grow in a shaded frame for planting out to flower in the same year, so replacement is easy if you lose it. It grows as a colony of fat rosettes of rather bronzy dark green leaves, deeply veined and slightly toothed at the edges. In June and July they put up a succession of slender stems from two to four inches long, each with the pair of flowers which earns their specific name. These are small bright yellow pouches, about half an inch across and are followed by nut-like seed capsules.

The soil should be on the leafy side and the best position is in semi-shade or shade outside the concrete of the pool. Unlike Primulas of the bog class, they prefer being splashed to having their feet in the water. The waterside Calceolarias want to come where the fall can splash them, and they benefit by the fact that the pump is turned off in winter, so then they receive only rain. The ravine bottom, with the side rocks keeping the cold winds off them, is an ideal place. As there is plenty of seed of *C. biflora* each summer, it is a good plan to try and establish some in the crevices round the fall by direct sowing, for they are longer lived edgeways than flat.

This applies even more strongly to another Chilean species, *C. tenella*, which has bright round green leaves, rather like duckweed and small slender stems that will climb with tiny clinging rootlets up the face of any damp rock in semi-shade, as well as spreading at its base. Though this is very good by waterfalls, it will also do well crawling up the 'risers' of shaded steps, provided the parent plant is growing in a light and leafy soil, standard leafy mixture with some extra sand does it well. It flowers from June to September, with half-inch-across slipper-shaped blooms, two and three to each two or three inches high stem, the same bright yellow as *C. biflora*, but with crimson lines and markings round the opening of the slipper. Increase is by division in April, or seed in February, but it is a plant to leave alone once you have it growing well.

171

Sow the seed thinly, and let each get to a good-sized patch before it is pricked out into pots with care, because it has rather brittle leaves and stems.

There are two other species, very near each other, *C. acutifolia* which has underground rhizomes and larger pointed leaves, more like those of *C. biflora*, but more pointed and arranged in tufts rather than rosettes. The flowers are single, and long slippers, over three-quarters of an inch in length with the same red markings on yellow as those of *C. tenella*. The other species is *C. polyrrhiza*, which has slightly larger flowers, up to an inch, and the spots are purple not red. Both flower from June to August. These are rather less hardy, good plants for those who garden in the south and waste their mild climate on planting nothing but Cerastium, Arabis and Aubrieta. The several other species, notably *C. Darwinii*, are best left to the expert with an alpine house.

Campanula

This race is a study on its own, and there are a great many species that look like Canterbury Bells that have taken the wrong turning, which are of more interest to the botanist than on the rock garden. As with Gentians and other large races, the purpose of this book is to tip a few winners for each garden purpose, and leave the rest for those who wish to expand their collection later.

The wall garden class is both easy and valuable to provide violet, near blues and whites in late summer. Perhaps the best of all is *C. isophylla*, which has a great profusion of near pale blue bell flowers of considerable size, on trailing stems which will hang down a wall at least a foot in July, August and September. This plant and *C. isophylla alba*, its white form, had the misfortune to be grown extensively by nurserymen for hanging baskets up to twenty years ago, and though fully hardy is rarely listed in alpine catalogues. The best way to get it is to ask for 'Hanging Basket Campanulas' at a wreathwork and bedding plant sort of nursery.

The toughest and strongest of all this group had a different misfortune to be discovered by an Austrian botanist. Once we had *C. muralis*, but now this very well known and easy species with clear violet trumpets, is called *C. Portenschlagiana*. This one will trail three feet and it flowers from June to August, after which it should be cut back so that it makes new shoots from the base, and will thrive in shade. It does not like shade, but takes this in its stride, even dry shade. Its comrade in name affliction is even lustier, *C. Poscharskyana*, which has grey leaves and star-shaped lavender blue flowers about an inch across. This is the

172

longest flowering of all the tribe, starting in May and finishing late in the autumn, often the end of October. A glorious plant if starved on the dry wall, but impossibly rampant and lush on the rock garden; on rich soil it will go up to a foot high and simply swamp, hiding its flowers in the leaping foliage. Cut it back when it is finally over and it will do this year after year.

The midway group which are suitable also for the rock garden with more room, are *C. fenestrellata*, which has the same small, notched, heart-shaped bright green leaves as *C. Portenschlagiana*, but is less powerful. Its flowers are very nearly clear blue stars with white centres, about three-quarters of an inch across, and come in a blaze in June and July. *C. garganica* is built on the same lines, but with rather smaller and more solid stars of pale blue only. Some forms are on the slatey side, and the plant is more of a dome former than a trailer, growing about four inches high and flowering at the same time of the year. Third comes *C. carpatica*, which is a clump maker with branching stems up to a foot high, and flowering from June to August. There are a great many varieties, and as it is usually raised from seed, these are all colours from deep violet to white through many shades of Campanula blue, and their shapes vary from deep cups to flat saucers into which a new typewriter eraser will just fit (the round sort with a hole in the middle). The seed is very easy, and mixed *C. carpatica* is a good one for sowing direct by scattering on the face of the dry wall in spring; or it can be raised in great quantity in the usual way, and will seed itself on the rock garden. This one needs caution if you have little room, and should be trimmed back after flowering.

The small Campanulas are many, and at the other end of the scale one reaches tiny ones which grow so slowly that they cannot recover between visits from even the smallest slug. The best of these is *C. arvatica* (correctly *C. acutangulare*) which grows as a low mat of dark green, notched, heart-shaped leaves, spreading modestly by underground runners, with a real show of almost stemless dark violet blue stars in June, July and August. It is only an inch high, and needs full sun and gritty limy soil, like all the other little ones. *C. pulla* is almost as nice, and is also a mat former, but with dark violet hanging bells on three inch stems. *C. pulloides* is the same though larger, reaching a couple of inches higher.

Then there is the great tribe of *C. pusilla*, which has now become *C. cochlearifolia*. This is a small and sturdy mat former with hairbells on three inch stems in many colours, white, lavender and pale blue. The best of all is the pale sky blue *C. Oakington Blue*. These are, perhaps, the best known small Campanula suitable for paving, paths, pan garden, the small rock garden, and everywhere but the wall as the thin layers of soil do not give its runners a chance.

C. haylodgensis fl. pl. is the only double of the race, and its flowers in July and August are a real clear blue on three inch stems; *C. Tymonsii* which is the same size and colour, but with bell flowers that look up at you instead of hanging down; and *C. Waldsteiniana* which also looks up, but with starry bells that are a rich dark violet, are all good in the 'third of a foot height group' for the small rock garden.

One of most unusual Campanulas is the dwarf form of our native Clustered Bellflower, *C. glomerata acaulis*. This grows three to four inches high with narrow, pointed, dark green leaves, rough on the undersides and fitted closely round reddish barked sturdy stems. From July to September these stems carry clusters of deep violet florets, each one of which is about an inch long and a little less than half an inch across the mouth. The original *C. glomerata* which is much more common, a two foot high border plant in the garden, is called 'The Twelve Apostles' in parts of Sussex, because there were supposed always to be twelve of these florets, but fifteens are as common as elevens, and so far as the alpine gardener is concerned, 'Rhododendron Campanula' would be a better popular name.

It should be planted in full sun in limy soil, ideally on the scree because it should not have a rich diet, and it is hardy, easy, and a really nice plant; the general effect is that of a low growing alpine Rhododendron of extra good deep colour and flower size. It spreads by making underground runners, and these give an easy method of propagation: either remove them with roots and plant where they are required, or take off the tips when these appear, with about an inch of buried stem and insert it as a cutting. Seed is not advisable, as it is a very variable species, and the best policy is to find yourself a good dwarf specimen, starve it, and increase it yourself. This is generally the best policy with this easy race.

The wall species can be divided in the autumn, with care because some grow a tap root, and built into the wall. The best general method of increase is by soft cuttings in spring; those which make runners prefer to be taken with about an inch of the buried stem attached. All the mat-forming ones here can be potted up and wintered in a frame after September division, or divided in the spring. *C. pusilla* can be divided almost any time and tucked where it is wanted, with adequate watering after planting. Seed is easy, but as so many species cross together, it is not recommended, except where quantity is required rather than

174

quality. Because most nurserymen are busiest in spring and therefore sow in early summer, we are losing our most lovely Campanulas. One can order the same species from six nurseries and get six entirely different plants.

Centaurium scilloides (formerly *Erythrea diffusa*)

A very nice little summer flowering alpine, carrying its small heads of shallow cups, about a quarter of an inch across at the mouths, on two inch stems. They are on view from June to the end of September and are rose pink, the rose being Caroline Testout, a good colour with nothing washy about it. The leaves are little pale green ovals on ground-hugging stems, and the plant grows as a neat evergreen mat which will spread to an eight inch circle, in the course of years.

The best position is in half shade, or in sun but fairly moist, in a ravine garden or by the water; not a damp position but where it will not get dry in summer, the same sort of place as the Gentians, which belong to the same natural order. It is not fussy about soil, normal alpine mixture will do, and it is easily raised from seed sown in March, division with care in April or September, or from soft cuttings in the sand frame of non-flowering wood in July or August. These are rather fiddling to make, but root quite easily.

Cerastium. Snow in Summer

In part of New Zealand there was formerly only one blackberry bush, but it was five miles across each way. There are many rock and wall gardens with only one plant on them, *C. tormentosum* with white flowers in May and June, which has spread and covered everything else. If this perennial Chickweed had seeds that blew like thistles, it would be the worst weed in these islands; don't plant it, even those who have it are always willing to give it away. Its roots are swine to get out, even after you have torn it up and burnt it.

Ceratostigma plumbaginoides

There are several Ceratostigmas but this is the only one which is hardy. It is a strong spreading bush with underground runner stems, which puts up flowering stems about a foot high carrying heads of flat florets, each rather larger than a sixpence, and vivid blue. It is not as dark as indigo, but a good clear colour with no mauve in it, flowering in August and September when this shade is rare on the wall where this plant belongs. The leaves are pale green changing to red in the autumn, and dropping then to leave the bare red brown barked stems.

The best place for it is on the dry wall, or on the dry bank. In a good sized pocket where its foliage can thrust upwards, as an example, above a thriving Aubrieta clump, but below it will be entirely hidden. In both places it will do well, for choice with some leafmould in the soil if the normal alpine mixture is not used, and in full sun. It is too large and powerful for a small rock garden.

Increase is from soft cuttings in July, taken from the smaller shoots which are not going to flower, in the normal sand frame. A rooting hormone is justified as you want to root it early; get it potted and have its roots run round the inside of the pot before it goes dormant for the winter, otherwise it will fail to come up next spring when it is removed from the cold frame for planting.

Claytonia australasica

This is a good carpeter for shade or half shade, for alpine lawns or paths; a strong grower with underground runners, and especially where it is a bit damp, it can creep about rather too much for the small rock garden. The leaves are small and pale green, forming a low mat on the surface and on which, from June to September, appear almost stemless rather blue-white daisy flowers about the size of a farthing.

The best soil is a leafy one, and it fits in well with the many carpeters for the standard mixture, good bulb cover for Erythroniums, and almost any early or late flowering type; over spring and autumn Crocuses it is ideal. Increase is by simple division in spring, but it is best to split and pot until established if this is done late, as it dislikes disturbance in the autumn.

Conifers

There are many dwarf Conifers for the rock garden, dwarf by nature and not by Japanese art. With all of them one should bear in mind that, unless they are so slow as to be delicate, they are going to increase in size with the years. Many a small rock garden is overshadowed and dried to sterility by a massive specimen planted ten or fifteen years ago. They are in general easy on good normal alpine soil, and need full sun on the lower slopes of the garden, not on the upper crags, where they not only look unnaturally windswept, but get too dry. All are relatively expensive, for all the time they are growing slowly from a cutting, the agricultural wage rate is rising, and every weeding, watering and re-potting costs more.

The most reliable for a small garden is *Juniperus communis compressa*, which is a perfect grey cone like a Noah's Ark tree, and the

176

17. *Acaena microphylla* has insignificant flowers but its spiny seed heads in July and August are bright crimson. It is a plant for the Alpine Path and is best in poor soil with plenty of sun. It can be walked on or used as bulb cover but should not be planted on a rock garden

18. *Polygala Chamaebuxus rubra* is a miniature shrub from four to six inches high, neat and non-invasive and very good as a companion for the smaller leafmould or peat lovers in the Alpine Border. Its foliage is like that of hedge Box, as its name shows, and its yellow and red pea flowers are plentiful in May

growth speed is roughly two feet in twenty years. *Chamaecyparis* (formerly *Cupressus*) *Lawsoniana Elwoodii* is a close growing flame-shaped Cypress, rather swifter, growing about three feet in twenty years. *C. obtusa tetragona minima* never leaves the ground at all, but grows as a sort of uncoiled hedgehog of bright green needles. There are many others; one can get other dwarf Junipers, of which *J. Sabina tamarisci-folia* grows perfectly flat as though blown by mountain winds with gnarled branches, but spreads and shadows far too fast to be allowed to stay on a small rock garden longer than five or six years. One can get dwarf Spruce, Pines and Yews, but as they do not of course flower, the best way to choose them is by going to a nursery and buying the shape you like.

Propagation for all species is from cuttings removed in June or July, about two inches long (one inch for *J. communis compressa*), and chosen from where they will not spoil the shape of the plant. Insert in the normal sand frame, with hormone treatment, and they will be ready to pot in the spring. They should be kept in pots, moving to larger pots as they grow, for from two to four years, until they have become shapely and have lost their juvenile growth, for the shades of the cutting frame linger round the growing Conifer; they cannot safely be lined out like stronger species because the roots are easily broken, and slow growth means slowly repaired damage, though one can chance it with *C. Lawsoniana Elwoodii* and usually get away with it. The main ingredients of their growth are time and patience. As with so many plants, they have their charm, and there are people so wrapped up in them that they grow nothing else, and quarrel bitterly over the names.

Convolvulus mauritanicus

As every gardener knows, Convolvulus is the worst weed on the rock garden. There is one sold as an alpine, *C. althaeoides*, with clear pink flowers, which is very showy but not too near a weed to be realised on even the wall garden. There are some un-convolvulus-like shrubby ones, *C. Cneorum* and *C. incanus*, with grey leaves and white flowers which are not really worth their room, but there is one really nice wall plant in this tribe of rampers and dullards.

C. mauritanicus sends out trailing stems up to two feet long from a central rootstock, which keeps in one place and does not runner and root from every fragment. These stems, with rounded greyish, pale green leaves, carry a most magnificent display of flat flowers shaped like an umbrella opened to its very fullest extent (looked at from the inside). These are the size of half-crowns, and deep lilac blue in colour, starting

M   177

off in June and carrying on in full swing until the end of October. In November the plant dies back, and if the dead branches are cut off it will keep up the show year after year.

This lovely thing is often regarded as part hardy, but in normal soil on the dry wall in full sun, it avoids winter damp on that big dormant root and stands up to the climate in any part of Britain. Keep it off the rock garden, however, as it is safer and happier hanging and blazing against the stone work.

Propagation is easy from seed sown in April, or from soft cuttings in June and July. Any buds that form in the sand frame should be pinched out, as it cannot flower and make roots at the same time.

Corydalis lutea

The Common Fumitory of Britain is *Corydalis lutea*, and unlike the many other Corydalis, most of which are rather here-today-and-gone-tomorrow plants for the amateur, it will thrive and flower on walls in shade. It is common growing in the crumbling mortar of churchyard walls in many villages, and like our native *Linaria Cymbalaria*, does well in damp and gloom, even with considerable dryness.

The foliage is rather like that of a Maidenhair fern, with small flower spikes of vivid yellow tubular flowers in May and June. It can be seeded directly in the wall, inserting the small black seeds with a dibber in the soil, and bearing in mind that it will make a clump with upward pointing flowers as it is not a trailer, and that morning or afternoon sun only will do as well. The seed pods are small and horn-like and when they turn yellow they are ready to gather. Take the seed and leave the plant if your source is wild, and be generous with it to allow for failures. Nature always sows plenty.

It can also be raised from wild or bought seed sown in April, but sow thinly and be careful when you are potting on into 60's for planting during the summer or following spring. The branches of the seedlings and their roots are soft and brittle, so do not squeeze them. It is also suitable for crevice planting on the rock garden, and is very good beside a small waterfall. Though, like many British natives, it will seed itself, it is easy to get rid of if it is not wanted.

Cotula squalida

This plant looks a charming miniature fern, with fronds about an inch and a half long springing from creeping stems that cling to the ground and root from the joints. It is not a fern, it is one of the *Compositae* and has flowers like daisy centres with no petals in May, but it has muscled in on the fern racket like the vegetable gangster it is. Cotula grows with fury in sun or shade, and in almost any soil. It is good bulb cover, fine for shaded paths, ideal for covering space quickly, but on no account plant it on the rock garden. Its bronzy green foliage is a perfect foil for the stronger bulbs that will thrust through and grow all the better for its moisture-retaining qualities in a dry and impossible place.

Fortunately it sets no seed in Britain. It comes from New Zealand, and if you dig it up in December, when it is feeling our climate and at low vitality, you can kill it easily. Increase is by digging it up at any other time but the depths of winter, and planting where it is wanted.

Cyclamen

The hardy Cyclamen are an ideal race for shade or semi-shade, and a leafy soil. They do not object to lime, if anything they like it, and provided the soil contains sufficient humus (the standard Lithospermum mixture is quite adequate), they will stand a good deal of dryness, which they tolerate better than damp for they naturally live in rather open woodland. On the small rock garden, where aspect means morning or afternoon sun only, they do well on the lower slopes. They have also been naturalised under trees where shade makes the grass thin, and a particularly fine planting of what is perhaps the best and easiest species can be seen in the grounds of the Bishop's Palace at Wells, Somerset.

This is *C. neapolitanum*, which has clear pale pink flowers like those of the greenhouse *C. persicum* but on a tiny scale, four-inch stems, and the flowers are about three-quarters of an inch from the centre to the tips of the turned-back petals. Their season is from September to November, and both this species and the white *C. neapolitanum album* should be part of the autumn glory of every garden. The leaves are mottled with white and shaped rather like those of ivy, which made their former name of *C. hederaefolium* quite apt. They are not exclusively Neapolitan, but are widely distributed in Southern Europe.

There are a number of other species, including *C. coum* with unmottled kidney-shaped leaves which flowers in February and March, and is apt to have its buds eaten by woodlice in the dead months of the year if naturalised. *C. coum album*, which is white instead of deep pink; *C. repandum* with ivy-like leaves with a white 'zone' or regular marking, and crimson flowers in April and May, which takes time to establish; and *C. europaeum* with rounded leaves like *C. coum* but mottled, and carmine pink flowers in August and September.

This race does not require drying off like the greenhouse species as the corms are never entirely dormant, so they cannot be planted as dry bulbs, but must go as small pot stuff. They should not be planted with covering carpeters which strangle them, but shallowly so that the top of the bulb, where the leaf and flower buds form, is just on the surface.

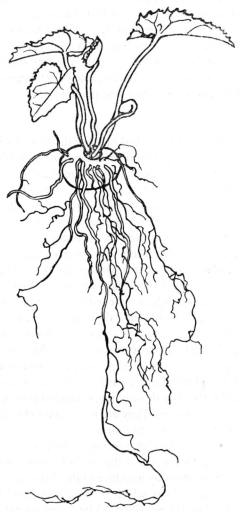

FIG. 10. Healthy, full flowering size corm of *Cyclamen neapolitanum*, note rounded base and position of roots.

In Britain an old bulb of *C. neapolitanum* is about as big round as a saucer, but they have been collected as big as dinner plates, and once they are established they should be left undisturbed. Gammexane

180

dusting against woodlice and slug baiting help the two-year-old flowering size corm, about half an inch across, to keep growing happily until it is a veteran capable of producing 200 blooms at just the season of the year when colour on the rock garden is dwindling.

Cyclamen are raised from seed, collected when it is ripe and black from the nutlike capsules. Those of *C. neapolitanum* and its ally are coiled up in a watchspring of stem which winds them down to ground level for some unknown reason, perhaps in defence against squirrels. Sow in April on the grit system but in leafy soil, pot in the growing mixture about September, when each will have one leaf and a tiny corm, and grow on through the winter in a cool greenhouse or cold frame. Like *C. persicum* they want watering when they are dry, but only when really necessary, though they want plenty in spring when they really start to grow. They can go out in May, but only if they have grown good corms; usually it takes two years to reach flowering size.

Delphinium

The miniature Delphiniums for the alpine border grow about a foot high, and the list is best restricted to two small groups, otherwise a search for further species leads to tall and not very striking approaches to the border of belladonna hybrids of full scale gardening.

The most striking of the small species is *D. nudicaule*, which has foliage rather like that of a belladonna hybrid, but more solid and on a smaller scale. The stems are branching and reach up to a foot high, usually about eight inches, and its short spikes of almost scarlet florets from June to August make a really good splash of colour at the back of the alpine border. These florets are long and slender, slightly drawn in towards the mouths, and those who grow the unusually belladonna variety 'Pink Sensation' (or *D. Ruysii*) will notice the *D. nudicaule* shape, for it was this species that brought pink, and perhaps some day will bring scarlet into the larger Delphiniums.

There are several varieties of *D. nudicaule*, all of which are scarce, mainly owing to the alpine grower's habit of raising everything from seed. The following are worth looking for if you like the original species: Chamois, apricot, Lemon Gem, yellow, sometimes known as *D. nudicaule luteum, aurantiacum*, orange, and *purpureum*, purple. All require a position in full sun, with if possible some shelter from the wind to save any staking problem in an exposed place, though they are less easily broken on the whole than the large Delphiniums, and a normal alpine soil. They are in fact treated exactly like ordinary Delphiniums and are just as hardy despite their small size.

The other miniature has more lacy leaves, and slightly longer spikes of pure blue florets with wider open mouths. This is *D. sinense*, or in full *D. grandiflorum var. sinense*, which is variable and will sometimes reach eighteen inches. The best forms are not taller than a foot, Blue Gem is the best, a pure bright Delphinium blue, and *D. sinense cineria* (or *cinerea*) is a good dark shade. Its treatment is exactly the same as the *D. nudicaule* group.

The miniature Delphiniums are usually raised from seed sown in pans in a cold frame during February, and potted when they are large enough to handle. They can also be sown in July or August and potted in winter in a cold frame, but as the first method produces plants that flower the same year (they have been grown as 'hardy annuals'), little is gained. Seed is plentifully set, and its only drawback is the variation that will occur with the named varieties and good forms you may select. If you start with seed, discard any inferior specimens and treat your best clumps like named border Delphiniums.

Dig up those you have marked, about January, and set them in a frame with leafmould or peat round the roots. The protection of the glass will warm the basal shoots along quicker than those in the open. When these shoots are growing well, shake off the leafmould and take your cuttings each with a piece of the hard wood from the main root stock at its base. All Delphinium cuttings are hollow tubes with pith inside them, without the divisions at the nodes or solid stems that make other species more easy. The bottom fragment of the solid bark of the root plugs this hole up, which water would such and rot off the cutting. The only difference between these miniature species and the others is one of size, and if the base of the cutting is dipped in a powder rooting hormone they will get away fast when inserted in the normal sand frame. This method also applies to border Lupins in named varieties.

Where only a few plants are required, the miniature Delphiniums can be increased by cutting up the main root and replanting the divisions where they are required in the early spring when the new shoots are just coming through the surface.

Dianthus

There are almost as many Dianthus as there are Campanulas, and there are, if anything, more hybrids. The general principle should be, as always, large and powerful ones on the dry wall and small ones for the rock garden, but many are dual purpose, and except for a few exceptions, all are tough and sturdy plants for full sun with a great liking for lime.

The purely dry wall kinds include any of the garden pinks, even Mrs.

Sinkins if you like double flowers, the 'Highland' hybrids, with single patterned flowers on eight inch stems in May and June, of which Highland Fraser, a deep pink with a white ground is one of the best, and of course our native Cheddar Pink. This is *Dianthus caesius*, now *D. gratianopolitanus*, with fringed rose pink flowers on six inch stems in June and July, with familiar grey foliage in a sturdy tuft, and its very nice double hybrid, Little Jock. The *D. deltoides* hybrids are also good on the wall; they have browny green, rather un-Dianthus-like foliage and small single flowers in great profusion, deep pink in the original, and a good crimson in *D. deltoides* Bowles variety. They flower in June, July or August, and should be cut back after flowering. One can, from some seedsmen, buy mixed Dianthus seed and raise a great many strong hybrids for the wall, but it is as well to remember that their usual season does not extend long after the Aubrieta, and too much space for them means less for later species.

The longest flowering of all Dianthus are the *Allwoodii alpinus* group, which flower from May to September, but are suited more for the small rock garden, not because they will not thrive on the wall, but with even more sun and drought, they will flower themselves to death. They include *D*. Elf, which is deep crimson, *D*. Jupiter, salmon, and *D*. Mars, bright crimson, all with double flowers, miniature Carnation foliage and growing about four inches high. Plant them in standard leafy soil, with extra lime, about a 48 pot of ground chalk to the barrowload, but there is no need to be exact about it, in full sun, and they will grow some foliage for next year's bloom. Another trick is to give them a spoonful of a general fertiliser about August and water it well in, even the self denial of pinching out all the buds on one side of a plant is often repaid if you keep losing them after the blaze of glory. The wise nurseryman keeps his stock plants from flowering, just a few to grow replacement cuttings.

This leafy soil device, which is usually all that is necessary, is also advisable for Dianthus with green rather wide foliage, which shows Sweet William blood (*D. barbatus*, well known as a biennial); these include Spark, a crimson single which flowers indiscriminately in June, July and August, *D*. Napoleon III, a double crimson with the same season, and Ariel, now called Crossways, which has cerise single blooms on a grand scale from May to September.

In another class to these brilliant high efficiency hybrids, come the small species with their quieter charm for the small rock garden.

Dianthus alpinus is one of the nicest of these, it has rather broad dark green leaves about half an inch long, set close together, and very short-stemmed clear pink flowers with a darker ring round the centres over the close packed clump which is about two inches high including the bloom. It flowers in July and August, and likes a limy soil in full sun among small Campanulas, though it should never be next to anything powerful. Seed is readily set and should be gathered and sown when the capsules split; sow at once thinly and leave it in the pan until the spring, pot when it starts to grow and plant out about May if they are big enough. It is easy and hardy but slow growing.

This Dianthus also hybridises, in fact there is little pure *D. alpinus* left; most of the plants sold are near *D. Boydii*, which is a bigger and stronger plant with larger flowers, growing as much as four inches high, but as this is just as good there is no need to worry, unless you get a chance to collect any true seed in Switzerland, or what is more likely, some more variations—a dark red one would be lovely.

There is a very good lost variety of *D. alpinus* that appears sometimes. This is *D. Jordans*, so called because it first appeared in the gardens of the Quaker meeting house at Jordans, Bucks. It has leaves like *D. alpinus*, but a more bluish green, about three-quarters of an inch long and set on small stiff branching stems, with deep rose pink flowers like *D. alpinus* but on the ends of the branches. The display is as brilliant as an *Allwoodii alpinus*, but the plant flowers itself to death by July after a blazing start in June. If you get a 'Bush *alpinus*' cut it back and treat it like *D.* Spark; with lime mixed with the leafmould, seed is worth saving, but the odds on getting it again are small. It is evidently what is called a 'recessive', a suppressed quality which only manages to get out now and again. Its last appearance was near Glastonbury in 1946.

Though *D. alpinus* is very easy from seed, good forms can be increased from cuttings in exactly the same way as all other small Dianthus. Take them as long as you can get them, with old wood at the base from where the clump can spare them. Pull off any dead foliage and insert in a pan of cutting sand. They root as easily as the bigger varieties, but you always have only a few. It is because of this slow increase that most are raised from seed, but it pays to use hormones, and to pot with care in gritty and limy mixture. The season for cuttings is April and May, before flowering; keep the pans in a shaded cold frame and pot about September or when well rooted and winter in pots in a frame ready for planting the following spring.

Small species for this treatment include *D. Freynii*, a short-stemmed species with small rose pink flowers in June and foliage like a tiny border Mrs. Sinkins, *D. haematocalyx* which is larger, about three inches, including rather purple red flowers in June and July, and *D.*

microlepis which is only an inch high with foliage rather green more than Carnation colour, and tiny clear pink flowers (about the colour of those of the ivy-leaved Geranium Marie Crousse) in May and June.

Another good one is *D. parnassicus* which is like *D. deltoides* in design, but with small bright green foliage and almost stemless pale pink single flowers. It is a small flat creature and, unlike the others,

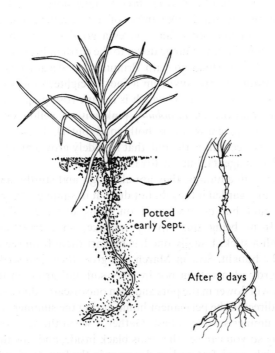

Potted early Sept.

After 8 days

FIG. 11. Stem-rooting division of *Dianthus caesius*, showing root development after eight days.

comes true from seed, which should be sown in February or March. The others vary from home saved seed as a rule, but one can always keep replacements coming on with a few cuttings of each every season.

Dodecatheon. American Cowslip

These have been in Britain since 1744 but very few people grow them, because most nurserymen will raise them from seed with no selection, so only washy colours survive. They are, however, very good shade plants for woodland conditions, needing a home in leafy soil in the Gentian bed, on the lower slopes of the small rock garden, or in with the less rabidly damp-loving Candelabra Primulas.

Two of the smallest and nicest are *Dodecatheon alpinum*, deep pink, and *D. integrifolium*, carmine red, the rarest and best. Their leaves are large, smooth and rather like those of an Auricula type Primula, both in shape and the sort of clump they make. In May and June they send up sturdy stems with heads of from three to nine florets, each with long petals pointing backwards like those of a Cyclamen. The American popular name of 'Shooting Stars' gives a good idea of the way they poise, as though about to plunge down to the earth in brilliance.

The larger kinds which go with Primulas (Dodecatheons belong to the same natural order) grow from a foot to eighteen inches high, and the best of these is *D. Jeffreyi* which is a dark rose pink, but deep red seedlings are known; *D. latilobum*, pink with a yellow eye, and *D. Hendersonii* with lilac flowers are both good, but *D. Meadia*, which will grow up to two feet tall is the one that is widely grown and variable; it can be a bright magenta, but usually is a washy pink.

Though they like humus, they are all tough and sturdy, and do well even in a chalky garden if they do not dry out in summer; they spend the winter dormant but do not insist on being dry then, though they often die from being dug up by mistake, so always mark their position with a stick. Usually one has to start them from seed as plants can rarely be bought. Sow in March and grow them in a seed box until they are sturdy plants, then pot in leafy soil and grow on in a shady place. They will flower in the pots and then one discards duds, or they can be planted direct in the permanent home during the summer. From your own seed, summer sowing is best. Gather it when the seed vessel is dry and opening so you can see the seeds black inside, and sow thinly; they come up quick, grow fast and go dormant in the box, to give fine plants when potted as soon as they start to grow, ready to go out about April and flower well the same year.

There are a great many other species that we do not have on this side of the Atlantic, *D. campestre*, clear pink with a blue purple eye, only four inches high in flower, *D. uniflorum*, just as small and with one deep purple floret to a stem, and *D. Frenchii* (or *D. Meadia membranacea*) which is a two foot high purple one, which would be good to have and plant for 'stud purposes' among our washy Meadia types.

Those who do get Dodecatheons in strong clear colours, or any that they really like, can increase them by dividing the clumps in the spring, just as they begin to wake up. Mark the good ones, dig them out and they will shake out into rooted fat buds. Pot them and grow on in the frame to plant when established. If you want a real quantity, grow them from root cuttings as described in Chapter 9.

Draba

The Drabas are useful plants for the scree or crevice, flowering early in the year, and the three that are described here are much tougher than they look; there are a great many species which are only suitable for the alpine house.

Draba Aizoon is the best known. It grows in a colony of rosettes of narrow dark green leaves, slightly incurved at the tips, and in March and April it carries on wiry two inch stems, a number of loose heads of up to fifteen tiny bright yellow florets. The rosettes are about an inch across and make a neat evergreen clump, which can be divided after flowering and used for crevice planting provided it can be watered until it has a good start. The white species *D. Dedeana* has broad grey green leaves, fitting closely into a cushion, much more like a Kabschia Saxifrage, with larger florets in a neater head on a stem only about an inch long. It flowers in April and May and though it grows slowly, it is very hardy and when it is well established, puts up a generous flower display for its size. *Draba sibirica* (formerly *D. repens*) is a rosette-forming species, and it sets down these rosettes on the end of their short stems like one of the *A. sarmentosa* type Androsaces. The small dark green leaves are pointed and slightly hairy and the plant makes a more quickly spreading cushion than the other two. The yellow flowerheads in April and May are larger, up to twenty florets, and their stems are about two inches long. This one is the best crevice plant, and September divisions are easily established.

All three species are easy from seed, which comes true and should be saved or bought when possible. Sow thinly on grit in June and pot when they have at least three good rosettes formed; as they are evergreen they keep growing through the winter in a frame and may be ready for spring planting. The stronger *D. sibirica* is easy from cuttings taken in June or July and inserted in the sand frame or pan, using a rosette with the dead leaves cleaned from the base and about an inch, more if available of the connecting stem. The other two species can be increased in this way if the clump can spare the pieces; the longest stems are secured by searching round the circumference of the clump on *D. Dedeana*; *D. Aizoon* is easier to find cuttings among.

Erica (Heather and Ling)

The Heather garden is a recognised feature in lime-free districts where the full range of species can be grown with a flowering season that ex-

187

tends right through the winter and covers the greater part of the year. If there is lime in the soil, then only the winter and spring flowering *Erica carnea* and its varieties can be grown; on solid chalk, no species at all. In general it can be said that where Rhododendrons do well, all the Ericas can be grown; with more lime than that one can manage with the same soils and precautions as lime-hating Gentians, and with a soil that is limy, the *E. carnea* varieties are well worth adding to any alpine border or rock garden.

The Ericas are all peat lovers, plants of the acid peaty mountain and moorland of Britain and Europe, and they therefore prefer peat to leaf-mould. They have microscopic fungi in their roots which enable them to obtain their food from peat, and lime destroys them by killing the fungi. The first group, for any soil with peat and leafmould, has evidently rather tougher fungoid helpers.

The original species, *E. carnea*, is from Central and Southern Europe, and it is a low, semi-prostrate evergreen shrub, which will grow to a foot high, but is more usually six to eight inches. Its leaves are short spines clustered along the branches (their colour varies with the variety), and its flowers are small bells under quarter of an inch across, but hanging from the stems in irregular clusters which may be as long as three inches. The parent species is a pale pink, but the cultivated varieties are greatly superior; their flowering season is roughly from November to April.

There are over thirty varieties known, some very near each other, and the following are merely a selection chosen for neat habit and strong colour: Cecilia M. Beale, six inches high, upright habit, January/April flowering, pure white; Eileen Porter, upright habit, also six inches, and clear carmine red, with the longest flowering season of any, October to April; Queen of Spain, six inches, pale pink, February to April, and *Vivellii*, which has dark green foliage, turning more browny in winter, four to six inches high, with almost dark red flowers in February and March. Others worth adding include Pink Beauty, a shell pink, and Ruby Glow, a slightly deeper *Vivellii*; the first four complete the colour range, and one can add more if further gradations are required. The other non-lime-hating Erica, *E. mediterranea*, is too large, even *E. mediterranea nana* is eighteen inches high, and *E. darleyensis* (formerly *E. mediterranea hybrida*) is no shorter and as they flower in March and April, they do not extend the season.

In the garden without lime, or with so little that Epsom salts will do the trick for *Gentiana sino-ornata*, the season continues with the varieties of *E. cinerea*, which is the Scotch or Bell Heather. Its leaves are more dense, on the young wood they are hairy and the bells are long, large and fewer in a cluster. Perhaps the finest is *E. cinerea coccinea*, which grows from three to six inches high, with real crimson flowers from June to August; *E. cinerea alba minor* is white and the same size and flowering period and *E. cinerea pygmaea* a good dwarf pink. The colour range can be completed with Mrs. Dill, who is a rich pink and about four inches high, and P. S. Patrick, who is taller, up to a foot, but a good purple with extra long flower spikes. There are many others, but most are in the foot high height group; all have roughly the same flowering season, June to July or August, so that the only gap is May and this is sometimes bridged by scattered early blooms.

Erica ciliaris, the Dorset Heath, flowers from July to October and links up with the first of the *E. carneas*. The leaves are also closely packed, and the bell flowers are puckered in at the mouths and about a quarter of an inch long. They normally grow up to eighteen inches, but two dwarf varieties are a foot high or less: Mrs. C. H. Gill has dark green foliage and flowers a really good red, and the older white variety, *E. ciliaris Maweana*; both are long flowering and compact, Two other long flowering summer varieties are *E. hybrida* Dawn, which is a cross between *E. ciliaris* and *E. Tetralix*, up to eight inches high, and with foliage like that of the first parent and flowers arranged in the manner of the second but in greater quantity, clear pink in colour and on view from June to October, and *E. hybrida* Gwen. This has the same parentage and flowering season, with rather paler pink flowers but is only from four to six inches high.

The really miniature Heathers are found among what are correctly Ling in England, or Heather in Scotland, botanically varieties of *Calluna vulgaris*, although here they are called *Erica vulgaris* because they are catalogued by nurserymen under this name. Their flowering season is August and September, and they are suitable for the front of the Heather garden, and on the lime-free rock garden they can be used like any other small mat-forming or cushion plants.

Their foliage is like that of the moorland Heather, on a much reduced scale and packed closely together in low clumps, and their small florets are carried in spikes between an inch and two inches long. *Erica vulgaris Foxii nana*, with erect bright purple flower spikes, was the first known, its free-flowering form known as *floribunda* is the best; both are about four inches high when in bloom. There are now a great many small varieties, and the following are especially recommended: *E. vulgaris minima*, purple flowers, growing as a two inch high mat; *E. vulgaris minima* Smith's variety, which is a two-inch cushion rather than a mat, with foliage that turns a reddish tint in winter and purple flowers; *E. vulgaris nana compacta*, also purple, a cushion former three inches high, perhaps the most free flowering, and *E. vulgaris* Sister Anne, with silvery foliage turning reddish in water and clear pink flowers on four inch cushions. The smallest of all is *E. vulgaris* Mrs. Ronald Gray, an inch high mat with rather more red in the purple its tiny flower spikes, in August and September like the other members of this charming group.

There are many taller varieties, and the nine inch, double flowered, clear bright pink *E. vulgaris* J. H. Hamilton, is about the very best. The amateur who wishes to go in for Heathers can add the many varieties of *E. Tetralix* (Cross Leaved Heather), especially the very compact six-inch-high Irish variety, *E. Tetralix Prageri*, with bright pink flowers from July to September, the usual flowering season of this species.

The Heather alpine border should be in full sun, but not excessively dry, and on the rock garden the lower slopes should be used. Though sandstone rock looks best with them, hard mountain limestones do not allow enough lime to dissolve to cause trouble. The general soil mixture is that for normal lime haters, but with acid peat in place of leafmould, another mixture is four peat, two sand, one loam; the *E. carnea* varieties will do well in normal alpine soil with about a third of its bulk of acid peat added.

In the past, when the mycorrhizal association of the fungus was first discovered, great stress was laid on the importance of mixing peat from where Heathers were growing in both the soil and the cutting sand, but this is entirely unnecessary, though high grade peat can be bought from Erica specialists; it is acidity and the right balance of plant foods it supplies. The fungi are distributed throughout the tissues of the plant, and even the small tip cutting of the topmost branch has an ample supply for life.

An established Heather bed needs no weeding because the evergreen foliage provides complete cover, though weeding will be needed until the plants meet in a solid mass. They will require a top dressing of fresh peat, usually applied in May, and this is worked down between the plants in roughly an inch thick layer every three years or so. If they have to be transplanted from the bed, May is also the best time to move them, but they should be dug out with as much root as possible and well watered. Large plants naturally go farther apart than the eight inches to a foot for young stuff from a nursery.

All Ericas should be allowed to grow ahead without pruning for a year after planting, and then each species should be clipped back after it has finished flowering, not hard pruned but merely removing the wood that has carried the blooms, a simple job with scissors or shears. They flower on the young wood, and therefore the need is to prevent long and leggy branches from forming and to keep the plants bushy and healthy. The sort of growth required is the type on which grouse feed, and scissors on the small rock garden provide young shoots in quantity— the gardener's equivalent to the controlled burning practised by those who manage Highland grouse moors.

Erica carnea varieties need less pruning than the others; if they are nice and bushy, restrict pruning to the removal of straggling shoots, and if any appear to be giving a reduced flower display because of excessive cutting back, miss a year, but in most gardens the race as a whole suffers from being allowed to make too much old wood. The propagation of Ericas is covered in detail in Chapter 8.

Erinus

Erinus alpinus is one of the best crevice plants for the small rock garden, and though it can be grown on the scree or anywhere on normal alpine soil in full sun or semi-shade, it is very much longer lived edgeways than on the flat where it is often regarded as a biennial. It makes rosettes of blunt ended, dark green leaves, deeply toothed at the edges, and puts up flower stems in May and June about three inches high with small clusters of lilac purple florets. There are several varieties, *E. alpinus* Dr. Hanele, a good carmine red, and *E. alpinus* Mrs. Charles Boyle, a clear pale pink, are perhaps the best; the white *E. alpinus albus* is less striking. All come nearly true from seed, which should be sown in February, for potting and planting to flower the same year.

They seed themselves on the rock garden, and as they are noninvasive, neat and free flowering, this is no disadvantage; plant on in the horizontal joint of two rocks and seedlings will appear in the vertical seam. Another method is to prick out strong seedlings in crevices not in direct sun, water them by spraying until they take hold, and a further variation is to grow some in very small pots so that the soil ball will fit in a narrow place without much squeezing. They can be sown direct on the dry wall, in paving or the rock garden in July and August, with sufficient growing time to come through in winter.

Seed is cheap to buy and easily saved, but a few plants in suitable positions sowing their own produce even better results.

Erodium (Heron's Bill is a popular name, but not often used)

The large Erodiums are splendid wall plants, long flowering, long lived and tough. They like full sun, plenty of lime, chalky gardens suit them, and though they start flowering in May or June, they keep it up until September or October.

They are in general plants with ferny leaves set on gnarled and twisted branches that cling close to the wall and clusters of flowers on stems four to six inches long, rather like those of a wild Geranium; after these are over the pistil in the centre stays protruding—it is very like the bill of a heron, in shape.

One of the nicest is *E.* Merstham Pink, a hybrid with deep pink flowers and closely matted red brown barked stems that will cover an area a foot up and down and eighteen inches across on the face of a wall; they do not trail like an Aubrieta. They are good on the fair-sized rock garden and make a nice show, especially if planted where they can lie on a large rock, or in a cleft; the stems do not want to root down and are best kept off the soil.

Other good species with the same general make up, ferny leaves and long flowering season, are *E. absinthoides* which is a lilac pink, not a clear one; *E. absinthoides amanum*, white; *E. cheilanthifolium*, with grey green foliage and clear pink flowers; *E. chrysanthum* with leaves and even more grey green and less ferny, more like those of a Corydalis and creamy yellow flowers in smaller clusters, a bit less vigorous than the others; *E. macradenum* with magenta pink florets with dark purple or black blotches in the centres, and *E. supracanum* with grey green leaves and clear pink flowers, a May to September flowering kind almost as good as Merstham Pink.

Increase is easy. One can sow seeds (there are five or seven little black ones gathered round the base of the heron's beak when this has withered and the remains of the flower head are brown and dry) in March and it is quite easy, but cuttings are even simpler. Every August or early September, cut the most straggling elderly branches away, or reach in and take some that can be spared from the mat. Pull the dead leaves from the base of the ferny and growing part, and cut off about two inches of that old brown barked wood. Insert this in a sand-filled cutting frame or pan, and they will root rapidly and easily.

When an old clump is tidied and long branches are cut right back to the middle so they will shoot again there and fill up a bare place, there is no need to throw away the length of gnarled 'bough' as rubbish. Slice it in two inch sections, keeping them the way up they grew, and insert these uprights in the sand frame with about a quarter of an inch of the top protruding from the sand. They will root as cuttings, small ferny growing points will develop round the top and roots at the bottom, but it is too much to expect them to do it upside down, as with root

19. An outcrop on a Welsh mountainside showing the backward dip of the strata. Though all types of bad amateur rock garden, other than the 'shark's mouth pool' can be found in nature, the rock garden takes its model from those that run the rain back into the soil; a forward dip acts like a shed roof

20. This small rock garden in Cheddar stone was built at Wells, Somerset, where this rock costs little for carriage. The bold outcrop at one end and in the middle (out of the picture) breaks up the rigid look of the thirty-foot-long cold frame in which it is built. The dip is in two directions, as nature often dips it

21. Sandstone has little dip in the strata, it is laid down by running water, and it breaks square. In this small outcrop garden the 'flight of steps' effect has been avoided by using pieces of varied thickness, a shallow dip, and backing on to a natural slope

cuttings; the part that was nearest the growing leaves must point to the sky.

There is one Erodium, *E. chamaedroides roseum* (also called *E. Reichardii*) which is an essential plant for the small rock garden. This grows as a low mound of the same sort of branches but shortened. The leaves are rather grey green and more like those of one of the smaller Campanulas but rounded at the tips and set in neat close rosettes. The flowers are shallow cups of five rounded petals, each half an inch across and they are a good deep pink with dark red veinings towards the centre. Their value lies in their flowering season, they start in May and go on until October, and the white variety which is also veined, *E. chamaedroides*, is just as long flowering.

Neither plant sets seed, but they can be increased as easily as the other Erodiums. Take the cuttings with some of the red brown barked old wood at the base and they root easily at any time in the summer, but do not make enough growth for branch cuttings. These two are not hardy enough in exposed gardens in the north; put a cloche over them in winter, grow them in a cleft, or make it a rule to have some rooted cuttings potted in a cold frame in case you get a hard winter so that replacements are ready in the spring.

Ferns

There are a great many species of small fern suitable for the rock garden which will not reduce it to a replica of a bracken covered hillside. The species that suit the alpine gardener are those which will grow modestly with or without lime and these are best selected from the British natives that grow in our own hills and on old walls. Many are rare, and like all native alpines, from *Fritillaria Meleagris* to *Gentiana verna*, there is no justification whatever for robbing our wild flora other than vandalistic meanness. Because they are hardy and grow fast and well in our climate, these British species are always the cheapest items in the specialist's catalogue, and as established pot plants they do far better than the results of hasty looting of our national treasures.

The Maidenhair Spleenwort, *Asplenium Trichomanes*, is an essential fern for the shaded wall or crevice and ideal beside the waterfall. This has small leaflets rather like those of the greenhouse Maidenhair fern but arranged in pairs along slender black stems. The fronds are from two to six inches long but size depends on the amount of soil and moisture. Normal alpine soil with some extra leafmould does them well and they live for many years in a slowly spreading clump, ideally with the fronds nodding in the splashes of a waterfall.

Another good one is *Ceterach officinarum*, the Scale Fern or Scaly Spleenwort, which was originally *Asplenium Ceterach* when christened by Linnaeus. This has triangular pale green leaflets in pairs on pointed fronds from four to six inches long, which curl at the ends like tiny fists. The leaflets too, on each side of the brown midrib, curl at the tips showing the undersides covered with the brown scales that give the plant its popular names, including that of 'Rusty Back' in some parts of Britain. Incidentally, the record number of popular names for one species is held by *Orchis mascula* with sixteen, not including the 'grosser name' that liberal shepherds used but Ophelia preferred to leave unknown, and is an example of the impossibility of using these names for horticulture.

Blechnum Spicant, the Hard Fern, with flatter and more slender leaflets on longer fronds is on the large side; these fronds can reach eighteen inches, but small specimens in crevices are good, while the possibility of a thriving monster is remembered. The miniature species, *B. penna marina* (sometimes called *Lomaria alpina*) from the Antarctic islands, is a very nice small and creeping variation but it is not hardy in all districts, though a good one for sheltered corners.

The Common Hartstongue Fern, which is *Scolopendrium vulgare* (now correctly *Phyllitis Scolopendrium*) also grows up to eighteen inches high with its familiar solid fronds uncurling in pale green ribbons, and, like the Blechnum, it is useful only on the small rock garden when it is small. All species, however, are extremely good on the heavily shaded dry wall, and with some damp and enough sun for Mimulus, or failing this, Corydalis and the Kenilworth Ivy, *Linaria Cymbalaria*, they are solutions for the impossible corner.

The species described are best increased from spring division, and planting direct, or by splitting in the autumn, potting in normal alpine mixture with extra leafmould or peat and growing on in a frame for spring planting. Their spores are so tiny that raising them is a specialist's job, though many species growing by water with splashed rock to germinate on will sow themselves and provide seedlings for potting and transplanting. Usually they pick their best positions themselves, often where you would never dare to plant them.

Frankenia thymifolia

This species is not our native Sea Heath, *F. laevis*, but it has very small blunt grey leaves rather like a tiny gorse bush on trailing brown barked stems, and flowers very generously in July and August, with later stragglers. The shell pink shallow cup blooms are small and stemless but they sit all over the low mat of foliage in real profusion. If you have *F. laevis* it produces only a few stragglers. After flowering, the leaves change colour to a red brown autumn tint and the older ones fall, though the plant is evergreen.

It is a good carpeter, about an inch high, but not a close carpet; it does not cling to the ground like a Thyme, but it is good bulb cover for spring or autumn species. The best position is in full sun in a dry place, it does well in chalky gardens but any soil will grow it, other than a peaty and leafy one, and it dislikes shade and damp.

Normally it is increased by spring or autumn division, but if you need a quantity, the tips of the soft branches can be taken about an inch long either in the spring or after it has flowered and inserted on the sand frame; there is no need to fiddle with trimming off the tiny leaves, put them in whole and they root very easily.

Gentiana

The common saying 'I can't grow Gentian, I've got lime or something' is just the same as saying 'I can't eat fruit because of the pips'; there are so many Gentians that it is merely a case of taking the trouble to find the one that will grow under your conditions. They are without question the most lovely of all alpines.

Start first with the very easiest species that likes town gardens, flowers generously every summer and grows in any ordinary garden soil with or without lime. This is *Gentiana lagodechiana*. It grows flat on the ground with strong branches radiating from it like the spokes of a wheel; these have dark green broad and sturdy leaves in pairs all the way along them and the sky blue trumpets with spotted throats look straight up at you from the tips in July and August. These trumpets are as wide as a two-shilling piece across the mouth, the throat is hairy inside and they are carried either singly or in clusters of three to five.

Plant it on the lower slopes of the rock garden where it will not get too dry in summer; this is its only 'hate' and where one has got it in full sun on solid chalk, give it plenty of leafmould, not because it is a humus lover, but to hang on to the moisture. In the winter time it dies down completely, so trim off the dead branches and mark the site, to save digging it up by mistake.

Its relation *G. septemfida* ('with seven lobes', it flowers also in July and August, *not* September) grows a foot high and has larger clusters, up to nine trumpets each, and the branches arch gracefully with their weight. Its tastes are the same, it is just as easy, so long as one remembers that it does not like being very dry in summer, and it is a good plant for the alpine border, or the front of a herbaceous bed. This one is quite good for cutting, and lasts well in water, especially if the cut stem is singed with a match before you put it in a copper vase with grey foliage or white Gypsophila.

There is another one often sold in the same group, *G. Hascombensis*, but this was originally a very fine herbaceous plant with up to twenty trumpets in a cluster and a tall strong stem over a foot high. As it is always raised from seed you get nothing but compromises between the first two which are its parents, and even these are inclined to be mixed. It makes one wish that the late Abbé Mendel had been a member of the Alpine Garden Society and done his work with Gentians instead of peas.

The best way to increase these Gentians is from soft cuttings in spring. When they wake up they produce a great many shoots straight up in a clump like Delphiniums and many other herbaceous plants. Choose those specimens which are either definite prostrate *G. lagodechiana*, or tall upright *G. septemfida*, or any variation you fancy—some of the half-and-half upright ones about six inches high are very attractive—and label them when they are flowering, you cannot tell them apart in the spring. Then select cuttings about two inches long and remove them with a sharp knife, taking small ones because they root best. Remove the lower leaves and insert in a sand-filled cutting frame or pan, after dipping in a plant hormone powder. They strike easily, and should be potted when growing well and brought on in a frame for planting the following spring. Do not plant them the first summer or autumn: they want time to get established in the pot and to build up a good crown for the first winter but they will flower splendidly the following summer, as like their parents in flower and habit as one scarlet Geranium is like another. They can be raised in great quantities from seed (see Chapter 9) but if you only want a few or even several dozen, it is better to increase them by this certain and easy method.

Another easy Gentian for any soil and the same conditions of sun or semi-shade on a soil that does not get too dry in summer, is *G. gracilipes*. This grows in a rosette or a colony of rosettes of smooth dark green willow-shaped leaves with a well marked midrib. These leaves are from two to three inches long, and on a very rich soil they can become rather swamping for nearby plants. In July and August it will send out a number of long slender stems which bear at the ends longer and narrower trumpets about the diameter of a shilling across the mouth, which also look upwards and are a rather darker blue with a touch of purple in it. Unlike the first two it keeps its foliage all the winter; trim back the flower stems in the autumn and clean up the dead elderly leaves.

This should be raised from seed, gathered when the seeds are brown, and if sown when they are still sticky from the pod, thinly on the grit system, they come up very well indeed and keep growing through the winter in a cold frame. Pot when ready and plant when the roots are well round the sides; it is an easy creature and most good tempered, even though its trumpets are not as large and brilliant as the others. Among the seedlings may be found some of the form which used to be called *G. Purdomi,* with broader leaves like a Zulu shield and whose flowers point along the stem. This is a less attractive plant and those who do not like it can throw them away before they intercross with the others.

When saving Gentian seed in a wet early autumn it is a good plan to peel back the withered remains of the trumpet from the swelling seed capsule in the middle. Especially with cluster-flowered species, the wet hangs up and may rot them off before they ripen. The early flowers, which give the best seed for immediate sowing, rarely need this except in a soaking August.

The next big group of Gentians is also easy to grow, but many of them are not easy to flower. They are evergreen and grow as close-packed domes of broad strong leaves up to an inch long. The best known is of course *G. acaulis,* which has really magnificent deep blue trumpets on stout two inch stems; they are great wide-mouthed massive flowers and what most people mean by 'Gentian'. It blazes in some gardens, edging the kitchen garden beds in parts of Scotland where (according to some local opinion) it only refuses to flower where Campbell blood has been shed. Various methods of making it bloom have been tried, sulphate of iron as used for blueing Hydrangeas, a teaspoonful to each plant in the autumn is the most promising, as it is most successful in the iron districts of Kent and Sussex, where the streams run red with the rust of the ore that cast the cannon for Drake's ships.

Try *G. acaulis.* It is relatively cheap and easy, and often if it misses March, April or May, it will come on in the autumn, and whenever it flowers well it is an event. There are, however, many species in the same group more generous and reliable with their great trumpet flowers (2-2½ inches across the mouth, they look huge over a small dome of foliage). Of these *G. angustifolia* has longer and narrower leaves, and carries a pair of them on its flower stems, which are a bit taller, three inches, and its trumpets are just as pure and brilliant a blue. Others are *G. Clusii,* with if anything bigger flowers, and *G. dinarica,* from the Austrian Alps, both worth trying for those who fail to flower *G. acaulis.* There is a smaller flowered Swiss species, *G. alpina,* which is free flowering but

197

likes its loam lime free; it has green spots inside the trumpet, small ones right down towards the bottom.

This group likes a normal loam soil, they do well on clay, and though it is best to cover the surface with limestone or granite chippings because the big trumpets get rain splashed, they can be grown as simply as Brussels sprouts. Like sprouts, they like firm planting; tread them round and leave them alone in a position where they will not get baked up, on the lower part of the rock garden. They can be grown in standard alpine soil, but they need more loam and less leafmould or peat.

Fig. 12. Pre-flowering cutting of *Gentiana sino-ornata*.

They can be raised from seed, and come true, but the best amateur method is to dig up a plant in the autumn or spring, split it up and replant the divisions where they are wanted or pot them to grow on for planting out when established; as they do not go dormant they grow quite a bit during the winter in the frame.

Finally, there are the thin leaved woodland species from the Far East, which give people the idea that all Gentians hate lime. The best known is *G. sino-ornata*, which flowers from September through the autumn up to Christmas in some cases, with splendid deep blue trumpets more than an inch across and two inches deep. These are so lovely at this time of year that it is the only Gentian sold regularly on Covent Garden for cut bloom. This has narrow pale green foliage which grows in a close clump but develops short branches that carry the generous display of rich and splendid flowers. There is a smaller-growing species with flatter, wider leaves, *G. Veitchiorum,* with indigo blue trumpets, which comes from Thibet, not China, and flowers early, July and August, even June; *G. Farreri,* which is clear pale Cambridge blue with a white throat in August and September and *G. hexaphylla* like a sky-blue *G. sino-ornata.* Two good hybrids are *G. Macaulayi,* the best and easiest next to *G. sino-ornata,* with turquoise blue flowers, rather more open trumpets like the sort of gramophone horn that came after the familiar H.M.V. label one or a loudspeaker in the days of 2LO, which flowers in July and August, and *G. stevenagensis* at the same time but a darker

FIG. 13. Rooted pre-flowering cutting of *Gentiana Macaulayi.*

blue. There are very many more hybrids; some of the best were raised by Mr. G. H. Berry whose book *Gentians* (Faber & Faber, 21s.) is essential for anyone who falls under the spell of these most lovely alpines of all, which range the sky and summer seas for the blues that no other flower can match.

Unfortunately they hate lime: if you have a chalky garden you cannot grow them, it is a great pity. If you have not, and with care and knowledge, you can grow them wherever you can grow Azaleas and Rhododendrons, they are the plants for whose sake expensive failure is most worth risking.

The soil should not be the pure peat in which they are often grown, but the leafy mixture given at the beginning of the chapter. *G. Farreri* and *G. Macaulayi* will grow in a normal John Innes type soil, but are best with leafmould instead of peat. They will all take roughly the same soil and a Gentian bed made up with this is a glorious feature from July onwards in any garden.

Dig out your bed at low level on the rock garden or anywhere else you like, with shade for some part of the day, not in full sun. Go down about a foot and put in six inches of drainage material in the bottom, filling up with the mixture, and firming it well. This is for clay soils and normal garden loams; those lucky enough to have a lime-free garden full of Azaleas need only choose the site and dig in a bit of leafmould on the surface.

Plant in the spring and keep the bed weeded, tidying up when they finally go dormant for the winter by cutting off the dead branches. If there is any trace of yellowing in the foliage, when they are growing the sign of too much lime, water with a tablespoonful of Epsom salts stirred up in every three gallon can. Epsom salts will keep these Gentians going in the most unlikely places. The action is that of base exchange, magnesium sulphate (the salts) swaps with calcium carbonate (the lime) and makes calcium sulphate which is insoluble and harmless. Buy the cattle grade, from any Boots branch and use it freely, it can do no harm. A Gentian bed once built lasts for many years. Scatter bone meal in the spring every other year and fork it in as a plant food, because these plants are often starved.

Increase is easiest in the spring. This group goes dormant to a colony of small buds with white roots attached and these can be separated and potted or planted as required; they should be divided when they are above the surface and just beginning to grow, then they have time to recover and flower well the same year. For slow ones and those one does not wish to disturb, take small soft cuttings about May, choosing shoots that are not the biggest, as these will not flower. They want to be about an inch long; take off the lower leaves and insert in pans of pure sand, or sand with some fine leafmould mixed with it. These root easily in a cold frame and should be potted into suitable soil as soon as they are well rooted. Wait to plant them until the following spring, they need to establish a good crown before they go out. Seed is difficult and is inclined to vary, but they are so easy from division or cuttings that there is no need to bother with it.

There is a very good white Gentian, the best of the New Zealand species, where the race usually runs to size and dinginess. This is *G. saxosa* which is an evergreen mat of red brown branches and small oval bronzy green leaves. The trumpets are single or in small clusters and are about an inch high; they curve in at the mouth, and their creamy white colour and blue black stamens have given them the wild flower name at home of 'Woodland Crocus'; they flower from August to October. This one is perfectly happy with the woodland species, and can be raised from soft cuttings in the same way, but it comes perfectly from seed, sown in the spring on the grit system.

There are a very great many more Gentians, including our own rare native *G. verna* with small solid flat star flowers on inch high stems. which needs the same conditions as *G. acaulis* but with a more gritty soil. This one hates being disturbed and is more delicate than any of those described here. The best complete book on the race is *Gentians* by David Wilkie (Country Life, 25/-), and this is useful as a guide to the unknowns which often turn out to be not worth growing, either because they are so difficult that they can never flower here as well as they do in their native mountains or because they are like *G. lutea*. This is the biggest of all, a great mass of foliage that slowly increases to cabbage size and then throws up a flower spike on which the very small yellow florets are hidden in the greenery.

Geranium. Crane's Bill

These have no connection with the bedding Geraniums which are Zonal Pelargoniums, but are good rock garden and dry wall plants, fully hardy and both long-lived and easy.

The best one for the small rock garden is *Geranium sanguineum lancastriense* which is now rare in Lancashire but is as sturdy as any north countryman. It likes full sun and plenty of lime, making it a good companion for Campanulas, and flowers best if the soil is not too rich. In the small rock garden its short jointed prostrate stems grow a maximum of three inches high with small leaves rather like those of a maple in design. The flowers are clear pink, shaped like saucers and about the size of a shilling; the plant looks as though it were covered with small dog-roses from June to August, though on close inspection they are seen to be veined with dark red.

Seed is not often set, but cuttings can be rooted with a hormone, especially when a section of the thick older branches can be used at the bottoms, as with Erodiums. The best time of year for propagation is in April or May before flowering.

The larger *G. sanguineum*, which can still be found wild, is more suited to the wall garden, it is much more powerful, growing to eight inches high and has magenta red flowers of the same type from June to August. Starved on a dry wall it can be very free flowering but gets big and coarse with too rich soil. Another good one for the wall is the Himalayan species *G. Wallichianum*, which has violet blue flowers an

201

inch and a half across on short stems among prostrate rather grey green foliage, in July and August. This is the plant that is sometimes sold as 'Blue Geranium, fully hardy, no greenhouse required' to the ignorant who expect an indigo Paul Crampel; it is rather big and floppy on the rock garden, but good starved on a sunny wall. It loses its leaves in winter and should be cut back in October, they shoot again from the base the following spring. Both these two are easy from seed sown about March.

There are several other Geraniums for the rock garden which lose their leaves in winter, *G. subcaulescens* (now *G. cinereum subcaulescens*) with leaves on four-inch stems and heads of rose pink flowers from June to September, is easy, and *G. Pylzowianum* with feathery foliage and pale pink flowers appearing above it in June and July is so easy that it will run about all over the place and become a problem. Those who like the Crane's Bills can find and try a number, those who only need good tough plants that flower well will just keep to *G. sanguineum lancastriense*.

Gypsophila. Chalk plant

The stronger Gypsophila species are good wall plants for chalky soils as their popular name reveals; they like lime and plenty of it, but will grow in almost any soil. The two strongest are *G. repens* and *G. repens rosea*, which have flowers like those of the border 'Gyp'; the single *G. paniculata*, white and pale pink respectively in June and July, in chalky gardens or on heavily limy soil in a real sheet; elsewhere it is not so generous. There is a double form, *G. repens flora plena*, which is attractive, but its flowers are far smaller than those of the big 'Bristol Fairy'.

Their foliage is small and fleshy, little half or three-quarter inch leaves on brown barked stems that weave into a close trailing mat, ideal hanging over a rock or down the face of a dry wall, reaching sometimes two feet long. A rather slower species with smaller leaves fitting into a closer and neater mat is *G. fratensis* (now *G. repens var. fratensis*) with single pale pink flowers at the same time of year, but more regularly with stragglers until September. For those who want a good wall Gypsophila that really will give a show on any soil, the hybrid *G.* Rosy Veil is excellent. It is large for a rock garden, about fifteen inches high with foliage more like a border variety, but on a dry wall it will produce a dome-like cloud of pale pink double flowers on eight inch stems that can be used for cutting. It is not strictly a rock plant, it is an early attempt at a double pink Gyp, and quite a pleasant creature.

All these Gypsophilas can be increased from soft cuttings either before or after flowering; take them with about three joints between the growing point and the bottom, from which the last two leaves are removed. They are rather hard to root normally but a powder hormone makes them easy in sand frame or pan.

The carpeting species *G. cerastioides* is entirely different. It is a mat of rosettes of pale green rounded leaves, with almost stemless flowers, white veined with purple. These are about the size of silver threepenny bits in June and July. This species likes lime but flowers equally well without and is good bulb cover but not strong enough to fight more powerful carpeters in the Thyme lawn. It is easy from division in autumn or spring and comes true from seed sown in March or April, if you can get any.

Helianthemum. Sun Rose

These are the best of all dry bank plants with only one handicap, the flowers will not open in tent or hall. This means that no one at Chelsea or any other flower show has ever seen the strong blaze of solid colour, almost every shade but blue or purple, that makes massed Helianthemums in summer rival the spring glory of Aubrieta. The best way for Londoners to see what these tough, easy and cheap hybrids can do, is to go to Kew in Helianthemum time, in June, July and August, where, though they are not massed, there is a good collection of modern varieties. The only three which are at all widely grown are the old doubles, Mrs. Earle (red) and Jubilee (yellow, Queen Victoria's Jubilee, not King George the Fifth's) and the rather straggling grey foliaged single pink, *Rhodanthe carneum.*

They are hybrids of *Helianthemum nummularium* (formerly *H. vulgare*) and grow as small bushes averaging nine inches tall, with wiry stems and small leaves of variable size and colour. The flowers of the single species range from the sizes of shillings to half-crowns (the 'Queen' range) and though each is individually short lived, they are produced in incredible numbers over a long season; those who cut back as advised in Chapter 1 will get a second crop in the autumn.

The following selection is not complete, there are others, and as there is no Helianthemum Society or 'Complete List of Sun Rose Hybrids' like the one for Orchids (at the opposite pole of price, ease of cultivation and number of gardeners who can grow them), those who buy unlisted varieties may get duplicates. Nurserymen are unable to show these plants and compare their variety with their neighbours, and often a kind may be listed by different firms as 'Mrs. Smith', 'Mrs. Jones' and

'Mrs. Brown', calling them in each case after the customer who gave them the cuttings, perhaps all of the same variety, with an entirely different name. Again, one may find a new name which is merely a misspelling of an old one; *H.* Mrs. Moules is the same as *H.* Miss Mould, as an example, and in the case of the following list the most widely used name has been chosen. The ordinary gardener can start sure that he has not got any of them and that whatever the name they will do their best for him. The best policy is to buy as many as possible, all different, from a big firm, in ones or threes, and propagate for massing; they are so easy that the term 'Helianthemum propagator' is an insult among nursery gardeners. Then one can add colours one has not, or (more cautiously) names that are new, from other catalogues.

List of Helianthemum Hybrids

All suitable for the dry bank or slope; prostrate varieties are also good wall plants.

Single Varieties

Amy Baring. Prostrate, bright orange.
Apricot. Prostrate, apricot yellow.
Ben Afflick. Orange, brown eye.
Ben Alder. Milk chocolate brown.
Ben Attow. Cream, primrose eye.
Ben Dearg. Grey foliage, compact habit, soft flame red, the only one suitable for the small rock garden.
Ben Fhada. Bright yellow, orange eye.
Ben Heckla. Soft red.
Ben Hope. Grey foliage, deep rose pink.
Ben Lawers. Pale orange yellow.
Ben Ledi. Deep crimson.
Ben Lomond. Clear pink, pale centre.
Ben Lui. Magenta crimson.
Ben Mare. Flame.
Ben Mohr. Orange flame.
Ben Nevis. Prostrate, yellow, red eye.
Ben Vane. Chocolate.
Ben Venue. Bright red.
Ben Vorlich. Coppery orange.
Chamaecistus. Crimson carmine. Erect habit.
Chamaecistus Brilliant. Coppery red. Erect habit.
Croftianum. Grey foliage. Large soft orange-pink flowers.

204

Alpines Plant by Plant

Firebrand. Bronzy scarlet.

Firedragon. Grey foliage, orange-bronze.

Firefly. Fierce red.

Golden Queen. Semi-prostrate, large yellow.

Jock Scott. Grey foliage, old rose.

Magnificence. Grey foliage, rosy copper.

Marigold. Large flowered yellow.

Miss Mould. Grey foliage. Salmon pink fringed edge.

Mrs. Clay. Grey foliage, compact, orange bronze.

Peggy. Soft rose, darker eye.

Praecox. Grey foliage, bright yellow.

Rhodanthe carneum. Grey foliage, pink.

Rose Queen. Semi-prostrate, large pink, orange centre.

Salmon Queen. Semi-prostrate, large salmon pink.

Sudbury Gem. Compact habit, deep rose, flame centre.

Supreme. Crimson maroon.

Taylor's Seedling. Greyish foliage, orange scarlet.

The Bride. Grey foliage, pure white.

Watergate Rose. Greyish foliage, large crimson.

Windermere. Dark green foliage, soft lemon yellow.

Wisley Primrose. Grey foliage, primrose yellow.

Double Varieties

Bronze Jubilee. Bronzy yellow.

Butter and Eggs. Orange yellow.

Golden ball. Yellow.

Cerise Queen. Rosy red.

Jubilee. Lemon yellow.

Mrs. Earle. Red.

Rose of Leewood. Large rose pink.

Rubens. Orange.

Tigrinum plenum. Deep orange.

Watlands Red. Dark red.

The doubles have mainly small 'pom-pom' flowers about half an inch across; Rose of Leewood is the largest and best but it has rather a sprawling habit. The reason why Mrs. Earle and Jubilee are well-known is perhaps because they hang on to their petals better at a flower show.

The growing routine will be found in Chapter 1 for dry banks, and on the rock garden, unless it is large, the varieties should be restricted to Ben Dearg, Mrs. Clay and the trough garden species. This is *H*.

alpestre serpyllifolium (sometimes called *H. alpestre oblongatum*) which grows as a neat mat of small branches with dark green oval leaves set in pairs, with bright yellow single flowers on short stems from June to August. This is a non-invasive semi-carpeting species with a maximum height of three inches. Like all the others it likes full sun on any soil except a peat, preferring somewhere poor and limy and tolerating wind, cold and winter rain in any part of Britain. The dead flower stems should be cut back in September, otherwise this small one is too slow growing to need trimming like the large varieties. It is also longer lived, for the bigger plants deteriorate after about five years, though raising replacements is so easy that one need merely replant a few every spring as a matter of routine.

Soft cuttings of non-flowering wood, the shoots which are not showing a bud, can be taken at any time when there are three good joints of stem available, trimmed and inserted in the sand frame for potting when ready. September is a good month and they will be rooted in about three weeks, ready to pot and grow on in a cold frame, pinching out the tips to make bushy growth for planting in April. They can be taken in May to make plants for autumn replacements, or in October and November to winter in the frame and pot in the spring.

Another method, for those with no frame, is to take longer cuttings, three or four inches long, and put them in along a spade cut in a shady place, treading them firm and watering well for a couple of days. These will not root 100 per cent, about half can be relied on, but they can be either lifted and potted or even planted direct, with care in lifting and ample water. Their home is usually somewhere dry and sunny, so replacements from the open ground are best planted in a wet spell or dull weather, if they are moved during the summer. The best specimens are, however, pot grown, as they can be put out at any time without root disturbance.

Helianthemums can be raised easily from seed, and where only a mixture is required, seed can be gathered from the relatively large capsules when these are light brown and the contents black on the existing plants, or bought for sowing about February for potting when large enough to handle. Pinch out the tips when they are growing well and even with this check they will flower the first year, and can be planted afterwards in autumn or spring.

This early flowering is important, because as they are all hybrids they are usually crosses between each other and their offspring will include the ancestors of both parents even when self-pollinated. Therefore the best system is to raise a quantity and expect to throw two-thirds of them away. Those who save their own seed should take it off the plants they like, so that at least one side of the family has some qualities that are attractive. Any lucky hits in the way of better habit, more moderate growth or striking colour can be increased from cuttings, but it is only just possible that one's best will be better than the many existing good varieties.

Those who wish to experiment would do well to try and produce ordinary rock garden size varieties, based on Ben Dearg or Mrs. Clay, or try and tilt the dark maroon Watergate Rose over towards the purples, but no one is ever going to make a fortune out of breeding Helianthemums though it would be a very pleasant hobby for someone ruthless enough to throw away his failures. The carpeting species has unfortunately only twenty chromosomes against the thirty-two of the large varieties and this 'colour bar' prevents crossing for a miniature race, but perhaps there may be wild Helianthemums somewhere in the world, even annual species that may make some persevering gardener the Russell of the Sun Roses.

There is one last species, also cut off behind the chromosome barrier from the hybridist, the forgotten Helianthemum, *H. Tuberaria,* which is completely unlike all the other members of the race. This is a very good hardy carpeter for the waterside. Its leaves are deeply veined, between one and two inches, about half as much across and carried in flat rosettes almost like a colony of small plantains. In June and July it flowers with four or five bright yellow Helianthemum blooms, often an inch and a half across each floret. These flower stems are usually between four and six inches long and make a real show, though like its bushy relations, they will not open in a flower tent and are individually short lived.

All it needs is a normal soil and a place that is damp but not wet and boggy, in sun or semi-shade. Its great handicap is that no one knows it, and those who try it, grow it dry and sunny like all the others. As a waterfall and stream-side plant it is hardier than either Calceolarias or Mimulus, but rare because its qualities are unknown to almost every gardener. It is increased from seed, sown in February or March, for potting and growing on to plant the following spring, but when it is in pots, it should not be allowed to get too dry, another reason for high mortality in the nursery. As it is so utterly distinct, seed comes 100 per cent true and should be saved on every opportunity; perhaps some day nature may defy the chromosome atlas and give us a whole race of these waterside plants as lovely as the brilliant hybrids for the alpine bank.

Alpines Plant by Plant

Hippocrepis. Horseshoe Vetch

Hippocrepis comosa is a British native, with feathery leaves like those of a Mimosa but on a small scale, an inch or so long and a darker green. It trails with short branches from a central root stock and from June to August carries heads of pea flowers on short stems, with the general effect from a distance of bright yellow honeysuckle, from the shape of the vivid clusters. There is a lemon yellow from *H. comosa* E. R. Janes and both are really good wall plants for a dry and sunny place, especially in a chalky garden. They trail about a foot and stick out roughly three inches, their height on the rock garden, where with better soil they run to leaf and fewer flowers. Both can be raised easily from seed, potted with care after early spring sowing because of the big *Leguminosae* tap root. They can be rooted from cuttings in the summer, soft shoots about two inches long, but these are difficult, unless a powder hormone is used, which makes them quite easy.

Hutchinsia alpina

This is a very useful bulb cover plant, or for paths in shade or semi-shade. It has small glossy dark green leaves, divided into threes, and makes a close flat carpet about two inches high with flowers in May and June like smaller and neater versions of those of the Iberis or perennial Candytuft.

It stands up to wear when not in flower and its only drawback is that it will get out of hand on a small rock garden and need drastic reduction. Division and replanting where it is required is the easiest method of increase, though it can also be raised from seed sown in the spring. It is called after a Miss Winifred Hutchins, an Irish botanist (1785-1815), and has no popular name.

Hypericum

The Hypericums are a lusty race for sun and a dry position on any soil; the best known is *H. calycinum* which will flower in shade under trees, the 'Rose of Sharon' which is a shrub and too large even for the dry bank.

On the wall garden there is room for many species and they are valuable in providing a good blaze of yellow in late summer after all the early flowering stuff is over. The most common, perhaps because it is the best, is *H. olympicum* and its pale yellow flowered ally, *H. olympicum citrinum*.

These are small bushes with grey green leaves set opposite each other on stems about eight inches long, making a kind of loose mound. In

22. A Gold Medal winning water garden at Chelsea Flower Show built by Messrs. G. G. Whitelegg. The electric circulating pump is behind the flat rock that juts forward to hide the concrete edge on the extreme left. A gentle curve on the pipe leads the water to the upper pool and gives the most waterfall for the smallest h.p. pump

23. *Primula Florindae*, the Giant Cowslip, flowers in July and even August, the latest of all the damp-loving Primulas. A water garden should grow the whole range, beginning with *P. denticulata* in March and April, and blazing in May and June with the many-tiered Candelabra type

24. *Ramonda Myconi* is an 'edgeways plant' for the sides of a steep ravine or a rock face. Plant it above the splash of the water, save that for Mimulus and hardy ferns which like nodding in the spray, and use the Sedums and Sempervivums where the sun blazes. *Ramondas* do well on dry walls in shade

July and August they are covered with large bright yellow flowers up to an inch and a half across the four petals at the back and about three-quarters through the fluffy dome of stamens and anthers in the middle. After they have flowered the stems should be cut hard back. The late shoots, or those which appear earlier in the year (about May), can be rooted as cuttings in the sand frame, or both species can be raised from spring-sown seed. Both plants are long lived and thrust upwards rather than trail down the face of the dry wall.

The trailing species, with grey foliage and rather smaller flowers also bright yellow, at the same time of year but with less central dome, *H. rhodopeum*, is also a good wall plant. This one is about six inches high and suitable for the small rock garden, and so is the smaller edition of *H. olympicum*, with six inch stems, *H. polyphyllum*.

The group of Hypericums which fit small size rock gardens best are those with dark green leaves, *H. nummularium* (which means, 'with leaves like Creeping Jenny, or Money wort'), which has red brown stems, small rounded leaves and small tuft-centred flowers and grows as a low carpet. Another is *H. reptans* with the same round leaves and dark stems, with foliage that takes on an autumn tint late in the year. Both are bright yellow but with centres reduced to a tuft; the outer petals form a broad cross, hence the popular name of our wild Hypericums, 'St. John's Wort' from St. John of Jerusalem.

There are a number of others, some with thin and spiny leaves like *H. Coris* and *H. fragile*, some tall lusty shrubs like *H. balearicum* and *H. orientale*, but all have the same type of flowers and all are yellow, and the four mentioned are not fully hardy.

There was once an orange scarlet Hypericum, *H. laevetrubrum*, which came from Persia, and though it received a First Class Certificate from the R.H.S. it died, and no one has yet been able to find it again. Even if it was part hardy it would be valuable in the hands of the hybridiser. We have one varying species, *H. anagalloides*, with prostrate stems, grey leaves and flowers, in June and July that are more like small cups with hardly any central tuft. This species grows about two inches high, and has orange yellow flowers, but apricot and salmon pink variations are reputed to exist. It is quite good on the small rock garden but prefers semi-shade and does not flower so freely as the others, so can be a disappointing plant.

All these species can be raised in quantity from seed, or in smaller numbers from soft cuttings in April and May; they do not root nearly so well after flowering, though hormones will level up the difference. They should be potted in normal soil and are easy to raise.

Hypsela longiflora

This charming carpeter from Chile, which grows down towards Tierra del Fuego and Cape Horn, is now a member of the *Lobeliacea*. It grows as a mat of dark green leaves about an inch long or less, rounded at the tips, and set closely on creeping stems that root downwards at the joints. It is about an inch high, including the flowers, which are on show from June to September. These flowers are very distinctive. They look up from the surface of the mat on very short stems, so that they seem to sit on the leaves, and each one has two petals on one side and three on the other. These petals are triangular, level across the tips, and pure white with a crimson blotch in the middle and veinings and edgings of dark red; inside the throat the colour changes again to yellow and the whole effect is neat but not gaudy.

They are happiest in part shade though they grow in full sun if not too dry in summer and they need a soil with plenty of leafmould in it— equal parts of this, loam and sand will grow it well on the small rock garden and anywhere that a good cheerful carpeter is needed. It does not grow fast and therefore it should be planted with the less rampant species.

Increase is by division, which is best in the spring, but where a great number is needed, the running stems can be snipped up into sections, each with a growing point, or merely three joints and a supply of fibrous roots, in the autumn and pricked out thickly in a pan of suitable soil to grow on through the winter to make plants for April potting.

Though some writers state that this species is the same as *Selliera radicans*, a species that is found in New Zealand, those who turn to page 261 will see how entirely different the two plants are. If they have grown either or both they will understand why some gardeners get rather impatient with orthodox botanists.

Iberis. Perennial Candytuft

The common Iberis is a large evergreen shrub with dark green leaves about an inch long on sprawling branches. It makes a round bush about nine inches high, it can be two feet across in time. Its species name is *I. gibraltarica* (it comes from this part of the Empire) and flowers with pale lilac heads, like those of the annual Candytuft but much flatter and about two inches across. It is good as a space filler on the dry wall and can be used on the dry bank, where its flowering season of April and May is an asset. This one is best increased by soft cuttings of the smaller shoots that are not going to flower, taken in May.

The smaller species are, however, better company for other plants. *Iberis sempervirens* Little Gem is a garden hybrid growing only four or five inches high and flowering in May or June. This is a superior miniature of the large *I. sempervirens* which is like *I. gibraltarica* but with pure white flowers. Little Gem has inch-across flowers and is better from June or July cuttings. It is very good on the dry wall, standing drought well, and suitable for the small rock garden so long as one remembers that a three year old plant can be a foot in diameter.

Smaller still is *I. saxatilis* which has gnarled dark brown stems and short stout leaves growing only three inches high, and looks like an expensive dwarf Conifer. Its small white flower heads are on view in March and April, sometimes later with a cold spring. Another little one is *I. taurica* with grey green leaves, hairy if you look at them closely, not shiny dark green, which makes a round bush between two and three inches tall with white flower heads that begin as violet buds between May and July.

These two miniatures are the best for the small rock garden; they can be increased by soft cuttings taken from where they can be spared without spoiling the shape of the plants, and as so few can be obtained each year, use a hormone. This is why they are rare, not because they are tender; both are tough little plants for any soil, for choice limy and poor. Like all the race, they need full sun.

Inula acaulis

Inula acaulis grows as a collection of flat rosettes of broad dark green leaves, on short jointed stems that root down from every elbow. It is slow growing and non-invasive, prefering a place in full sun on any soil. It is good on the small rock garden, and has no objections to summer drought. The flowers in April and May are big yellow daisies two inches across, and have sturdy stems so short that the total height, foliage and all, is barely the width of the relatively large blooms.

This easy and hardy plant is rare because it sets little seed. If this can be found those who have it are recommended to break up the dried flower heads and sow the lot in February or March, on chance that something will come up. If you have a clump it is best to remove some of the rooted rosettes in June or July, pot and keep in a cold frame until well established, and replant either in the autumn or spring.

There is a more common species, *I. ensifolia*, which is an upright bush with pale green, sharply pointed leaves, growing between nine inches and a foot high, and with smaller yellow daisies about an inch across in July and August. This needs the same conditions and is no more fussy about

211

its soil, but is not fully hardy in all districts. In a sheltered place it is suitable for the larger rock garden, but it dies down in winter and may easily fail to come up again. This one makes plenty of cuttings easily rooted in June and July, or it may be split up in the spring.

Iris

Those who are growing the large wet-loving Primulas can add round the pond the Japanese Iris *I. Kaempferi*. This has large lower petals, four of them spread out flat, and very tiny 'standards' (the part of a border Iris that points up, the petals that go down being the 'falls') and can be obtained mixed or in separate colours with Japanese names. These grow nearly a yard tall and though they are handsome in July, the flowers are soon over and there is a great deal of foliage. *I. sibirica* which flowers in sprays of florets like smaller border Irises, can also be obtained in blue, both deep and pale, and also in white. Their brief flowering season fits in with the later Primulas, but unless there is a wet patch that must be *filled*, they are not recommended for the small garden where space is a problem. Both kinds can be increased by division in March when they start to grow, for they die right down in winter.

Those who have only a small concrete pool can secure the effect of water Irises, narrow leaves and dancing flowers plus the colour the Primulas lack, with *I. ruthenica;* it has violet blue standards and falls with white veins in May and June, nearer the main Primula time, with a height of only nine inches. A yellow June flowering 'flag' on a smaller scale, is *I. Forrestii*, about a foot high. Both like about the same degree of damp as Primulas, and go dormant in winter. Increase by dividing in July and replanting where they are wanted, like the border Iris, which is always better moved soon after flowering than in the autumn.

Small size Irises for the alpine border are provided by *I. pumila* and its allies. *I. pumila* is about six inches high and is about an eighth scale replica of the border Iris, but with shorter stems in proportion. It can be used as an edging, or planted anywhere dry and sunny; it flowers in April and May so is best divided in June. The usual varieties are *I. pumila atroviolacea*, purple blue; *I. pumila azurea*, pale blue; *I. pumila lutea*, yellow, and *I. pumila alba*, white and the rarest one. Near these in habit and flower, are *I. Chamaeiris*, yellow and a bit taller and not losing its leaves in winter; its dwarf form, four or five inches high, *I. Chamaeiris Campbelli*, sky blue standards and violet falls; *I. Reichenbachii*, yellow and May and June flowering and about nine inches high.

This group look out of place on the small rock garden, where it is best to stick to the real miniatures. The nicest is *I. minuta* from Japan, with narrow pale green leaves like young grass blades, but two or three inches high, and tiny yellow flowers in April and May with brown markings on the falls. Another good one is *I. mellita* from Jugo-slavia, which is about the same height but with short, wide Iris leaves edged with dull red. Its flowers are about the size of a penny and a rich smoky crimson, usually in May and with another crop in September. (These two were once *I. minuto aurea* and *I. rubro-marginata.*)

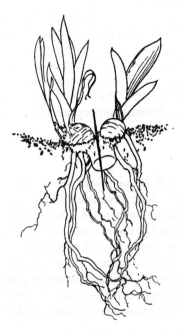

FIG. 14. *Iris pumila*, thick line shows knife cut.

Both species prefer the limy mixture for small Campanulas and Dianthus, and need a position in full sun where they will not be swamped by stronger plants. Plant them so that the rhizomes, the fat roots which store the food, are at ground level; they like to have the sun on these, just as border Irises always do best when planted shallow. When the blooms go over pinch off the remains; neither plant sets seed easily and it is better to spare them the effort of the attempt.

Iris lacustris from the Canadian lakes is just as lovely. It is a three inch high miniature border Iris, with pale blue flowers crested with gold, that spread their season through the summer from May to September.

213

This one is not fond of lime, it prefers a poor soil but one with plenty of leafmould, or John Innes Compost with leafmould instead of peat. It is not a water Iris, but should not be planted where it will get baked dry in summer. There is a larger species *I. cristata* (either one is a larger form of the other or vice versa) which grows up to nine inches tall, and usually concentrates its flowers in June and July. These are the same in colour but on a bigger scale. Both make a solid mat of surface rhizomes spreading flatly like the fingers of a small hand, and both die down in winter until this mat is all that shows.

These four little Irises are best left undisturbed for three years or so, and then they can be lifted and divided in July after flowering, sliced up so that each has leaves and some growing roots, on the rhizomes, and potted to grow on in a frame for spring planting. The cut ends of the rhizomes can be dipped in lime as a precaution against rotting, just as you would with the big ones. These small species are rare not because they are difficult, but because nurserymen can increase them no faster than gardeners.

Jasminium Parkeri

This is a dwarf bush Jasmine with almost half size yellow Jasmine flowers in June. It has dark green spiny leaves and the older branches twist into a neat shrub that may reach a foot high, but six inches is more normal. Its home should be on the small rock garden, in normal soil and in a sunny sheltered place, for it is not fully hardy.

Increase is best from soft cuttings an inch to an inch and a half long, rooted with a hormone in the sand frame or pan in July or August. Grow through the first winter in the frame and plant about April. It will be small but sturdy and will increase in size very slowly.

Leontopodium alpinum. Edelweiss

The remarkable thing about this plant is how anyone ever broke his neck trying to gather it. It is easy to understand people reaching over too far for some of the Gentians, but not this dingy plant that flowers like two grey starfish one on top of the other.

The leaves are grey and furry in small low tufts, and the flowers on six inch stems in June and July may bring back memories of a Swiss holiday. It is easy from spring-sown seed, but if you are going to fetch back seed bring something more attractive than this smug and overrated creature. It is best on a poor soil and sun-baked slope in a chalky garden, but its best is nothing to yodel about.

214

Linaria. Alpine Toadflax

There are two sorts of Linarias, the biennial or annual species, and the perennial, which are sometimes called Cymbalarias, though not in catalogues.

The first group are about three inches high with small blunt grey leaves on floppy stems, and ones and pairs of miniature Snapdragons with long lower lips from June to September, The best are *L. alpina*, deep violet with an orange splash on the lip; *L. alpina rosea*, pink and orange; *L. faucicola* which is Spanish not Swiss, and has pure violet Snapdragons with no orange at all. There is another species, *L. supina*, which comes from Majorca and is taller, being about six inches and variable in colour including red, purple, pink, yellow and brown. This is less hardy and seeds itself freely. The brown predominates so that the result, unless one keeps pulling up the dull colours, is a race of floppy and sad flowered weeds.

The true mountain species are better. They like full sun and a dry place with lime in the soil, and if they are trimmed back after flowering will last for a second season. They are, however, so easy from seed that there is no need to worry; save some each summer and sow it where it is needed in February or March, thinly so that it can grow on without thinning. These seeds can be used in a number of ways; dropped down cracks between paving too narrow to plant, inserted in the soil of dry walls where plants have died, put in with a dibber to take their chance in the crumbling mortar of an old wall, and into unplantable crevices on the rock garden. With starvation and in awkward places they do their best, but on rich soil they are fleshy and weedy.

The best of the Cymbalaria group is *L. globosa rosea*. This makes a round tuft about two inches in diameter studded with shorter and fatter pink Snapdragons from May to August. This species has small pale green rounded leaves, entirely like the *L. alpina* type. The Kenilworth Ivy, a British native found on many churchyard walls, is *L. Cymbalaria*, and though not a striking plant is good on a dry wall in shade where few things will grow. It has grey green ivy-shaped leaves, and thin trailing stems with thin lavender Snapdragons on and off through the summer. Both these two can be raised from spring-sown seed, or from cuttings of the soft shoots in July and August.

The carpeting Linarias are unsuitable for the rock garden, but are good as bulb cover or on paths; they will take shade and are quite happy with sun for only part of the day. They like a light sandy soil with plenty of leafmould or peat. John Innes Seed Compost as for the alpine lawn does them well and saves weed trouble under them.

These are *L. aequitriloba,* which is never more than in inch high, spreading flat on the ground as a carpet of small leaves, divided as the name implies into three, and studded with small lavender Snapdragons from June till September. Do not disturb it once it is going well, except to trim it back if it gets out of bounds. The other species of this type is *L. hepaticifolia,* which has white underground stems and dark green kidney-shaped leaves veined with white, so the effect is like that of a small Cyclamen. This is an even stronger grower and these runners can make dives below the soil and come up a long way off. Its total height is half an inch, and the small stemless Snapdragons are pale pink with the same flowering season as its comrade. Both are increased easily from division in spring, planting direct where required, firming well, and watering until they take root. Despite many warnings, these are good plants in the right place.

Linum. Perennial Flax

The best species for the dry wall is *L. alpinum,* if possible in its rather larger flowered variety, *L. gentianoides.* This has small and sharply pointed blue grey leaves on prostrate wiry stems in a thick mat. From May to August it sends up six inch stems topped with a cluster of shallow cup flowers in great abundance. They are a glorious pale blue, and as they drop their large petals these resemble the wings of the Chalk Hill Blue Butterfly. It is a tough and sturdy plant that likes full sun and lime, one of the best pure blue plants for any dry wall in summer.

It is best to keep to this one variety because the others cross-pollinate, and one gets compromise kinds which are upright stemmed and tall like the eighteen inch *L. narbonense,* and the two foot *L. perenne.* It is easy from the shiny black seeds which are set generously, sown in March for planting about May or in the autumn. Those who get a really good prostrate *L. gentianoides* can increase it from soft cuttings, taken from the young shoots in the spring as soon as these are about an inch and a half long. These root easily in a sand frame or pan but should be taken after flowering, as the plant goes dormant in winter and it is best to get the cuttings well established in pots by then. The taller Linums are attractive with their feathery arching stems and clear blue flowers, but are large for the small rock garden and less suitable for walls, where they are inclined to droop and break.

Though *L. alpinum* in a good small form is attractive on a small rock garden where its blue is against grey stone, there are several more suitable species. *L. flavum*, which has pointed oval brownish green leaves, grows as a compact bush but goes down to a basal tuft every winter. It can be tidied up in October and usually grows about nine inches high during the summer when it will carry cluster heads of golden yellow flowers from June to September; on the same general plan as those of *L. alpinum*, four overlapping petals gathered into a tube in the centre, but smaller and individually longer lived. Its relation *L. arboreum* makes more of a bush, and as it does not die down in winter and keeps its old branches, it can in time be twelve inches high and as much across. There is a trailing member of this group, *L. capitatum*, but it is not hardy, and like the white *L. monogynum* with narrow grey leaves rather like those of the first group, it vanishes in winter.

These two yellow hardy Linums can be increased from young shoots in July and August; they need about an inch of stem between the base of the cutting and the growing point, three-quarters is the minimum, and a hormone makes sure of a good plant. When they are potted and growing in a cold frame they keep moving through the winter, as it is only our climate that brings the outdoor ones to a stop.

The best small rock garden and alpine border species is *L. salsoloides nanum* (the last word is more correctly *alpinum*). This makes a small round mat of evergreen branches like those of a heather but more slender and grey, rather on the lines of *L. alpinum* when it first wakes up, but neater and more compact. The flowers are pure white with faint grey pencil markings, five petalled shallow trumpets that last for several days, as every evening they furl themselves neatly like umbrellas and open again next morning. The display goes on from May till September for, as with *Erodium chamaedroides*, though the plant sets no seed, it is not for want of trying. With its neat habit and barely three inches of height including flower stems, this is a real treasure. I had a favourite specimen bought in 1937 which was moved four times, once after bombing, which died in 1946 from being robbed of too many cuttings for post-war demand on a nursery. Left alone, it might have lived twenty years and exceeded a foot in diameter.

The best soil is a good Campanula mixture, though it will grow on any standard alpine soil with lime. It needs a position in full sun and has no objection to drought or winter cold and rain.

The problem with this species is propagation, because it is hard to root and slow growing. The best time of year is July or August; take the shoots from round the edges about an inch long, using a powder hormone for quicker and better rooting, and insert in a pan of sand. Pot when rooted in a limy mixture and grow on in a cold frame. Do not plant until its roots are well round the pot and it is growing well as a small copy of its parent, which may take until the second spring. Those nurserymen who list it expensively are not greedy, it has taken them over eighteen months to grow.

Lithospermum

There is one Lithospermum which has earned a popular name, like *Aethionema* Warley Rose, by its garden merit; everyone knows what 'Heavenly Blue' is, *L. diffusum* Heavenly Blue, and its colour is exactly that.

It is not a plant for every soil; like the woodland Gentians, if you have a very limy soil or are on solid chalk you cannot grow it. You can do wonders with Epsom salts, as it is not a true lime hater but a humus lover, and with plenty of leafmould even those on heavy clay can grow it well. Its trouble on clays is that it is unable to force its very tender feeding roots through the hard stiff soil, and this is more often its difficulty than the presence of lime.

On the rock garden it is best either in a pocket where it can cascade over an outcrop, or low down where it can become a thriving mat. It can reach two or even three feet in diameter in course of years, but is rarely as much as six inches high. The leaves are long ovals, curled over at the edges, dark green with a paler underside (if they are yellow green use Epsom salts as for Gentians, it means lime trouble) on trailing, black barked branches that weave thickly into a mat; this mat can be rolled back in the spring to allow a top dressing of bone meal or dried blood to be scattered round the central root stock.

The flowers are shaped like single florets of Lilac but larger, nearly half an inch across. Their main display is in May and June, but stragglers and lesser crops are produced far into the autumn. They are the colour of the sky on a summer day, the type that one feels is too good to last.

The best situation is in full sun or sun for part of the day, without excessive drought in summer—the reason why it is not a good dry wall plant. On a light sandy loam where Azaleas and Rhododendrons grow well all that is necessary is to dig in some leafmould and plant it, and in this sort of garden one can also use it along the top of a wall to trail down.

For most people it is best to dig out about a foot and make up a bed exactly as one would for woodland Gentians. Two parts leafmould, one loam and one sand is a traditional mixture; peat can be substituted for half the leafmould, but Lithospermum does not normally grow in peat bogs and it prefers a woodland soil. Once planted do not disturb;

218

it rarely recovers from root damage, but encroaching or straggling branches can be cut back in April with no ill effects. The branches are not tender and the plant is hardy, but the roots are neither.

Increase is from cuttings, which root best in July, for choice the first half of the month; you can do them in August, but it is better to take your cuttings on the top of the short season if you are only doing a few. They should be soft young stuff about two inches long, and though they should be cut through neatly below the joint do not remove any side leaves; in this case it pays to be lazy. Insert in a mixture of three parts

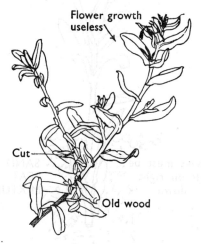

Fig 15. Branch of *Lithospermum* Heavenly Blue, showing good cutting.

sand to one of fine peat in a pan or cutting frame, and keep well watered; never let them flag, that is the secret. With a hormone the cutting season can be extended to September, but the July plants will still be the best.

When the cuttings are dug out for potting, take great care not to break the pink-tinted semi-transparent roots; a broken tap root, the largest one, is a common cause of the hard and struggling plants often sold. Like the woodland Gentians these Lithospermums (there is another and slightly larger flowered variety called 'Grace Ward'), are worth taking the trouble to grow. If they were less beautiful and hardy once planted in the right soil they would not be so widely popular.

Those with limy soil and chalky gardens, or who use only the dry wall for growing alpines, can still grow Lithospermums, the type which are now Moltkias, not quite so strikingly but with the same pure blues in June and July. They prefer the same type of soil as a Campanula, and can be built into the dry soil in the same way. Crush the soil ball of a pot-grown plant, do not break it, for the roots are nearly as tender as those of Heavenly Blue. Full sun is the best aspect, they need no special soil even though they like lime, and they have no objection to normal summer drought, especially when well established.

Leaves must be left on right down   SAND PEAT MIXTURE

FIG. 16. Cutting with lower leaves on, to encourage axillary rooting.

Perhaps the most attractive is *L. graminifolium* (now *Moltkia suffruticosa*) which has dark green narrow leaves rather like those of one of the border Thrifts, but shorter, wider and stiffer, springing directly from woody creeping stems. These form a low bush about six inches high and on the small rock garden, where it also grows well, it will reach a foot across in a few years; a round clump three feet in diameter in ten years is a record. In June and July sturdy stems up to eight inches high thrust up in a regular thicket above the evergreen rosettes of leaves, each with a cluster of tubular flowers, the individual florets being over an inch long and the same authentic sky blue as the better-known species. The allied species *L. intermedium* (or *Moltkia intermedia*) has taller flower stems, up to a foot high, and deep indigo florets. It can be distinguished when not in flower by the leaves, which are shorter and broader than those of *L. graminifolium*.

Seed of both species is sometimes available and should be sown in the spring, but it is only rarely set, and the usual method of increase is from soft wooded cuttings in August and September. These should be treated with a hormone in the same way as those of Heavenly Blue. They should be four joints long, about an inch and a half between growing point and base, as the grassy leaves are longer than the cutting. They are easier to root, though they need the same care in potting, and a leafy mixture with additional chalk grows them fast and well in a cold frame through the first winter.

Lychnis

The best Lychnis for the small rock garden or as a clump plant on the dry wall or in paving is *L. Lagascae* (correctly *Petrocoptis Lagascae*). This is a small bushy plant, with long oval grey green leaves, that grows in a loose clump about six inches high, springing from a woody central root stock. It flowers very freely from June to August with starry, Maltese-cross-like blooms, about three-quarters of an inch across, rose-pink in colour but with a pale centre when they are first open.

It is very easy from seed, which is set in great quantity and comes completely true. Sow in February, pot and plant to flower the same year. It is as a direct-sown crevice plant that it is at its best; the new name, from the Greek meaning 'Rock breaker' because it will thrive in the narrowest crack, is much more descriptive than the earlier one which links it with species of very different qualities. It should be sown direct in spring where it is required, and though it is usually regarded as a biennial, this is merely because it does not live so long when it is grown on the flat.

There are other species of Lychnis; *L. alpina* (now *Viscaria alpina*) which has grass-like foliage of a brownish green and not very striking cluster heads of rose pink flowers on sticky four inch stems, which hates lime, or rather is not perennial when lime is present, and *L. Haagaena*. This has large scarlet flowers rather like single florets of *L. chalcedonica*, the 'Turk's Cap' of the herbaceous border, but though it sounds striking from catalogue descriptions, the colour fades, the flowers are hidden among the leafy bracts, and it grows about twelve inches high, dying down each winter to a semi-tuberous root. Both are very easy from seed, and are the kind of plants often included in 'a dozen all different'. *Lychnis Lagascae* is a very much better plant, even though one should

221

watch to see that its self-sown seedlings are not invading where they interfere with other species.

Mazus

Mazus Pumilio, a New Zealand species, and *M. reptans* from the Himalayas are two useful carpeters for shade or semi-shade. Neither is fussy about soil, though both are fond of leafmould and some moisture in summer, like so many shade lovers. Both are good bulb cover, and highly suitable for the alpine path.

The New Zealand one grows in small rosettes of rather brownish green leaves, about two inches long, joined together by red-brown stems that root like strawberry runners but less rapidly. The flowers are relatively large, rather like those of a Mimulus (Musk) but with a much longer lower lip, white or varying shades of lilac with yellow centres. Their season is July and August and for a shade plant, the display is quite a good one.

Mazus reptans, with small more willow-shaped leaves with rugged edges set opposite each other on more slender stems that root downwards from every joint, is far more vigorous, a thickly weaving carpeter with a surprising talent for town gardens. Neither Mazus likes cold winds, though they stand frost, and if *M. reptans* is planted in a sheltered place it can be used as weed-preventing cover even under bush roses in the open border. It is not therefore a plant for the rock garden where space is limited. It flowers from June to August with the same type of flower as its colleague, though the lower lip is more prominent and divided into three. The colour scheme is pale lilac, with a white throat and an orange spot on each division of the lower lip; the flowers sit on short stems above the weaving mat of leaves and branches and give the distant effect of single Antirrhinum florets on a small scale but scattered with a lavish hand. This plant is sometimes wrongly called *M. rugosos*.

Both species are easily increased by division, either planting them directly where they are wanted about April when they are growing well, or lifting in September, potting and wintering in a frame; they do not recover quickly when disturbed in the autumn.

There is reputed to be a deep red purple *Mazus reptans*, and those who can get seed to sow in the early spring should watch for it, and increase it only by division. Neither species sets seed freely in this country.

Mimulus (Musk)

The one thing everyone knows about Mimulus is that it has lost its scent, which vanished during the 1914-18 war. The accepted theory is that the Musk grown on cottage window-sills before this time, *M. moschatus*, was all descended from one wild plant that by chance was a scented freak. The quality was not permanent and was bred out because seedsmen did not select only scented ones. There is no real proof that the first World War had anything to do with it, and so far no one has found any flower that lost its perfume after World War II. The species and hybrids of interest here never did have any real scent to lose.

They are hybrids of *Mimulus cupreus*, long-flowering plants in vivid colours for a moist place, but none are completely hardy in all districts in all winters. The best for the small rock garden, by the pool or in a semi-shaded place on the lower slopes, is *M.* Whitecroft Scarlet. It grows two or three inches high in a compact clump of short-jointed, sturdy stems and small, pointed, rather browny green leaves. The flowers are wide-mouthed scarlet trumpets, and they are a generous blaze from June to September. It comes true from seed, which is freely set, and should be gathered to sow in a frame or cold greenhouse about February to make plants to go out in April. It is also easy from cuttings, and by either method one can make sure of it in case it fails to come through the winter.

The other hybrids are larger and have longer jointed stems which run up to six or eight inches. *Mimulus* Plymtree is the nicest, with pink trumpets and is nearly as compact as Whitecroft Scarlet; *M.* Prince Bismark is a clear cherry red, *M.* Chelsea Pensioner is a good crimson, and Bee's Dazzler a bright scarlet. The first two are rare but worth finding and there are many more, but mostly scarlets very little different from each other. The yellow varieties all run tall, but Dainty, which is a cream yellow, is a neat grower in the six inch height group. The wild Mimulus of the south of England is *M. luteus* from Chile, which grows a foot high and taller and should only be used on a stream side with plenty of space.

All these hybrids are hardier as cuttings than as plants in winter. Take a few soft cuttings of each about September and insert them in a mixture of two parts of sand to one of any normal alpine soil, in labelled pans in a cold frame and they will need no more attention bar the removal of dead leaves until March or April. Then by topping them and rooting cuttings, ample stock can be raised for replanting. Those who like Mimulus and have the rarer hybrids, or discoveries of their own, should do this every year to avoid the risk of loss; very little room is needed and they are worth the trouble.

Morisia hypogaea

This charming species is correctly *Morisia monantha* but it is rarely known by this name. It makes a colony of flat rosettes each about two inches across, dark green saw-edged leaves like a more fairylike and far

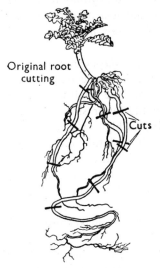

FIG. 17. Plant of *Morisia hypogaea* lifted for propagation.

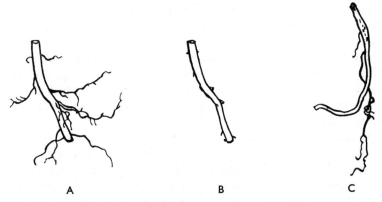

FIG. 18. Root cuttings of Morisia, twice natural size,
(a) as removed, (b) with fibre trimmed off, (c) the smallest type.

neater dandelion. In March, April and May, each tuft of leaves is ringed with half inch diameter, bright yellow, Maltese-cross-shaped flowers. These are not only very attractive in their own right, a good colony of

224

Morisia will outshine many yellow Saxifrages in spring; they have a most curious habit.

As they go over, a growing point forms instead of a seed and these thrust themselves deep into the ground, for the seeds to develop on the ends, in exactly the same way as those of the Monkey or Ground Nut (*Arachis hypogea*), which is no relation. The probable reason for this habit, unique in the order *Cruciferae* where wide seed scattering is the rule, is because the plant grows on beaches in Corsica and scattered seed might simply drift out to sea.

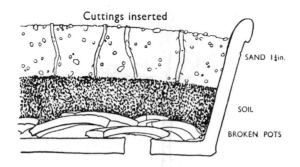

FIG. 19. Root cutting pan.

Morisia likes a light soil, a normal John Innes Seed Compost does it well, and on heavy clays plenty of leafmould and sand should be used. The tufts will lift themselves out of the ground with the force of the frustrated seed sowing pushing against hard ground. The best position is in full sun and it is an ideal small and interesting species for the miniature rock garden; it can go with Dianthus and the lesser Campanulas as it does not object to lime.

Though the carefully sown seed will germinate if removed from round the plant when it is ripe (about September), this is the most famous rootcutting subject of all. Dig up a plant in June, July or August, and remove some of the long white main roots, just a few, not more than one-third of the total, then replant your Morisia and water it well. In hot weather a broken branch of a Conifer or a cabbage leaf provides welcome temporary shade while it is recovering.

Cut up these roots into sections about half an inch long, lay them in a row with the upper ends all the same way, because there is so little taper in half an inch that once they are cut up it is almost impossible to tell which is right way up. Insert them in a pan of sand, with the tops, the upper ends, just level with the surface. Water them in and leave the pan in a closed cold frame, like any other pan of soft cuttings. Leaves and growing points will develop at the tops and roots at the bottoms, then in about six weeks after insertion the root cuttings are ready to pot, and grow on in a frame for spring planting.

If a struggling leaf appears at the base of a cutting, it has been inserted upside down, so dig it out and reverse it; any that lag behind usually have an unfortunate white shoot fighting to the surface. This plant has been used as a nature study subject in schools, but as a root-cutting demonstration, with the same sort of sections in sandy soil, with

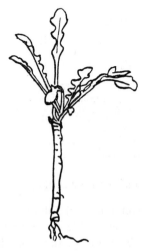

FIG. 20. Root cutting with two months' growth.

a pane of glass over the pan, turned night and morning to remove condensed moisture, the dandelion is better. It is larger and quicker, and points the lesson that some weeds you can dig in and some you should burn because even little bits of root will grow, however small and whichever way up they are. Docks, thistles, convolvulus and couch grass will all do it, but the dandelion is the most striking.

Nepeta. Catmint

The Common Catmint is common because it is a good tough plant for a poor soil, very hardy, easy and drought tolerant. It is not suitable for the rock garden, but is good with Helianthemums on the dry bank, as a wall plant, or as a perennial edging for the herbaceous border. Its correct name is *Nepeta Faassenii*, but as its incorrect one of *N. Mussinii* is always used by nurserymen it is best to keep to it.

Its grey foliage, and sprays of lavender flowers from May until late autumn are as well known as its smell of tom cats, which is not oppressive unless it is crushed. Remember that it will spread and flop over an eighteen inch circle, more in rich soil, and cut it back every autumn. It can be increased by tearing the clump to pieces in March or April and replanting where required, or from soft young shoots taken during April and inserted in the sand frame. Propagation is easy then, those who have difficulty with it are usually trying cuttings and division in the autumn. It is, however, a space filler rather than a plant to treasure.

Nierembergia rivularis

This small South American carpeter is fully hardy and a very useful plant for the small rock garden, paving, the alpine path or bulb cover. The flowers are large deep cups, about a shilling's diameter, creamy white and with a yellow pistil that shows at once the kinship with the tomato and the potato, which are also members of the order *Solanacæ*. They look upwards on very short stems in July and August from the thicket of small pointed oval leaves springing from the thickly woven branches that hug closely to the ground. Its total height is about an inch. Any ordinary light soil will grow it, with extra leafmould on heavy clay, and it can be relied on as a sturdy bread-and-butter plant. Propagation is by spring division and where a great number are needed the stems may be sliced up into lengths about an inch long and pricked out in a box for potting when they have filled it. This plant is now officially *N. repens*.

The shrubby Nierembergias, *N. caerulea* (which is also *N. hippomanica*) and *N. frutescens*, are not only on the tall side for the small rock garden but in most parts of Britain are not fully hardy.

Oenothera

The popular name of 'Evening Primrose' applies only to *Oe. biennis* which is a tall border plant; the species for the rock garden and dry wall have no English names, and they have just recovered from a botanical catastrophe. About 1934 the race was split into *Kneiffia*, *Lavauxia*, *Megapterium*, *Spahaerostigman Taraxia*, and other genera, but now, according to leading botanical authorities, they are all thankfully back as Oenotheras.

The best all-round Oenothera for the rock garden and dry wall is *Oe. riparia* (once *Kneiffia riparia*). This has long prostrate branches with narrow, pale green, willow-shaped leaves and pale yellow four-petalled flowers as wide across as a half-crown, which open from red-brown buds from June to about October. In the autumn it changes over to a different habit altogether. Small flat rosettes of rather longer leaves of a brownish deep green develop at the base of the stems, which can then be cut back like those of any other herbaceous plant. The easiest means of increase is to split up these rosettes in March before they change back again and either pot them for later planting when they are beginning to develop flower stems, or to go direct as rosettes where they are required. It can also be raised from seed sown in February, or from summer cuttings, taken from the flowering wood, with any buds that form pinched out, but these should not be put in later than August; July gives them more time to root and then change over to their winter habit. This species is now (1953) regarded as a variety of *Oe. tetragona*, but not by nurserymen.

This trailing species is best as a long-flowering dry wall plant, and the more upright *Oe. pumila* (ex *Kneiffia pumila*, formerly *Oe. pusilla* and latest name *Oe. perennis*) is better for the rock garden. This grows eight or nine inches high with golden yellow flowers rather smaller and set on short stalks where the narrow pointed leaves join the slender flower stems. Its winter habit, flowering season and increase are the same as *Oe. riparia*, and very roughly it can be regarded as a smaller flowered and upright variation on the same theme.

Both species grow well in any ordinary soil, are fully hardy and do best in full sun, but there are many more with even more names in their pasts for those who like them. Perhaps the most striking is *Oe. missourensis* (*Megapterium missourense* and quite often *Oe. macrocarpa*). This is a big sprawling plant with thick red-brown stems and dark green willow-shaped leaves, three or four inches long, with a strongly marked white midrib and veins. The flowers sit among these great branches, a plant two feet across is quite common, and resemble giant Evening Primroses. Each one is made up of four overlapping petals and is about four inches across, some as much as six. When they are first open they are a golden yellow, opening in the evening only, but as they age they stay out all day and change to an orange or apricot shade. They are on view from June until September in successive crops. In the winter this one drops all its leaves and the branches die back to a central root stock; it does not make a winter rosette.

This species is worth growing on a dry bank or the dry wall, never on the rock garden except a large one, and is easily raised from seed sown in the spring.

There are thirty-five Oenotheras in cultivation, many of them tall biennials and none really long lived, and except for those who get really fond of them, it is best to restrict the collection to these three.

Alpines Plant by Plant

Omphalodes cappadocica

This is a scarce but thoroughly useful plant which should be in every alpine garden. The leaves are broad, pointed ovals about 2½ inches long, dark green, and spring on short stalks from strong creeping stems. In June, July and August, flower sprays about eight inches high, of bright blue florets, each as wide across as an old-fashioned threepenny bit, are thrust up in great abundance. They are a real pure blue and rather resemble those of the dwarf Anchusa, *A. mysotidiflora*, but more compact, deeper and in greater quantity.

Put this plant on a rich soil and it will run to leaf and stem and give a far inferior display. It is best on a dry bank in semi-shade, even in dry shade, and thrives on a wall, needing a poor sandy soil with some leaf-mould though it is quite happy in a chalky garden. It is best increased by division in March or April for direct replanting where it is wanted; autumn division is not so effective as it is a species that loses its leaves in winter.

There is another species with the same needs, that is more strongly growing, that prefers more shade but flowers less freely, *O. verna* with a white centre to the florets that flowers earlier, in April and May. The slow growing species with blue-grey foliage, *O. Luciliae*, is not hardy for most people and is best kept for the alpine house by those whose pleasure in alpines comes from victory in battles with difficulties and slugs.

Onosma

The Onosmas are plants with furry leaves from the dry mountains of Turkey and Persia. On most rock gardens they are regarded as part hardy, the plants that flower one year and die before the next. Like the shaggier Androsaces they are, however, perfectly hardy on the dry wall and well worth growing there.

The least rare and perhaps the best is *Onosma echioides*, which has a woody root stock, and a thick mat of grey-green blunt-tipped hairy leaves. In May and June it puts up thick stems with more stout hairy leaves pointing along it until it curves over like a shepherd's crook, with large bell flowers hanging below it both single and in pairs. These bells are about an inch long and pucker in at the mouths, clear yellow in colour and so striking that they have earned the plant the popular name of 'Golden Drop'. This name is also applied to *O. tauricum*, which is rather bigger, with stems up to a foot high (the Onosmas are upward thrusters, not trailers, and this should be considered when planting a dry wall) and inch and a half long yellow flowers, but with the same hairy dark grey-green leaves. The flowers, like those of all Onosmas, have a scent of almonds.

Onosma albo-roseum (now officially *O. albo-pilosum*) has rather smaller leaves and these are a greyer green with denser hairs. The habit and flowering season are the same, but the bells open white with a red edge to the mouth, and turn pink as they grow older. This one is supposed to be less hardy than the others, it resents damp more, but it is usually quite safe on the wall.

All species are increased from cuttings, which should be taken after flowering, getting as long a shoot as possible, going back to the old wood; about two inches of young shoot is enough. These should be inserted in sand into a normal cold frame, and a powder hormone is an advantage to speed up the process. Their problem is that the furry leaves rot off with the moist conditions of the cutting frame. It is best to insert each cutting singly in a small pot of sand, or three spaced round the edges of a 48 pot, so that they do not touch each other and if one goes the rest are safe. They need much less water than normal cuttings—the hairy leaves are designed to reduce transpiration and economise water in a dry rock cleft—therefore they should always be rooted where their tastes can be considered. Some nurserymen have a separate dry cutting frame for these and other fur-leaved plants.

In the autumn it is a good plan to clean up established Onosmas. They are evergreen, but the over-age leaves die off and remain a black and slow decaying collection against the wall. If these are pulled off with care there is less chance of the general humidity of our winters rotting off even *O. albo-roseum* in our wetter districts.

Ourisia coccinea

There is some doubt as to whether this species is really *O. elegans*, but by now there is probably only the Ourisia that Reginald Farrar found easy left in cultivation; the difficult one, which may have a better right to the name, is extinct. *Ourisia coccinea* has jagged-edged, heart-shaped leaves, pale green and set on thick ridgy barked stems that root to the ground from the undersides and is a good mat forming plant for a leafy soil of the kind that does woodland Gentians, or a place among the damp-loving Primulas. Out of flower it is about two inches high, but in June and July the many flower stems, with narrow, scarlet trumpets in twos and threes, bring it up to six or eight.

The trumpet mouths have three divisions at the bottom and two at the top and are about half an inch across. Seed is not often set, but increase is easy from division in spring about April. The plant comes from the Cape Horn end of South America; there are a number of species from New Zealand but as yet it is not known if they are going to be fully hardy for they are still mainly in botanic gardens.

Penstemon

The Penstemons are a huge race and many are massive herbaceous plants; the few species described here are those which are not only small, but flower well, for so many species make a massive bush with merely a few florets in meagre spikes here and there.

The best is still perhaps *P. rupicola*, which used to be called *P. Roezlii*. This is about six inches high including flower spikes and is a low bush which can grow to a foot across. The leaves are small and leathery, slightly toothed at the edges, and grey green with a reddish tint that is shown more strongly in the young stems. The flowers are long narrow tubes of bright coral red in spikes of up to eight; they appear from May to July, and as many as a dozen at once are common on established plants.

The best position is in full sun, with some shelter from wind, on any normal alpine soil, but a limy one is preferred; the plant is fully hardy and should be on every small rock garden. It is sometimes incorrectly called *P. Newberryi var. rupicola*, but it is an outstandingly good species in its own right. There is a dwarf form, or hybrid with *P. rupicola* blood, called *P.* Weald Beacon, which is as hardy and free flowering, but in June and July only, that grows no higher than three inches.

The other Penstemons are rather a let down after this. There are *P. confertus* with larger oval leaves and creamy yellow florets, about four inches high; *P. Scouleri*, an eight inch bush with narrow pointed leaves and lilac flowers; and the hybrid *P.* Six Hills which has rosy lilac flowers in a succession from June to August, but not in any real quantity at once, also a six incher.

Those who like Penstemons, and the race has keen fans willing to argue fiercely in defence of their dingiest and floppiest treasures, will find many more, but most of them are more fitted to the large herbaceous border than for alpine gardening.

The blue Penstemon, *P. heterophyllus*, is quite a good wall plant and for those who do not mind eighteen inch plants on the rock garden it is an alpine shrub. It has long pointed leaves and upright, red-barked stems, with long flower spikes of small florets from June to August. These should be cut back after they are over to maintain the display. There are many forms. 'True Blue' is reputed to be the best but all the blues have got pink in them and where the standard is set by Gentians, they are rather messy colours. This species is not as hardy as the others in the north and is best used on the dry wall facing south; it is inclined to get greenfly, and, as with the others on occasion, derris dusting may be needed in summer.

The Penstemons are all increased easily from soft cuttings after flowering; many can be raised from seed but so many species are variable, which gives great scope for argument, that those who have one they like should stick to the sand frame. They will root quite well from late cuttings wintered in the frame for spring potting and later planting.

Petrocallis pyrenaica

This plant, once *Draba pyrenaica* but now no longer linked with a rather unrewarding race, is one of the essential small alpines. It grows as a neat low mound of tiny rosettes and in May and June has a generous show of small star-like flowers, lilac purple in colour and sweetly scented.

It likes a sunny place and a gritty, limy soil, exactly like its best companions, the Kabschia Saxifrages, and it is increased and grown in exactly the same way, and is even more pleasant to have.

Phlox. Alpine Phlox

The alpine Phloxes can be split into three groups, the subulatas, with narrow gorse-like foliage, the Douglasiis, which have smaller, shorter and wider leaves and grow more slowly, and the broad-leaved type, of which *P. stolonifera* is characteristic.

The hybrids of *Phlox subulata* are ideal wall and dry bank plants, good in the alpine border and better still on the large rock garden. They grow in any soil but a peaty one, and will thrive in dried-up chalky gardens as well as in soot and smog. Next to Aubrieta they are the most essential alpines for beginners. Their foliage varies but the leaves are spiny and evergreen and the flowers like clusters of rather smaller and much less solid florets of those of a border Phlox, on short stems in real sheets in May and June. Any one of the following will spread to two feet across, but they can be cut back freely in spring or autumn if they get out of hand.

Increase is very easy from soft cuttings in July and August in the normal sand frame, it is not even necessary to remove the lowest pair of leaves. Those who need a few for replacements need merely put some leafmould among the outer branches and place a stone on them, the plants layer themselves naturally, and these rooted branches can be cut off about April and replanted where they are needed. One can also fill a plant with leafmould (simply to encourage rooting; peat or even light soil will do) during the summer and build the rooted fragments into the dry wall in the same way as Aubrieta.

The best of all is perhaps *P. Temiscaming*, the new almost crimson variety, which completely outclasses the old *P. atropurpurea*; it averages six inches high and is a strong grower like the pale slaty violet *P. G. F. Wilson* and *P. Margery* which is a pale rose pink. Rather more compact, the 'gorse spines' closer together and about four inches high with a slightly slower rate of spread, are *P.* Apple Blossom, pale pink; *P.* Brightness, rather deeper; *P.* Eventide like a smaller, paler G. F. Wilson; *P.* Fairy, lilac with a dark eye; *P. Moerheimii*, rose pink with a dark central ring; *P. Nelsoni*, white with a pink ring; and *P.* Sampson, deep pink with a darker eye. The best white is May Snow (or Snow Queen) which is a Douglasii type with subulata vigour. Its leaves are broad and a paler green, the plant is flatter, three to four inches, and the florets are more solid and less stary, released in one snow white sheet in April and May. The nearest to a salmon pink is *P.* Betty, which is a six incher but more compact, making a neater bush than the others in this height group; it is reputed to be a good form of the old *P. Camlaensis* (or Camla Var.) raised by the late Mr. F. W. Millard, which was a good colour but not robust. The other salmon, *P.* Vivid, seems to have deteriorated like some varieties of potato. It was always a weaker grower with smaller spines and less powerful branches, but those in cultivation now are a shadow of the plants of the 1920's. The old form, or something near it, is reputed to survive as '*P.* Sensation' which was a name formerly used for *P.* Vivid.

Like Helianthemums, with which they should be associated as often as Lobelia and Geraniums in the bedding of the past, on the dry bank of today, the *Phlox subulata* hybrids are a bit muddled. Any collection from a number of nurserymen will contain duplicates under different names, and often the same plant from three firms will be three separate varieties. The best policy is to get the main batch from one firm with a good collection, and then pick up new kinds with caution; there is no standard list with *R.H.S. Colour Chart* references, but it is easy enough to increase those you like and replace the less attractive.

The *P. Douglasii* hybrids can be used on the front of a dry bank, but they are more suited to the small rock garden; they are less vigorous weed suppressors. The spines are shorter, more like pairs of small triangles, usually about a quarter of an inch long, set alternate ways and closer together on the shorter stems. The flowers are more solid, the petals overlap a little and the florets are smaller but can be produced in even greater quantity. The best is perhaps *P. Douglasii* Boothman's Variety, lavender with a deeper eye; *P. Douglasii* Eva is nearer pink with a dark eye; *P. Douglasii* Lilac Queen is lilac without the eye; and *P. Douglasii* Rose Queen (also known as *P. Douglasii rosea* and *P. Mabel*) is a clear self pink. This one is unfortunately difficult to flower, it can give a splendid show or hardly anything and a great mass of foliage. *P.* Beauty of Ronsdorf is reputed to be a *P. Douglasii* hybrid that is both pink and free flowering.

This group are best with full sun and a limy soil, not too rich, on the normal rock garden; they are increased by soft cuttings in the same way as the *P. subulata* hybrids, but they cannot be increased by rough layering so easily. The true *P. Douglasii* is much smaller and slower, a two inch high mat former with almost stemless flowers, sometimes a real pale blue, but this treasure for the pan and the small rock garden seems to have vanished in World War II.

First of the broad-leaved Phloxes (which is not a botanical classification, just an unscientific group for gardeners' use only), is the lovely *P. bifida*, which is just coming into cultivation. This makes a creeping surface stem or rhizome from which spring short sturdy branches with relatively long (half to one inch) flat pointed leaves. It makes a compact bush from three to six inches high, with heads of pure white flowers in May, June and July (if the dead ones are snipped out). The individual florets are about an inch in diameter and are shaped like Maltese crosses with an extra arm. As this species has fourteen chromosomes, like the other members of the race, there is scope for the hybridiser to produce a third class of good all round alpines for everyone, which may even surpass the parents in garden merit, as the *P. subulata* hybrids outshine the original species. Meanwhile, *P. bifida* is a good all-round non-invasive alpine for a normal soil on any small rock garden, increased by spring division, or soft cuttings after flowering.

The broad-leaved Phloxes in general like plenty of leafmould in the soil—many do not have sufficiently powerful roots to force through hard ground. A John Innes Compost will do them nicely, but leafmould is better than peat as a lightener and moisture retainer. They prefer less dry conditions than the other two groups and are best on the small rock garden or in the alpine border.

The strongest and most popular is *P. stolonifera* (formerly *P. reptans* and *P. verna*), which has oval leaves on stems that root into the ground at the joints like strawberry runners, making a low, evergreen mat. In April and May it puts up stout six inch flower stems with clusters of

Phlox florets about three-quarters of an inch across, a good deep pink in colour. It is a woodland plant from Pennsylvania, U.S.A. and grows well in semi-shade. Even better is the new variety *P. stolonifera* Blue Ridge which is the first really blue Phlox, even though there is a touch of violet in it. The clusters are even larger, and it flowers in May and June. Both are increased by division of the runners after flowering, July or August, or soft cuttings, about three joints long, at the same time.

Phlox amoena varies. It has dark green, pointed leaves about an inch long, in pairs, making what is almost a small bush, the stem joints are so short; and though it will spread to about a foot across, it is slow growing and a very good plant for any rock garden, in full sun on a normal alpine soil. Its usual height is four inches, but in May and June its compact clusters of solid florets bring it up to six. The true plant is a bluish purple, but white forms are known, and there is a variegated form with creamy edges to the leaves. The most common form is, however, deep rose pink and this is often called *P. amoena rosea* by sensible nurserymen. All variations root rather better from soft cuttings in April than the harder-stemmed shoots which can be taken in August and September, though a hormone is a great help where the best season has been missed. They are easy in sand frame or pan, and make good stuff for spring planting from April cuttings, wintered in pots.

The last of the really useful amateur Phloxes is *P. procumbens*, which is a cross between *P. amoena* and *P. subulata*. This is prostrate and more of a trailing plant, with smaller leaves, half or three-quarters of an inch long, but also flat and pointed, not spiny and gorse-like. It flowers in May and June with clusters of pinkish mauve flowers, and a total height of four inches; it is also suitable for wall planting where it will not get excessively dry.

Among the remainder of the race are many taller species, half way to border Phloxes with less brilliant flowers. *P. divaricata*, and *P. divaricata Laphamii* are pale violet blue, and *P. pilosa* also violet with long hairy leaves, are characteristic; they are of value to the hybridist and those who specialise. *Phlox adsurgens* is often grown as an alpine. It is semi-prostrate and trailing, with bright green pointed oval leaves and clusters of salmon pink flowers in June and July, but is a lime hater, and curiously chancy in its choice of soils. It is increased by soft cuttings after flowering and is best in semi-shade on the rock garden. Still more difficult is *P. nana ensifolia*, usually known as *P. mesoleuca*, which has long slender leaves and rather a *P. subulata* type habit, with varying flowers, white, purple and even yellow. It is reputed to grow well in light dry soil where it can become a 'veritable weed' but it is rarely seen except in an alpine house. This plant is also confused with *P. triovulata* and possesses all the qualities of *The Times* crossword puzzle for the Third Programme type alpine enthusiast.

Polygala

The Polygalas are charming small shrubs with decided tastes, and all are really good subjects for the small rock garden.

Polygala calcarea is a round mat of wiry branches with small (half inch) long oval dark green leaves, which is well covered in May and June with short spikes of pure blue flowers; The height is rarely as much as two inches and this is mostly flower; the spikes are more than an inch long with up to twelve florets. A plant eight inches in diameter is a veteran. They need a position in full sun and a chalky soil—this Polygala is a native of British chalk hills, and it insists on its normal diet. A good lump of chalk broken up and mixed with the soil before planting is all that is required and prevents the sulky growth usually seen on nurseries where this plant is grown in plain John Innes Compost. Blackboard chalk is insoluble calcium sulphate and so is plaster; ground limestone seems too slowly available. Like the British tourist demanding a nice cup of tea in all the countries of the world, *P. calcarea* insists on chalk and does its very good best on the diet.

The plant can be increased by division in spring, about April, from soft cuttings after flowering, which are small and fiddling but easy to root, or seed when available, sown in the early spring.

The other Polygalas are humus lovers and lime haters, for sun or semi-shade on the small rock garden; they are utterly different in appearance so there is no chance of confusion. The humus lovers do well in a John Innes Compost with leafmould instead of peat, or a Lithospermum mixture. They are *P. Chamaebuxus*, whose name derives from its resemblance to box edging; its leaves are shaped like those of a box but rather larger and narrower in proportion, dark green and set on short branch stems making a bush from four to six inches high. These shoots spring from underground runners, which are not invasive, and solve the propagation question: they can be divided in the early spring, though soft cuttings after flowering are easy to root. The flowers are rather like those of a gorse bush but more slender though about the same size, cream on the upper portions and golden yellow on the 'keel' which deepens to almost a bronze when the flowers have been open some time. Their main display is in May and June, but they will keep producing stragglers through the rest of the summer. There are two variations, *P. Chamaebuxus purpurea* (also known as *P. Chamaebuxus grandiflora*) which has larger flowers, magenta purple below and with yellow above, and a carmine and pale yellow species, *P. Chamaebuxus var. rhodoptera* which is rare but worth finding.

A lime-hating species, which needs *Lithospermum* Heavenly Blue soil and situation, is *P. paucifolia* which has narrower leaves a darker and more bronzy green, and with trailing stems which are bare for quite a bit of their length, hence the specific name. The flowers are bright rose purple, with an orange upper portion, and their season is from May to August. The second of this type is *P. Vayredae*, which has the same leaf type—they tend to point upwards along the stem—but is more of a bush, about four inches high. The flowering season for the pink and yellow, pea-like blooms is May and June.

Both these species are best in some shade, they resent getting too dry in summer, and are increased from soft cuttings after flowering or from non-flowering wood during the display; June and July are the best months. They are both hardy under the right conditions; a 'round Polygala in a square hole' is the usual cause of the loss.

Polygonum

The best of the race, which includes our native weed Redshank, is *P. vacciniifolium*. This is a plant it pays to starve on the dry wall or bank; its thick mat of red brown barked branches and brownish green, willow-shaped leaves will become a flowerless and swamping mass on the rock garden with richer soil.

In the right place it is a valuable 'after the Aubrieta' alpine. An established plant will produce a long succession of clear, pale pink flower spikes, about two inches high, of tightly packed florets like small beads, from July to October, usually with the main show in September. It has no special soil tastes, is fully hardy and very long lived. On the dry wall it is a downward trailer and is best cut back with shears in April after it has begun to make new growth, if it is inclined to get bare at the base.

Propagation is easy by cutting up the trailing branches that root into the ground at the joints, by soft cuttings, not only tips but two jointed sections all the way down a stem, or cuttings six inches long inserted upright in trenches in the open ground. Taken in June or July these large cuttings are suitable for direct building in the dry wall, like Phlox layerings. There are forms of this plant which are less free flowering so the best specimens only should be increased; the time to secure this species by visiting a nursery is in September when the parent stock plant should be in bloom.

237

Polygonum affine is rather better known. It has wide, pale green leaves up to four inches long, springing directly from creeping stems; these leaves turn bronzy red in the autumn and winter and are replaced in the spring. It is a mat former not a trailer. Its flowers are upright spires like those of *P. vacciniifolium*, also pink, but six or even eight inches high, in August and September. A dark red form has been raised at Wisley, *P. affine* Darjeeling Red (the plant is from the Himalayas) which is less powerful and when this is in commerce it will be a real treasure.

These two large Polygonums are suitable for the dry bank and the alpine border, in full sun on any soil, but not the rock garden, except a very large one where it is desired to cover the ground to reduce weeding. They are easily increased by division and direct replanting in March or April.

Potentilla

The most desirable Potentilla for the small rock garden is *P. verna nana*, which grows flat on the ground as a mat of small bright green leaves rather like those of an Acaena, studded with stemless yellow Geum-like flowers from April to August. It is as good on the rock garden as in the pan, an inch high and slow growing, preferring full sun and happy in any normal alpine soil. The other species in this class, *P. aurea* and *P. ambigua* (now *P. cuneata*), have the same type of foliage, low growing and bright green; those of the latter are divided into five parts instead of three, and they flower in May and June with larger short stemmed buttercups up to three-quarters of an inch instead of under half an inch, but less generously. They are equally easy on any soil, and they both will reach three inches high.

The white flowered species, *P. alba*, also grows three inches tall but is much stronger; its leaves are grey green and white on the undersides, it has stronger branches that push out and extend the area, and the flowers are in clusters of two and three and each individual is up to an inch across. They are spread over from April to September and the display is most generous on a poor, lime-lovers' mixture; with a richer soil this plant can be a disappointment. This sort of situation suits the slower growing and far more attractive *P. nitida*, which has grey green or silvery white foliage and clear rose pink flowers in June and July. It is two inches high, and has leaves divided into three parts (like all Gaul), not five like *P. alba*, but neither will flower unless starved.

All these small rock garden Potentillas root from small, soft cuttings between June and August—a hormone is a help for those who need plants quickly; they do not divide easily because the branches go back to a central root stock, though *P. verna nana* can usually be split, in March or April. When the seed is available it should be sown about February, and any more generous variations of the less free flowering species propagated from cuttings.

Charles Darwin's *Origin of Species* did more unseen damage to the Linnean system, based on the idea that each species was fixed and unchanging, needing only description and cataloguing like a stamp collection, than to the Catholic Church. Some plants vary less than others, but the number 'of Garden origin' bears witness not only to natural hybridisation but to Darwinian variation, when a species is collected in some other country of the world, and 'originates' one that suits our gardens but may not fit the description made from the collected dried specimen in the herbarium. That semi-impossible plant from the Straits of Magellan, *Calceolaria Darwinii*, seems to have been trying hard for years, to judge by reports of hardy forms; some day it may become a good waterside species, by evolution, helped by appreciative gardeners.

The taller and more floppy Potentillas are best on the dry wall, their foliage is not dense enough for weed strangling on the dry bank. Among these *P. fragiformis*, with very near-strawberry leaves, dark green and hairy, is tough and easy, the flowers in May and June are in clusters and up to an inch across. This plant has a close relation, *P. megalantha*, which differs mainly in having larger flowers, up to an inch and a half diameter. Both are yellow, and the nine inch flower stems are far more freely produced when the plants are starved on a sunny wall. Seed is freely set and spring sowing produces great quantities of plants. *Potentilla rupestris* is a large white flowering species, with leaves more like those of a wild strawberry, and red-barked, foot long stems with flower clusters in July and August, equally easy from seed and suited for the wall garden.

The best wall Potentilla is *P. Tonguei*, which is a hybrid, with dark green, five divisions, wild strawberry leaves, and strong red-barked stems about a foot long with clusters of apricot yellow flowers, each with a crimson centre. Their season is from July to September and after flowering, about October, the plant should be cut back hard. It can be divided in the spring, or when it starts to produce new growth from the base, in April, shoots about two inches long can be removed and rooted with or without a hormone. One of the parents is *P. nepalensis*, which will grow two foot branches though not in the dry wall, with crimson flower clusters; another hybrid with this parent is *P. nepalensis* Miss Willmott, rose pink, and *P. nepalensis Roxana*, which is orange scarlet. All are 'of Garden origin' and flower as long as *P. Tonguei*; they need

239

much staking in the herbaceous border, and run to foliage, but on the dry wall they have a new sphere of usefulness.

There are many other border Potentillas which are better on the dry wall than in the border, hybrids of *P. argyrophylla* with three-division leaves more solid than the *P. nepalensis* group. These include Gibson's Scarlet, William Rollinson, large double orange flowers; Yellow Queen, double yellow; Monsieur Rouillard, crimson with an orange blotch on the petals; and Hamlet, a double dark red. They flower from June to August and are increased in the same way as the *P. nepalensis* varieties. They are not plants for the alpine purist, but they do give a good show on the dry wall.

Primula

The Primulas are an overwhelming race: the number of species, varieties and hybrids is almost beyond counting, and they range in size from the tiny jewel-like *P. minima* to the giant *P. Florindae*, a monster Cowslip over three feet high. By careful selection you can have Primulas in flower for eight months of the year, and in mild winters the Primrose type flower continually and inspire many letters to the Press.

The colour range of Primulas is very wide and in one group or another almost every colour is represented. Another attraction of this great and lovely family is that many are sweetly scented. The scent of *P. capitata*, *P. involucrata*, *P. sikkimensis* and *P. Florindae* is delicate and charming, and the fragrance of *P. alpicola* rises in waves to meet you as you pass on a still summer day.

Just like Gentians, Primulas have a reputation for being difficult and this is true of many species, but there are plenty of easy ones for all soils from chalk to peat, and all aspects from dry and sunny positions to the wettest corner in shade. In fact, unlike Gentians, the most lovely are the easiest to grow.

Let us start with those which will grow in full sun on the small rock garden. The easiest and hardiest are the hybrids of *P. pubescens*, a subdivision of the large Auricula family of Primulas which keep their leaves all winter. They can be described most easily as miniature Auriculas. They have the same tough, leathery, grey green leaves, and grow as neat clumps with compact heads of often sweet-smelling flowers on small but stout stems; a feature of these flowers is the depth and clarity of their colours. A selection of the best and easiest varieties includes Faldonside, a compact hybrid with rich crimson flowers and a height of two inches including bloom and stem; Mrs. J. H. Wilson, very free flowering with larger heads of violet florets with white centres, three inches high; and

25. *Campanula gargauica* is a clump former rather than a trailing species and a very good wallplant for June and July flowering. The star-shaped flowers are clear pale blue, those of the variety W. H. Paine are deeper blue with white centres, but both should be increased from cuttings; seedlings can be very poor

26. *Erodium macradenum*, pale purple with black centres, flowers from May to September. This long-flowering race, some of which go on until October, is essential for dry walls, alpine borders, and rock gardens. *Erodiums* are one of the many answers to the ignorant who consider annuals should be sown for summer colour, after Aubrieta

The General, with terra cotta flowers, also three inches. They come easily from seed though not true to name, and a batch of mixed seedlings will give a colour range with variations that may include something really good. The flowering season is May, though stray blooms often appear in the course of the summer.

The named varieties can be increased by careful division after flowering, about July, or where the small short-stemmed bush can spare some branches, from soft cuttings in August. These need about an inch between growing point and bottom joint; remove the lower leaves and insert in a pan of sand so that the neat little cabbages do not touch each other, and keep them relatively dry, like Onosmas. They root well and should be potted in a rich gritty soil with some lime, which is what they prefer to grow in on the rock garden.

Another good Primula for the same soil and situation, but with a taste for more lime, is *P. marginata*. This has longer stems that trail in a modest way, and grey powdered leaves with rather saw-edged margins. The flowers are larger heads of up to twenty florets on four inch stems in March and April, a bluish lilac usually, but red violet is known. It has a lovely but expensive hybrid Linda Pope, with lavender blue flowers, and a good form *P. marginata rosea*, which is nearer a lilac pink. These are increased from seed, sown like that of *P. pubescens* as soon as it is gathered, or in the spring if it is bought, on the grit system. Also, cuttings may be taken in July and rooted as above.

On the lower slopes of the rock garden and where there is damp and shade, a further group of Primulas can be grown. They need standard leafy mixture which retains the moisture anyway, but with rather more loam than normal. One of the earliest and loveliest is *P. Clarkei*, which grows as more of a mat than a clump of rounded leaves, with heads of from one to six small clear pink flowers on very short stems in April and May. See that it does not dry out and is away from stronger growing plants, and increase from division after it has flowered. This species is from high in the Himalayas, and it has only recently been discovered that it is the toughest of the 'tinies' (about two inches high) for ordinary gardens.

Another good one for this situation is *P. farinosa*, our native 'Bird's Eye Primrose' from damp upland meadows in English and Scottish hills. When it is grown from seed (the best way to increase it) sown in July or August, you get a range of colours; purple, lilac, pink and even white, all with a yellow eye. The rounded heads of florets are carried on six inch stems in May and June, though it has been known to flower earlier. Both *P. farinosa* and *P. Clarkei* lose their leaves in winter.

Q

Primula frondosa, from Bulgaria, has small florets of the same type and size, pale purple, but on three inch stems, in April and May. It has very mealy leaves, almost white underneath, and likes the same leafy soil and a cool shady place. Another species for this position is *P. capitata Mooreana*, which also has mealy leaves but they are gathered into small compact rosettes. This flowers usually from July to September with stems from six to twelve inches high, each topped with a flat disc of florets each about two inches across, shaped almost exactly like the small hammer a doctor uses to test one's knee jerk. Their colour is deep violet blue, and they are sweetly scented. They often flower at other seasons, and stand up to more drought than *P. frondosa*. Though the individual plants may flower themselves to death in two seasons, they set plenty of seed in nut-like capsules, and spring-sown replacements are very easy to raise.

Two other good Primulas for the small rock garden are *P. rosea grandiflora* and *P. involucrata*. The first flowers in April and May with heads of five to twelve florets, each three-quarters of an inch across, on stout stems from six to eight inches high. Their colour is a good clear pink, and the leaves, which are pointed and a rather bronzy green in low rosettes, develop rather later than the first flowers. This one can be increased easily from division after flowering, or in quantity from seed sown as soon as it is ripe, for choice from early heads to give more time to grow good plants before they go dormant for the winter. *P. involucrata* has narrow oval leaves and stems nearly a foot high, with loose heads of large white florets tinged with lilac, blooming in April and May. It is one of the most sweetly scented of all Primulas and worth growing for this alone. Both these two will thrive in a damp place and are reputed to dislike lime, but with ample leafmould they will do well on the normal rock garden on any soil.

The European, Primrose or 'Wanda' type Primulas, are not really suited for the small rock garden, except one that must be made in a sunless corner. Their best use is under trees, as edging for beds, in the alpine border, and everywhere with moderate moisture where something easy is required. The original Wanda is too well known to need description, with its purple Primrose flowers and compact Primrose leaves. Its only real enemy in a town garden is the London sparrow, which will pick the blooms.

There are a great many other hybrids, and the following are a selection of those which are entirely different from the sparrow's friend in colour: Betty Green, bright scarlet; David Green, intense crimson with a yellow eye, robust, early and free flowering, one of the best; E. R.

Janes, orange rose; Romeo, large parma violet flowers; Snow Queen, good white; and *Altaica grandiflora*, clear pink. The Garryarde hybrids have bronzy leaves and a small head of flowers like a neater and true perennial Polyanthus; Garryarde Guinevere is the best known, with lavender pink flowers; Lady Greer is a neat small cowslip, with a generous display of creamy yellow flower heads, and Mrs. J. H. Wilson is a lavender version. The thicker main stems of these two seem to defeat most sparrows.

Original root
cutting—dead

FIG. 21. Plant of *Primula denticulata* lifted for propagation,
straight lines show individual root cuttings.

These Primulas will grow in almost any soil and situation, and are increased by division as soon as their spring flowers are over; if they are planted somewhere damp they can be split up again in the autumn.

There are a number of Double Primroses and these seem to be returning to favour. They need a richer soil with more leafmould, and those who can give them cow dung or good compost will grow them best. It is essential to divide them at least every other year in June or July, as they seem to resent *not* being disturbed. Many of these are very slow to increase, but the following are the easiest for those who like them: Bonaccord Lavender, lavender; Bonaccord Purity, white; Marie Crouse, royal purple, edged white; Red Paddy, crimson with silver lacing; Our Pat, nearest to blue, and Quaker Bonnet, lilac.

The most splendid Primulas of all are the 'wet' ones, the species from the Himalayas and the Far East, for the bog garden, the artificial wet corner, and the woodland garden. They vary in the amount of damp they need; some will grow wherever you can grow a Polyanthus well, and if you have sufficient damp during the hottest part of the summer, they will thrive in full sun. Their glory is that they grow and flower brilliantly in shade, and though they come from the sides of mountain streams and in deep gorges on the roof of the world, they do well in town gardens. Practically all of them lose their leaves in winter, thus not only dodging the winter smoke but the fresh crop of foliage is working at its best when the flower stems need the food.

They prefer an acid soil, and the standard leafy mixture with some extra loam is ideal for them. A John Innes potting soil with some of the peat replaced by leafmould is good, though a complete recipe is given in Chapter 6. They are not suitable for the small rock garden, though they will thrive on a large one in damp pockets, and can be seen every year in all their splendour on the rock gardens at Kew and Wisley.

The first to flower is *P. denticulata*, which is so tough that it will grow anywhere that *P. Wanda* will, though it is a good bog species. It has long leaves with a strongly marked white midrib, and drumstick heads of flowers, lilac, pink, dark purple and even red. The white form is dignified as *P. denticulata alba*; the others are seedling variations, except the dark violet which is *P. denticulata* Hay's variety. The hybrids known as *P. denticulata* Ascot Red are nearest this colour. Those who have a good colour should increase from root cuttings taken during the winter, and keep it true. These drumstick heads on six to twelve inch stems are about two inches across, though they vary in size, and they are on view from March to April. Like all this group, their stems are too thick for sparrow beaks.

The others can be divided into Candelabra types, with whorl upon whorl of florets going up and up the flower stem, and Cowslip types, with a head of hanging florets on a long stalk. The last group is usually scented.

The best Candelabras are *P. japonica* and *P. pulverulenta* and their hybrids, many of which come perfectly true from seed. The two leading hybrids of *P. japonica* are *P.* Millers Crimson and *P.* Postford White, but the original *P. japonica* varies from red to pale pink. The flower spikes in May and June are tall, up to two feet, and they run to as many

244

as six tiers of bloom. Each layer is made up of florets more than three-quarters of an inch across the mouths, and their solid circle is often wider than five inches through. They are strong enough to stand Polyanthus conditions, but are at their best in wet situations. A very good Primula corner of my acquaintance receives the overflow of a septic tank; there they have now proved immune to modern detergents and bathwater soap.

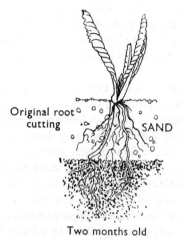

Original root cutting   SAND

Two months old

FIG. 22. *Primula denticulata* root cutting, two months old, half natural size.

Primula pulverulenta is magenta crimson, with a mealy stem and a taller spike, up to three feet high. The whorls are smaller but greater in number, twelve being the record. It is the parent of many hybrids, and *P. pulverulenta* Bartley Strain, with its splendid shell pink whorls, is the most striking and the best. *P.* Red Hugh is almost a scarlet, but it is not so hardy and long lived as the first two.

In this height group comes the best yellow Candelabra, *P. helodoxa*, which is the vivid yellow of butter in Cornwall when the butter is made locally. This one has a popular name 'Glory of the Bog', but it will take moderately dry conditions. It has fewer florets to a whorl, which are rather larger than those of *P. pulverulenta*, and it runs up to two feet high, and more if by a stream side in a lucky garden. Very near in flower shape, though with leaves that are bluntly rounded not pointed, is *P. Wilsoni*, which is for practical purposes a purple *P. helodoxa*. Grown together the two make a lovely contrast; both flower in June and July and as they are distinct species they come true from seed.

245

Coming down in height among the Candelabras are *P. Bulleyana*, with orange whorls paling slightly to orange yellow, in May and June, about eighteen inch level; *P. Beesiana* is the same size but lilac, and both have good solid whorls and plenty of them. They hybridise freely, and the offspring include many good pastel shades; the race is usually known as *P. Asthore*. *P. aurantiaca* is apricot orange, with red flower stems and midribs, and its hybrids are the same size but ring the changes on the others, with many shades in between.

Where these Primulas are going well they seed themselves freely. The seedlings can be moved with plenty of soil and planted in a damp and shady bed to grow on, but it is just as well to leave them; the result is charming.

The grandest of the Cowslip type is *P. Florindae* which has large roundish leaves; a great powerful thing in a wet place, though smaller with drought, and stems as much as half an inch through, going up to three feet, and bearing a head of hanging florets, as many as forty of them, on a grand scale. It flowers later than the others, beginning in June and often going on until August, the latest of all the bog Primulas. It comes true from seed, and is so tough that attempts have been made to naturalise it in the west of Scotland. The Sikkim Cowslip, *P. sikkimensis*, has longer, narrower leaves compared with others of its type, and hanging florets of a soft pleasing yellow in a loose head on top of an eighteen inch stem. It begins to flower early in May and keeps going well into June, with odd flowers even later. It sets plenty of seed, which comes true to colour but not always leaf shape, and the flowers are scented.

Even more sweetly scented is *P. alpicola* (formerly *P. microdonta*, and now *P. sikkimensis var. alpicola*) which is sulphur yellow with a very mealy stem about a foot or fifteen inches high. It flowers in May and June, and its leaves are rather like those of *P. sikkimensis* but rounder. There is a reddish violet species with yellow inside the florets, *P. alpicola violacea*, and a white one *P. alpicola alba*, but if seed is saved from any one of these it results in all three colours and variations between them, so it is best to regard the plant as a charming mixture.

Two other species of this type are worth adding; *P. secundiflora* with narrow leaves in a more compact rosette, mealy white on the under sides, and thickly clustered heads of florets, the colour of good port, with silver markings on the backs of each, a good contrast. It is about eighteen inches high, a May and June species, not so fond of damp as the others and preferring more woodland conditions. *P. Waltoni* is a crimson Cowslip type, eighteen inches tall, and is later in flowering, usually June and July. *P. secundiflora* comes true from seed, but *P. Waltoni* varies in shade.

All these strong Primulas suffer greatly from pot cultivation. If they get their roots coiled round in a tight ball, it takes them ages to reach any size, and they remain stunted and starved. Those who buy Primulas should insist on open-ground plants for the spring or autumn; there is no gain at all in potting them. The cheapest method is to buy small plants as seedlings to plant direct, with watering to start them, as though they were Polyanthus; these are usually half the price of a plant no larger that has been starved in a pot.

The seed should be sown either as soon as it is ripe—sow thinly in boxes and prick out like Antirrhinums, about twenty-four plants in a good deep box for spring planting—or sow in the spring, and prick out for summer planting. It is possible to divide these wet Primulas in the early spring, when they start to wake up, putting them directly where they are required; or after they have finished flowering. September is a good time so that they can take hold before they go dormant for the winter.

This of course does not apply to the difficult ones, only to the hardy easy species that should tower in every garden where they can have damp and shade to enjoy. Those who wish to specialise in Primulas are refered to the excellent book *Primulas in the Garden* by Kenneth C. Corsar (Lindsay Drummond).

Pterocephalus

Pterocephalus perennis Parnassi is a dwarf Scabious (formerly *Scabiosa pterocephalus*) and an excellent wall plant, good also for paving and on the small rock garden. It needs a poor soil and plenty of sun and lime, otherwise it will give more foliage than flowers. The leaves are silver grey and make a thick mat of foliage with woody creeping stems four inches high, less when well starved. The flowers are relatively large, pale pink Scabious heads, rather like those of the annual species (with a cushion in the middle) in July and August.

These flowers are often as much as an inch and a half across and are carried on short stems low down on the dome of grey leaves. There is, according to the *R.H.S. Dictionary of Gardening*, a purple flowered type, the true *P. Parnassi* (the pink should be *P. perennis*); and a real good purple, not a pale lilac, would be a splendid plant, for there is insufficient colour difference between leaf and flower to make the Pterocephalus stocked by every nursery more than attractive in a quiet way. A holiday in Greece could well provide seed of the best and deepest colours, which would be worth far more climbing than any Edelweiss.

Increase is best from division in April or soft cuttings in May. They root best before flowering and should be taken from the longer shoots round the edges, avoiding the buds.

Ramonda

Ramonda Myconi (formerly *R. pyrenaica,* it comes from the Pyrenees) is one of the best wall plants for shade or semi-shade; on the small rock garden it should be squeezed in between two rocks, either on a horizontal or an upright joint. It is one of the several plants that are tender on the flat and perfectly hardy edgeways, because they naturally grow in crevices. This is an advantage on the rock garden because it is occupying otherwise unused vertical space.

The comparatively large dark green crinkly leaves often form a flat clump the size of a saucer, increasing to a colony along the crevice, with clusters of violet blue flowers with buttercup yellow eyes on three inch stems from May to September. In the dry wall it is the longest flowered species that is happy in shade, for the shade lovers usually give only a brief display. The pink *R. Myconi rosea* varies from seed; a good one is a strong and clear rose pink, a poor one is washy and verges on the white *R. Myconi alba.* Two separate species are *R. Nathaliae,* which has more oval, less deeply toothed leaves and rather larger flowers with orange eyes and a bigger flower display, but in May and June only; and *R. serbica,* which is like a smaller *R. Myconi* but with longer hairs on the backs of the leaves and these hairs are golden brown.

All the Ramondas like a soil that is both leafy and limy, and extra ground chalk and leafmould added to the normal alpine soil is much appreciated. They do not like being excessively dry in summer; they are plants for moderately damp conditions, the sort of place that will grow ferns well.

The easiest method of increase is by taking up an old plant in March, dividing and potting in suitable soil to grow on in a frame until the divisions are well established. The other good method, which should always be used in preference to seed to increase the white and pink varieties, is from leaf cuttings, and as Ramondas are the only alpines propagated in this way, it is described here.

In June or July remove leaves from where they can be spared, taking those from the lower parts of the saucer-shaped plant, but not those which are going yellow or brown at the tips. The action is a slow steady pull sideways and downwards, holding the leaf well down on the stalk;

those who wish to practise can use plantains from the lawn. The object is to get the leaf off with the portion that clasps the stem intact because this holds a dormant bud which will grow into the new Ramonda. Insert the leaf so that two-thirds of the leaf blade is protruding, in a pan of sand with some fine peat added, about one part to five, and water them like any other cuttings. They should be ready by the end of August but do not hurry potting, the peat is there to provide some food, and when they have good roots and a growing point, pot in their normal soil. Do not remove the remains of the parent leaf when potting; it can go on gathering food until it dies off completely. This routine sounds more difficult than it really is, and it is far easier than seed raising.

Ramonda seed should be sown in the spring on the grit system, with leafy soil below the grit. It is very tiny and needs careful watering by soaking the pan from below. Watering with potassium permanganate, about enough to tint the water to the colour of a threepenny stamp, will help to keep down moss while the seed is slowly germinating. Once a crop of seedlings has been dug out, do not throw away the pan; it will produce more because the seeds seem to be designed to produce a succession of crops—three from one sowing is a record. If seed is gathered from the black-coffee-brown ripe pods from the early flowers and sown at once, it may all come up with a rush, and here it is important to see that it is very thinly sown, so that each plant can reach the size of a sixpence without rotting off through overcrowding during the first winter. *R. Myconi* is by far the easiest from seed and sets it most often, which is why it is the only one listed by most nurseries.

Rhododendron

The Alpenrose of Switzerland (Rostrothe Alpenrose is its full popular name to distinguish it from *Rhododendron hirsutum*, which is Bewimperte Alpenrose) is *R. ferrugineum*, and though this will grow to over three feet high it rarely does on a British rock garden. This species, with miniature evergreen Rhododendron leaves about an inch long, rusty brown on the undersides, is a very good shrub for the small rock garden, as it tolerates more lime than the other Rhododendrons. On any soil, in part shade such as on a north slope, it will do well in the standard leafy mixture. It flowers in June or July with small Rhododendron heads of up to twelve florets, about three-quarters of an inch across the mouths, and varying in colour from carmine pink to a real red.

There are many more species, but it is very easy to obtain some nice little bush raised from seed which is not going to flower until it is five feet high, or one that is going to start small and go on to a size that will dwarf the flowers. Now that what used to be Azaleas have been added, there are over 300 species of Rhododendrons in cultivation, not counting hybrids like Pink Pearl, which is the best known of still more hundreds. The few which are covered here are merely those which are small and suited for the smaller rock garden; it would be possible on the right soil to plant one entirely with the race, with the addition of heathers to extend the flowering season. The problem would be their high price, and therefore the descriptions that follow are of species that give value for money.

Apart from *R. ferrugineum*, the alpine Rhododendrons need a lime-free soil, and though they can be grown in pockets of leafy soil with Epsom Salts as a defence, like *Gentiana sino-ornata*, they are not for the chalky or limy garden. The commonest and one of the nicest is *R. keleticum* which has bright green, long oval leaves on a compact bush about eight inches high, with bright purple flower heads in June. *R. campylogynum* has leaves more rounded at the tips and is even more of a dome-like mass, about six inches high. The flower heads are not, however, large Rhododendrons in miniature; each floret of the four in a cluster is carried on a two inch upright stem, from the top of which they look sideways as red purple wide-mouthed bells. Another good one is the Chinese species *R. imperator*, still more compact, three or four inches high, and with pairs of red buds that open into relatively large pinkish purple funnels, sometimes over an inch and a half across the mouths, in May and June.

The real gem is *R. radicans*, which is a carpeter with tiny Rhododendron branches hugging the ground, and rounded half inch long leaves. It flowers in April, May or June, with large single florets as wide across the mouth as a two-shilling piece, shallow bells of pale red purple nodding from stems that just hold them clear of the two inch high mat beneath.

The best means of increase for all these species is cuttings of the soft shoots after flowering, taken with about four joints and inserted in the cutting sand mixture recommended for Ramondas. A hormone is advised, and they should go in a pan in the cutting frame to wait until they do root. Pot in standard leafy soil and grow them slowly, watering well in summer, and pinching out the growing point to make a shapely bush if they are growing tall on a single leader. Before they are any real size they will have been two years in the pots, which is why they are all as expensive as miniature Conifers. Seed is difficult, slow to germinate, and the seedlings are even slower still to raise.

Alpines Plant by Plant

Rosa. Miniature Roses

On the sunny windowsill the miniature Roses are the most long-flowering pot plants that can be grown, and they are essential in every pan garden. In the open on the small rock garden they are equally essential, but they have a grave disadvantage. Most gardeners forget they are Roses and find themselves with a bush a foot high, with much dead wood, yellowing leaves and flowers only here and there. This is a miniature Rose neglected into the condition of a Hugh Dickson eight feet high, unpruned for years in the garden of a derelict mansion.

Miniature Roses in the open should be cut back hard, using secateurs if necessary, in March when full sized bush Roses are pruned. As they are grown on their own roots, not on a briar stock, an elderly plant that is overgrown is best cut back to ground level, and the shoots from the base are then pruned the following year in the normal way, being cut back to about three joints. In the open spraying should not be neglected, for though the small Rose seems immune to black spot, greenfly can be very bad, because the pests are full sized and in proportion to flower and stem size, as big as young mice. The miniature Roses are easy and very hardy, but they should be treated as Roses.

They grow well on any soil other than a peaty one, and are best in full sun on the small rock garden. There are today many new varieties, but *Rosa pumila* (correctly *R. gallica var. pumila*) six inches high when properly pruned, with double pink flowers about three-quarters of an inch across, and *R. Oakington Ruby* or *R. Lawrenceana*, with equally perfect miniature crimson Roses, are still about the best. Others are *R. Peon*, a single crimson; *R. Rouletti* (correctly *R. chinensis minima*), single or semi-double pink; and Little Dot, a double white. Their flowering season in the open is from May to October.

They are easily increased by soft cuttings including about three joints of the green-barked young shoots; so long as there is a side shoot going well on each, one can go on making cuttings all down the stem. The best time is in July and August, but the cuttings root well in the sand frame at almost any time during the growing season. It is always best to re-place the big plants every four or five years, but this is simple with such an easily raised race.

Saponaria

Saponaria ocymoides is too rampant for all but the largest rock gardens, but it is ideal planted in the upper courses of the dry wall. It will trail as much as three feet in a season, a mat of many branched red-barked stems with pointed oval rather pale green leaves. The flowers are pale pink, in clusters of florets about half an inch across of the Maltese Cross shape of so many of this branch of the order *Caryophyllacea*. The season is from May to September, but some plants will produce one burst of bloom early in the season and stragglers afterwards, a habit most common in the slightly deeper pink variety, *S. ocymoides splendens*. There is also a white one which is rather scarce, *S. ocymoides alba*.

They should be cut back every year in the early autumn or spring because, like Aubrieta, they lose vigour if allowed to continue from where they left off, apart from having them half way across the path. The best method of increase is from soft cuttings from non-flowering shoots in July and August. These root easily in the sand frame, but after potting the plants will need stopping back, as if they develop a long 'leg' in pots the young plants are easily broken off short.

Seed is also very easy, sown in February and making very good plants by September, but because it is so easy the original *S. ocymoides splendens* has been lost. Good deep pink forms should always be increased only from the cuttings, and if the carmine flowered variety appears it should be treasured. The sport of this plant, *S. ocymoides var. rubra compacta*, with deep pink flowers and a very compact stunted habit is delicate and rare, and opinions differ on its cultivation. One half way between this plant which grows at two speeds, dead slow and stop, and the rampant parent, would be worth having.

One natural hybrid is *S. Boissieri* (a cross between *S. ocymoides* and *S. caespitosa*, an alpine house species), which is an excellent scree plant. It grows as a mat of slowly spreading stems with rather fleshy pale green leaves and flowers in May and June like those of the larger parent but bigger. Give it full sun on the scree and it is quite hardy. Increase is from soft cuttings in July, which root easily, ready for potting into normal alpine soil and growing on for late spring planting. There are other small species, including *S. lutea*, the only yellow member of the race, but these are of interest to the specialist or hybridiser, as none are good amateur's plants.

Saxifraga. Saxifrage

These are a huge race, and the best way to deal with the great bulk of species and hybrids is to sort them into three batches according to their general garden uses. First there are the Encrusted Saxifrages, with silver powdered foliage in rosettes and relatively tall flower stems of clustered florets. These are suitable for the dry wall and crevices on the rock garden. They like plenty of lime and full sun, and stand up well to being very dry. Secondly the Kabschia Saxifrages, which (again only broadly speaking) are neat dome-like plants with small cup-like flowers on short stems in early spring. These are ideal for the small rock garden and need a limy gritty soil, but do not like being baked up in summer. Finally, there are the Mossy Saxifrages, with loose rosettes of pale green foliage and heads of cup-like florets on slender upright stems. These prefer semi-shade, will grow in complete shade and do not like getting too dry, and they are fond of lime and very hardy. They are botanically divided into sixteen groups, including the mighty border species known as 'Elephant's Ears' (once *S. Megasea* and now a *Bergenia*) and several trees, but we are concerned only with a few, and their grouping here is for alpine gardeners only.

There are three species which do not fit into these groups and as they are usually lumped under 'Miscellaneous' in catalogues and books, they are discussed first.

The best of the three is *S. oppositifolia*, which is found widely in Europe and is quite common on the mountains of Scotland, and on the cliffs of many small and rocky islands of Britain. It is a close mat former with prostrate branches and small round tipped leaves, about a quarter of an inch long, set closely together in pairs. They are dark green or dark grey green when the plant is healthy, and slightly hairy at the edges. In March and April the plant flowers generously, covering itself with almost stemless, five-petalled flowers about half an inch across. The original species has purple flowers, but the range includes white, pink, red purple and almost crimson. Those most worth searching for include *S. oppositifolia coccinea*, the nearest to crimson; *S. oppositifolia grandiflora* (also called *S. oppositifolia major*), a good red purple with extra-large flowers; *S. oppositifolia latina*, the nearest pink, the white form of this being called '*S. oppositifolia alba*' (the true plant is a poor weak thing), and the most common of all, *S. oppositifolia splendens*, which is simply a free flowering form of the original.

This very attractive race prefers a sandy or gritty soil with plenty of leafmould, part shade and a place where they will not get too dry in summer. If they are grown in a dry place with a lot of lime they become yellow and starved, but anyone who has seen them growing in peat among rock fragments will understand why they fail so often on the rock garden. They should be regarded as semi-shade carpeters, and they grow well on the lower slopes of the rock garden, or even in an alpine lawn with such species as *Hypsela longiflora* and *Selliera radicans*, and autumn flowering Crocuses beneath. Their soil requirements are very nearly the same.

Increase is either by division and direct replanting or potting after flowering, or from cuttings about an inch long taken from the tips of the branches and inserted in a sand pan with some fine peat mixed in. They root easily, but once potted do not let them get dried out in summer; the need is not for dampness, like Primulas, but for moisture with free drainage, the normal conditions in summer on a Scottish mountain.

Saxifraga umbrosa var. primuloides is a neater version of the ordinary London Pride, with round green leaves and sprays of pale pink flowers in May. It grows on any soil and is valuable because it does so well on the almost sunless small rock garden. If more are needed it is simply split and planted where it is required after it has flowered. A hybrid, with this variety as one of the parents, is *S. Primulaize*, which has dark green rosettes of tooth-edged leaves, making a mat about an inch tall, with short flower stems about two inches high and heads of variable flowers, salmon, orange, even a good bright red on and off from May to August. It is ideal in semi-shade on normal alpine soil, and on the lower slopes of the rock garden, where it will not get too dry.

The most common of the Encrusted Saxifrages (botanically speaking the *Euaizoon* section) is *S. Aizoon*, if its many varieties and hybrids are included. The original plant is a colony of many leaved rosettes, each leaf rimmed with the white 'encrusting'. These leaves are up to two inches long and half an inch wide, bluntly pointed and incurved at the tips, and the stout six inch flower stems in June carry large sprays of creamy white florets with small red purple spots on the petals. The flower is very much bigger than that of London Pride, the florets are as much as half an inch across, and on a wall or in crevices on the rock garden they can give a very good display, dwarfing the plant beneath. There is a pale yellow ground colour variety, *S. Aizoon lutea*, and a pink, *S. Aizoon rosea*, which have small flowers, and leaves that are a paler green.

There are a number of species in this class which are good on the small rock garden, domes of reduced-scale rosettes, with the same type flowerheads in June. Of these, *S. Aizoon baldensis* (correctly *S. Aizoon minutifolia*) is two inches high, with very grey leaves and two inch high white flower clusters; *S. cochlearis minor*, with half inch across rosettes also white, and a hybrid, *S. Esther*, which is pale yellow, a small plant, but with large sprays on six inch stems.

Among the big ones again there are *S. Cotyledon*, with large rounded leaves, margined with white, up to three inches long, and flower stems that branch low; the tallest is *S. Cotyledon pyramidalis* which can put up a flower stem four feet high, though eighteen inches is more common in gardens. The stems are red, and the cloud of white florets is more of a cone-shaped mass. They take about two years to reach flowering size, and the rosette spends itself in one great burst, but there are always plenty more coming on round it. After it is over, the dead stems should be cut out, to give the smaller growth a chance to recover. The variety *S. Cotyledon caterhamensis* is so heavily spotted with red that it appears pink, and is perhaps the finest of all these June flowering glories. They are best in crevices on the rock garden, because of the great size of the flowers which are awkward if there is a path at the foot of the dry wall. Another species with smaller flowers in longer sprays is *S. lingulata* (also called *S. callosa*) which has longer leaves, incurved at the tips in smaller rosettes. There are several varieties and hybrids, but all have white flowers at the same time of year.

These Saxifrages are increased easily by division in August, potting to get them established for spring planting in limy soil, or lifting in September, dividing and planting where they are required. It is possible to raise them from seed, but the result is only more variations, and though their display is good while it lasts, and they are neat and ever-green when out of flower, no one really needs more than a clump or two of some representative kinds.

Those who like great sprays of white florets arching down from the rocks, can grow the hybrids of *S. longifolia*. The old variety *S.* Tumbling Waters had the disadvantage of making very few offsets, its three foot flower spray meant the complete loss of the plant, but *S. longifolia var.* Symonds Jeune, or *S. longifolia* Walpoles var. both flower and produce offsets. They have narrow leaves, very silvery, in a dense rosette that grows larger year by year—the longer before flowering the bigger the spike—and their cultivation is a special branch of alpine gardening. They are usually grown in large pots or pans for display in the alpine house. The offsets, with the lower leaves cleaned off, can be rooted in pans of sand, and any non-rooted rosettes of the other En-crusted Saxifrages can be inserted in this way; they need very little stem but dead leaves round the base should be removed or they cause rotting off in winter.

The Kabschia Saxifrages are equally bewildering in their variety; it is possible to collect over a hundred species and hybrids, but for the sake of space and sanity only a few of the more usual are described.

The most common and perhaps the best for the normal rock garden is *S. Irvingii*, which is a close-packed half cricket ball of tiny, spine-leaved grey rosettes, with a thick scattering of almost stemless pale pink flowers, which are deep, open-mouthed upright bells. It spreads slowly in an inch high dome, flowers in March and April, and is ideal on the small rock garden with limy gritty soil where it will not get baked dry in summer. Even smaller and slower is *S*. Faldonside, which has rather larger individual spine leaves, and splendid golden yellow bells; *S*. Cranbourne is like an inch high Encrusted Saxifrage, with small pink flowers; *S*. Aubrey Pritchard is deep reddish mauve; and C. M. Pritchard is creamy white. Then there are the varieties of *S. Burseriana*, with the same sort of low mound of tiny leaf tufts and larger upright bells but on two inch stems. The original species is pure white, but *S. Burserina sulphurea* is pale yellow, *S.B.* His Majesty pale pink, and *S.B.* Gloria has even larger white cups, several on a stem. All flower, with the other members of the group, at Kabschia Saxifrage time, March and April, and the best way to select among the many kinds available is to go to one of the early spring shows at the Horticultural Hall, Westminster, and choose those which are most personally appealing.

They are increased from soft cuttings in May or June, and raising Kabschia Saxifrages is a standard routine that fits also *Petrocallis pyrenaica*, and almost anything that grows as a small cushion even if it is no relation. Small and unknown plants should always be treated *as* Kabschia Saxifrages, and the reader who has launched out on the tiny Androsaces, the more tender Saponarias or the minute Silenes will find the system a guide. It is the one used at Kew, for new plants from high mountains.

Take your cuttings from the lower parts of the dome with a safety razor blade, and pick off any dead leaves: the cutting is often barely half an inch long and though forceps can be used they are rather clumsy. Insert them in pans of cutting sand so they do not touch each other; it used to be a test of a propagator's skill to get perfect circles each smaller than the next for 500 cuttings in one pan, but this is not important; they want to go about half an inch apart, or a little less.

Set the pan in the cutting frame buried to the rim in sifted coke breeze or boiler ash, not house coal ash, and keep it watered like any normal cutting pan. The cuttings will grow slowly through the summer and winter (when less water is required) until in the spring they should be ready for potting. Pot in limy, gritty soil, with plenty of drainage material in the bottom of the pot, and set them again in a frame with a three inch layer of ash under them, and more ash between the pots, so that each row sits with the rims level with the surface. Keep them watered, with plenty of ventilation, and shading on the lights to prevent scorching by fierce sunlight. The ashes retain the water that the pots let soak through the pores, so that the plants spend a moist summer with

27. *Gentiana lagodechiana*, the easy gentian for almost any soil that flowers for everyone. Its blue clusters of trumpets should be a feature of every rock garden and Alpine border in August and September, and it thrives in town gardens

28. The *Edelweiss* has a flower like two grey starfish one on top of the other, it is *Leontopodium alpinum* and except as a curiosity, is not worth growing. It is easy from seed and cheap to buy

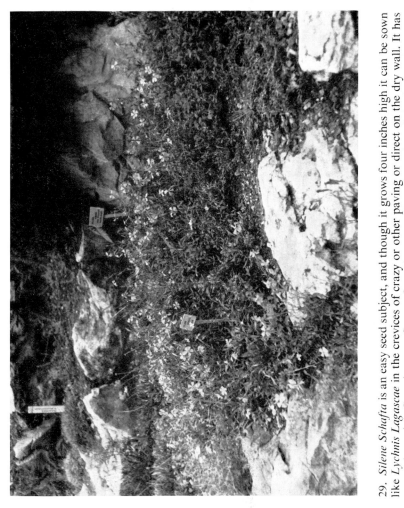

29. *Silene Schafta* is an easy seed subject, and though it grows four inches high it can be sown like *Lychnis Lagascae* in the crevices of crazy or other paving or direct on the dry wall. It has deep pink Campion type flowers from August to October and no fads about soil

free drainage below, and in the winter, when the shading is washed off, the lights keep them dry.

Their speed varies: *S. Irvingii* will be ready to plant by the autumn, *S. Faldonside* may take another year, but it is the best and quickest way to grow small plants from tiny cuttings, when their speed is about an inch in diameter in a season, or under. There is of course no need to take this trouble; it is easy to buy good plants, but one should remember that the nurseryman has done it, and at modern wage rates for a job no machine will do, so do not grumble at the price. With every small alpine you pay for skill and knowledge and waiting—an Atlantic liner takes about as long to build as a good big Faldonside.

There are a number of swifter species in the same group, with larger green rosettes, and stronger branches, which spread as powerful turves rather than mats. Of these, *S. apiculata* is the most common; it has sprays of small bright yellow florets on two or three inch stems about a three inch high plant in February and March, but not in any real quantity, and its white variety, *S. apiculata alba* is no freer. Others are *S. Borisii*, with single yellow florets, and *S. Boston Spa*, rather deeper yellow in March and April. The best of this group is *S. Elizabethae*, with rather pale yellow florets at this season but in good measure; the worst is *S. Haagii*, which has sprays like *S. apiculata*, but so rarely that it is almost a foliage-only plant. These easy species are increased by division in September for potting or direct replanting, and they are suitable for the dry bank or alpine border with plenty of lime and sun, as well as the normal small rock garden which is not cramped for space.

The Mossy Saxifrages are especially useful because they will stand up to a great deal of shade and are happiest in semi-shade. They can be split up in September and October and built into the dry wall, like Aubrieta, to develop into sturdy pale green mounds where shade prevents other planting. With these to flower in April and May and Ramondas for later, the shaded wall can give a display over a long season where other plants dwindle and die. They can be used for edging beds, in the alpine border, and on the lower slopes of the rock garden, where the need is to fill space. They grow in any soil, with lime as a first choice, and though they do not like getting too dry they will grow in full sun. Deep shade is not advised and really dry shade is no more suited to them than any other plant. As this race is what most people mean when they say 'Saxafrage' or 'ordinary Saxifrage' no detailed description need be given.

The hybrids of *S. moschata* have red flower stems and clusters of open bell cups that look straight up, with heights varying from four to six inches. Of these Sir Douglas Haig is a good crimson; General Joffre very near it; Mrs. Piper, a good pink; Pompadour, carmine red; Triumph, almost scarlet; and Carnival, a deep pink, with florets about the diameter of a shilling. The smaller sizes, below four inches, have the blood of our native *S. hypnoides* or Dovedale Moss, and include Peter Pan, a dwarf red; Stormonth's Variety, rose crimson, three inches; James Brenner with very big white florets as large as florins; Pixie, deep red, three inches; and Kingii, a good three inch white.

It is not possible to say which are hybrids and which varieties, and for garden purposes it does not matter, as they are not raised from seed. They are on most nurseries in a state of mixture, and those who like them, or have a place where they will thrive and nothing else will, should follow a Helianthemum or Phlox policy: buy from a firm with a large number of varieties, and then pick up additions in ones and twos, without surprise that some are duplicates.

Where they are not built into the dry wall, increase is exactly as for Aubrieta. Gather three or four strands together with the foliage in a bunch, and pot firmly, standing the pots in a shaded closed frame with moderate watering until they are established. For large numbers, individual cuttings can be taken with one or two inches of brown mature stem and inserted in the sand frame any time in the summer or autumn. It pays to dig up and divide or cut back elderly clumps, as in time these grow bare in the centres.

Sedum

The Sedums are not exciting plants. They are very tough, tolerating some shade, but at their best in full sun on poor limy soil in a dry place. They are very easy to increase, and some of them will produce quite a good flower display as well as evergreen fleshy foliage, but they are like some people whose good qualities we have to recall after every meeting.

The small rock garden is best restricted to the few low and slow-growing species, which can also be planted as a kind of dry alpine lawn with bulbs beneath, excellent for those who are trying the rarer bulbous Iris such as *I. Danfordae* and *I. histrio*. These are *S. dasyphyllum*, which is a carpet of tiny egg-shaped leaves, pale grey tinged with pink, about an inch high, with sprays of little white or pink flowers; *S. hispanicum minus* (now *S. bithynicum*) with pale grey green leaves in small rosettes packed into a turf and very pale pink flowers on two inch stems; its variety *S. hispanicum aureus* with yellow green foliage; and *S. lydium*, which is very much the same but a brighter green that is tinged with red in the autumn, and white flowers, all of them in June and July.

These are not invasive under dry conditions, though they should not be grown near small and treasured plants, and they can be established in almost impossible clefts in very little soil by just thrusting in rooted pieces. They are good also in paving and on paths, where some stronger species can be added. The rather slower form of our common Stone Crop, *S. sexangulare*, with bright green foliage and heads of yellow flowers about three inches high, is a good one, and so is *S. album murale* (also called *S. murale*), with half inch long egg-shaped leaves on creeping stems, red brown in colour in a dry place and with pale pink heads. These two are June-flowering and can be used to fill a dry place solid with weed-suppressing foliage; they have been used to cover graves as a 'non-attention' planting.

Other rock garden species are *S. kamtschaticum*, with large notched dark green leaves shaped rather like those of an Arabis, but thicker and more fleshy, set on short trailing branches, with orange yellow flower heads and a flowering season from July to September; its form, *S. kamtschaticum variegatum*, with white edges to the leaves; and *S. spathulifolium*, which makes thick domes of packed rosettes of fat fleshy leaves with sprays of bright yellow flowers in June and July. This one is about three inches high, and it has two varieties, *S. spathulifolium var. capablanca*, which is about an inch high with very silvery foliage that sets off the smaller flower sprays well, and *S. spathulifolium purpureum*, which has foliage that is dull purple, brightening in dry places with ample lime to pickling-cabbage colour, and the same type of flowers. This group is all neat plants, increased by cuttings which root very easily or by division.

The plant that most people call just 'Sedum' is *S. rupestre*, with plump grey green spine-shaped leaves that curl in at the tips which are set around thick trailing branches. The flower heads are yellow and on nine inch stems that hang down among the foliage or thrust up floppily and they can be as much as two inches across. It is a wall plant that is best built in and even unrooted lengths sandwiched between the courses will take hold and grow. A more attractive group is *S. spurium* and its allies. These have round leaves slightly notched at the edges on thick trailing stems, and they flower more generously, but in August and September the foliage turns slightly red in a dry place and they can be built into a wall in the same way. The original species has pale pink flower heads, flat across the top and about two inches across, but *S. spurium splendens* has red purple flowers and the new variety *S. spurium* Schorbuser Blut., is a real crimson and perhaps the strongest colour in the whole race.

259

Where these varieties are not used in a wall they can be dug up and planted where they are required; all are suitable for clothing a very dry bank or anywhere where something tough is needed, but except for the last one, they are not really worth a place on the small rock garden, if there are better plants available. If broken fragments are left lying on the ground, they can root themselves, and one gardener who threw his

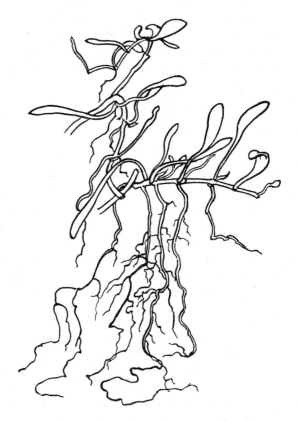

FIG. 23. A division of *Selliera radicans*, for direct replanting.

rubbish over the fence into a railway cutting grew far better plants half-way down where the discarded branches rolled, than in his own garden. He had them on too rich a soil in shade. Starve them with plenty of lime in full sun and they do their best, just as many dull characters have shown up well, in the lifeboats of a torpedoed ship.

Those who take a lucky dip among Sedum names are advised to

ignore *S. coeruleum*, an annual, and *S. Hobsonii*, *S. humifusum*, *S. Stahlii*, *S. spinosum* and *S. Winkleri*, which are not hardy.

Selliera

Selliera radicans is a charming carpeter for semi-shade or sun, preferring a rather leafy soil, though a John Innes will grow it well. It is a good bulb cover, an alpine lawn plant, excellent in the alpine path, and suitable also for the lower slopes of the small rock garden. The leaves spring from underground stems, they vary from one to four inches long, and are bluntly pointed and narrow. They form a thick mat of dark green and from June to September the flowers are dotted over the surface, almost stemless and very curiously shaped.

This habit of saying 'curiously shaped' is largely to blame for the confusion between this species and Hypsela. Selliera has five white petals with rounded tips all on one side of the stamens and pistil, so that they look like tiny white-gloved hands with the fingers widely spread. The two plants grown together give a very charming effect, with the dark red centres and 'three one side, two the other' flowers of Hypsela, in complete contrast.

It is a native of New Zealand and Australia, and is best kept sheltered from cold winds in chilly districts, but in most of Britain it is fully hardy. It is propagated by division, either by direct replanting in April, or dividing more drastically and potting the fragments to grow on in a frame until established, either in spring, or in October after flowering.

Sempervivum

For practical purposes the Sempervivums can be divided into two kinds, the Spider or Cobweb plants and the House Leeks.

The first type, *S. arachnoideum*, and its variations, consists of colonies of small rosettes covered with fine white hairs; *S. arachnoideum tormentosum* has rather larger and more hairy rosettes, *S. arachnoideum Stansfieldii* has foliage that turns red in summer. They are good plants to tuck in crevices, to put in small hollows in the surface of a rock, or for a really dry place on the small rock garden. The best soil is one that is poor and limy and they are easily increased by division at any time during the spring or summer.

The common House Leek is *S. tectorum*. It has large rosettes of pointed leaves rounded at the back, flat on top and up to two inches long. The colour varies partly with the kind and partly with the soil; in the same sort of poor, dry and limy situation as the Spider plant, it will be much more red than on better feeding. Its variations and allied species are legion; *S. tectorum calcareum* has white powdered grey green rosettes with dull red leaf tips; *S. tectorum glaucum* has blue grey leaves; and *S. tectorum triste* no longer exists, it was a reddish foliaged variety, but it has now been decided that it is no different to a well-starved *S. tectorum*.

The Sempervivums are foliage-only plants, for they flower by growing a thick, much-leaved flower stem with a few small and dingy daisies concealed in the fleshy greenery; this is usually during the summer and only occurs to a few rosettes a season. Those who like neat evergreen rosettes in crevices can have far better value from the Encrusted Saxifrages.

These plants have a fascination: some nurserymen and gardeners take to them like drink, but any discussion of the shifting sands of species and hybrids near and between these two types is out of place here. Those who are interested in Sempervivum Gardening, not Alpine Gardening, are referred to the monograph by Dr. Lloyd Praeger, published by the Royal Horticultural Society in 1932 and repeatedly brought up-to-date, which deals with more kinds than the total number of plants mentioned in this present book.

If more varieties are required it is easy to order an assorted dozen from a nursery; they will be different to look at but not very much, but the names will certainly be all wrong in the opinions of several of the many authorities whose disagreements in this department of botanical nomenclature are perhaps more fierce and acrimonious than in any other.

Serratula

Serratula Shawii is a relation both of the Cornflower and the Thistle but smaller than either. It is a plant for the small rock garden in full sun with lime and a poorish soil, growing about six inches high when in flower. It has slowly creeping buried stems, from which spring short upright branches with much serrated (hence the generic name) rather bronzy green leaves. The flowers in September and October are crimson and rather like those of the heraldic Scots Thistle, but it does not have blowing seeds, in fact it sets very few.

It is a rare but easy alpine, flowering at a time when there is always a need for good plants, and it is increased by spring division for direct replanting or potting. The plant is probably a dwarf and free-flowering form of the Swiss species *S. nudicaulis*, and as long as it is increased only by division it will stay one.

Alpines Plant by Plant

Silene

Silene Schafta is a good easy species, always true from seed, for crevice and paving sowing, and for planting on the moderate sized rock garden or in the dry wall. It has pointed rather pale green leaves on four inch stems rising from a central root stock, making a neat clump up to six inches high that does not spread—one eight inches across is large. It flowers generously and late, roughly from August to October, with five-petalled bloom about three-quarters of an inch across, but in a shade of rather pale magenta pink many people dislike. Any normal soil suits it and it prefers full sun.

Another easy species is *S. alpestris*, now correctly *Heliosperma alpestre*, which forms a low clump of brownish-green grassy leaves, with white starry flowers about half an inch across on slender stems about six inches high in May and June. This is a good wall plant but not a striking one and it is also suitable for direct sowing; it will tolerate quite considerable shade, and though regarded as a biennial, like *S. Schafta* it lives longest in a crevice.

Our native Sea Campion, *S. maritima*, has fleshy pale grey green leaves in pairs on creeping stems which make a low and spreading clump. The flowers come singly or in pairs from the shorter stems in the middle of the clump; these blooms are about three-quarters of an inch across, and the calyx behind the frilled bloom is swollen like those of our Bladder Campion (*S. inflata*). They are usually white, but there is a pale pink form, sometimes called *S. maritima rosea*, and they are usually in evidence in May and June. It can be raised easily from seed sown in February, but soft cuttings in July from the young shoots root easily and are a means of making sure of keeping any good deep pink seedlings.

The small Silenes for the scree or the pan garden, are neat domes with stemless Campion flowers in May and June, but though *S. acaulis* is a British native, it never flowers as well here as it does in the Alps. It makes a two inch high, slowly spreading dome of tightly packed, spine-leaved pale green foliage very like a Kabschia Saxifrage, and the flowers that appear are between a quarter and a half an inch across. There were a number of forms in cultivation: the best and most free flowering seems to be *S. acaulis exscapa*, and all are worth trying, and if they flower well, increasing from division about March or from summer cuttings. The cuttings are as small as those of a Kabschia and they should be increased in exactly the same way. A good form of *S. acaulis exscapa* is a really lovely miniature plant, and the lost salmon pink one collected by Mr. Clarence Elliott, *S. acaulis* Elliotts Variety, would be a prize worth propagating if one survives in some lucky garden.

Sisyrinchium

The usual Sisyrinchiums are small, Iris-like plants which flower out of the tips of the narrow sword-like leaves. *Sisyrinchium angustifolium* is nine inches high, with roughly star-shaped flowers, three or four in a cluster, deep violet blue; *S. bellum* is a smaller, six-inch version; and *S. Bermudianum* is up to a foot high, with yellow markings on the flowers. They are more foliage than bloom, but do put out a considerable number of flowers from the leaf tips between June and September.

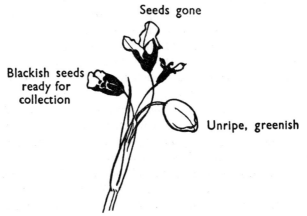

Seeds gone

Blackish seeds
ready for
collection

Unripe, greenish

FIG. 24. *Sisyrinchium bellum* seed head.

They are easily grown on any normal soil, and though they make good 'imitation water Iris' beside the cement pool, they take quite dry conditions and semi-shade, though not a Sedum standard of drought. All are easily increased by dissecting the clump in March or April and direct replanting, or they can be raised in great quantity from spring-sown seed, which can be saved in plenty.

There are, however, two rare ones which, unlike the first type, lose their leaves in winter, coming through as dormant underground roots; they are so often thrown away on nurseries or dug up in gardens that they are almost out of cultivation. Both are lime haters, needing the standard leafy mixture and a position with the woodland Gentians. One comes from the United States, *S. Douglasii* (formerly and with visual justification, *S. grandiflorum*), which has round, rush-like leaves, not flat Iris type, and clusters of red purple bell flowers, each as wide as a

264

shilling, in February or March. There is a white species, *S. Douglasii album*, and both are rare and beautiful. After flowering the leaves will sometimes die down again to re-appear during the summer, so the plant should always be marked and never dug up until it has not been above ground for two years. Both grow to about nine inches high.

Increase is by division in June, when it should be growing, but seed should be saved and sown immediately it is ripe; anyone with a real colony of this plant in the Gentian bed would be very lucky, and it is possible that natural selection may fix variations which would be more reliable garden plants.

The other rush-leaved Sisyrinchium is *S. filifolium*, which comes from the Falkland Islands. Its popular name there is 'Pale Maiden', and it is the national flower of these treeless islands in the extreme South Atlantic. This one is far tougher, as one would expect from a native of a colony with a climate rather colder than that of the Orkneys or Shetlands. It is about eight inches high with round slender dark green leaves and separate flower stems which have shorter leaves that point up alternately from the sides. Each stem carries two to three large five-petalled shallow saucers, pure white and pencilled with pink lines, with a maroon centre; each floret is more than an inch across. The flowering season is May and June, and the foliage stays on view until about October when it is dormant until it wakes up in March or April.

The Pale Maiden needs standard leafy soil and a position in sun or part shade, the Gentian bed suits it well, and it can be increased by division after flowering, about July, or from spring-sown seed, which is set quite freely. It is by far the toughest of the deciduous Sisyrinchiums, and worth searching catalogues to find; both plants are scarce but very rewarding in the garden.

Solidago

Solidago brachystachys (now regarded as a form of *S. Virgaurea* though this makes no difference to the plant) is a miniature Golden Rod. It grows six inches high, and though it is possible as a plant for the small rock garden, in a dry sunny place, it is best on the dry wall. Here it makes an upward pointing clump with reduced-scale Golden Rod leaves and familiar bright yellow feathery flowers in August and September.

Cut it back after flowering, divide it in April and plant direct if more are needed, and root soft cuttings in May from the young shoots in the sand frame if you require a large quantity.

Stachys

There are a number of species of Stachys, but only one is of real interest to the alpine gardener. This is *S. corsica* which is a good carpeter for bulb cover or the alpine path, needing semi-shade and preferring a leafy soil to hold on to the moisture and prevent its drying out excessively.

It has small pale green leaves about half an inch long on prostrate branches with a total height for the carpet of about an inch. The flowers from June to August are almost stemless, cream white and flushed with pink at the lips of the small slender double tubes, which vaguely resemble single Antirrhinum florets. Increase is easy from division in September, and it is as well to raise a few plants each year, wintering in a cold frame. The main plant is inclined to go bare in the middle with age and the 'hole' should be forked over and young stuff replanted.

Thymus

The Thymes are a pleasant race, hardy, easy and suitable for any soil. They divide roughly into two groups, the bushy ones and the prostrate carpeters, which are ideal in the alpine lawn and give their name to a development of this composed of them entirely. In the alpine path they are delightful to walk on and the crushing that releases the scent does not seem to harm them in moderation. Several can be pressed into use in emergencies in the kitchen.

The lemon-scented Thymes are really hybrids with the common species used in cooking (*T. vulgaris*) as one of the parents. They grow six or eight inches high as upright evergreen bushes, and have small lilac flowers on rare occasions. The original *T. citriodorus* has dark green leaves, and so strong a lemon scent that it can be used as a variation for culinary flavour; *T. citriodorus argenteus* has silver-edged leaves and many more flowers, from June to August, and *T. citriodorus aureus* has yellow variegations; both can be regarded as small foliage bushes, and they have been clipped into a cheaper and more snail-proof version of box edging. The variety *T. citriodorus* Silver Queen is best for this.

Thymus carnosus is a much more free-flowering little bush, about six inches high with stiff upright stems, small, thick, pointed leaves, and little lilac or white flowers of the standard Thyme type in June and July; *T. nitidus* is often confused with it, but the true *T. nitidus* has oval leaves, also grey, and the flowers in definite spikes, about an inch and a half tall. The total height of this last bush varies, it is usually not more than five or six inches and it flowers at the same time of year as its fellow.

Smaller still, making bushes that verge on mats, are *T. caespititius*, and *T. Herba-barona*. The first has also been *T. azoricus* and *T. micans*; it grows about three inches high with spiny, rather browny-green foliage and not very many pale purple flower heads in July. The other is from Corsica and is distinctive in having the scent of caraway seeds. It has oval leaves, is about three inches high, and has small pale lilac flower heads, also in July.

The group as a whole is not striking, but they are tidy and evergreen, and if they are given the sort of poor soil and dry sunny situation that they have at home, they will give themselves a 'good blossom season' every now and then, like some varieties of fruit tree. Increase is easy for them all, from cuttings with hard wood at the base inserted in the sand frame about May, or they can be divided. Elderly clumps with a quantity of old trailing branches can be torn up and built into the dry wall, with only the growing tips protruding, but they need some of the original fibrous root from the main stem to give them a start.

Before the main body of carpeting Thymes there are two strong-growing species with grey foliage more suited to the dry wall, not only because of their vigour, but because here only will they flower on any real scale. *Thymus Doefleri* (or correctly *T. hirsutus Doefleri*) is a trailing mat of branches with grey hairy leaves, about two inches high when grown on the flat, and small pink flower heads in June or July. The other common grey Thyme is *T. lanuginosus*, or rather the plant that is grown as this is really *T. pseudolanuginosus*, but few nurserymen have space for the new name. It is also grey with woolly leaves, the stems are square like those of several of the *Labiatae*, and it has individual pink florets on short stems at the leaf joints, not heads. There is a reputed variety *T. pseudolanuginosus floribundus*, which trails rather further and flowers more freely from June to August. Both these are very easy from cuttings or division, tearing them apart in September and planting where they are required.

The really good Thymes are all varieties of *T. Serpyllum*, and of these, *T. Serpyllum major* is a wall plant worth all the rest put together. It has relatively large dark green leaves, about quarter of an inch long ovals, on red barked stems, with a much looser growth than that of the carpeting Thymes, and heads of crimson florets an inch or more across from June to August. It should be increased from cuttings of the young shoots in the spring or after flowering, inserted in the normal sand frame; division is easy in September, but those who have this splendid plant on their walls will want more of it. It is sometimes called '*T. Serpyllum superbus'*, but it is so distinctive that it has avoided the muddle of the main body of the creeping Thymes.

These are varieties of our native species from the South Downs and other hills of the British Isles, just as our cultivated Ericas are mainly collected as wild variations of Heather species. They spread as a flat carpet with interlacing branches clothed in tiny oval leaves, rooting down where they rest. A Thyme lawn made of all varieties weaving together, with both spring and autumn bulbs below it, is a lovely sight during their June to August flowering season, and they can be said to be the best all-round carpeters for full sun on any soil. The principal varieties are: *albus* with white flowers and paler foliage than the rest; Annie Hall, also pale foliage and pale pink; *aureus*, golden foliage, lilac; *carmineus*, dark foliage (normal) and deep pink or carmine with a touch of lilac; *coccineus*, which is brilliant crimson and the finest of all; Pink Chintz, which has rather grey foliage and is slightly salmon pink; and *minus*, which has very small foliage and lilac flowers. In addition to these *T. Serpyllum* varieties, *T. nummularius* (sometimes called *T. Serpyllum nummularius*, but now a separate species) has larger rounder leaves, a looser habit of growth, and rosy lilac flower heads which go on as late as September.

One of the beauties of the Thyme lawn is the contrasting of the colours, strong crimson among the pinks, the foliage colour of *T. Serpyllum aureus*, and the extended season secured by adding *T. nummularius*, and for this one needs pure and distinct varieties. Buying Thyme is, however, a chancy business, because one can get *T. Serpyllum coccineus* from half a dozen nurseries and find that most are variations of the original *T. Serpyllum* verging on *T. Serpyllum carmineus*.

All are easily increased from division in September or in the spring, but like all easy plants of no rarity, few people take the trouble to cherish them, and when they are out of flower it is very easy to mix all but those with distinctive foliage. The best way to buy Thyme is to choose it in pots and in flower.

The Thyme lawn is not a good propagating bed because the branches are usually interwoven and easily confused, so stock plant of the most '*coccineus*' *T. Serpyllum coccineus* available should be planted on its own. This can be increased in great quantity from cuttings very slender but they need no making, in the normal sand frame at any time between June and October. They root easily through the winter for spring potting. This variety, like *T. Serpyllum major*, should be treasured and increased. Thyme flies, and once it has vanished from your garden it may be gone beyond recall.

Alpines Plant by Plant

Umbilicus

Umbilicus oppositifolius is a very good wall plant, enjoying normal or limy soil and drought; it is a member of the order *Crassulaceae* like the Sedums. It is most un-Sedum-like in its flower display, producing hanging tassels of bright yellow florets from six inch branching stems, with the distant effect of Laburnum blossom, or large and brilliant hazel catkins. The season is in May and June and it is sufficiently non-invasive to be grown on the small rock garden as well as the wall in full sun, though not next to miniature species. It forms a spreading mat of stout prostrate branches with broad oval rather fleshy leaves slightly notched at the edges, and is a thoroughly easy and dependable plant for everyone. Propagation can be by division in September with direct replanting, or in the spring, from soft cuttings of non-flowering wood, kept dry in the pan, or from seed which is set and comes perfectly true, sown for choice about February.

This plant was formerly *Cotyledon simplicifolia*, but it has now been awarded the dignity of a genus all on its own. It is officially *Chiastophyllum oppositifolium*. All the other species of Umbilicus are part hardy and nothing like it, and the same applies to the Cotyledons, both of which are nearer Sempervivums in appearance, so this change is thoroughly justified, if it is allowed to stay where it is long enough for people to get used to it. It is no use trying to buy a *Chiastophyllum*, the nurserymen have it under one or other of the earlier names, usually as *Umbilicus oppositifolius*, but sometimes as *Sedum oppositifolium*, which was earlier still.

Veronica

There are a great many species of Veronica, including many part hardy shrubs now renamed 'Hebes' but the following account is restricted to those which are suitable for the alpine garden.

The Veronica everyone knows is *V. rupestris*; it is now *V. prostrata* but it was for a short time *V. teucrium dubia*. It is a powerful wall plant with narrow dark green leaves, notched at the edges, on strong but slender trailing branches capable of about two feet of growth in a season when it is at maximum speed. Plant it in the upper courses of the wall and let it cascade down; attack it with shears every second or third spring, cutting back to the main mass, and it will do well for anyone. Keep it off the small rock garden, there is no room.

The flowers from June to August are small clear blue spires; those of the best pink variety, *V. rupestris* Mrs. Holt, are considerably larger, and the growth is more moderate; the old *V. rupestris rosea* is completely

269

outclassed; *V. rupestris alba* has white spires and is also quite attractive.
These bread and butter Veronicas are good on the dry bank, in bulk they
can suppress many weeds and are very easy to increase. Soft cuttings in
June, or any time during the summer, root 100 per cent for even those
with 'red' fingers, and by cutting off larger branches and treading them
in along a trench in May or June in a shady place with watering to start
them, one can have plenty of large rooted pieces for building into the
dry wall. Curiously enough very little seed is set, and if it is there are
only three in a pod, but there is no need to bother with it.

A very much better plant, though scarce, is *V. armena*, which has
pale bright green rather lacy foliage and slender branching stems from a
centre root. The flower spikes are short but large and a glorious sky blue,
and keep going from June to October. This is by far the best Veronica
for the dry wall, and it is sufficiently modest in growth speed to go on the
rock garden; its height on the flat is about two inches. It is fully hardy,
has no soil fads, and is increased from soft cuttings of the branch tips
in August or in May.

Two grey foliaged species complete the wall Veronicas. They have
rather hairy oval leaves, bluntly notched at the edges and set thickly
on trailing branches, making a mat about three inches high. One has
blue spires, from three to five inches long on floppy stems, *V. pectinata*,
and *V. pectinata rosea* has pink, both in May and June, but not very
freely; they do their best on the dry wall. Increase is as for *V. rupestris*.
They are the kind of plant one gets in 'a dozen all different', and good
space fillers.

The small rock garden Veronicas include three nice but very scarce
creatures well worth long searching. Two of them have been Paederotas
but are now back as Veronicas, *V. Bonarota* which is a collection of
tufty rosettes of rounded leaves, notched at the sides and deep green in
colour with short spikes about an inch and a half long of pure blue
florets, and *V. lutea*. This is the only yellow Veronica, and though it is
not so free-flowering, and grows up to six inches high, while its fellow is
about four, it is reputed to hybridise with it. Both are increased by soft
cuttings in August, spring division or spring-sown seed. Those who can
secure seed—both species flower in May and June—should watch for
variations that are neat and flower well, to increase from cuttings and
enjoy in quantity. *Veronica lutea* was formerly *Paederota Ageria* or
Egeria and both thrive on a normal soil, not too rich in full sun.

Veronica pyroliformis from Western China is another treasure, with
oval leaves in a close mat, bronzy green and slightly hairy on the under
sides. The flowers are on four to six inch stems, with florets that hang

with the effect of little bells, in June and July. It needs a rather leafy soil
in sun or semi-shade, and is a most un-Veronica-like species but as hardy
as any of them. Increase is from seed sown in the spring, or from division in August, potting and wintering in a cold frame; when there are
more about it will probably be found suitable for direct replanting but
at the moment no one risks it.

More common and quite attractive are *V. Allionii* and *V. spicata
nana.* These are both mat formers, with creeping stems usually underground and oval leaves about three-quarters of an inch long, dark green
and plentiful. The first has clear blue flower two-inch spikes in June and
July, and the second violet spikes at the same time but about four
inches tall; its leaves are more pointed and it may be only a form of the
other species. Both are easy on any soil, increased by division in spring
or autumn.

The best of the shrubby Veronicas for the small rock garden is *V.
saxatilis*, which is correctly *V. fruticans*. This has oval dark green leaves
about the shape and size of those of box edging on a neat bush with
gnarled little branches, from four to six inches high. It flowers in April
and May with loose spikes of deep blue florets, each with a red central
eye and about half an inch across. Another is *V. satureioides*, which is
lower on the ground, about three inches, with darker blue flowers in
May and June, but not so many of them. These two are very easily
increased from soft cuttings after flowering.

The New Zealand Veronicas, which are now correctly Hebes, though
this is usually abbreviated to an 'H' against their names even in reference
works, are in general too large for the small rock garden. One, *V.
catarractae*, with rather brownish green, long, oval tooth-edged leaves
and red brown stems, growing about nine inches high, is quite a good
wall plant with sprays of white florets in June and July. The others
flower sparsely and can be regarded as foliage-only plants, like *V.
cupressoides*, which is a pale green 'imitation Conifer' rather on the lines
of *Chamaecyparis (Cupressa) macrocarpa.*

The best carpeting Veronica is *V. repens.* This has small oval leaves,
bright green on creeping stems, making a solid inch-high mat with single
Speedwell-like florets in May and June; these are often in real quantity.
It is an easy thing for any soil and makes good bulb cover, it takes
semi-shade and is suitable for the alpine path.

There are very many more Veronicas, and those who take a lucky
dip among the names, bearing in mind that though catalogues give
flower colour, they do not give frequency, should beware of *V. filiformis.* This is a creeping species like a more slender *V. armena*, but

the most fearful weed in the garden, in the alpine lawn especially, for it is usually described as a carpeter; it gets everywhere. Even when given its head it is not attractive, and though its weak stems break, one can never get the roots out.

Viola

The normal Violas of the border, such as *V.* Bluestone and *V.* Chantryland, are always out of place on the rock garden, and the species which are grown as alpines fall into two groups, apart from alpine house species.

First there are the impermanent types like small and free-flowering border Violas, but with lighter and more dainty blooms. These seed themselves and seed should always be saved for spring sowing as they are scarce in cultivation because they vanish from the nurseryman's stock beds as easily as from the small rock garden.

Viola saxatilis aetolica (often *V. aetolica saxatilis*) is a tiny prostrate species with a total height of two inches when in flower in May and June; it is vivid yellow and lovely while it lasts. The best way to be sure of it is to sow seed every September and winter it in pots so that a fair-sized plant is built up before flowering. Another rather larger species, about three inches tall, is *V. elegantula* (formerly *V. bosniaca*) which is a neat tuft of border Viola foliage on a small scale with rose pink flowers from May to July in great profusion; but again it is here today and gone tomorrow.

A more permanent species, which is neat and appropriate, is *V. cornuta minor*, a small form of one of the parents of the garden Violas. This is an inch-high tuft of slow-spreading foliage with tiny lavender flowers from May to October. It is not only a true perennial and long flowering, but a really good small rock garden plant for any soil. It should be raised from cuttings of the soft shoots in June, and the problem is that there are only relatively few of these. Seed is set, but it will cross with the border hybrids and when it is sown in September one should be prepared to throw away all the large ones, for it is a real beauty if only it can be secured true. The Rouen Pansy, *V. rothamgensis* (correctly *V. hispida*), is a larger version with small lilac flowers reaching six inches high and with the same long flowering season. It can be divided in the autumn or increased from summer cuttings, it is a more vigorous plant and much more easy to find.

The other group of Violas are those that need semi-shade and plenty of leafmould, with flowers and habits that come nearer our native woodland Violet. One of the best of these is *V. arenaria rosea,* a neat tuft plant with small dark green leaves (they go pale when it has too much sun and not enough leafmould) and a real quantity of small very deep pink Violets in May and June. It is best increased by September division for potting until established and it also comes true from seed, sown in the spring. Like very many species of garden value, this plant has many names: *V. sylvestris rosea* is one and the most correct is probably *V. Reichenbachiana*, but the one in which we are interested may well be of garden origin and never occur wild as we know it. Two other good ones are *V. biflora* and *V. hederacea*, the first mainly from North America and the other a New Zealander.

21st September

Fig. 25. Pot plant of *Viola arenaria rosea*, showing green seed pod.

Viola biflora has permanent creeping root stocks and the kidney-shaped leaves, from an inch to an inch and a half across at the widest part, are bright green and die down every autumn, so beware of digging it up by mistake. Its flowers appear from April to June and they are small, vivid yellow Violets, two on a stem as the name suggests. The total height in flower is from three to six inches, usually about four, and seed comes true from spring sowing. Normal increase is best by division in March, just as the plant is waking up, and direct replanting or potting. *Viola hederacea*, which was once *Erpetion reniformis*, is a very good little carpeting species, but not fully hardy in all districts, so seed should be saved and sown in September, to winter in a frame, as it is evergreen and keeps growing ready for planting after potting about April. It has pointed kidney-shaped leaves, or like rounded ivy leaves—the two specific names each describe it in one of its resemblances—and running stems that root from the joints in a slow spreading mat. The flowers are on two inch stems, four-petalled, one at the top deeply divided, two at the sides, slightly twisted and one broad one at the bottom. They are

s   273

deep violet in colour, with white tips, and stand above the foliage mat
from May to September.

There are many other Violas for woodland conditions, many of
which are inclined to flower on a scale that is meagre in proportion to

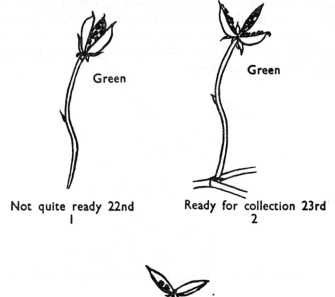

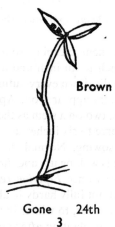

FIG. 26. Progress of the Viola pod.

the foliage; the worst is *V. conspersa* with heart-shaped leaves that are
slightly tinted with purple, and scarce flowers which are a pale violet
blue.

Alpines Plant by Plant

Wahlenbergia

This race spends its time becoming Edraianthus and then turning back again, so they are all described here because after more than twenty years of confusion, most nurserymen have decided to leave them as Wahlenbergias and wait for them to change again. The gardener searching in a catalogue for these very good species for limy conditions in full sun on the small rock garden, should look under both names.

The best of all is *Wahlenbergia serpyllifolia major*, which has tufts of small narrow leaves widening slightly at the tips, up to three-quarters of an inch long and dark purple green (if there is such a colour). It makes a neat clump about an inch high, spreading only slowly and from it in May and June come red-brown-barked flower stems with small leaves along their length, bearing very large bell flowers of rich royal purple. These are Gentian-like in their magnificence, and about an inch across.

It can be increased from tiny cuttings taken round the edges of the clump in July and August, the small non-flowering shoots that develop at this season; removed with great care, they should be about three joints long and go in a sand pan in the cutting frame. Seed is sometimes set and comes true but it is scarce, and it is best to cut back the stems after flowering to take the strain of trying to ripen the pods off the plant. This is one of the perfect small alpines, to go with such creatures as *Dianthus alpinus*, *Armeria caespitosa* and *Petrocallis pyrenaica* in limy gritty soil in full sun; it is scarce but hardy and a real treasure.

Another good small one is *W. pumilio*, quite often an Edraianthus, with grey green rather grassy foliage, the leaves about an inch long, and almost stemless lavender upturned bell flowers in June and July. The plant dies back to a central root stock in winter but produces another neat two inch high clump next spring. A larger relation is *W. graminifolia* (or *Edraianthus graminifolius*) which has the same grassy leaves, but up to two inches long, and the flowers in clusters on stiff stems about six inches high. It is, however, an evergreen and varies a great deal in its habit. Both plants need the same conditions as *W. serpyllifolia major*, and are easily raised from seed sown thinly in March.

Others in this group are *W. dalmatica* (correctly *Edraianthus caudatus*) which has wider leaves, two inches long and grey green rather than the silver grey of *W. pumilio*, with cluster heads of from six to ten violet blue bells in July and August, on six inch stems; and *W. dinarica* which is a smaller version with inch and a half leaves, rather more hairy on close inspection and with three inch flower stems.

These narrow-leaved species which grow as slow-spreading tufts with

275

cluster heads (those of *W. pumilio* are a cluster that has just got clear of the foliage), are at the moment most likely to be Edraianthus, and it would be a good solution to draw the line there, leaving *W. serpyllifolia major* on its own as a Wahlenbergia as it is so widely different.

Waldsteinia

Waldsteinia trifolia is a good carpeter for semi-shade and shade. It makes a mat of dark green leaves in rosettes at the ends of the underground branches; they are rather like those of a carpeting Potentilla and take on a bronzy tint in the autumn. The flowers are in sprays of buttercup yellow florets, about half an inch across and about six in a cluster on four-inch stems. Its season is May and June, and in effect it is a robust Potentilla that will flower well in the shade, on any normal alpine soil. It is increased easily by division in September or the early spring for direct replanting. The correct name is *W. tenata*, and it was previously *W. siberica*, but neither is in wide use. Another and rather more vigorous species is *W. fragarioides*, which has, as its name suggests, leaves like those of a strawberry, and the same type of flower heads in May and June. It is increased in the same way, and for practical purposes there is little difference between them; if anything the second one has rather shorter flower stems, about four inches, but makes a less compact mat.

Zauschneria

This is perhaps the latest to flower of all the wall plants, and its slender scarlet tube flowers in September and October should be as essential a feature as the deep blue trumpets of *Gentiana sino-ornata* on the rock garden.

Zauschneria californica makes a bush about a foot high or a bit less with a central woody stem and crowding slender branches clothed with narrow pointed grey leaves each about half an inch long. The flowers are carried in the joints of the upper leaves so that the effect is of a spike, and when a plant is doing well the scarlet and the grey make a splendid contrast. Its American popular names are Hummingbird Flower, and Californian Fuchsia, and their shape is very like that of the varieties of *Fuchsia fulgens*, such as *F.* Fireman, grown in greenhouses. They are about three-quarters of an inch long and open in a narrow-mouthed trumpet.

This species is sometimes regarded as not hardy, but on the wall with freedom from winter damp it is tough, and if the frost cuts back the branches, the spring trim-up which is always advisable brings plenty of new growth. The soil can be anything other than a peat, and though it does not mind a lime-free soil, it does its best in a chalky garden.

Increase is from soft cuttings taken in June or July. The best place to find these is low down by the woody stem, turning back the branches to hunt. These rather stouter basal cuttings are reputed to produce the toughest and sturdiest plants, they certainly root the best and grow well. They should be rooted in the normal sand frame and the plants grown on in a frame for spring planting, after stopping to produce bushy growth. One of the reasons why this plant is rarely seen in its glory at flower shows is because it hardly ever flowers in a pot; they take about a year or eighteen months after planting to get sufficiently established to give a good display.

8

Propagating Alpines

In the normal garden the object of propagation is merely to provide replacements and plants for extensions, but the principles of propagation are exactly the same as they are on a nursery where thousands of some species are grown, though the amateur has the advantage that he can select the best cuttings and the ideal time of year for his few.

Open-Ground Propagation without Glass

The easiest method of increase is by division, and the toughest of the division subjects can be multiplied by direct replanting. This should be done in the spring, firstly because the plants are coming into growth and secondly because there is less strong sun and more moisture about. Dig up your plant, divide it into fragments, bearing in mind always that it is better to have four good specimens that grow well than four survivors from a dozen broken up more drastically, and replant them where they are needed. Firm the soil well: the broken roots must put out new root hairs into the fresh soil and they do this more quickly if the surrounding earth is packed firmly against them, and water thoroughly. There should always be some undisturbed soil round the roots of the division, so that some of the root hairs are still able to draw in water. In dry weather, the clump should be watered also before dividing, both to make the soil hang on to the roots and to give a starting stock of moisture.

If this operation is carried out in later spring, or summer, shading is advisable, and this may enable the process to be successful with many unlikely division subjects among the less powerful carpeters. Use Conifer branches, the flat hand-like foliage of *Thuya Lobbii* or Lawson's Cypress used for hedging is ideal, and thrust them in the ground so that they lean over and shade the transplanted division. The outer leaves of cabbages are a good temporary cover, but wilt, flag and attract slugs. Conifer branches last for several weeks and are without these disadvantages.

Propagating Alpines

Soil layering, as advised on page 232 for alpine Phlox is best restricted to this race, because though Ericas have been increased in this way, the plants have always a large amount of old stem which has higher sap resistance, and they never grow so well. With alpine Phloxes, however, the system of filling a plant with fine soil during the summer or even leaving it to the soil that washes down an alpine bank, means that in March or April one can cut out a number of well-rooted divisions for direct replanting. The procedure is to feel round the edges of the clumps for those that have rooted fast down, and then to get to work with a fork. Any which turn out to have few roots can be replanted still attached to the parent; those which have plenty are removed. Their foliage will want to be drastically reduced: cut them back so that they have only about one-third of the growing leaves and stems, to reduce the expenditure through transpiration because they have lost the income from the parent stem. They will not of course flower the same year, but should do well the next.

There are a number of cuttings which can be inserted in the open ground, and because Helianthemums are among them, the alpine bank can be maintained without even using cloches. Losses are high by this method, which is only used for the very easiest subjects, but as plenty of cuttings are available and only a few replacements required, this is no drawback when not even cloches are available for propagation.

Put down a line in a shaded bed in part of the kitchen garden or other out-of-the-way place, and make a continuous cut about six inches deep against it with a spade held upright. Sprinkle some sand down the trench and insert your cuttings along it so that only the top few leaves protrude, but do not touch each other. Then tread firmly along both sides and water well with a rosed can. They will need watering daily in dry weather—the idea is to keep the ground round them moist—and later on they will need weeding. Many will die, but from summer cuttings between a third and a quarter will make plants for lifting in the autumn for use on the dry wall, or in the spring for removal to the dry bank.

These cuttings should be taken very much larger than normal: a branch of Helianthemum four to six inches long will root, one of *Polygonum vacciniifolium* of this size will root far more easily, and both *Veronica rupestris* and *Nepeta Mussinii* taken at this length will have an excellent chance. If the row can be covered with cloches the number rooted goes up very greatly. The method has been used for several of the tougher Dianthus, and it is commercial practice for Garden Pinks and Lavender, but in this case the operation is carried out in autumn. Aubrietas have been raised in this way, but as they do well in the dry wall as bare stems

279

Propagating Alpines

in October and November, and suffer when lifted in the spring, they are best pot grown as autumn divisions, or if no frame is available, planted directly from divisions at this time.

The Cutting Frame

If anything like a range of alpines is to be grown, some sort of frame is essential for propagation from cuttings; other operations including seed raising can be carried out under cloches. The cutting frame must be airtight for though, as the cuttings root, they need ventilation, when they are unrooted they need what used to be called a nice 'growy' feel in the air, in the words of scientific horticulture 'a microclimate of favourably high humidity'.

When a soft green cutting is removed from a plant and inserted in sand it can only draw water through the cut stem like a flower in a vase. Its leaves, however, are transpiring (breathing out water) through the stomata pores at the same rate as when they were on the parent plant with a full supply from the roots. The cutting therefore first wilts to reduce the size of the pores that are throwing away the water, the economy cuts in every plant budget, and then dies. If it is in a comparatively airtight cutting frame, with plenty of water in the sand, the humidity of the air in the frame rises until there is so much water vapour that the transpiring leaves can only force a limited amount into it; therefore they do not flag, or quickly recover if they do, and remain alive until they can grow roots to provide a normal supply.

The simplest form of frame is made from the sort of wooden box that once contained soap or tinned food, which could be bought for a shilling from any grocer. It is sometimes possible to obtain strong wooden boxes today, but construction needs only hammer, saw and nails. You require a bottomless box which can be any size so long as it is not shallower than six inches and not larger than eighteen inches square. It is covered with a single pane of glass—the size limitation is the risk that a larger piece will break in handling. If the glass is cut with a diamond, the sharp edges may be dangerous to handle, so round them off with emery paper which has had its abrasiveness increased to glass-cutting quality by wetting the surface with turpentine. A very good way out is to use one of the shorter and broader bathroom shelves made from thick rounded glass, and in this case the frame box can be made to fit it.

Fig. 27 shows the construction. The side pieces are to prevent the glass blowing away, and the lower blocks are shaped or extended a bit further from the end of the box by nailing another piece on first so that the lower edge of the glass can overlap by about half an inch for easy

280

handling. The essential slope is not provided by shaping the wood, but by setting one end of the box—and that faces south to catch the sun—lower than the other, to avoid accurate sawing. It is possible to buy 'prepared' or ready planed boarding six inches wide and half an inch thick ready cut to size, and the edge pieces can be bought in the same way, cut from $\frac{1}{2} \times 1$ or 2×1 in. planed wood, so no carpentering skill is involved, even if you cannot secure a box and use the discarded bottom to provide the other wood required.

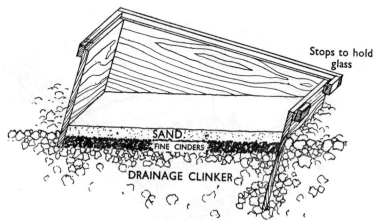

FIG. 27. Cutting frame from a grocer's box, with glass removed.

It is common practice in a greenhouse to put a pane of glass over a pan of seedlings or cuttings, to give higher humidity, but as this is flat, the moisture in the imprisoned air condenses on the underside of the glass, and will splash in the cold night on to the cuttings, often rotting them before they can root. The remedy is to turn the glass over night and morning so that the condensation evaporates outside. In the cutting frame the condensed water runs down the underside of the glass and trickles away into the sand at the lower end where no cuttings are inserted—an automatic time saver that is far more efficient in preventing drip.

As the frame itself is no more than a very large seed box, it is best filled solid with sand. Before it is put in place, a hole rather larger than its area should be dug out a foot deep and filled in with drainage material, ideally clinkers from a central-heating boiler, but coke, small stones or anything of this type will do. On top of this layer put about an inch of finer grit, cinders or small coke sifted through a fine sieve to remove dust and a coarse one to get out the lumps; the idea of this second storey is to prevent the fine sand washing down between the larger fragments of the drainage layer and yet to allow the water to pass through easily.

Finally, fill in a two inch layer of cutting sand, packed firm and level. It should reach to roughly four inches from the glass at the top end of the box and two inches at the lower one, though it does not matter if there is more space above than this. The frame in the illustration was a foot deep and about the largest possible with this type of construction.

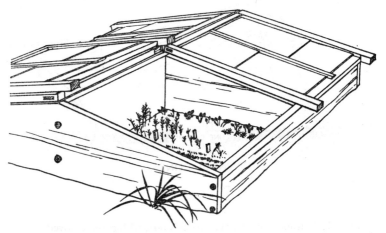

Fig. 28. Precast concrete cutting frame, with divisions.

The single pane frame is merely the easiest made, smallest, and cheapest device for rooting a full range of alpine cuttings; any other garden frame will do as well, provided it is airtight and the drainage layers are made with equal care. Not only do they give the rapid run through of water that cuttings need, but they are worm proof, and worms play havoc with propagating frames. A frame made from a single dutchlight is excellent, for size is not required in a propagating frame as the cuttings go through in batches during the summer, occupying space only for periods ranging from three to six weeks, though some take longer.

A box cutting frame a foot square should, between June and September, be able to produce between four and five hundred rooted alpines of the easier type, and better results are secured with three or four small ones, keeping slow rooting stuff or that which requires less watering on its own with one large, awkward, brick frame covered with a leaky old six foot by four foot light, rotten at the corners. If you already have an old fashioned brick frame, dig out the weeds and soil to give space for a good drainage layer, partition off one division with a rough brick wall, fill up any holes with cement, and use the soundest light over it.

The cutting frame needs good drainage and lack of leaks and draught holes, but it is only relatively small; frames used for new potted or growing alpines require far less care and airtight covering. The most common cause of failure in propagation, wasting time and cuttings in high mortality, is neglect of these simple principles.

Soft Wooded Cuttings

The greatest number of alpine cuttings are soft shoots removed after flowering, and of these the Helianthemum is both characteristic and the

Useless. with a flowerhead

FIG. 29. Helianthemum shoot, with bud.

amateur's best first attempt, especially as quantities are needed to give a good show on the alpine bank. A shoot with a bud in the tip, as shown in Fig. 29, is generally useless because it will use its strength trying to open the flower and set seed instead of growing roots.

Consider first the large branch of a Helianthemum drawn life size in Fig. 30. The second cut gives an ideal shoot, with a growing point, not a flower head, and if you are using a frame the cutting should be removed there, leaving the side shoots and others to come on either for next season's flowering, or further cuttings when they are large enough. Remove the cuttings with a sharp knife, selecting with care among the branches; a slow growing species supplies cuttings at the expense of next year's flowering, and an easy one has so many to spare that it is just as well to pick the best.

The cutting should now be 'made' by removing the bottom leaves to provide enough bare stem to enable it to hold firmly in the sand and to

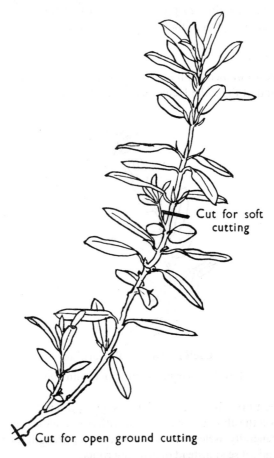

Cut for soft cutting

Cut for open ground cutting

FIG. 30. Ideal Helianthemum cutting shoot.

avoid burying the leaves, which may cause rotting off. Many commercial growers miss this operation, especially with alpine Phlox, to save time, but the amateur has fewer cuttings and needs a wider margin to make up for lack of skill.

A sharp knife is the usual tool, but used safety razor blades, discarded as soon as they are dulled, make the cleanest cut and save constant sharpening of a good knife that is quickly blunted on the fine grit the rain splashes on to alpine stems as they grow low on the ground. The blade is held between the first and second fingers of the right hand and the thumb pressed against the other side so that even a slotted blade is rigid as it is bent on a slight curve. The cutting is held between the finger and thumb of the left hand with the growing end pointing back towards the palm, and the leaves are removed close to the stem, cutting against the tip of the left thumb. The extreme sharpness of the blade makes the action almost one of resting the edge on the underside of the leaves to be removed, and the only time that a cut thumb is likely is when extra force is used on a tough cutting with a blunt blade. Then turn the cutting so that the lower end of the stem lies across the ball of the left thumb, and

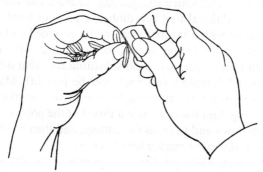

FIG. 31. 'Making' a Helianthemum cutting.

cut it through cleanly below a joint; the cut when it was removed from the plant may be ragged, or too much length of stem may have been left below this joint, or 'node'. With a sharp knife and care in removing the cutting from the parent, so that it comes off about an eighth of an inch below the joint, this last operation can be avoided.

All this is far more complicated to describe than to do; the propagator whose hands are shown in Fig. 31 has often carried out the whole process three hundred times an hour. It is exactly the same if a knife is used except for the difference in holding, and it also applies to propagating herbaceous plants and shrubs, though for hard cuttings and those thicker than a quarter of an inch, the knife is best. If the branch shown in Fig. 30 was to be used as an open ground cutting, the leaves below the second cut would be removed, also the growing side shoot just above the first cut.

Prepare your batch of cuttings: if they are all one species in a number of varieties either put a row of a different species between each, or, especially when you are doing say a couple of dozen each of a range of Helianthemums, part those with the same type of foliage with another; alternate grey leaved and dark green kinds save confusion when you dig them out rooted for potting.

First water the cutting sand with a fine-rosed can, and leave it a little while to soak in. This sand should contain no clay at all, it wants to be sharp and gritty, the sort of stuff that a builder uses to mix good mortar— the better for building the better for cuttings, and as it is used by the ton it is always cheaper than 'silver sand' which may have wind-rounded grains and therefore be without the sharp edges that make cuttings root best. It holds together in the frame in the same way as sand on the sea shore, because it is moist.

Use a piece of wood with a straight edge to mark out your first line of cuttings. The traditional tool is a dibber, a piece of hard wood about three inches long with a tapered point and a rounded end (the tip of a large sized wooden knitting needle, sawn off and with the cut end rounded with sand paper, is a good substitute now that dibbers turned from beechwood dowelling can no longer be bought). Make a row of holes with the point along the straight edge of your marker, put in the stem of a cutting, firm the sand with a thrust of the point of your dibber directed both down and towards the cutting, and then do the next right across, moving down the marker for each row.

Another system, which gets the cuttings in more firmly, is to take out a long narrow cut along your marker, like ruling a pencil line, with the tip of a builder's pointing trowel, or an old putty knife—anything with a thin blunt metal blade and an easily gripped handle. Put the stem of your cutting in the trench and press the sand firm round it with your finger and thumb on each side of the stem, a straight down push each time, leaving the cuttings standing upright in a line, so that their leaves just do not touch each other; if one rots off then, it will not spread to neighbours. It should take a slight pull to remove a cutting; if they lift out, press more firmly.

Both methods leave the sand disturbed with depressions round the cuttings, but this does not matter. Water them well with a rosed can; the sand washes smooth and level and the water grips round the packed grains ready for the cut channels in the stems to take as much as they can. Each kind should be labelled after it is inserted while the name is fresh in your memory, and here plastic labels, written, rubbed off and written again for a second batch are very useful, for with a small rock garden the cuttings of one variety may be taken in several goes as they are ready and this may mean four labels used for a mere dozen rooted.

On a commercial nursery, cutting frames in full sun can be watered several times a day, and canvas shades pulled over if they get too hot inside, but the amateur wants to be able to propagate by evening or week-end work, even though the speed of rooting is reduced. Therefore, either the frame should stand in a shaded place or the glass should have a coat of limewash or even white distemper on the underside; on the upper one

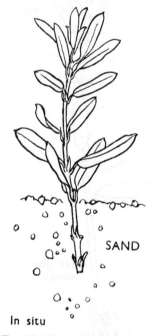

In situ

FIG. 32. The cutting inserted.

the rain will wash it off. The need is not heat but humidity inside. With this shading one good watering with a rosed can in the evening will keep them going, though in very hot weather a mid-day damp over with the rosed can is an advantage. The sand should stay firm and wet; if the surface becomes dry and powdery, it needs watering. In wet weather, or on dull days, waterings can be missed, because the hotter the air in the frame, the more water it will hold, therefore, the cuttings get to flagging stage more quickly. The water, too, sinking in the sand, sucks down air to the roots, which they need.

After a week or so, the cuttings will show some growth at the tips, but they should not be potted until the roots are well away, but as this is a sign that they are rooting, the lower edge of the glass can be propped up to give some ventilation when there is no doubt that all of them are definitely making new growth. If it is not convenient to pot them at once,

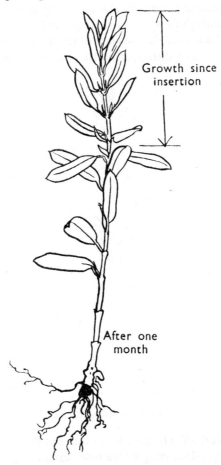

Growth since
insertion

After one
month

FIG. 33. Helianthemum cutting ready to pot.

take the glass off, and they will keep growing for some time, but there is no feed in the sand and they should be handled before they slow up and go hard from starving.

Rooting Hormones

The synthetic plant hormones developed within the last twenty years are extremely useful. They have removed the necessity for grafting

288

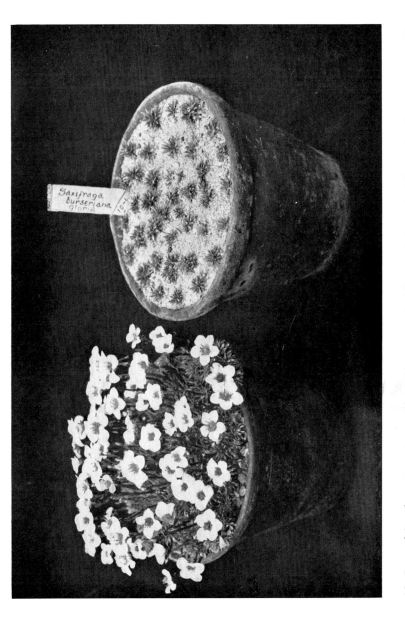

30. Pans of *Saxifraga Burseriana* cuttings. The pan on the left was photographed 8 months after insertion and is ready to pot as soon as it finishes flowering. On the right is a pan of single rosette cuttings of the same species, just inserted

31. The Kabschia system of plunging the pots in ashes in a cold frame is the best method of raising small Saxifrages quickly and also for all tiny cushion formers, especially *Petrocallis pyrenaica*. Photographed at Kew

dwarf Conifers and several shrubs, and are a very real help in rooting bad cuttings at the wrong season, or in giving good ones a better start.

The most trouble-free system is to buy them as a powder, mixed to the strength required, without any of the old messing about with glass

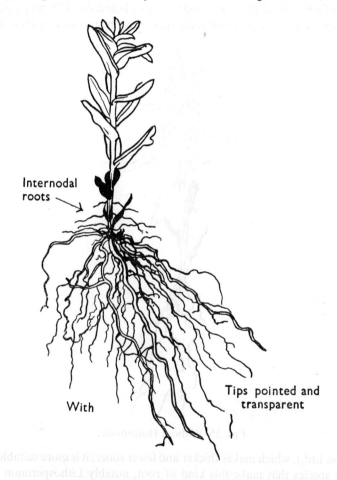

Internodal
roots

With

Tips pointed and
transparent

FIG. 34. Rooted cutting (Lithospermum treated with Hortomone 'A').

measures graduated in c.c.'s. The general all-purpose strength for alpines is the soft wood cutting dilution. Seradix 'B' (made by Messrs. May and Baker), strength one, is a pink powder sold by any good chemist. Stand your cuttings upright in a small dish of water—the shallow small size potted meat jar is ideal—and as you insert them, dip the moist tip in the powder. It clings to the wet stem, and the dish device is also good because it enables a large batch of cuttings to come off and be kept even overnight without flagging, in a shaded shed.

This preparation is beta indolyl butyric acid, and it produces a quick mass of roots which are as fine and thick as a beard. Another preparation, based on alpha naphthalene acetic acid, is Stimcut (made by Plant Pro-

FIG. 35. Without Hortomone.

tection Ltd.), which makes thicker and fewer roots; it is more suitable for those species that make this kind of root, notably Lithospermum and Miniature Roses. One or the other can be used: my own choice is the first, perhaps because I have rooted so many thousands of Delphiniums (miniature and border) and Gypsophila (including something near 50,000 Bristol Fairy) with it, apart from alpines in great quantity. The cost per cutting is very low, and if a little of the powder is tipped into another small dish, there is no risk of spoiling it by dripping in the water off wet stems; it seems to keep indefinitely. This artificial stimulation of the roots makes no difference to the alpine in after years, though it may be a better specimen because it has had a good start. All that happens is that the cutting turns its energies to root making in quantity; if the cuttings stay in the frame too long they starve just as fast. The advantages of modern science are easily thrown away by neglecting something quite simple that any illiterate gardener two or three hundred years ago learnt as a boy.

For the amateur they greatly increase the chances of rooting his first cuttings; they turn many slow and difficult plants into quick and easy ones, and secure the results that skill secured in the past. They are, however, no substitute for a good tight frame, sharp sand, good drainage and watering when required. Hormones are no help to open-ground cuttings and they also prevent the development of growing points, in fact, another powder hormone is now on sale to dust on potatoes to stop them sprouting in the clamp.

Therefore, do not use them for very tiny cuttings with the growing point near the stem like Kabschia Saxifrages, because you may spill some on the point and injure the cutting. They are also less effective for very slow growing species; their ideal subject is one that grows well but refuses to root because its natural hormone is either produced in very small quantity or strictly seasonably, like a Lithospermum. The amateur advantage is that they make easy plants easier still, though some experts refuse to use them at all.

Other Types of Cutting

Preflowering cuttings are used mainly to increase Campanulas and Gentians. They need the same methods as normal soft cuttings, but they come off before the main batch of summer alpines. The difference is that in the case of Campanulas, some buried stem should always be included; therefore, there are no leaves to trim off, they finish with about an inch of stem ready for insertion, and with Gentians and most other cuttings taken at this stage, the bud problem.

Always select the smaller growths as cuttings, not only to avoid reducing the flower display of the parent but to miss the ones with buds. Those which do develop while the cutting is rooting should be pinched out as soon as they are seen. They have the handicap of building up a new growing point as well as roots and therefore are always slow. When shortage of stock, as an example of a new hybrid that deserves maximum propagation, compels the use of flowering wood cuttings, use a powder hormone at the base to speed the root production, the sap pressure from the large root system brings out dormant stem buds quickly. Pre-flowering cuttings are best taken at least six weeks before normal flowering time to reduce the number of cuttings with buds. Campanulas in April, with no flowers possible before June, are always easy.

Small and compact plants provide another type, the tiny cutting, which often has to have old wood at the base, like an Aubrieta, not only

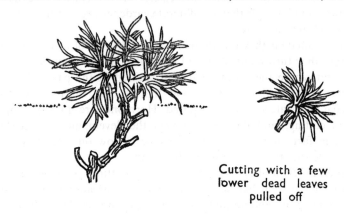

Cutting with a few lower dead leaves pulled off

Shown with earth cleared from the upper part of the root for clarity

FIG. 36. *Armeria caespitosa*, propagation.

because they root better with it, but because they take longer than a year to reach enough length to insert. *Armeria caespitosa* is an example, and Fig. 36 illustrates a branch and a complete cutting. The extra task is to

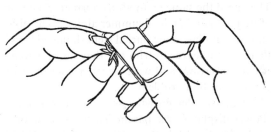

FIG. 37. Hand action in making small cuttings.

pull off the dead old leaves to clear the tiny stem for insertion. Where live leaves have to be removed from the lower part of the very small cuttings, like those of *Wahlenbergia serpyllifolia major* as an example, the making action is slightly different. The cutting is held between the thumb and forefinger of the left hand, pointing back in between them,

292

and the cuts are made upwards as it were towards the growing point. Fig. 37 shows the process of making a Kabschia Saxifrage cutting, but it applies to all tinies.

Heel cuttings are rarely made today. They were a favourite means of increasing shrubs, by tearing off some of the parent branch to provide a seal for the hollow stem of the young growth. Miniature Delphiniums with a small slice of the old wood at the base are a type of heel cutting, but unless the only available growth is hollow, as with Cytisus, cuttings without heels root best, especially with a rooting hormone.

Root cuttings are used for *Morisia hypogaea* and *Primula denticulata* named varieties, but these are described on page 225 under 'Morisia' and the same applies to the only leaf cutting subject, the Ramonda, discussed on page 248. Layerings are rarely used today, except as a rough method of increasing alpine Phlox without a frame.

The idea was to root a branch to the ground while it was still attached to the parent, a species difficult to root, and cutting it away when and if this took place. The layering, especially for Ericas, always meant a relatively small root supply for a branch of some size that always had a good deal of old wood at the base through which water had to force its way—a lasting handicap. A seedling or cutting has a fresh start and develops into a young plant; a layering from a hard wooded subject never becomes so well shaped as it is always old at root level. This disadvantage does not apply to border Carnations which are layered on young wood. The use of rooting hormones has removed the necessity and the amateur gardener has now learnt that a large layered Erica is a very bad bargain compared with a small bushy plant in a pot, grown from a cutting which has the root system to give vigorous growth and long, free flowering life in the Heather bed.

Ericas are ideally suited to the pan system of cutting raising, used for those which must stay a considerable time in the frame as they start very small indeed. Eight inch diameter seed pans are best, and these are filled first with some broken flower pot in the bottom, placed concave side downwards, then enough peat to cover them and finally a mixture of five parts sand to one of a good acid peat which will break down to fine particles so it mixes well. The object of the peat is to provide some feed for the rooted cuttings.

The cuttings are tiny. They are taken from the young wood, the tips of fine soft shoots, and in the case of *E. carnea* and varieties, are about an inch long; the minimum is roughly half an inch for the small side shoots of the miniature varieties of *E. vulgaris*. There is fortunately no need to cut off the minute leaves that cover these fraction-thick stems. Press the finger and thumb together about half way up, and strip them off; the bark does not seem to tear and so long as the soft stem is not squeezed too hard the process does no harm. Many nurserymen have done the

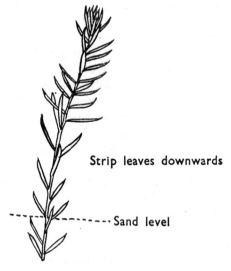

Strip leaves downwards

Sand level

FIG. 38. A 'stripping' cutting of *Linum alpinum*.

first thousand slowly and painfully with a razor blade and stripped the next ten thousand in reckless disgust at the prospect of working on this fiddling job for days and found that the stripped cuttings rooted best. The method applies to *Linum alpinum* also—*L. salsoloides nanum* is more easily damaged—but in general it is only used for Ericas.

Cutting—lower leaves
to be removed

FIG. 39. Kabschia Saxifrage cutting.

Insert the cuttings with a dibber, firming them in so that they need a slight pull to get them out, and then water them in with a rosed can. These pans should now stand in a shaded frame, with rather less water than a normal cutting frame, because the peat hangs on to the water to some degree, where they stay until they are rooted and growing well, with several side shoots at the base, ready to pot. If they are taken in May or June, this will be by the autumn. August or September cuttings should be potted in the spring, about February—pot in plain sand without peat; they need handling sooner. Very many alpines can be rooted in pans, or even seed boxes stood in a cold frame or greenhouse, but though they are portable, they still need cutting-frame humidity, and the best place for them is in a frame tight enough for good propagating conditions, until they are rooted. With other small cuttings, soil should replace peat over the crocks, and in the sand.

Inserted—with lower
leaves removed

FIG. 40. Kabschia Saxifrage cutting
'made' and inserted.

The Alpine Frame

This can be any ordinary cold frame, but it does need a good clinker and ash bottom to allow free drainage from the holes in the bottom of the pots, and to keep out the worms which will creep in through these holes to cause great root damage before they get out again. Its first purpose is to provide higher humidity for newly potted plants, all of which, whether they are root cuttings, divisions, or seedlings, have had their roots broken and their water supply reduced. It does not need such airtight construction as a cutting frame; it need only be kept closed for a few days until the new potted plants pull round, after which the lights should be propped up for ventilation in the day time.

During the winter and spring, however, it acts as a sun trap to give evergreen species a longer growing period. In summer, the underside of the glass is shaded like a cutting frame, to keep the temperature down, and avoid leaf wilting and scorching; for the rest of the year, the shading is washed off (which is why limewash is best as it comes off easily), and by closing the lights down about four or five p.m. a great deal of warmth can be stored for the night. The short wavelength heat from the warmed inside cannot radiate back through the glass, though it came in that way as light, which is the principle of all frames, cloches, and greenhouses, though in the last case the sun heat is usually supplemented with hot water pipes. In the depths of winter the alpine frame is kept closed, with ventilation only on sunny days, not because the alpines are not hardy, but to make them keep growing slowly through the winter. If the cutting frame is used in winter for a late batch, the shading should be removed from the glass. As a rough guide, shading is wanted from mid-May to mid-September when there is a chance of too much sun.

Cloches

As newly potted plants need less humidity than cuttings, those who have a few cloches of the 'Growers Barn' type, made of four pieces of glass, can do without a frame entirely. Level off some spare ground and spread it with a drainage layer of coarse ashes, stand your freshly potted alpines in rows of about four abreast, and place the cloches over them, first shading these on the inside, to reduce the amount of watering needed. When the plants are growing well, they can make room for another batch, but the ends of each row should be blocked with a pane of glass supported by a stick, or there will be a draught through that will undo all the benefit; a single lone cloche over a few plants is useless.

As cloches are used mainly for winter and spring vegetable crops, especially lettuce, and then to go over early outdoor tomatoes, they are usually free in summer, and therefore, if a little-used path or corner can take a single row, the same cloches can serve both purposes. They are not so useful as a substitute for a frame in winter, the gap along the top leaks in long continued rain, but for those who propagate only replacements in summer from the easier species, they are ideal. Helianthemums, Sedums and alpine Phlox need no cloches even, if they can be stood along a shaded path, they do better with them, but are sufficiently tough to endure without any assistance.

Divisions and Potting

The less vigorous carpeters and division subjects cannot be directly replanted but if the fragments are potted and placed in the alpine frame to recover they are far easier than cuttings or seed.

Dig up the stock plant, shake off sufficient soil so that the run of the roots can be seen, and cut these so that each fragment has a supply of fibrous roots as well as plenty of growing points. It is the root area that counts and if any fragment is left with a meagre share, cut back the foliage where a large subject is concerned. The method of chopping a clump in quarters with a spade, or the time honoured one of levering it apart with two forks back to back apply only to herbaceous plants. Small alpines need more care and deserve it: the most frequent cause of failure is too greedy division for the size of the plant. Some species can be cut up very small and grown on in pans until they are ready for potting, and this process is described under *Hypsela longiflora* on page 210.

It has been found that some of the smaller cushion plants, particularly *Petrocallis pyrenaica*, do best from tiny divisions of a single rosette with roots; these are removed with care and pricked out in a pan to grow on until they are well established. The method cannot be used for the slower small Saxifrages, because they seem to suffer from the resistance of the old stem, so a fresh but slow start as a cutting is superior.

One of the first needs of the alpine gardener is a collection of small pots, and because these are going to be used in a frame and a plunge bed before they are returned to stock when the alpines are planted, they are best all one size. An assortment of oddments means wasted space as a frame is rectangular, and will hold roughly 370 2½ in. or 'small 60' pots, the best size for alpines under a single dutchlight, which is 3 ft. 11 in. long and 2 ft. 10½ in. wide. It wastes room because they cannot fit together like cells in a honeycomb if the pots are mixed.

The procedure of potting is the same for alpines as divisions, seedlings or rooted cuttings. Place in the bottom of the pot some small stones, small cinders or broken flower pots as drainage material, enough to cover the drainage hole. Put in a small quantity of soil, then hold the plant central with the finger and thumb of the left hand and scoop the soil round it with the right. Finally use the thumbs of both hands to firm the soil, revolving the pot in the fingers and even lifting and banging it on the bench. Firm potting is as important as firm planting; the soil should not be hard, but it should take some little force to push a finger into it, and if one is knocked out at once, the soil should hold together in the shape of the pot. Care should be taken that the growing point of any cutting or seedling is not covered, and the surface of the soil should be about a quarter of an inch below the inner rim of the pot, to allow room for water. Like all operations it is easier to show in practice than to describe. I have potted very many more alpines than I have written words about them; it is a quick and simple job, when your hands learn their way about with plants and soil.

The many forms of block pot or soil block are unsuitable for alpines because these root through the large undersurface, and they are not

297

designed to stand for long periods in a frame or to be plunged. These pots should be restricted to quick growing species such as tomatoes, or for herbaceous plants where the different root action in them is an advantage.

Care of Newly Potted Alpines

The potted plants should stand carefully level on the ash floor of the frame or cloche site, so that they can hold their full share of first watering, with a rosed can leaving each pot full to the brim. Then close down the shaded light or put the cloches over them. There is plenty of water in the soaked soil for their needs restricted by broken roots, but after the third day some will be found to have dried out as shown by the lighter colour of the soil surface. Water these with the rosed can, filling them up completely, and only those; you cannot water alpines with a hose or can, filling up every one for about three weeks, otherwise the ones that do not need water will suffer. During this first period, the lights are kept closed; ventilation is given after this, increasing gradually, until after a month or so; the lights or cloches can come right off when they are established, in summer.

The main item in successful alpine growing in pots is careful watering: never dribble or give 'just a damp over', either water well or not at all. For those who work in the day time, evening watering is best, but in the winter, when much less is required, weekend watering at midday or thereabouts is best. The light with a leak is a big danger; one steady drip on the same plant every time it rains will kill any alpine.

Plunge Beds

If a frame can be spared during the summer, even without lights, it can grow alpines on for spring planting because its sides act as windbreaks and reduce the amount of watering required. The plunge bed is a more effective method of growing alpines to planting size with the minimum of watering. On a commercial nursery they are moved from the frames when the new roots can be seen round the sides of the pots (knock a plant out, take a look and put it back, to see when they are ready) into plunge beds where they remain until they are sold. The amateur with a frame or cloches can transfer his plants to plunge beds to save frame space in the same way.

Prepare the ground by replacing about three inches of top soil with ashes to keep out the worms and provide drainage, and surround the area with either bricks on edge, or rough wood the height of the pots used. Some growers make the sides and ends higher than this so that lights can be put over the plants in winter, making a very shallow frame, but as it is used mainly for hardy subjects that are well grown by September and October, this is not necessary. The width should allow easy weeding: two feet wide and as long as will fit the room is a good standard for a small garden, commercial sizes fit either a dutchlight or a 6 ft. × 4 ft. pitlight.

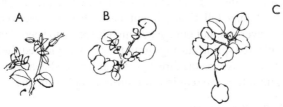

Fig. 41. (A) Chickweed, (B) Cardamine or 'poppers', (C) Lesser Chickweed.

The plants are buried in sifted ash up to the rim of the pot, and though sand has been used, central-heating or boiler ash, or coke breeze (ask your gas works for this excellent drainage material, it is cheap fine refuse coke) are best. For young Ericas and other lime haters, horticultural peat is good. Its purpose is to retain moisture and to prevent the pores of the pot from losing it as the wind blows against the exposed sides; the value of the system is demonstrated by anyone who has a few

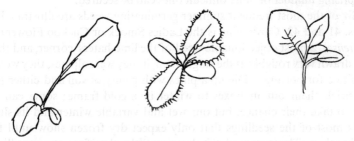

Fig. 42. (D) Dandelion, (E) Common Thistle, (F) Woody Nightshade, all at the potting stage, if they were alpine seedlings.

pots standing outside a frame and some in a bed. Shovel a fillet of ash against the end of your frame, press your first row of pots against it, then put in another strip of ash and repeat the process; with practice it is easy to make a neat job. If the plunging material contains no weeds, little weeding is required, but there may be some from those that blow on from the rest of the garden.

The plants stay in the bed, readily portable until they are required for extensions and replacements. If any of the more robust suddenly start growing fast, this is usually a sign that the main roots have gone through the drainage hole and ash layer and reached soil. Therefore, a replunge is advisable if plants stay in the bed more than a year. Cut off the protruding roots, and cut back the foliage; those which have rooted through badly will always be strong and woody subjects like Hypericums and Helianthemums, and unless this is done, the loss of the supply of water from the root may kill them; if cut back they will recover. In most gardens, however, a small plunge bed merely serves to keep Campanulas, as an example, for spring cuttings until they can be planted the following spring, or to hold Aubrietas direct potted and rooted in a frame through the winter, until they are required for autumn replacements.

The Easiest Seedlings of All

The simplest method of raising seedlings is to wait for the plant to sow its own. All alpine seeds are sown when they are ripe under natural conditions, though they do not always germinate at once, and the seedlings may be too small to stand our unnatural (for many alpines) winter. Therefore, if the seedlings of the more common weeds are known by sight, and any sudden crop during the summer is left until it can develop its first true leaves (apart from the rounded seed leaves or 'cotyledons') so it can be identified, many of the easier species, and a surprising number of more difficult ones can be secured.

Six of the most frequent summer germinating weeds are illustrated in Figs. 41 and 42. Cardamine is the Ladies Smock or Cuckoo Flower (*C. pratense*), a most objectionable weed of the lime-haters' corner, and they are drawn very roughly at the stage when, if they were alpines, they would be lifted for potting. Dig up alpines with plenty of soil and either pot or prick them out in boxes to winter in a cold frame; some can be left to take their chance, but our wet and variable winter and its slugs kills most of the seedlings that only expect dry frozen snow until the spring thaw. The rock garden is dug very little; therefore, stray seedlings have a good chance, and apart from deliberate direct sowing in crevices and paving, these self-sown alpines should always be remembered. Rather than miss a good 'hybrid of garden origin' or something scarce that has grown by luck, it is better to pot strange weeds and throw them away when they can be identified.

Seedboxes and Pans

The standard seed tray, two inches deep, is really too shallow for alpines; it also grows more expensive every year. The following substitute will do for the easier and quicker growth subjects, or for pricking out or anything that only has a six months stay in the box. Collect some firmly made, shallow, cardboard boxes, three inches deep and not larger than six inches across and nine inches long; bigger than this they are too floppy. Boxes that hold fifty or a hundred cigarettes are ideal, and so are those used by drapers to hold ties or some makes of collar.

Place the bottom of the box against a block of wood, on the end grain for choice, and punch out one quarter-inch drainage hole to every two square inches of surface, using a flat headed punch, which can be bought cheaply at an ironmonger's, or a large old bolt with the screw end filed flat across the tip, and a hammer. The object is to drive out a neat disc of cardboard, like a piece of confetti, without weakening the box or causing rotting or closing up afterwards as with holes jabbed with a nail or a pair of scissors. It is very much quicker and easier than making up wooden seed trays and splitting the inferior modern wood with bad nailing.

Then paint your box with ordinary cheap enamel and leave it to dry; for a good job give a second coat, taking care to get some on the cut edges of the holes. When they are dry they can be used like any other seed tray, but must stand on a good drainage layer of ash so that the surplus water can get away through the holes. They can be used for any seedlings; their inventor was experimenting on the influence of light and varying wavelengths on pasture grasses and his trial boxes stayed for a year without rotting, and though they cannot be used a second season, their cost is trifling. A small tin of enamel and a brush will provide for over a hundred, and once dry, they can be stored until required.

The kipper box, obtainable from fishmongers, is both cheaper and better than the two inch seed tray, because it is roughly three inches deep—three inch seed trays are the size to buy if these are used. Kipper boxes last about two seasons if they are outside all the time, but all wooden containers are best painted with Cuprinol, Solignum or other harmless preservative, not creosote which contains oils harmful to plants. This applies even more strongly to frames; creosote never dries properly and heat brings the smell out of the wood and makes a creosoted frame a death trap. Good paint or a sound brand of wood preservative should always be used.

The standard eight inch seed pan is permanent; those who have them should treasure them, as it is one of the problems of the makers that fewer and fewer men today will sit at a potter's wheel, so prices rise with wages, for machines cannot replace the potter's skilled thumbs. The $3\frac{1}{2}$ inch pot or 48 makes a very good seed pan especially for the smaller quantities sown on a garden scale, and any which come in to the family as pot plants from florists should be saved for alpine seeds. Broken pots for drainage material are also of value and should be hoarded, and washed after a pan or box has been emptied for use again.

Seed-Raising Systems

The easier species can be raised exactly as though they were any half hardy annual. First cover the bottom with a layer of drainage material, crocks or cinders, about half an inch deep, then fill up with soil which is pressed firm, levelled off and flattened with a flatter. This is made from a suitably sized piece of wood fitted with a handle, the sort of metal trowel called a 'float', used by plasterers, is good, and a round one to fit pans is a further refinement.

The soil should either be standard sterilised John Innes Seed Compost or a mixture based on the following two mixtures: six parts sandy loam, four parts good leafmould, four parts sharp sand, or, for lime haters, four parts lime-free loam, four parts leafmould, one part peat, six parts sharp sand. Seeds need a grittier soil than grown plants, and one that has been sifted fine, a quarter inch mesh is ideal.

The main need is thin sowing because some alpines from fresh sown seed will germinate like hairs on a cat's back, and others must wait for a considerable time to grow large enough to handle, so they cannot go in as casually as tomatoes. The better the spacing the stronger and sturdier the plants and the aim should be one to every quarter inch of surface, one every half inch for large seeds. The best way of securing thin sowing is to mix small seed with a fine grade of red hard-tennis-court dressing; shake the seed up with ten times its bulk or more in a suitable tin. Then sow thinly; the red dressing shows exactly where you have been, for it is not easy to see tiny seeds on a surface of flattened soil. Fine sand can be used, but it is heavier and therefore the seeds may sort themselves out a bit as you shake.

The old method was then to cover the surface with fine soil sifted on, ideally just the thickness of the seed, but a grit covering is superior, because it is less favourable to the growth of weeds and moss, and less easily driven aside by careless watering. Cover the surface of the soil with very coarse sand grains up to quarter of an inch, or granite or limestone chippings as used on the rock garden, roughly a single layer of them. The surface cannot cake and there is no need to worry about too deep a covering, within limits, because alpine seeds are accustomed to pushing their first shoot through a layer of chippings flaked by frost from the rocks; a too deep layer of a clay is another matter.

Propagating Alpines

A variation of this method is to cover with a mixture of two parts of coal dust to one of sand in a layer quarter an inch thick or preferably less. The coal dust (it makes no difference if it is anthracite or domestic coal, but coke dust is unsuitable), should be the fine powder that can be scraped up off the floor, and first it needs to be washed by stirring up in a bucket and pouring away the finest particles, leaving a coarse black grit, that should have any lumps bigger than quarter of an inch across picked out; the ideal method is to sift through a small sieve made by tacking perforated zinc on to the bottom of a bottomless small wooden box.

This material is of special value for slow growing lime haters where these are raised from seed, because though the coal makes no difference to the seed, moss seems to hate it, and moss is the great enemy of seeds, especially in a lime-free mixture. It is very effective for Ramonda and Astilbe seeds.

The normal rule for all alpines should be grit on the surface, granite or even smashed up flowerpot or slate for lime haters, limestone for others, even really coarse sand. The worst substance for any seed pan covering (or cutting frame) is a sand with some clay in it, the sort of low level subsoil which can sometimes be obtained free for taking away. Such small quantities are needed that the best pays every time.

The first watering is of considerable importance, for it is with this that the amateur usually washes all his seed to one corner of a box that stands on the tilt as he uses a coarse-rosed can. The propagator's skill or its lack is mercilessly exposed when his pans germinate. The most satisfactory method for a few is to have a large baking dish or even a washing bath beside you as you sow. This is filled with water about an inch shallower than the height of the pan, and as it is sown, each pan is stood in the water until the surface is damp, the last fraction is damped by capillary attraction as the soil sucks up the water like blotting paper. As the pans are removed the bath needs topping up from a waiting can; each is thoroughly wet, and will need no rose watering for a long while, perhaps more than a week.

Failing this system, used on some nurseries to water fresh potted plants by standing in a shallow box beside the potting bench, made watertight with pitch or sheet lead, water the box first before the seed is sown, using a fine-rosed can, leave it until the water has soaked in, then fill up again. Then wait until the wet box has stopped dripping, say an hour, flatten the surface gently and sow. Put on the chips and then leave the pan without any surface water, the chips will damp by their own suction.

Propagating Alpines

The 'soak from below' method is the basis of the 'suck down system' for very fine seeds. Make up your pan with a chipping surface, stand it in the soak tank and wait until the surface is damp, then sow your seed on top of the chips. Lift out the pan and place it where it is wanted, for as the water-level falls in the soil there is a sucking down of air, which pulls the fine seeds under. The method is not often used but is quite effective; most growers prefer a straight 'sown on soil and covered with grit' routine. Many are, of course, still using a soil covering, which is obvious and easy, but those who live by their skill in raising difficult seedlings to sell to specialist nurseries, use grit.

The Care of Seedlings

It is not necessary to keep alpine seeds in the dark, but it saves space in the spring and watering to cover each pan with a suitable sheet of flat asbestos sheeting. This material is slightly absorbent so there is little condensation trouble, and the pans or boxes can stand one on top of each other, with the labels laid on their sides. After about a week they will need searching through, to remove those that have germinated to the greenhouse stage or a cold frame, for before this they can go under the staging, or in a frame, or even a shed. The drawback is handling them, because if any are forgotten for two or three days the seedlings can suffer, and the method should only be used with sterilised soil, otherwise the first seedling through is almost always a weed.

It pays with Gentians, especially when stale seed is used, to stand the new sown pans outside to get them frozen, then bring them into a cold or even slightly warmed greenhouse. Alpine seeds expect to be frozen, though most will do without it, so this trick is often of value, and no ungerminated pan should ever be thrown away until it has been tried. This applies especially to Ramondas, and Rhododendrons as well as Gentians, for all three are erratic germinators. There is nothing to prevent a domestic refrigerator being used for this if room can be spared in it during the winter, but the seedlings should come out into mild conditions before they will germinate. There have been cases of rare and precious seeds left in by mistake for months, with a perfect germination as a result.

The normal routine of February or March sowing, with the fresh seed species about midsummer, needs no frost, neither does it need heat or high humidity. The seed frame has three jobs; first to provide a slightly milder climate, secondly to keep the drying winds off the seedlings while providing good ventilation, and thirdly, to prevent overwatering by excessive rain. Therefore, once the seedlings are up, block up the

32. Rooted cuttings of *Chamaecyparis Lawsoniana Fletcheri*. The upper cutting has been treated with Hortomone 'A', the lower is untreated. Seradix 'B', the powder rooting hormone, contains a different substance that makes very many small roots instead of a few strong thick ones. These chemicals give plenty of roots quickly and make no more difference to the plants afterwards than the advantage of a flying start. Their discovery has removed the need to graft difficult plants and they are very valuable for small Rhododendron species that are slow, difficult and variable from seed

33. A pan of *Ramonda* leaf cuttings photographed in August just after insertion

34. Leaf cuttings of *Ramonda Myconi*. A: two rooted cuttings showing the developing bud on the longer of the two. B: right and wrong cuttings; the shorter one has had the petiole (where the leaf clasps round the parent rosette) and stalk removed and so, like the cutting on the extreme left, it may root but can never form a bud and grow to a new plant

lights, which are unshaded in spring or winter, shaded in summer, and give plenty of ventilation.

Though some people consider a chipping surface means that it is hard to tell when water is required, it grows lighter in colour when it is dry and should be damped over on the surface lightly. The golden rule for watering seeds is 'when in doubt, don't'. The larger the seedlings, the more they need, but watering depends on weather, and it is impossible to give any hard and fast rule. Especially in winter, water with caution, and if a seed pan or plant gets so desperately dry that the soil cracks away from the edge, stand it on the soak tray. If a pan of seedlings flags right down flat, do the same; do not water on the surface if they are as dry as that, the water will not be able to replace the air in the pores and may run through the cracks. Always use a rose for seeds, on a florist's or other long spouted can of any size; the galvanised iron type with a screw-on rose is too coarse and heavy. Without a rose, even on pot stuff, the water just jumps in and out again; a hose with a fitted rose is better than any bare can.

Damping off is a problem that should not be much trouble on the grit system with good ventilation and careful watering. If it does develop, use Cheshunt Compound according to the directions on the packet. If moss appears, water with permanganate of potash; put sufficient crystals in the can so that you can see a rose pink colour as it jets through the fine holes, and use it if you see anything in the way of a green slime on the chippings, but next time the pan wants watering. Excessive water is the usual cause, and it may be due to drip; watch for the hole in the surface splashed by the drips and move the seeds to safety.

Slugs are another problem, and these are best destroyed with a slug bait, usually meta solid alcohol in bran. When you examine your pans or boxes, lift them high and look underneath where slugs hide so that these can be removed and squashed—it is the small ones that do the damage. Anyone fortunate enough to have the chestnut brown Slow Worm, a legless lizard usually about a foot long, in their gardens, should rejoice. This harmless creature which lies stiff on the hand when picked up, lives on slugs which it eats in incredible quantities; it is entirely different to the large and swift Grass Snake which eats frogs, or the rare, zig-zag marked Adder or Viper, the only snake which is dangerous and deserves destruction.

Because seedlings require these cool airy conditions, it is possible to use only cloches to raise all seeds. With a good ash standing ground, and glass at the end of the rows, one can sow, in spring, summer or autumn, cover down with cloches, lifted weekly for inspection and watering (more often in late spring and summer), and raise every species without using a frame or cold greenhouse. They may get cold in winter, but this is what they are designed to take.

Pricking out Alpines

The usual procedure is to pot alpines when they are large enough to handle, but in some cases, as an example when a lucky germination gives very many more of something good than the available pots or frame room will hold, they can be pricked out. Use a dibber and make a fair sized hole to take as much root as possible, and put them, usually in six rows of eight, in a standard size seed tray, filled like a seed box but with potting soil, and no chippings.

In this they occupy very much less room, but before they are planted they will need potting, because, except for very robust species, the root breakage on digging them out of the box for direct planting gives them a very severe check. Species like Primulas which have a dormant period can be planted direct while they are under an anaesthetic as it were, but as a general rule, alpines should be planted from pots without root disturbance.

Pricked out in boxes, however, they can keep on growing until room is available, standing under cloches or in a frame while they are recovering from the move, and then anywhere sheltered from drying winds where they can be watered, until they can be handled again. It is important that they should stand level, so that even watering is secured; a high dry end or a wet low one means mortality.

Seed Saving

Though alpine seeds can be bought from a few specialist growers, very many species never set enough to be sold, and fresh, home saved, seed always germinates best. The aim should be to gather your seed when it is ripe, not before and not later or the plant will have scattered it. The usual guide is the splitting of the seed vessel, or the ready break up of a fluffy head, and those who save seed should watch their plants and snip, carrying a pair of garden scissors, a few old envelopes and a pencil in readiness.

The collected seed should be placed pods and all in trays with paper in the bottoms so that it does not sift through and these trays should stand in the sun on a greenhouse shelf, a sunny windowsill or a dry shed. Break up the pods when they are dry, and remove the debris before storing in envelopes, labelled and dated for future sowing. If there is any doubt, as there is with one's first saving of some species, as to what exactly is the seed, sow the lot; it is as well to remove rubbish, but not essential, though those who sell seed are not entitled to do this.

Gentians, the Asiatic Primulas and Ramondas grow best from seed

Brown flower

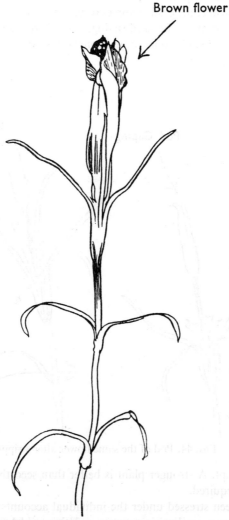

FIG. 43. Dying flower of *Gentiana Farreri*.

sown as soon as it is ripe; therefore, take it off the earliest blooms so that it has the longest growing season before winter. Later than August savings should be left until spring, which is the standard sowing time. With

Gentians of all types, it is a good plan to peel the petals that are dead and holding moisture away from the developing pods which can be felt fattening inside; this helps ripening in our wet summers, but is not required for other species.

If a plant will come easily from cuttings or by any other method there is no need to bother with seed saving, and where a species does not set seed easily the dead blooms should come off, as they weaken themselves

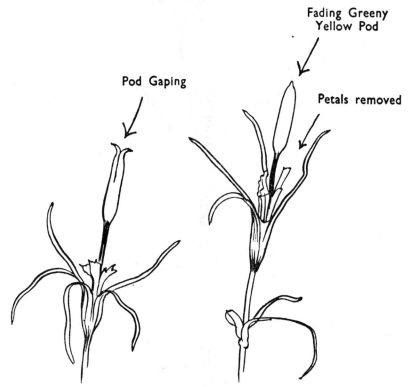

FIG. 44. Pod of the same flower after stripping.

in the attempt. A stronger plant is better than seed that may not ripen and is not required.

As has been stressed under the individual accounts of the species in the last chapter, seed raising means variation, widely where a hybrid is concerned and over narrower limits with many species, for alpine seed is never subjected to the careful selection of the seedsman. Many species breed true, but there are always some minor variations, which may not matter in the garden. Therefore, regard seed raising as a

Propagating Alpines

method of securing a plant which cannot otherwise be obtained, a means of gaining a large increase quickly, or a source of new variations from which to select plants of merit for propagation vegetatively. Those who wish to take up the production of new hybrids are recommended to read *Practical Plant Breeding* by R. D. Crance and W. J. C. Lawrence (Allen and Unwin) and to be utterly ruthless in discarding their 'also ran' variations.

Conclusion

In this book I have tried to give a guide to alpine gardening in all its aspects, dodging no issue and evading no problem. This is not because alpine gardening is more complicated than any other branch, but because it involves knowing more plants well, and my aim has been to give fuller descriptions and more precise details and instructions rather than to race over the subject to make it sound simple. I may have laboured the obvious and bored those with more knowledge than can be gathered from briefer books, I may have disgusted the expert, but failure in the modern garden with alpines is usually from lack of some simple principle that was common knowledge among gardeners twenty-five years ago when I grew my first alpines. Then I found when I read to increase my knowledge that the books never told me enough, so I have tried to say enough about the plants of which I write. I like them; they are all plants worth growing and taking the trouble to know well. They deserve to be used in our hasty gardens which run down hill towards lawns and shrubberies and I hope that among the 'Labour Saving Gardens', 'Trouble Free Gardens', 'Gardens Without Soil', and 'Gardens for Profit', there will still be room for an alpine garden, for those who like small plants from the mountains of the world, which have only beauty in miniature to recommend them.

If when you have read this book you find that the answer to your alpine problem is not here, and you wish, as I did, that instead of talking of other things, the author had dealt with your particular question, write to me c/o Faber and Faber, and I will do my best to make up for my neglect—that is if I know the answer, for however long one gardens, there is always more to learn.

APPENDIX

On Botanical Names, with a Glossary of special interest to the Alpine Gardener

THOUGH this subject would seem to have little to do with alpine gardening and alpines, even in an appendix, the author has, for many years, felt the need of a brief account of some of the principles and conventions of botanical Latin, and adds the present section* for the benefit of those whose life has been among plants, rather than books.

The botanical name of a plant is normally in Latin or of Latin form, and is a precise, internationally current, scientific term; it enables a species to be designated with accuracy, and purchased without misunderstanding, provided the name is correctly applied. Though the names used in some countries and by some nurserymen may not be in accord with the latest conclusions of systematic botanists, it is generally possible by consulting reference works to reduce them to common terms. These scientific names form an Esperanto for gardeners and botanists, in the same way that certain medical and chemical terms are international; many of them yield important clues to plant identification, and they deserve respect and study. They should not be regarded as a jargon, intelligible only to the expert; often their meaning is self-evident, even to the non-Latin scholar, and behind those whose meaning is obscure there are often interesting and complicated histories.

The history of botanical names is, however, less important than their correct application. The gardener needs to name his plants correctly so that he can consult reference books to learn more about them, can describe them accurately to others, and sell or buy them in confidence that he is handling the right goods.

One of the botanical conventions which many gardeners find puzzling is the *correct use of capital letters*. All botanists are agreed that the first

*The following notes and glossary are mainly the work of W. T. Stearn; grateful acknowledgment is also made to H. Gilbert-Carter, T. A. Sprague and D'Arcy W. Thompson for constructive criticism and suggestions.

311

part of a botanical name, *i.e.* the generic name such as Alyssum, Campanula or Meconopsis should begin with a capital letter. Concerning the second part of the name for a species, *i.e.* the specific epithet or trivial name, there is a divergence of usage. Many botanists now write all specific epithets with a small letter, hence we find *Gentiana farreri, Campanula wockei*, etc. in their works. This certainly makes the writing of botanical names simpler but involves the loss of a certain amount of historical information and most botanists at the present time prefer to follow the recommendation of the *International Rules of Botanical Nomenclature* 3rd ed., no. XLIII: 'Specific (or other epithets) should be written with a small initial letter, except those which are derived from names of persons (substantives or adjectives) or are taken from generic or vernacular names (substantives or adjectives).' Both usages are legitimate.

Geographical epithets nowadays take a small initial letter. Some examples are *āpennīnus* (from the Apennines, Italy), *arvaticus* (from Arbas, N. Spain), *austriacus* (Austrian), *baetĭcus* (from Andalusia, S. Spain), *bălĕārĭcus* (from the Balearic Isles), *cappădŏcĭcus* (from Cappadocia, Asia Minor), *carduchorum* (of the Kurds, hence from Kurdistan), *cenisius* (from Mont Cenis, France and Italy), *cōus* (from Cos, Aegean Sea), *ĕmōdi* (of the Himalaya), *graecus* (Greek), *helvētĭcus* (Swiss), *hispānĭcus* (Spanish), *monspeliensis* and *monspessulanus* (from Montpellier, France), *nĕāpŏlītānus* (from Naples, Italy), *novae-zelandiae* (of New Zealand), *pedemontanus* (from Piedmont, Italy), *sabaudus* (from Savoy), *saharae* (of the Sahara), *sinensis* (Chinese), *yunnanensis* (from Yunnan, China). Note the variety of terminations.

Commemorative names are many and present little difficulty: *Calceolaria Darwinii, Ceratostigma Willmottianum, Gentiana Farreri,* × *Penstemon Edithae, Ramonda Myconi, Saxifraga Burseriana* are examples. Generic names used as specific epithets are less easy to recognise because so many old generic names have passed out of use, though some of them may from time to time be revived, owing to differences of opinion among botanists as to the definition of genera. *Antirrhinum Asarina* (alternatively *Asarina procumbens*), *Cotyledon Umbilicus* (alternatively *Umbilicus rupestris*), and *Linaria Cymbalaria* (alternatively *Cymbalaria muralis*) are common examples. A generic name used as a specific epithet retains its original gender, which may be different from that of the modern generic name with which it is now associated. Such an occurrence may trap the unwary, especially if no warning capital letter is used. One of these tricky names is *Sedum Rosea* (not *Sedum roseum*), the epithet *Rosea* here being a feminine noun (not a descriptive epithet agreeing

Appendix on Botanical Names

with Sedum which is neuter) which was used by the old herbalists and botanists as the Latin name for the roseroot. Another is *Lythrum Hyssopifolia* (not *L. hyssopifolium*), the specific epithet *Hyssopifolia* being here a feminine noun, an old generic name, whereas in *Dianthus hyssopifolius*, *Centaurea hyssopifolia* and *Hypericum hyssopifolium* the specific epithet is simply a descriptive adjective and agrees in gender with the generic name. The specific epithet in *Sisyrinchium Bermudiana* (not *S. bermudianum*) is an old generic name; some botanists consider this the correct epithet for *Sisyrinchium angustifolium*, which does not grow in Bermuda! Vernacular names used as specific epithets are likewise unaffected by the gender of the generic name. They are based on native names in languages other than Latin and Greek; characteristic of this type among alpines are *Gentiana Kurro* (Indian, ? Nepali), *Pinus Mugo* (Italian), *Codonopsis Tangshen* (Chinese). Though these last two classes are comparatively uncommon, they are worthy of attention. The capital letter indicates that here is a name which conveys little or no information about the character of the plant or even its country of origin and therefore is not worth pursuing through a botanical glossary or dictionary in search of a translation.

Another convention, this one derived from the usage of the Romans, is that of *agreement in gender*. In Latin and Greek every noun has a gender; irrespective of whether it represents an animate or inanimate object, it is regarded as masculine (*e.g.* Dianthus, Schizocodon), feminine (*e.g.* Gentiana, Daphne), or neuter (*e.g.* Alyssum, Onosma). A specific or varietal epithet of adjectival form such as *barbatus*, *caespitosus* or *mollis* agrees in gender with the generic name and this usage has become so well known that a wrong gender as exemplified by *Dianthus alpina* or *Campanula alpinus* immediately hits one in the eye. However, a noun ending in *-us* is not necessarily masculine; names of trees such as Quercus, Pinus, Laurus are feminine; Acer, however, is neuter. Nor does the ending *-a* necessarily indicate a feminine noun; all generic names derived from Greek which end in *-ma* are neuter.

The Latin generic name-endings *-us*, *-a* and *-um* are the most frequently used for alpines, but without going into the question of Latin declensions, it is perhaps of value to note that names ending in *-es*, as in Omphalodes, *-e*, as in Jasione, and *-is*, as in Meconopsis and Oxalis (but not Cucumis, which is masculine), are treated as feminine (although certain of them were considered masculine by the Greeks and Romans), and take specific epithets with feminine adjectival endings. The gender of a name derived from Greek is less obvious than that of one derived from Latin. Generic names ending in *-pōgōn* (-beard), *-stēmōn* (-stamen)

313

Appendix on Botanical Names

-*cōdōn* (-bell) are masculine; those ending in -*mēcōn* (-poppy), -*daphnē* (-daphne), are feminine; those ending in -*děndrŏn* (-tree), -*stigma* (-stigma), -*nēma* (-thread) are neuter, like other Greek nouns ending in -*ma* or *ŏn* (i.e. -ον, not -ων).

Exceptions are few, and the practical gardener is little concerned with the reasons for them; by looking through a reliable plant list, he can ascertain the gender from the majority of the epithet-endings in the genus. The man who wishes to run to earth the reasons for anomalies can always do so by means of reference works. Thus, the name Onosma is neuter, not feminine, because it is a Latin loan-word taken directly from the Greek, and retains its classical gender, this being neuter in both Greek and Latin, so that *O. albo-roseum* is correct, not *O. albo-rosea*.

A few examples of these *adjectival endings* are given below, and with each word in the glossary will be found the masculine, feminine and neuter endings that apply; those without any are the same whatever the generic name.

Masculine	*Feminine*	*Neuter*
parvus (small)	parva	parvum
neglectus (neglected)	neglecta	neglectum
niveus (snowy)	nivea	niveum
asper (rough)	aspera	asperum
niger (black)	nigra	nigrum
pulcher (beautiful)	pulchra	pulchrum
ruber (red)	rubra	rubrum
tristis (sad)	tristis	triste
humilis (low)	humilis	humile
acer (sharp)	acris	acre
campester (of fields)	campestris	campestre
paluster (of marshes)	palustris	palustre

monticola (a mountaineer); the same in all genders
felix (happy); the same in all genders
radicans (rooting); the same in all genders

This last type of specific epithet (grammatically a present participle usually ending in -*ens* or -*ans*) is quite common.

Although the general public is apt to consider plant-names difficult, most gardeners soon acquire a rough working knowledge of 'botanical Latin', which is a simplified and somewhat mongrel tongue, dating from the Middle Ages and by no means identical with the language of classic Latin literature. It contains many words derived from other languages, more especially Greek and Late Latin. Thus, out of 727 specific epithets applied to Rhododendron, only 259 are of Latin origin; 246 come from Greek, 162 commemorate persons, and 80, mostly geographical, are from languages other than Greek and Latin. Moreover, a number of pure Latin words when used in modern botany have meanings other than those associated with them by the ancient Romans. Hence dictionaries of classical Latin, such as Lewis and Short's *Latin Dictionary* and W. Smith's *Latin-English Dictionary*, while giving guidance as to pronunciation, may lead one astray as to the meanings of botanical names. They must be supplemented with botanical glossaries such as those compiled by Lindley and Daydon Jackson.

However, one cannot grow plants for long without learning somehow that *-carpus* refers to the seed vessel or fruit, *-florus* to the flower and *-folius* to the leaves, and that the endings *-oides* (Greek) and *-formis* (Latin) indicate a resemblance to the plant named in the first part of the word, as *anemonoides* (resembling an Anemone) or *fragiformis* (resembling a strawberry or Fragaria).

The glossary which follows is designed to extend the 'carpus, folius, florus' rule of thumb knowledge of the gardener over a wider range of names, all of which apply to alpine plants, but it does not aim at completeness. Epithets which commemorate persons, or are vernacular or old generic names, have been omitted, together with those that refer to places of origin. It is primarily a beginner's guide to the meaning and pronunciation of some five hundred or so descriptive words which tell one a little about the character of the plant.

When well chosen, specific epithets are valuable aids to identification in genera which include only a few species, and every gardener should be acquainted with the meanings of a considerable number of them. It should be remembered, however, that names indicative of size are purely relative and that many plants were first named by botanists working with scrappy herbarium specimens, which did not give a good impression of the whole plant in the living state. Consequently a number of species have been branded for all time with rather misleading names, which the *International Rules of Botanical Nomenclature* compel us to accept, though such names are surprisingly few.

The *pronunciation of botanical names* seems to vary from person to person; there are no universally accepted hard and fast rules. Classical scholars have now fairly definite opinions as to the manner in which the ancient Romans spoke Latin, but the majority of English gardeners hearing plant names pronounced like that would either fail to guess the names intended or regard the speaker as highly eccentric. Most gardeners attempt to pronounce botanical names as if they were English words—

Appendix on Botanical Names

with results that classical scholars, as well as Continental gardeners and botanists, find equally amazing and unintelligible. Hence it is good policy to be acquainted with both the academic and the conventional English systems, at least as far as words of Latin origin are concerned, for about eighty per cent of botanical generic names and thirty per cent of specific epithets are derived from languages other than Latin and Greek; to pronounce *Mlokosewitschii, Maximowiczii* and *Przewalskii* as if they were Latin words is impossible. Such awkward names, being mostly commemorative of persons or else geographical, are not included in the glossary below, where an attempt has been made to indicate the correct vowel quantities and the place of stress.

Vowels and the syllables in which they occur are described as 'long' or 'short' according to the comparative time spent in saying them. Thus *o* in *rŏt* is short, in *rōte* long; *a* in *hăt* (or *ăpart*) is short, in *hāte* (or *psālm*) long; *i* in *kĭt* is short, in *kīte* (or *machīne*) long. In the following glossary the quantity mark ˘ indicates a short unstressed vowel and the mark ¯ a long unstressed vowel.

In words of two or more syllables, one syllable tends to be especially stressed or emphasised. In a two-syllable word, the emphasis is on the first syllable, *e.g. ál-bus, bó-nus*. In other Latin words, the stress falls on the next to last syllable (the penultimate or last but one) when this has a long vowel, *e.g. al-pì-nus, de-al-bà-tus*, or ends in a consonant if it has a short vowel, *e.g. pu-síl-lus*, but when the penultimate syllable is short, the stress usually falls on the one preceding it (the antepenultimate or last but two), *e.g. ol-e-à-ce-us, e-le-gan-tís-si-mus*. In the following glossary an acute accent, ′, marks a short stressed vowel, a grave accent, ‵, a long stressed vowel. It should be remembered that in Latin words every vowel is pronounced; hence, there are as many syllables as there are vowels. With regard to accentuation, all diphthongs are treated as long vowels. In pure Latin words, when two vowels come together without forming a diphthong, the first vowel is short, *e.g. lūtĕus*. This rule does not apply to words of Greek origin, *e.g. gĭgantēus*.

The vowel quantities of Latin words below have been taken from the standard *Latin Dictionary* of Lewis and Short or determined by analogy with words listed there, while for Greek words reference has been made to the *Greek-English Lexicon* of Liddell and Scott and the 'Pronouncing Dictionary' by P. W. Myles in Nicholson's *Illustrated Dictionary of Gardening*, **4.** 356-361 (1889). Following Lewis and Short, the *o* in *-folius* is here treated as short (*i.e. -fŏlius*) but English gardeners commonly pronounce it long (*i.e. -fōlius*), by analogy with English *fōliage*.

For further information the reader is referred to these dictionaries and those devoted to botanic terms by John Lindley and B. Daydon Jackson. It must be confessed that on a number of points there is some divergence between these works, and consequently the following list makes no pretence to infallibility.

A Glossary of Specific Names of special interest to the Alpine Gardener

Long stressed vowels indicated by ˋ (*e.g.* English *hàter*).
Long unstressed vowels indicated by ¯ (*e.g.* English *hāte*).
Short stressed vowels indicated by ˊ (*e.g.* English *hátter*).
Short unstressed vowels indicated by ˘ (*e.g.* English *hăt*).

Academic Pronunciation	*Conventional English Pronunciation*
ā (or *à*) as in *fāther*	*fāte*
ă (or *á*) as in *ăpart*	*făt*
e (or *è*) as in *thēy*	*ēvil*
ĕ (or *é*) as in *tĕnd*	*tĕnd*
ī (or *ì*) as in *machīne*	*īce*
ĭ (or *í*) as in *bĭn*	*bĭn*
ō (or *ò*) as in *vōte*	*vōte*
ŏ (or *ó*) as in *rŏt*	*rŏt*
ū (or *ù*) as in *rūle*	*rūle*
ŭ (or *ú*) as in *fŭll*	*stŭb*
ȳ (or *ỳ*) almost like *i* in *machīne*	*cȳpher*
y̆ (or *ý*) almost like *i* in *bĭn*	*cy̆nical*
ae nearly as *ai* in *pain*	*ae, oe* as *ee* in *meet*
ei nearly as *ey* in *grey*	*ei* as *eye*
oe nearly as *oi* in *boil*	
au as *ou* in *house*	*au* as *aw* in *bawl*
ui as *ui* in *ruin*	
c always as in *cat*	*c* before *a, o, u* as in *cat* (*i.e.* like a *k*)
	c before *e, i, y* as in *central* (*i.e.* like an *s*)
g always as in *good*	*g* before *a, o, u* as in *gape*
j like *y* in *yell*	*g* before *e, i, y* as in *gentle*
ch (of Greek words) like *k*	*ch* (of Greek words) like *k*

ăcàulis (-*e*) : Stemless or with only very short stalks.

ăcĕròsus (-*a*, -*um*) : Chaffy.

ăcĭcŭlàris (-*e*) : Needle-like (from *acicula*, a small pin).

ăcūminàtus (-*a*, *um*) : Acuminate, *i.e.* drawn out into a long sharp point.

ădĕno- : Gland (used in compound words, and derived from the Greek *aden*).

ădscéndens : }
ădsúrgens : } Ascending.

ădúncus (-*a*, -*um*) : Hooked.

ăffìnis (-*e*) : Neighbouring, related, hence, akin to a plant already known.

ăgērătĭfólĭus (-*a*, -*um*) : *Ageratum*-leaved.

ăīzòŏn : Evergreen (Greek origin).

álbĭdus (-*a*,-*um*) : }
albídŭlus (-*a*, -*um*) : } Nearly white.

álbŏ-margĭnàtus (-*a*, -*um*) : White-edged.

álbŏ-rósĕus (-*a*, -*um*) : White and rose.

álbus (-*a*, -*um*) : White, always referring to the flowers.

ălchĕmĭllŏìdēs : Like lady's mantle, *Alchemilla*.

álgĭdus (-*a*, -*um*) : Cold (see *frigidus* below).

ălpéstris (-*e*) : Alpine, but at moderate elevations.

ălpícŏla : A dweller in high mountains.

ălpìnus (-*a*, -*um*) : Alpine : applied both to natives of the European Alps and to those found at high elevations on other mountain ranges.

ăltíssĭmus (-*a*, -*um*) : Very tall.

ămàbĭlis (-*e*) : Lovable.

ămàrus (-*a*, -*um*) : Bitter.

ămoènus (-*a*, -*um*) : Lovely, delightful.

ămplĕxicaùlis (-*e*) : With leaves embracing the stem.

ăngŭlòsus (-*a*, -*um*) : Full of corners, *i.e.* angular.

ăngŭstĭfólĭus (-*a*, -*um*) : Narrow-leaved ; used to distinguish a plant from members of the same genus with broader leaves.

ănīsŏdòrus (-*a*, -*um*) : Smelling of anise, *Anisum*.

arbórĕus (-*a*, -*um*) : Tree-like ; usually applied to plants with one main sturdy stem, not necessarily of large size.

argéntĕus (-*a*, -*um*) : Silvery.

argillàcĕus (-*a*, -*um*) : Of clay, *i.e.* growing on clay.

argùtus (-*a*, -*um*) : Sharply toothed.

argўrŏphýllus (-*a*, -*um*) : Silver-leaved (Greek).

argўrótrichus (-*a*, -*um*) : Silver-haired (Greek).

ărĭĕtìnus (-*a*, -*um*) : Like a ram's head.

-ascens : Nearly, becoming (Latin suffix).

Appendix—Glossary of Specific Names

ăssĭmĭlis (*-e*) : Similar (see *affinis* above).

ātràtus (*-a, -um*) : Blackened, dressed in mourning.

àtrŏ-caerúlĕus (*-a, -um*) : Dark blue; referring always to the flowers.

àtrŏ-purpúrĕus (*-a, -um*) : Dark purple; referring to flowers or foliage.

àtrŏ-rúbens : Dark red; referring to flowers or foliage.

àtrŏ-sanguínĕus (*-a, -um*) : Dark blood-red : referring to flowers or foliage.

àtrŏ-vĭŏlàcĕus (*-a, -um*) : Dark violet.

aūrántĭăcus (*-a, -um*) : ⎫ Orange yellow; refers only to flowers.
aūrăntĭăcus (*-a, -um*) : ⎭ (from a Sanskrit word)

aùrĕus (*-a, -um*) : Golden.

aūstràlis (*-e*) : Southern, not always Australian.

aūtumnàlis (*-e*) : Autumnal.

ăzùrĕus (*-a, -um*) : Pure blue, or sky-blue (from a Persian word).

barbàtus (*-a, -um*): Bearded; refers to either leaves or flowers; hairs weak, not stiff.

bĕllĭdĭfólĭus (*-a, -um*): With leaves like those of a lawn daisy, *Bellis perennis*, in general shape, *i.e.* narrowly obovate.

bícŏlor : Two-coloured.

bĭfĭdus (*-a, -um*) : Divided in two parts.

bĭflòrus (*-a, -um*) : Two-flowered *i.e.* with flowers in pairs or two on a stem.

bĭfólĭus (*-a, -um*) : With two leaves.

bĭfùrcus (*-a, -um*) : Two-pronged.

blándus (*-a, -um*) : Attractive, or pleasant.

blĕpharŏphýllus (*-a, -um*) : Having leaves fringed with hairs (Greek).

bombỳcĭnus (*-a, -um*) : Silky.

bŏrĕàlis (*-e*) : Northern.

brăchy- : Short; as the first part of a name, indicates that flowers, leaves, spines, or some parts of the plant are relatively short (Greek).

brăchyphýllus (*-a, -um*): Short-leaved, in relation to other members of the same genus.

brăctĕàtus (*-a, -um*): With bracts, or small modified leaves at the bases of the flower stalks.

brĕvĭcaùlis (*-e*): Short-stemmed: usually with flower-stem more developed than *acaulis*.

bullàtus (*-a, -um*) : Puckered, or crumpled.

bŭxĭfólĭus (*-a, -um*): With leaves like those of the common box, *Buxus sempervirens*.

càesĭus (*-a, -um*) : Bluish grey.

caespĭtòsus (*-a, -um*) : Growing in close tufts.

319

Appendix—Glossary of Specific Names

calcāràtus (*-a, -um*) : Spurred ; *Aquilegia* is an example.

călcàrĕus (*-a, -um*) : Lime-loving, or growing on chalk or limestone.

căllizònus (*-a, -um*) : With a beautiful zone (Greek).

cályx : The outermost part of the flower.

campanulàtus (*-a, -um*) : Bell-like, of flowers (from Late Latin).

campéstris (*-e*) : Dwelling in fields or plains.

cándĭcans :
cándĭdus (*-a, -um*) : } Shining white ; brighter than *albus*.

cānéscens : Becoming hoary, white or grey.

cānus (*-a, -um*) : Hoary, white or grey.

căpillàris (*-e*) : Hair-like.

căpĭtàtus (*-a, -um*) : Closely clustered, in a head.

cardĭnàlis (*-e*) : Scarlet (in Latin first meant 'pertaining to a door-hinge', then 'chief', later transferred to the colour of a Cardinal's robes.)

cardĭŏphýllus (*-a, -um*) : Heart-leaved (Greek origin).

carmìnĕus (*-a, -um*) : Carmine, about the colour of our present 2½d. stamp. (Arabic, not Latin, origin.)

cárnĕus (*-a, -um*) : Flesh-pink.

-carpus (*-a, -um*) : Referring to the fruit, used in compound words (Greek suffix).

cauléscens : Having a stem.

cérnŭus (*-a, -um*) : Drooping.

chămaedrĭfólĭus (*-a, -um*) : With leaves shaped like those of *Teucrium Chamaedrys*.

chĭŏnánthus (*-a, -um*) : With snow-white flowers (Greek).

chrȳsánthus (*-a, -um*) : Golden-flowered (Greek).

cĭlĭàtus (*-a, -um*) : Edged with fine hairs, like an eyelid.

cĭnérĕus (*-a, -um*) : Ash-grey or pale grey ; applied to leaves.

cĭtrìnus (*-a, -um*) : Lemon-yellow ; always of flowers.

clȳpĕŏlàtus (*-a, -um*) : With a little shield.

cŏccínĕus (*-a, -um*) : Scarlet, usually the brightest in the genus.

cŏchlĕārĭfólius (*-a, -um*) : With spoon-shaped leaves.

coeléstis (*-e*) : Heavenly, hence blue.

cŏllìnus (*-a, -um*) : Growing on hills.

cŏmmùnis (*-e*) : Common, widely distributed.

cŏmmūtàtus (*-a, -um*) : Changed.

cŏmòsus (*-a, -um*) : Hairy ; hence shaggy or leafy, often with a crown of leaves or sterile flowers at the top of the inflorescence.

cŏmpáctus (*-a, -um*) : Pressed together, hence compact in growth.

cŏmpréssus (*-a, -um*) : Pressed down, flattened ; found as a name mostly among Conifers.

320

Appendix—Glossary of Specific Names

cōnfértus (-a, -um): Crowded together.

cōnfùsus (-a, -um): Confused, usually referring to a plant that has been known by a wrong name, through confusion of identity.

cōngéstus (-a, -um): Pressed together, crowded; usually of the flowers.

cōnspérsus (-a, -um): Sprinkled.

cōntòrtus (-a, -um): Involved, intricate or twisted.

cordàtus (-a, -um): Heart-shaped (in classical Latin, however, it means 'wise, prudent').

cŏrĭandrĭfólĭus (-a, -um): Coriander-leaved.

cŏrĭdĭfólius (-a, -um): With leaves like *Hypericum Coris*.

cornùtus (-a, -um): Horned, or spurred.

cortūsŏìdēs: Like a *Cortusa*.

cŏrymbòsus (-a, -um): With flowers in flat clusters.

crăssĭfólĭus (-a, -um): Thick-leaved.

crĕnàtus (-a, -um): Crenated, that is with scalloped edges (Old French, used in heraldry).

crīnìtus (-a, -um): Long-haired.

crĭstàtus (-a, -um): Crested.

crócĕus (-a, -um): Saffron-coloured, a deep bright yellow.

crŭéntus (-a, -um): Blood-red.

cŭnĕàtus (-a, -um): Wedge-shaped.

cŷánĕus (-a, -um): Dark blue, or sea-blue (Greek origin).

cŷlĭndrostáchyus (-a, -um): With a cylindrical flower-spike (Greek origin).

dăsy-: Thick, hairy; used in compound words (Greek).

dĕalbàtus (-a, -um): White-washed.

dĕca-: Ten- (Greek).

dēfléxus (-a, -um): Bent back.

dĕltŏìdēs:
dĕltŏìdĕus (-a, -um): Shaped like the Greek letter *delta* (Δ), *i.e.* more or less equilaterally-triangular (Greek but derived from Phoenician word for a tent-door).

dēmíssus (-a, -um): Lowly, humble.

dentĭcŭlàtus (-a, -um): Furnished with little teeth; having the edges finely toothed, more sharply than *crenatus*.

dĕòrum: Of the gods.

dēpréssus (-a, -um): Flattened.

dēsertòrum: Of deserts.

dĭastróphis (-e): Twisted (Greek).

dĭffùsus (-a, -um): Spread out, often loosely prostrate.

dĭssĭtĭflòrus (-a, -um): Remote-flowered.

x 321

dīversĭfólius (-a, -um) : With leaves of more than one kind.

drўădĭfólius (-a, -um) : *Dryas*-leaved.

dúbĭus (-a, -um) : Doubtful.

dūmòsus (-a, -um) : Of bushy habit.

ĕbúrnĕus (-a, -um) : Ivory-coloured.

ēcalcāràtus (-a, -um) : Spurless.

ĕchīnàcĕus (-a, -um) : Spiny (*echinus* is Greek and Latin for hedgehog).

ĕchĭŏìdēs : Like an *Echium*.

ēlàtus (-a, -um) : Tall.

èlĕgans : Elegant.

ĕmpĕtrĭfólĭus (-a, -um) : With leaves like those of the black crowberry or crakeberry (*Empetrum nigrum*), *i.e.* small, thin and heatherlike.

ĕnnĕăphýllus (-a, -um) : With nine leaflets, or with leaves divided into nine parts (Greek origin : *ennea* means 'nine'.)

ĕnsĭfólĭus (-a, -um) : With leaves shaped like the two-edged short Roman sword.

ēréctus (-a, -um) : Of upright habit.

ĕrīcĭfólĭus (-a, -um) : With leaves like those of an *Erica*, or heather.

ĕrĭŏcárpus (-a, -um) : With woolly or hairy fruits.

ērŭbéscens : Pale red, turning red, blushing.

ĕrўthrŏ- : Red- (Greek).

exímĭus (-a, -um) : Distinguished, excellent.

fărīnòsus (-a, -um) : Mealy, covered with powder (*farina* is Latin for 'flour').

fastīgĭàtus (-a, -um) : With all parts parallel and pointing upwards (typical example : Irish yew).

fĕnestràlis (-e) : Pierced with holes (the Latin *fenestra* was an opening in a wall to admit light, hence a window).

fĕrrŭgínĕus (-a, -um) : Rust-coloured.

-fĭdus (-a, -um) : Cleft or divided ; used with a number, as in *trifidus* (cut in three).

fīlĭfólĭus (-a, -um) : With thread-like leaves.

fīlĭfórmis (-e) : Of thread-like growth.

fĭstŭlòsus (-a, -um) :Pipe-shaped, tubular.

flăbellàtus (-a, -um) : Fan-shaped, referring to the leaves.

flàvus (-a, -um) : Golden yellow.

fléxĭpēs : With bent pedicels, literally with crooked feet.

flòre plèno : With a full (*i.e.* double) flower, usually abbreviated to *fl. pl.*, always a varietal epithet.

Appendix—Glossary of Specific Names

flŏrĭbùndus (-a, -um) : Having many flowers.

flòrĭdus (-a, -um) : Full of flowers.

fōlĭòsus (-a, -um) : Leafy, having more or larger leaves than related species.

formòsus (-a, -um) : Finely formed, beautiful.

frāgārĭŏìdēs :
frāgĭfórmis (-e) : }Like a strawberry (*Fragaria*) plant.

frágĭlis (-e) : Fragile, either in appearance, or with easily broken branches.

fràgrans : Scented.

frìgĭdus (-a, -um) : Cold, chilly, *i.e.* growing in an arctic or high mountain region.

frŭtéscens : Becoming shrubby.

frŭtĭcòsus (-a, -um) : Shrubby or bushy.

fúlgens : Gleaming, usually referring to a bright red or orange flower.

fúlvus (-a, -um) : Tawny, or reddish yellow.

gélĭdus (-a, -um) : Icy cold (see *frigidus* above).

gĕrănĭĭfólĭus (-a, -um) : With leaves like Cranesbill, *Geranium*.

gĭgăntèus (-a, -um) : Gigantic, the largest of the race (Greek origin).

gĭgàs : Giant (Greek origin).

glăbéllus (-a, -um) :
gláber (glabra, -um) : }Hairless, smooth.

glăbréscens : Becoming more or less hairless.

glăcĭàlis (-e) : Frozen, glacial (see *frigidus* above).

glăndŭlòsus (-a, -um) : Having many glands i.e. usually glandular hairs.

glaùcus (-a, -um) : Blue-grey in colour ; usually with a grey bloom like a cabbage (Greek origin).

glŏbòsus (-a, -um) : Ball-shaped, spherical.

glŏmĕràtus (-a, -um) : Clustered into a close head.

glūtĭnòsus (-a, -um) : Sticky.

grăcílĭpēs : Slender stalked ; literally, slender-footed.

grácĭlĭs (-e) : Thin, or slender.

grāmínĕus (-a, -um) : Grassy, *i.e.* with narrow grass-like leaves.

grāmĭnĭfólĭus (-a, -um) : Grass-leaved.

grăndĭflòrus (-a, -um) : Large flowered, compared with others of the same genus.

grándis (-e) : Large, grand.

grănítĭcus (-a, -um) : Growing on granite (Italian).

grăvéŏlens : Strong smelling.

guttàtus (-a, -um) : Spotted, speckled.

323

Appendix—Glossary of Specific Names

haemătócălyx: Having a blood-red calyx; the prefix *haem-* (from the Greek *haima*) means 'blood'.

hăstàtus (-a, -um): Halbert-shaped, *i.e.* with two diverging basal lobes; literally 'armed with a spear'.

hĕdĕràcĕus (-a, -um): Ivy-like.

hĕdĕrĭfólĭus (-a, -um):With leaves resembling those of ivy, *Hedera Helix*.

hĕdrēánthus (-a, -um): With sessile flowers (Greek origin).

hĕlŏdóxa (-a, -um): Marsh-glory (Greek origin).

hĕtĕrŏchròmus (-a, -um): Of various colours (Greek origin).

hĕtĕrŏdòn: Irregularly toothed (Greek origin).

hĕxándrus (-a, -um): Having six stamens (Greek origin).

hĕxăphýllus (-a, -um): Having six leaves or leaflets (*hex* is Greek for six).

hirsùtus (-a, -um): Hairy, usually with long distinct hairs.

hìrtus (-a, -um): Rough, or shaggy.

híspĭdus (-a, -um): Shaggy, or bristly with long stiff hairs.

hŏlŏsērícĕus (-a, -um): Very silky (Greek origin).

hŏrīzŏntàlis (-e): Horizontal in growth (Greek origin).

hórrĭdus (-a, -um): Sticking out; hence, rough, bristly or prickly; does not necessarily indicate an unpleasant plant.

hŭmĭfùsus (-a, -um): Spreading over the ground.

húmĭlis (-e): Lowly, small, not necessarily prostrate.

hўăcínthĭnus (-a, -um): Hyacinth-like.

hýbrĭdus (-a, -um): ⎱ Hybrid; sometimes applied by the older botanists to
hýbrĭdus (-a, -um): ⎰ species intermediate between others.

hўĕmàlis or *hĭĕmàlis (-e)*: Belonging to Winter, Winter flowering.

hyssōpĭfólĭus (-a, -um): Hyssop-leaved.

ĭánthĭnus (-a, -um): Violet-blue.

ĭbērídĕus (-a, -um): Resembling *Iberis* or candytuft (Greek).

īlĭcĭfólĭus (-a, -um): Holly-leaved.

ĭŏn-: Violet- (Greek).

ĭmbrĭcàtus (-a, -um): Overlapping, like tiles on a roof.

ĭmpúnctus (-a, -um): Unspotted.

ĭncànus (-a, -um): Hoary or grey.

ĭncānéscens: Becoming hoary or grey.

ĭncúmbens: Prostrate, leaning on, overhanging.

ĭnnōmĭnàtus (-a, -um): Un-named.

ĭnŏdòrus (-a, -um): Scentless.

ĭnsígnis (-e): Remarkable.

ĭntĕgrĭfólĭus (-a, -um): Entire-leaved, not divided.

324

Appendix—Glossary of Specific Names

ĭnvŏlūcràtus (*-a*, *-um*) : Provided with an involucre, *i.e.* a whorl of leaves or bracts below the inflorescence.

īsŏphýllus (*-a*, *-um*) : Equal-leaved, *i.e.* with all leaves of roughly the same size (Greek).

jūcúndus (*-a*, *-um*) : Pleasant, delightful.

júncĕus (*-a*, *-um*) : Rush-like.

K. This letter was absent from the Latin alphabet, its place being taken by 'C', so nearly all specific names beginning with 'K' are commemorative, or from the Greek.

lăbròsus (*-a*, *-um*) : With a large lip (or lips).

lăcĭnĭàtus (*-a*, *-um*) :⎫
lăcĭnòsus (*-a*, *-um*) :⎭ Much jagged or torn.

láctĕus (*-a*, *-um*) : Milky.

lăctĭflòrus (*-a*, *-um*) : With milky white flowers.

lăcùstris (*-e*) : Found by or in lakes, but not necessarily damp-loving.

laevĭgàtus or *lēvĭgàtus* (*-a*, *-um*) : Smooth, as if polished.

laevis or *lèvis*(*-e*) : Smooth, *i.e.* free from hairs or roughness.

lānàtus (*-a*, *-um*) : Woolly, covered with fur, usually thickly.

lăncĕŏlàtus (*-a*, *-um*) : Lance-shaped, *i.e.* often about three times as long as broad and broadest below the middle.

lānūgĭnòsus (*-a*, *-um*) : Woolly, downy.

lăsĭŏcàrpus (*-a*, *-um*) : With hairy seed vessels or fruits (Greek origin); the first part of the word denotes hairiness, the second refers to fruit or seed-vessel.

lātĭfólĭus (*-a*, *-um*) : Broad-leaved.

laxĭflòrus (*-a*, *-um*) : With loosely arranged flowers, *i.e.* not closely clustered.

láxus (*-a*, *-um*) : Loose, open.

lĕĭómĕris (*-e*) : With smooth parts (adapted from Greek).

lĕptŏpétalus (*-a*, *-um*) : With slender petals (adapted from Greek).

lĕptŏsépalus (*-a*, *-um*) : With slender sepals.

léptus (*-a*, *-um*) : Slender.

leucánthus (*-a*, *-um*) : White-flowered (Greek).

leucŏnòtus (*-a*, *-um*) : White on the back (Greek origin).

līlăcĭnus (*-a*, *-um*) : Flowers the colour of those of the common lilac, *Syringa vulgaris* (of Persian origin).

līmōnĭĭfólĭus (*-a*, *-um*) : With leaves like sea-lavender, *Limonium*.

līnĕàtus (*-a*, *-um*) : Marked with lines.

ĭngŭlàtus (*-a, -um*) : Tongue-shaped, usually of leaves.

līnĭfólĭus (*-a, -um*) : With leaves like those of the common flax, *Linum*.

lītŏràlis (*-e*) : Pertaining to the sea-shore.

lŏbàtus (*-a, -um*): Lobed; sometimes used with number-prefix, as *trilobus* or *trilobatus* (from the Greek *lobos*, the lobe of the ear).

lŏngĭflòrus (*-a, -um*) : Long-flowered.

lŏngĭfólius (*-a, -um*) : Long-leaved, compared with others of the group.

lùcĭdus (*-a, -um*) : Shining.

lùtĕŏlus (*-a, -um*) :⎱
lūtéŏlus (*-a, -um*) :⎰ Yellowish.

lùtĕus (*-a, -um*) : Yellow ; usually indicates a deeper colour than *flavus*.

măcrŏcárpus (*-a, -um*) : With large fruits (Greek).

măcrŏphýllus (*-a, -um*) : With large leaves (Greek).

măcrŏstèmōn : With large stamens (Greek origin).

măcŭlàtus (*-a, -um*) : Spotted or blotched.

măgnífĭcus (*-a, -um*) : Splendid.

màjor : *majus* : Greater.

mălăcŏìdēs :⎱
màlvàceus (*-a, -um*) :⎰ Mallow-like.

margĭnàtus (*-a, -um*) : With conspicuous margins to the leaves.

mărítĭmus (*-a, -um*) : Of the sea, coastal, seaside.

máxĭmus (*-a, -um*) : The largest of a genus, *minutissimus* being the opposite extreme.

médĭus (*-a, -um*) : Middle-sized, moderate, standing between two others.

mĕgălánthus (*-a, -um*) : Large-flowered (Greek).

mīcránthus (*-a, -um*) : Small-flowered (Greek).

mīcrŏphýllus (*-a, -um*) : With small leaves.

mĭnĭmus (*-a, -um*) : Least, smallest, very little.

mínor, mínus : Smaller ; small.

mĭnūtíssĭmus (*-a, -um*) : Smallest.

mĭnùtus (*-a, -um*) : Very small.

móllis (*-e*) : Soft.

mŏnánthus (*-a, -um*) : One-flowered (Greek).

mŏntànus (*-a, -um*) : Belonging to the mountains.

mŏschàtus (*-a, -um*) : Musk-scented (ultimately from Sanskrit).

mūcrŏnàtus (*-a, -um*): Pointed, *i.e.* abruptly ending in a sharp point, usually of leaves.

mŭltĭcàulis (*-e*) : Many-stemmed.

mŭltĭcŏlor : Many-coloured.

mŭltífĭdus (*-a, -um*) : Many-cleft.

Appendix—Glossary of Specific Names

mŭltĭflṑrus (-a, -um) : Many-flowered.

mūràlis (-e) : Of walls.

mŭscarĭŏidēs : Like a grape-hyacinth, *Muscari.*

mŭscŏìdēs : Moss-like.

mūtàtus (-a, -um) : Changed.

nànus (-a, -um) : Dwarf, compared with others of the genus.

nĕgléctus (-a, -um) : Neglected, overlooked, despised.

nĕmŏròsus (-a, -um) : Growing in open woodland, or in glades.

nervòsus (-a, -um) : Nerved, *i.e.* with prominent veins.

níger (-gra, -grum) : Black.

nítĭdus (-a, -um) : Polished, glossy, well groomed.

nĭvàlis (-e) : Growing in snowy places (see *frigidus* above).

nòbĭlis (-e) : Noted, excellent, superior.

nummŭlārĭĭfólĭus (-a, -um): With leaves like moneywort or creeping jenny, *Lysimachia Nummularia.*

nummŭlàrĭus (-a, -um): Like a coin, round and flat; strictly speaking, concerned with money-changing.

nùtans: Nodding, always of flowers.

obscùrus (-a, -um) : Dark, obscure.

obtūsàtus (-a, -um) : Blunted.

obtūsĭfólĭus (-a, -um) : Blunt-leaved.

obtūsílŏbus (-a, -um) : Blunt-lobed.

obtùsus (-a, -um) : Blunt.

ŏctōpétalus (-a, -um) : Eight-petalled.

ŏdōràtus (-a, -um) : Sweet-scented.

ŏffĭcīnàlis (-e) : Of medicinal use; sold in the shops, *i.e.* by herbalists (from the Latin *opificina*, a workshop).

-ŏìdēs: -òdēs, or -ìdēs : Like, or resembling (suffix of Greek origin).

ŏlĕĭfólĭus (-a, -um) : Olive-leaved.

ŏphĭŏcàrpus (-a, -um): With a long, slender, twisted snake-like fruit (Greek origin).

ŏppŏsĭtĭfólĭus (-a, -um) : With opposite leaves.

-òsus (-a, -um) : Abounding in, possessing, remarkable for (Latin suffix).

ōvālĭfólĭus (-a, -um) : Oval-leaved.

ōvàtus (-a, -um) : Ovate, *i.e.* of egg-shaped outline, often about twice as long as broad and broadest below the middle.

ŏxýlŏbus (-a, -um) : With pointed lobes (Greek origin).

pállĭdus (-a, -um) : Pale.

327

palmàtus (-a, -um): Divided like a hand; the leaf of a border Lupin is palmate.

pălùster (palustris, -tre): Growing in marshes.

pānĭcŭlàtus (-a, -um): With loose, branching inflorescence.

parvĭflòrus (-a, -um): Small-flowered.

pátŭlus (-a, -um): Spreading widely, outspread.

paucĭflòrus (-a, -um): Few-flowered.

pĕctĭnàtus (-a, -um): Like a comb.

pĕdàtus (-a, -um): Divided somewhat like the foot of a bird; palmate, with the lateral divisions themselves cleft in two, like a leaf of hellebore.

pĕduncŭlàris (-e):
pĕduncŭlàtus (-a, -um): } With a stalked inflorescence.

pĕrénnis (-e): Perennial; used to distinguish a plant from annual members of the genus.

pĕtraèus (-a, -um): Growing among rocks.

phlŏgĭfólĭus (-a, -um): *Phlox*-leaved.

pĭnnātĭfólĭus (-a, -um): Pinnate-leaved; with leaflets arranged on each side of a stalk; Mimosa, *Acacia dealbata*, is an example of a pinnate leaf.

plăntāgínĕus (-a, -um): Like a plantain, *Plantago*, especially in leaf.

plăntāgĭnĭfólĭus (-a, -um): Plantain-leaved.

plătýpĕtalus (-a, -um): Broad-petalled (Greek origin).

plūmòsus (-a, -um): Feathery.

pŏlўchròmus (-a, -um): Many-coloured (Greek).

pŏlўphýllus (-a, -um): Many-leaved (Greek).

pŏlўrrhìzus (-a, -um): With many roots (Greek).

praetérĭtus (-a, -um): Passed over, overlooked, omitted.

prōcèrus (-a, -um): Tall, elongated.

prōcúmbens: Prostrate.

prōcúrrens: Extending, spreading.

prōrèpens: Crawling.

prŭĭnàtus (-a, -um): } Pruinose, *i.e.* with a waxy granular secretion on the
prŭĭnòsus (-a, -um): } surface; literally, covered with hoar-frost.

ptĕrócălyx: With a winged or flanged calyx.

pūbéscens: Covered with fine soft hairs.

pūbígĕrus (-a, -um): Down-bearing.

pŭdĭbúndus (-a, -um): Modest.

pŭlchéllus (-a, -um): Dainty and small.

pŭlchérrĭmus (-a, -um): Most beautiful.

púllus (-a, -um): Dark coloured, blackish.

pŭlvĕrŭléntus (-a, -um) : Powdered, dusty.
pŭlvinàris (-e) : Cushion-shaped, making a small tuft or mound.
pūmílĭo : Dwarf.
pùmĭlus (-a, -um) : Small, dwarfish.
pŭnctàtus (-a, -um) : Dotted.
púngens : Piercing, usually with thorny twigs.
pūnícĕus (-a, -um) : Reddish, red-purple.
pŭrpŭráscens : Purplish, or turning purple.
pŭsíllus (-a, -um) : Dwarf or small.
pўcnólŏbus (-a, -um) : With close or crowded lobes (Greek origin).
pўgmaèus (-a, -um) : Dwarf.

quadri- : Four- (used in compound words).
quin- : *quinqu-* : *quinque* : Five- (used in compound words).

răcēmòsus (-a, -um) : With flowers in a raceme, *e.g.* the common laburnum.
rādĭcans : Taking root readily ; refers usually to a prostrate species rooting from the nodes.
rāmòsus (-a, -um) : With many branches.
rāmŭlòsus (-a, -um) : With many small branches.
rĕcúrvus (-a, -um) : Curving backwards or downwards.
rĕfléxus (-a, -um) : Bent back sharply.
rēnĭfólius (-a, -um) : With kidney-shaped leaves.
rēnĭfórmis (-e) : Kidney-shaped, referring to leaves.
rĕpándus (-a, -um) : With an unevenly wavy leaf-edge.
rèpens : Creeping ; compare *Hypericum reptans* and *H. repens* to see the difference.
réptans : Creeping flat on the ground.
rētĭcŭlàtus (-a, -um) : Net-like, made like a net.
rĕtùsus (-a, -um) : With the tip rounded but shallowly notched.
rhŏmbŏĭdàlis (-e) : Of rhombic shape, *i.e.* in outline somewhat like a rhombus, a four-sided figure with the sides equal but the angles not right angles.
rígens : Stiff or rigid, not necessarily erect.
rígĭdus (-a, -um) : Stiff, not always upright.
ríngens : Gaping, wide open, always of the flower.
rīpàrĭus (-a, -um) : Frequenting river-banks.
rīvŭlàris (-e) : From brook-sides.
rŏsĕĭflòrus (-a, -um) : With rose-coloured or rose-shaped flowers.
rósĕus (-a, -um) : Rosy pink.

Appendix—Glossary of Specific Names

rŏstràtus (-a, -um) : Beaked.

rŏtundĭfólĭus (-a, -um) : Round-leaved.

rúber (rubra, -brum) : Red.

rùfus (-a, -um) : Red, reddish.

rūgòsus (-a, -um) : Wrinkled, creased.

rūpéstris (-e) : Growing in rocky places.

rūpícŏla : A dweller among rocks.

rūtĭfólĭus (-a, -um) : With leaves like rue, *Ruta graveolens.*

săgĭttàtus (-a, -um) : Shaped like an arrowhead.

sălĭcĭfólĭus (-a, -um) : With leaves like a Willow, *Salix, i.e.* pointed, long
    and narrow.

sălmònĕus (-a, -um) : Salmon-pink.

sălsūgĭnòsus (-a, -um) : Growing in salty places, *e.g.* a salt-marsh.

sănguínĕus (-a, -um) : Blood-red.

sarmentòsus (-a, -um) : With many runners, like a strawberry, *Fragaria.*

săxàtĭlis (-e) : Living among the rocks.

scáber (scabra, -brum) : Rough to the touch.

sēclùsus (-a, -um) : Separated, remote.

sēcŭndĭflòrus (-a, -um) : With all the flowers turned towards the same
    side.

sēcŭndĭfólĭus (-a, -um) : With all leaves pointing the same way.

sēmĭ- : Half- (used as the first part of a word).

sĕmpĕrflòrens : Ever-flowering, not always in this country, however.

sĕmpĕrvírens : Evergreen, or ever living and growing.

sĕptémfĭdus (-a, -um) : Cut in seven divisions (not September-flowering).

sĕptĕntrĭōnàlis (-e) : Northern.

sērícĕus (-a, -um) : Silky ; clothed with close-pressed fine hairs.

sēròtĭnus (-a, -um) : Late, *i.e.* Autumn-flowering.

sĕrpȳllĭfólĭus (-a, -um) : With leaves like wild thyme, *Thymus Serpyllum.*

sĕrràtus (-a, -um) : With many teeth at the edges, like a saw.

sèrtulum : A little garland.

sĕssĭlĭfólĭus (-a, -um) : Without leaf-stalks, the leaves sitting directly on
    the branch.

sētòsus (-a, -um) : Bristly.

sĭmplĭcĭfólĭus (-a, -um) : With simple leaves, *i.e.* in one piece, undivided.

sŏnchĭfólĭus (-a, -um) : With leaves like sow-thistle, *Sonchus.*

sŏròrĭus (-a, -um) : Sisterly (see *affinis* above).

spăthŭlĭfólĭus (-a, -um) : With leaves like a spatula.

spĕcĭòsus (-a, -um) : Good-looking, handsome.

spĕctàbilis (-e) : Notable, remarkable.

Appendix—Glossary of Specific Names

-spermus (-a, -um): -seeded (used in compound words of Greek origin).
sphaerocéphalus (-a, -um): Round-headed (Greek).
spīcàtus (-a, -um): With flowers in a spike, *i.e.* flowers sessile along the terminal part of the stem.
spīnòsus (-a, -um): Spiny, thorny.
spléndens: Brilliant, glistening; may be the best of a dull race.
spúrĭus (-a, -um): Of illegitimate birth, hence false.
squarròsus (-a, -um): Rough, with scales or bracts spreading outwards.
statĭcĭfólĭus (-a, -um): With leaves like sea-lavender, *Limonium*, often known as *Statice*.
stellàtus (-a, -um): Star-like.
strāgŭlàtus (-a, -um): Covered.
strāmínĕus (-a, -um): Straw-yellow; literally, made of straw.
strĭàtus (-a, -um): Streaked or marked with longitudinal parallel lines.
stríctus (-a, -um): Drawn together; hence upright, or growing stiffly with the stems close together, not so close or so pointed in habit as *fastigatus*.
stylòsus (-a, -um): With a long or persistent style.
sūàvĕŏlens: Sweet-smelling.
sŭb-: Nearly, slightly, partly, almost; used as a prefix in compound words.
sŭbăcaùlis (-e): Nearly stemless.
sŭpìnus (-a, -um): Lying on the back, *i.e.* prostrate, with flowers facing upwards.
sȳlvátĭcus (-a, -um): Growing in woods.
sȳlvéstris or *sĭlvéstris (-e)*: Growing wild, in contrast to a related, cultivated kind.

tănăcētĭfólĭus (-a, -um): Tansy-leaved.
tărăxăcĭfólĭus (-a, -um): With leaves like those of a dandelion (*Taraxacum*).
tărdĭflòrus (-a, -um): Late-flowering.
tárdus (-a, -um): Slow in growth, or late in flowering.
ténax: Tough, holding fast.
tĕnéllus (-a, -um): Rather delicate, of frail appearance.
tĕnŭĭflòrus (-a, -um): Slender-flowered.
tĕnŭĭfólĭus (-a, -um): Slender-leaved.
tĕnŭíssĭmus (-a, -um): Very or most slender.
tĕtra-: Four- (Greek).
tĕtrăgónus (-a, -um): Four-sided, square, with blunt angles (Greek).

331

Appendix—Glossary of Specific Names

tīnctòrius (-a, -um) : Used in dyeing, now or formerly.

tōmĕntòsus (-a, -um) : Densely hairy with short hairs (*tomentum*, literally, is 'stuffing for cushions').

trĭándrus (-a, -um) : With three stamens (Greek origin).

trícŏlor : Three-coloured.

trifĭdus (-a, -um) : Cut in three.

trĭŏvulàtus (-a, -um) : With three ovules.

tríquĕtrus (-a, -um) :⎫ Sharply three-cornered, triangular, with acute
trĭquètrus (-a, -um) :⎭ angles.

trístis (-e) : Sad, mournful, hence dull-coloured.

tūbĕròsus (-a, -um) : With tuberous roots, literally, 'full of lumps'.

turbĭnàtus (-a, -um) : Inversely conical, top-shaped.

ūlícĭnus (-a, -um) :⎫
ūlĭcìnus (-a, -um) :⎭ Like gorse, *Ulex*.

ŭmbĕllàtus (-a, -um) : Having flowers in an umbel, *i.e.* an inflorescence with the flower-stalks radiating from the stem like the ribs of an umbrella.

ŭmbròsus (-a, -um) : Shady, *i.e.* liking shade.

ŭndŭlàtus (-a, -um) : With a wavy edge.

ūni- : One- (Latin prefix synonymous with Greek *mono*).

ūnĭflòrus (-a, -um) : With one flower on a stem.

ūtrĭcŭlàtus (-a, -um) : With a small bladdery fruit.

văccīnĭĭfólĭus (-a, -um) : With leaves like whortleberry, *Vaccinium*.

vágans : Wandering, widely distributed.

vărĭĕgàtus (-a, -um) : Of two or more colours.

vĕlūtìnus (-a, -um) : Velvety (Italian origin).

vēnòsus (-a, -um) : With many, or well-marked veins.

vĕnústus (-a, -um) : Beautiful (from the goddess Venus).

vĕrnàlis (-e) :⎫
vèrnus (-a, -um) :⎭ Pertaining to Spring.

vĕrsícŏlor : Of changeable colour, or of various colours.

vēsícàrĭus (-a, -um) : With a bladder, referring to the fruit.

vĕstìtus (-a, -um) : Clothed, usually with hairs.

vĭllòsus (-a, -um) : Shaggy, with hairs longer than in *tomentosus*.

vĭncĭflòrus (-a, -um) : With flowers like periwinkle, *Vinca*.

vĭŏlàcĕus (-a, -um) : Violet.

vīrgàtus (-a, -um) : Of twiggy habit.

vīrgĭnàlis (-e) : Virginal, hence pure white.

vĭrĭdĭflòrus (-a, -um) : Green-flowered.

332

Appendix—Glossary of Specific Names

vírĭdis (-*e*) : Green.
vĭttàtus (-*a*, -*um*) : Striped lengthways.
vŭlgàris (-*e*) : Common, or well known.

W. The Latin alphabet contained no such letter, so specific names beginning with this letter are all commemorative or geographical.

xĭphĭŏìdēs : Shaped like a sword (Greek).
xĭphĭŏphýllus (-*a*, -*um*) : With sword-like leaves (Greek origin).

Y. All specific names beginning with Y are commemorative or geographical.

zōnàlis (-*e*) :
zōnàtus (-*a*, -*um*) : }Marked with a belt or ring.

INDEX

Acaena, 93, 148–9
Buchananii, 101, 149
inermis, 101, 149
microphylla, 101, 148
Achillea, 149
Clavenae, 75, 149
Kellereri, 75, 149
King Edward, *see* A. Lewisii
Lewisii, 25, 40, 75, 104, 149
tomentosa, 75, 149
umbellata, 75, 149
Aconite winter, *see* Eranthis
Aethionema, 149–51
cordatum, 151
coridifolium, 75, 151
grandiflorum, 75, 150, 151
iberideum, 75, 151
moricandianum, 151
pulchellum, 75, 151
Warley Rose, 25, 29, 40, 75, 129,
149–51
Ajuga, 151–2
Brockbankii, 26, 40, 129, 152
genevensis var. Brockbankii, *see* A.
Brockbankii
reptans, 21, 56, 84, 151
Alpenrose, *see* Rhododendron ferrugineum
Alpine bank, 13–23
construction, 16
planting, 18
plants, 19–21
soil treatment, 17
upkeep, 21–3
Alpine border, 24–60
construction, 27
planting, 25, 26, 28, 30
plants, 28-31, 37-60
Primula corner, 31–7
site, 28
soil, 27, 28, 37

Alpine border, upkeep, 28–31
Alpine frame, 295–6
Alpine lawn, 97–105
plants, 99–105
Alpine path, 89–97, 99–105
planting, 93–7
plants, 99–105
soil, 93
Alpine Phlox, *see* Phlox
Alpine soils, 138–46
lime-haters mixture, 144, 145
lime-lovers mixture, 144
scree mixture, 144
seed-raising, 302
testing, 144
sterilising, 145–6
woodland-plant mixture, 144
Alpine Toadflax, *see* Linaria
Alyssum, 152–3
saxatile, 75, 88, 152
saxatile citrinum, 152
serpyllifolium, 152
spinosum, 40, 153
spinosum roseum, 40, 153
American Cowslip, *see* Dodecatheon
Androsace, 30, 144, 153–6, 256
carnea, 155
carnea var, Halleri, 127, 155, 156
lanuginosa, 75, 153, 154
lanuginosa var. Leichtlinii, 75, 153
primuloides, *see* A. sarmentosa
sarmentosa, 75, 154, 155
sarmentosa Chumbyi, 75, 154
sarmentosa Watkinsii, 75, 154
sempervivoides, 40, 129, 154
Anemone, 167–8
apennina, 168
blanda, 49, 56, 167
blanda alba, 167
blanda atrocaerulea, 26, 49, 56, 167
blanda rosea, 49, 56

335

Index

Anemone, fulgens, 168
 nemorosa, 168
 nemorosa Allenii, 168
 nemorosa Blue Bonnet, 168
 nemorosa Robinsoniana, 168
 Pulsatilla, 168
Anthyllis, 156
 montana, 76, 103, 156
 montana rubra, 156
 Vulneraria, 76, 103, 156
 Vulneraria var. Dillenii, 76, 103, 156
Antirrhinum Asarina, 72, 76, 88, 156,
 157
 glutionosum, 157
 nanum Dazzler, 157
 nanum Flame, 157
Ants, 31
Appendix on botanical names, 311–33
Aquilegia discolor, 40, 158
 pyrenaica, 40, 129, 158
Arabis, 158–9
 albida, 76, 88, 158
 aubrietioides, 76, 88, 158
 blepharophylla, 158
 carduchorum, 40, 159
 rubella, 158
Arenaria, 99, 159–60
 balearica, 93, 101, 159
 caespitosa, 101, 159
 caespitosa aurea, 101, 159
 montana, 73, 76, 159
 purpurascens, 40, 129, 160
Armeria, 160–1
 caespitosa, 26, 40, 129, 144, 160, 292
 corsica, 76, 88, 103, 161
 maritima, 76, 88, 103, 161
 maritima Vindictive, 76
 Vindictive, 161
Artificial fertilisers, 141, 143
Asperula suberosa, 127, 129, 161
Asplenium Ceterach, see Ceterach
 officinarum
 Trichomanes, 84, 193
Astilbe, 162, 303
 chinensis pumila, 56, 162
 glaberrima saxatilis, 56, 162
 simplicifolia, 56, 162
Aubrieta, 162–5, 279, 292
 alpine bank, 21

Aubrieta, dry wall, 62, 63, 65, 71, 76, 88
 soil, 144
 Barkers Double, 76, 164
 Blue King, 76, 164
 Carnival, 76, 164
 Dawn, 76, 164
 deltoidea, 164
 Gloriosa, 76, 164
 Godstone, 76, 164
 Gurgedyke, 77, 164
 Henslow Purple, 77, 164
 Magnificent, 77, 164
 Rosea splendens, 77, 164
 Russell's Crimson, 77, 164
 Vindictive, 77, 164
Azalea balsaminiflora, see Azalea
 roseaflorum, fl. pl.
 roseaflorum, 135
 roseaflorum fl. pl., 52, 165

Bell Heather, see Erica cinerea
Bird's Eye Primrose, see Primula
 farinosa
Blechnum penna marina, 194
 Spicant, 85, 194
Bone meal, 143
Botannical names, 311–33
Brodiaea uniflora, 168
Bulbs, 49–51, 56, 57, 165–70
 alpine border, 25, 26, 29

Calamintha alpina, 77, 170
 grandiflora, 170
 suaveolens, 170
Calceolaria, 124
 acutifolia, 172
 biflora, 127, 135, 171–2
 Darwinii, 172, 239
 polyrrhiza, 172
 tenella, 135, 171
Californian Fuchsia, see Zauschneria
Calluna vulgaris, see Erica vulgaris
Campanula, 172–5
 alpine bank, 21
 dry wall, 72, 73
 pre-flowering cuttings, 291, 292
 soil, 144
 acutanula, see C. arvatica
 arvatica, 40, 129, 173

Index

Campanula, carpatica, 77, 88, 173
cochlearifolia, *see* C. pusilla
fenestrellata, 40, 77, 88, 103, 129, 173
garganica, 40, 77, 88, 103, 173
glomerata, 174
glomerata acaulis, 129, 174
haylodgensis fl. pl., 40, 104, 174
isophylla, 77, 172
isophylla alba, 77, 172
muralis, 172
Oakington Blue, 173
Portenschlagiana, 21, 73, 77, 85, 172, 173
Poscharskyana, 21, 77, 172
pulla, 40, 105, 129, 173
pulloides, 25, 41, 85, 173
pusilla, 25, 41, 101, 129, 173, 174
pusilla alba, 41, 101
Tymonsii, 41, 174
Waldsteiniana, 41, 174
Catmint, *see* Nepeta
Cement, 33, 89, 90, 91
Centaurium scilloides, 41, 175
Cerastium, 175
tomentosum, 175
Ceratostigma plumbaginoides, 77, 175–6
Ceterach officinarum, 85, 194
Chalk Plant, *see* Gypsophila
Chamaecyparis Lawsoniana Elwoodii, 177
obtusa tetragona minima, 177
Cheddar Pink, *see* Dianthus gratianopolitanus
Cheshunt Compound, 305
Chiastophyllum oppositifolium, *see* Umbilicus oppositifolius
Chionodoxa sardensis, 25, 49, 167
Claytonia australasica, 26, 51, 56, 101, 176
Cloches, 279, 280, 296, 305
Clustered Bellflower, *see* Campanula glomerata acaulis
Cobweb Plant, *see* Sempervivum arachnoideum
Common Fumitory, *see* Corydalis lutea

Common Hartstongue, *see* Scolopendrium vulgare
Concrete, 33, 89, 90, 91
Conifers, 176–7
Convolvulus althaeoides, 177
Cneorum, 177
incanus, 177
mauritanicus, 77, 177–8
Corydalis lutea, 85, 88, 135, 178
Cotula squalida, 56, 93, 101, 178–9
Cotyledon simplicifolia, *see* Umbilicus oppositifolius
Crane's Bill, *see* Geranium
Crazy paving, 96
Creeping Bugle, *see* Ajuga
Creeping Snapdragon, *see* Antirrhinum Asarina
Crocus, 165–6, 169
Balansae, 49, 166
Fleischeri, 49, 166
Kotschyanus, *see* C. zonatus Kotschyanus
longiflorus, 49, 166
medius, 50, 166
ochroleucus, 50, 166
pulchellus, 26, 50, 166
susianus, 50, 166
Tomasinianus, 26, 50, 166
Tomasinianus Whitwell Purple, 50, 166
zonatus Kotschyanus, 50, 166
Cross Leaved Heather, *see* Erica Tetralix
Cupressus Lawsoniana Elwoodii, *see* Chamaecyparis Lawsoniana Elwoodii
Cutting frame, 280–3, 296
Cutting sand, 286
Cuttings, 283–95
heel, 293
leaf, 248, 293
miniature, 292–3
open-ground, 279–80, 285
pan system, 293
pre-flowering, 291
root, 225, 293
soft-wooded, 283–8
Cyclamen, 179–81
coum, 41, 56, 179

Index

Cyclamen, coum album, 41, 56, 179
europaeum, 41, 56, 179
hederaefolium, *see* C. neapolitanum album
neapolitanum, 41, 56, 129, 179, 180, 181
neapolitanum album, 41, 56, 129, 179
rapandum, 41, 56, 179
Cymbalaria, *see* Linaria

Daffodil, *see* Narcissus
Damping-off, 305
Delphinium, 29–30, 181–2, 290, 293
cinerea, *see* D. sinense cinerea
grandiflorum var. sinense, *see* D. chinense
nudicaule, 26, 41, 181
nudicaule autantiacum, *see* D. nudicaule Lemon Gem
nudicaule Chamois, 181
nudicaule Lemon Gem, 181
nudicaule luteum, *see* D. nudicaule Chamois
nudicaule Pink Sensation, 181
nudicaule purpureum, 181
Ruysii, 181
chinense, 25, 41, 182
chinense cineria, 182
Dianthus, 29, 88, 182–5, 279
alpinus, 41, 129, 183–4
Allwoodii alpinus, 183
Ariel, 183
barbatus, 183
Boydii, 41, 184
caesius, 41, 77, 88, 103, 183, 185
caesius Little Jock, 42, 78, 105, 183
Crossways, 42, 78, 183
deltoides, 78, 183
deltoides Bowles variety, 78, 183
Elf, 42, 78, 183
Freynii, 42, 184
gratianopolitanus, *see* D. caesius
haematocalyx, 42, 129, 184
Highland Frazer, 78, 183
Highland Queen, 78
Jordans, 184
Jupiter, 42, 78, 129, 183

Dianthus, Mars, 25, 42, 78, 130, 183
microlepis, 42, 185
Mrs. Sinkins, 182–3
Napoleon III, 42, 78, 183
parnassicus, 26, 42, 130, 185
Spark, 42, 78, 183
Division, 278, 296
Dodecatheon, 135, 185–7
alpinum, 53, 56, 186
campestre, 186
Frenchii, 186
Hendersonii, 53, 57, 186
integrifolium, 53, 57, 186
Jeffreyi, 54, 57, 186
latilobum, 54, 57, 186
Meadia, 54, 57, 186
Meadia membranacea, *see* D. Frenchii
uniflorum, 186
Dog's Tooth Violet, *see* Erythronium
Dorset Heath, *see* Erica ciliaris
Dovedale Moss, *see* Saxifraga hypnoides
Draba, 187
Aizoon, 127, 187
Dedeana, 127, 187
pyrenaica, *see* Petrocallis pyrenaica
repens, *see* D. sibirica
sibirica, 127, 187
Dry wall, 61–88
building, 62–71
double-sided, 72
planting, 62–70, 72–3
plants, 61, 70, 72–88
soil, 73
steps, 70–1
stone, 62
upkeep, 71–3
Dwarf Thrift, *see* Armeria caespitosa

Edelweiss, *see* Leontopodium alpinum
Edraianthus, *see* Wahlenbergia (Wahlenbergia is now obsolete)
caudatus, *see* Wahlenbergia dalmatica
graminifolius, *see* Wahlenbergia
graminifolia

Index

Edraianthus, Elephant's Ears, *see* Saxifrage Bergenia
Encrusted Saxifrage, 88, 110, 252, 254, 255, *see also* Saxifraga
Eranthis hyemalis, 25, 50, 57, 167
Ereption reniforme, *see* Viola hederacea
Erica, 187–91
  alpine border, 38
  miniature cuttings, 293, 294
  soil, 142
  soil for plunge bed, 299
  carnea, 38, 42, 188, 190, 191, 293
  carnea Cecilia M. Beale, 42, 188
  carnea Eileen Porter, 25, 42, 188
  carnea Pink Beauty, 188
  carnea Queen of Spain, 42, 188
  carnea Ruby Glow, 188
  carnea Vivelli, 42, 188
  ciliaris, 189
  ciliaris Maweana, 189
  ciliaris Mrs. C. H. Gill, 52, 189
  cinerea, 188
  cinerea alba minor, 189
  cinerea coccinea, 52, 189
  cinerea pygmaea, 52, 189
  cinerea P. S. Patrick, 52, 189
  darleyensis, 188
  hybrida Dawn, 52, 189
  hybrida Gwen, 52, 189
  mediterranea, 188
  mediterranea hubrida, *see* E. darleyensis
  mediterranea nana, 188
  Tetralix, 189. 190
  Tetralix Prageri, 190
  vulgaris, 189, 293
  vulgaris Foxii nana, 189
  vulgaris Foxii nana floribunda, 189
  vulgaris J. H. Hamilton, 52, 190
  vulgaris minima, 52, 189
  vulgaris minima Smith's variety, 189
  vulgaris Mrs. Ronald Gray, 190
  vulgaris nana compacta, 52, 190
  vulgaris Sister Anne, 52, 190
Erinus, 191
  alpinus, 103, 130, 191
  alpinus albus, 103, 191
  alpinus Dr. Hanele, 103, 191

Erinus, alpinus Mrs. Charles Boyle, 103, 191
Erodium, 191–3
  absinthoides, 78, 192
  absinthoides amanum, 78, 192
  chamaedroides, 193
  chamaedroides roseum, 25, 42, 105, 130, 193
  cheilanthifolium, 78, 192
  chrysanthum, 78, 192
  macradenum, 78, 192
  Merstham Pink, 78, 130, 192
  Reichardii, *see* E. chamaedroides roseum
  supracanum, 79, 192
Erythraea diffusa, *see* Centaurium scilloides
Erythronium, 169, 170
  californicum, 57, 169
  Dens-canis, 57, 169
  revolutum Johnsonii, 57, 169
  revolutum Watsonii, 57, 169

Ferns, 69, 85, 118, 119, 124, 135, 193–4
Fertilisers, artificial, 141, 143
Fish, 125
Frames, *see* Alpine frame; Cutting frame
Frankenia, 99
  laevis, 194, 195
  thymifolia, 25, 51, 93, 96, 101, 130, 194–5
Fritillaria, 169
  Meleagris, 50, 169
Fumitory, *see* Corydalis lutea

Galanthus byzantinus, 50, 167
Gammaxene, 180
Gardener's compass, 71
Gentiana, 195–201
  alpine border, 25, 29, 38
  pre-flowering cuttings, 219
  seed saving, 307, 308
  seedlings, 304
  small rock garden, 116
  soil, 144
  acaulis, 28, 43, 197
  alpina, 197

Index

Gentiana, augustifolia, 43, 130, 197
  Clusii, 43, 197
  dinarica, 43, 197
  Farreri, 199, 307, 308
  gracilipes, 196
  Hascombensis, 196
  hexaphylla, 53, 135, 199
  lagodechiana, 25, 43, 130, 195, 196
  lutea, 201
  Macaulayi, 26, 43, 130, 199
  Purdomii, 197
  saxosa, 26, 43, 130, 200
  septemfida, 43, 195, 196
  sino-ornata, 28, 38, 53, 135, 198
  stevenagensis, 199
  Veitchiorum, 53, 136, 199
  verna, 43, 201
Geranium, 201–2
  cinereum subcaulescens, see G. subcaulescens
  lancastriense, 26, 43
  Pylzowianum, 202
  sanguineum, 79, 201
  sanguineum lancastriense, 79, 105, 130, 201, 202
  subcaulescens, 127, 202
  Wallichainum, 79, 201
Glory of the Bog, see Primula helodoxa
Glossary of specific names, 317–33
Gold Dust, see Alyssum
Golden Drop, see Onosma echioides; Onosma tauricum
Golden Rod, see Solidago brachystachys
Grape Hyacinth, 167
Gravel drive, 89
Greenfly, 31
Gypsophila, 144, 202–3, 290
  cerastioides, 25, 51, 101, 130, 203
  fratensis, 79, 105, 202
  paniculata, 202
  repens, 79, 202
  repens flora plena, 202
  repens rosea, 79, 202
  repens var. fratensis, see G. fratensis
  Rosey Veil, 79, 202

Hard Fern, see Blechnum Spicant
Hartstongue, see Scolopendrium vulgare
Heather, see Erica
Hebe, see Veronica
Heel cuttings, 293
Helianthemum, 203–7
  alpine bank, 14, 15, 19–22, 279
  alpine border, 38
  dry wall, 63, 71, 79, 88
  newly potted plants, 296
  soft-wooded cuttings, 283–5, 288
  soil, 146
  alpestre oblongatum, see H. alpestre serpyllifolium
  alpestre serpyllifolium, 130, 205–6
  Amy Baring, 79, 204
  Apricot, 79, 204
  Ben Afflick, 204
  Ben Alder, 204
  Ben Attow, 204
  Ben Dearg, 79, 130, 204, 205, 207
  Ben Fhada, 204
  Ben Heckla, 79, 204
  Ben Hope, 79, 204
  Ben Lawers, 204
  Ben Ledi, 19, 204
  Ben Lomond, 204
  Ben Lui, 19, 204
  Ben Mare, 204
  Ben Mohr, 204
  Ben Nevis, 79, 204
  Ben Vane, 204
  Ben Venue, 204
  Ben Vorlich, 204
  Bronze Jubilee, 205
  Butter and Eggs, 205
  Cerise Queen, 205
  Chamaecistus, 204
  Chamaecistus Brilliant, 204
  Croftianum, 204
  Firebrand, 205
  Firedragon, 205
  Firefly, 205
  Golden ball, 205
  Golden Queen, 79, 205
  Jock Scott, 205
  Jubilee, 203, 205
  Magnificence, 205

Index

Helianthemum, Marigold, 205
  Miss Mould, 205
  Mrs. Clay, 79, 205, 206
  Mrs. Earle, 203, 205
  Mrs. Moules, *see* H. Miss Mould
  nummularium, 203
  Peggy, 205
  Praecox, 205
  Rose of Leewood, 205
  Rose Queen, 80, 205
  Rubens, 205
  Salmon Queen, 80, 205
  Sudbury Gem, 205
  Supreme, 205
  Taylor's Seedling, 205
  The Bride, 205
  Tigrinum plenum, 205
  Tuberaria, 127, 135, 207
  vulgare, *see* H. nummularium
  Watergate Rose, 205, 207
  Watlands Red, 205
  Windermere, 205
  Wisley Primrose, 205
Heliosperma alpestre, *see* Silene
  alpestris
Herbaceous border, *see* Alpine border
Heron's Bill, *see* Erodium
Hippocrepis, 208
  comosa, 80, 88, 104, 208
  comosa E. R. Janes, 80, 104, 208
  Hormones, 288–91
  Horseshoe Vetch, *see* Hippocrepis
  Horticultural peat, 142
  Hortomone, 289, 290
  House Leek, *see* Sempervivum tec-
  torum
Hummingbird Flower, *see* Zausch-
  neria
Hutchinsia alpina, 57, 85, 93, 101, 208
Hypericum, 20, 65, 95, 208–9
  anagalloides, 80, 209
  balearicum, 209
  calycinum, 208
  Coris, 209
  fragile, 209
  laevetrubrum, 209
  nummularium, 130, 209
  olympicum, 80, 104, 208
  olympicum citrinum, 80, 104, 208

Hypericum, olympicum polyphyllum,
  80, 104
  orientale, 209
  polyphyllum, 209
  reptans, 26, 43, 209
  rhodopeum, 80, 209
  sanguineum nummularium, 43
Hypsela, 261
  longiflora, 26, 51, 96, 101, 130, 210

Iberis, 210–11
  gibraltarica, 80, 210
  saxatilis, 43, 130, 211
  sempervirens, 80, 211
  sempervirens Little Gem, 43, 211
  taurica, 43, 131, 211
Inula acaulis, 26, 43, 131, 211
  ensifolia, 211–12
Ipheion uniflorum, *see* Borodiæa uniflora caerulea
Iris, 170, 212–14
  Chamaeiris, 43, 212
  Chamaeiris Campbelli, 212
  cristata, 44, 214
  Forrestii, 54, 212
  Kaempferi, 212
  lacustris, 25, 44, 131, 213–14
  mellita, 44, 131, 213
  minuta, 44, 213
  pumila, 212, 213
  pumila alba, 212
  pumila atroviolacea, 44, 212
  pumila azurea, 212
  pumila lutea, 44, 212
  minuto aurea, *see* I. minuta
  Reichenbachii, 212
  reticulata, 25, 50, 167
  reticulata Hercules, 50, 167
  reticulata J. S. Dijt, 50, 167
  reticulata Krelagei, 167
  rubromarginata, *see* I. mellita
  ruthenica, 54, 135, 212
  sibirica, 212

Japanese Iris, *see* Iris Kaempferi
Jasminum Parkeri, 44, 214
John Innes Compost, 27, 32, 138, 145
Juniperus communis compressa, 176,
  177

341

Index

Juniperus Sabina tamariscifolia, 177

Kabschia Saxifrage, 29, 252–3, 255, 256, 293, 294, 295, *see also* Saxifraga
Kenilworth, Ivy, *see* Linaria Cymbalaria
Kew, ravine garden, 111
Kidney Vetch, *see* Anthyllis
Kneiffa pumila, *see* Oenothera pumila riparia, *see* Oenothera riparia

Labels, 30–1, 286
Lady's Fingers, *see* Anthyllis Vulneraria
Latin names, 311–33
Leaf cuttings, 248, 293
Leafmould, 141, 142
Leontopodium alpinum, 127, 214
Limestone, 109–11
Linaria, 215–16
  aequitriloba, 57, 101, 216
  alpina, 44, 72, 80, 88, 104, 131, 215
  alpina rosea, 44, 80, 88, 104, 215
  Cymbalaria, 85, 215
  faucicola, 44, 80, 88, 104, 215
  globosa rosea, 44, 131, 215
  hepaticifolia, 57, 101, 216
  supina, 215
Ling, *see* Erica
Linum, 216–18
  alpinum, 80, 216, 294
  arboreum, 44, 217
  capitatum, 217
  flavum, 44, 217
  gentianoides, 216
  monogynum, 217
  narbonense, 216
  perenne, 216
  salsoloides alpinum var. alpinium, *see* L. salsoloides nanum
  salsoloides nanum, 25, 44, 105, 131, 217, 294
Lithospermum, 126, 218–221, 289, 290, 291, *see also* Moltkia
  diffusum Heavenly Blue, 38, 53, 73, 136, 144, 218
  diffusum 'Grace Ward', 219
  graminifolium, 44, 80, 105, 131, 220

Lithospermum, intermedium, 44, 80, 105, 220–1
Loam, 141
Lomaria alpina, *see* Blechnum penna marina
London Pride, *see* Saxifraga umbrosa var. primuloides
Lychnis, 221–2
  alpina, 221
  chalcedonica, 221
  Haageana, 221
  Lagascae, 88, 221

Maidenhair Spleenwort, *see* Asplenium Trichomanes
Mazus, 93, 222
  Pumilio, 26, 51, 57, 102, 222
  reptans, 57, 102, 222
Megapterium missourense, *see* Oenothera missourensis
Milla uniflora, 168
Millfoil, *see* Achillea Lewisii
Mimulus, 69, 104, 124, 135, 222–3
  Bees' Dazzler, 54, 85, 223
  Chelsea Pensioner, 54, 85, 223
  cupreus, 223
  Dainty, 54, 85, 96, 223
  luteus, 223
  moschatus, 223
  Plymtree, 54, 85, 96, 223
  Prince Bismark, 54, 85, 223
  Whitecroft Scarlet, 54, 85, 96, 104, 131, 223
Miniature Columbine, *see* Aquilegia pyrenaica
Miniature Roses, 290, *see also* Rosa
Minuartia, *see* Arenaria
  verna caespitosa, *see* Arenaria caespitosa
Moltkia, 220, *see also* Lithospermum
  intermedia, *see* Lithospermum intermedium
  suffruticosa, *see* Lithospermum graminifolium
Morisia, hypogaea, 25, 44, 131, 224–6, 293
  monantha, *see* M. hypogaea
Moss, on seedlings, 305

Index

Mossy Saxifrage, 65, 253, 257, *see also*, Saxifraga
Municipal compost, 143
Muscari azureum, 50, 167
Musk, *see* Mimulus

Narcissus, 166, 170
asturiensis, *see* N. minimus
Bulbocodium, 50, 166
cyclamineus, 50, 166
juncifolius, 51, 166
minimus, 166
nanus, 25, 51, 166, 169
Nepeta, 226–7
Faassenii, 226
Mussinii, 81, 226, 279
New Zealand Burr, *see* Acaena
Nierembergia caerulea, 227
frutescens, 227
hippomanica, *see* N. caerulea
repens, *see* N. rivularis
rivularis, 51, 102, 227

Oenothera, 227–8
macrocarpa, *see* O. missourensis
missourensis, 81, 228
perennis, *see* O. pumila
pumila, 25, 45, 81, 104, 131, 228
pusilla, *see* O. pumila
riparia, 81, 227–8
tetragona, 228
Omphalodes cappadocica, 57, 85, 88, 229
Luciliae, 229
verna, 57, 85, 88, 229
verna alba, 85
Onosma, 229–30
albo-pilosum, *see* O. albo-roesum
albo-roseum, 81, 230
echioides, 81, 229
tauricum, 81, 229
Open-ground propagation, 278–80, 285
Organic manures, 143
Ourisia coccinea, 54, 58, 135, 230–1
elegans, *see* O. coccinea
Outcrop rock garden, *see* Small rock garden

Paederota Ageria, *see* Veronica lutea

Paederota Egeria, *see* Veronica lutea
Pale Maiden, *see* Sisyrinchium fili-folium
Pans, seed, 300–2
Paving, 94–7
Peat, 142
Penstemon, 231–2
confertus, 45, 231
heterophyllus, 26, 45, 81, 231–2
heterophyllus 'True Blue', 231
Newberryi var. rupicola, *see* P. rupicola
Roezlii, 29, *see also* P. rupicola
rupicola, 26, 45, 131, 231
Scouleri, 45, 231
Six Hills, 231
Weald Beacon, 45, 231
Perennial Candytuft, *see* Iberis
Perennial Flax, *see* Linum
Pests, 31, 305
Petrocallis pyrenaica, 127, 131, 144, 232, 256, 297
Petrocoptis Lagascae, *see* Lychnis Lagascae
Phlox, 232–6
alpine bank, 20, 21
alpine border, 38
dry wall, 63
newly potted plants, 296
soil layering, 20, 232, 279, 293
adsurgens, 235
amoena, 25, 131, 235
amoena rosea, 45, 235
bifida, 45, 131, 234
divaricata, 235
divaricata Laphamii, 235
Douglasii Beauty of Ronsdorf, 45, 234
Douglasii Boothman's Variety, 45, 131, 234
Douglasii Eva, 45, 131, 234
Douglasii hybrids, 88, 105, 233–4
Douglasii Lilac Queen, 45, 81, 132, 234
Douglasii Mabel, *see* P. Douglasii Lilac Queen
Douglasii rosea, 81, 234, *see also* P. Douglasii Rose Queen
Douglasii Rose Queen, 45, 234

343

Index

Phlox mesoleuca, *see* P. nana ensifolia
nana ensifolia, 235
pilosa, 235
procumbens, 45, 81, 235
reptans, *see* P. stolonifera
stolonifera, 45, 234–5
stolonifera Blye Ridge, 45, 235
subulata, 20, 88, 232–3
subulata Apple Blossom, 81, 233
subulata atropurpurea, 233
subulata Betty, 81, 233
subulata Brightness, 81, 132, 233
subulata Camlaensis, 233
subulata Camla Var. *see* P. subulata Camlaensis
subulata Eventide, 81, 233
subulata Fairy, 81, 233
subulata G. F. Wilson, 20, 81, 233
subulata Margery, 82, 233
subulata May Snow, 82, 132, 233
subulata Moerheimii, 82, 233
sublata Nelsoni, 82, 233
subulata Sampson, 82, 132, 233
subulata Sensation, *see* P. subulata Vivid
subulata Snow Queen, *see* P. subulata May Snow
subulata Temiscaming, 82, 132, 233
subulata Vivid, 233
Temiscaming, 20
verna, *see* P. stolonifera
Phyllitis Scolopendrium, *see* Scolopendrium vulgare
Plunge beds, 298–300
Polygala, 236–7
calcarea, 26, 45, 132, 236
Chamaebuxus, 46, 132, 236
Chamaebuxus grandiflora, *see* P. Chamaebuxus purpurea
Chamaebuxus purpurea, 26, 46, 132, 236
Chamabuxus var. rhodoptera, 237
paucifolia, 53, 237
Vayredae, 53, 237
Polygonum, 126, 237–8
affine, 58, 84, 238
affine Darjeeling Red, 238
vacciniifolium, 21, 63, 82, 88, 237, 279
Potentilla, 238–40

Potentilla, alba, 82, 105, 238
ambigua, 238
argyrophylla, 240
argyrophylla Gibson's Scarlet, 82, 240
argyrophylla Hamlet, 82, 240
argyrophylla Monsieur Rouillard, 82, 240
argyrophylla William Rollinson, 82, 240
argyrophylla Yellow Queen, 82, 240
aurea, 238
cuneata, 238
fragiformis, 82, 239
megalantha, 239
nepalensis, 82, 239
nepalensis Miss Willmott, 82, 239
nepalensis Roxana, 82, 239
nitida, 238
rupestris, 83, 239
Tonguei, 83, 239
verna nana, 25, 51, 105, 132, 238, 239
Potting, 296–8
Pre-flowering cuttings, 291
Pricking out, 306
Primula, 240–7
corner, construction and planting, 31–7, 90, 119
dry wall, foot of, 69
pricking out, 306
seed saving, 307
alpicola, 54, 240, 246
alpicola alba, 246
alpicola violacea, 54, 246
altaica grandiflora, 86, 243
Asthore, 54, 246
aurantiaca, 54, 246
Beesiana, 54, 246
Betty Green, 86, 242
Bonaccord Lavender, 244
Bonaccord Purity, 244
Bulleyana, 55, 246
capitata, 46, 240
capitata Mooreana, 132, 242
Clarkei, 46, 132, 241
David Green, 86, 242
denticulata, 55, 58, 135, 137, 244, 245, 293
denticulata alba, 55, 58, 244

Index

Primula, denticulata Ascot Red, 55, 58, 244
denticulata Hay's variety, 55, 58, 244
denticulata rosea, 243
E. R. Janes, 86, 242–3
farinosa, 46, 241
Florindae, 55, 240, 246
frondosa, 46, 242
Garryarde Guinevere, 243
helodoxa, 55, 245
involucrata, 46, 240, 242
japonica, 33, 55, 244
japonica Millers Crimson, 55, 244
japonica Postford White, 55, 244
Juliana altaica grandiflora, 58
Juliana Betty Green, 58
Juliana Bonaccord Lavender, 58
Juliana Bonaccord purity, 58
Juliana David Green, 58
Juliana E. R. Janes, 58
Juliana Carryarde Guinevere, 58
Juliana Lady Greer, 58
Juliana Marie Crouse, 59
Juliana Mrs. J. H. Wilson, 58
Juliana Our Pat, 59
Juliana Quaker Bonnet, 59
Juliana Red Paddy, 59
Juliana Romeo, 58
Lady Greer, 243
Marie Crouse, 244
marginata, 241
marginata Linda Pope, 241
marginata rosea, 241
microdonta, see P. alpicola
minima, 240
Mrs. J. H. Wilson, 243
Our Pat, 244
pubescens, 46, 240
pubescens Faldonside, 46, 132, 240
pubescens Mrs. J. H. Wilson, 46, 132, 240
pubescens The General, 46, 241
pulverulenta, 55, 244, 245
pulverulenta Bartley Strain, 55, 245
pulverulenta Red Hugh, 55, 245
Quaker Bonnet, 244
Red Paddy, 244
Romeo, 86, 243
rosea grandiflora, 26, 46, 132, 242

Primula, secundiflora, 55, 246, 247
sikkimensis, 55, 240, 246
sikkimensis var. alpicola, see P. alpicola
Snow Queen, 86, 243
Waltoni, 55, 246–7
Wanda, 58, 86, 88, 242
Wilsoni, 55, 245
Propagating alpines, 278–309
alpine frame, 295–6
cloches, 279, 280, 296, 305
cutting frame, 280–3, 296
cuttings, 283–95
division, 278, 296
open-ground propagation, 278–80, 285
plunge beds, 298–300
potting, 296–8
rooting hormones, 288–91
seeds and seedlings, 300–9
soil layering, 20, 232, 279, 293
Pterocephalus, 247–8
Parnassi, 247
perennis, 247
perennis Parnassi, 83, 104, 247
Ptilotrichum spinosum, see Alyssum spinosum
spinosum roseum, see Alyssum spinosum roseum

Ramonda, 137, 248–9, 293, 303, 304
Myconi, 83, 86, 132, 248, 249
Myconi alba, 86, 248
Myconi rosea, 86, 132, 248
Nathaliae, 86, 248
pyrenaica, see R. Myconi
serbica, 248
Ravine garden, Kew, 111
Redshank, see Polygonum
Rhododendron, 142, 249–50, 304
campylogynum, 53, 250
ferrugineum, 46, 132, 249
imperator, 53, 250
indicum var. balsaminaeflorum, see Azalea roseaflorum fl. pl.
keleticum, 53, 250
radicans, 53, 250
Rock, 109–13, see also Stone

Rock Candytuft, *see* Aethionema grandiflorum
Rock Cress, *see* Aubrieta
Rock garden, small, *see* Small rock garden
Rock Jasmine, *see* Androsace lanuginosa
Rock Millfoil, *see* Achillea
Rock garden, list of plants, 127, 129–36
Root cuttings, 225, 293
Rosa, 29, 251
  chinensis minima, *see* R. Rouletti
  gallica Little Dot, 46, 251
  gallica var. pumila, *see* R. pumila
  Lawranceana, 251
  Maid Marion, 46
  Oakington Ruby, 25, 46, 133, 251
  Peon, 46, 251
  pumila, 26, 47, 133, 251
  Roulettii, 47, 251
Rose of Sharon, *see* Hypericum calycinum
Rostrothe Alpenrose, *see* Rhododendron
Rouen Pansy, *see* Viola rothomagensis
Rusty Back, *see* Ceterach officinarum

St. John's Wort, 209
Sagina, *see* Arenaria
  glabra, *see* Arenaria caespitosa
Sand, for cuttings, 286
Sandstone, 111, 118
Sandwort, *see* Arenaria
Saponaria, 251–2, 256
  Boissieri, 127, 252
  caespitosa, 252
  lutea, 252
  ocymoides, 83, 251, 252
  ocymoides alba, 83, 252
  ocymoides splendens, 83, 252
  ocymoides var. rubra compacta, 252
Saxifraga, 252–8, 297
  Aizoon, 83, 254
  Aizoon baldensis, 47, 133, 254
  Aizoon lutea, 83, 254
  Aizoon minutifolia, *see* S. Aizoon baldensis

Saxifraga, Aizoon rosea, 83, 254
  apiculata, 257
  apiculata alba, 257
  Aubrey Pritchard, 256
  Bergenia, 253
  Borisii, 257
  Boston Spa, 257
  Burseriana, 133, 256
  Burseriana Gloria, 47, 256
  Burseriana His Majesty, 47, 256
  Burseriana sulphurea, 47, 256
  callosa, *see* S. lingulata
  cochlearis minor, 254
  Cotyledon, 254
  Cotyledon caterhamensis, 83, 254
  Cotyledon pyramidalis, 254–5
  C. M. Pritchard, 256
  Cranbourne, 256
  Elizabethae, 86, 105, 133, 257
  Esther, 254
  Faldonside, 127, 133, 256, 257
  Haagii, 257
  hypnoides, 88, 105, 258
  hypnoides James Brenner, 59, 258
  hypnoides Kingii, 59, 86, 258
  hypnoides Peter Pan, 59, 86, 258
  hypnoides Pixie, 59, 258
  hypnoides Stormonth's Variety, 59, 258
  Irvingii, 47, 133, 255, 257
  lingulata, 83, 255
  longifolia, 127, 255
  longifolia Tumbling Waters, 255
  longifolia var. Symonds Jeune, 255
  longifolia Walpoles var., 255
  Megasea, *see* S. Bergenia
  moschata, 88, 105, 257–8
  moschata Carnival, 59, 258
  moschata General Joffre, 59, 86, 258
  moschata Mrs. Piper, 59, 86, 258
  moschata Pompadour, 59, 86, 258
  moschata Sir Douglas Haig, 59, 87, 258
  moschata Triumph, 59, 87, 258
  oppositifolia, 47, 133, 253
  oppositifolia alba, 253
  oppositifolia coccinea, 47, 253
  oppositifolia grandiflora, 253
  oppositifolia latina, 47, 253

Index

Saxifraga, oppositifolia major, *see* S. oppositifolia grandiflora
oppositifolia splendens, 25, 47, 253
Primulaize, 47, 133, 254
umbrosa var. primuloides, 59, 86, 88, 254
Scabiosa Pterocephalus, *see* Pterocephalus perennis Parnassi
Scale Fern, *see* Ceterach officinarum
Scaly Spleenwort, *see* Ceterach officinarum
Scolopendrium vulgare, 194
Scotch Heather, *see* Erica cinerea
Sea Campion, *see* Silene maritima
Sea Heath, *see* Frankenia laevis
Sea Pink, 161
  see Armeria
Sedum, 258–61
  alpine bank, 21
  alpine border, 27
  alpine path, 95, 96
  dry wall, 62, 88
  newly potted plants, 296
  rock garden, 110
  acre, 21
  album murale, 102, 259
  bithynicum, *see* S. hispanicum minus
  coeruleum
  dasyphyllum, 51, 102, 133, 258
  hispanicum, 51
  hispanicum aureus, 258
  hispanicum minus, 102, 133, 258
  Hobsonii, 261
  humifusum, 261
  kamtschaticum, 47, 83, 133, 259
  kamtschaticum variegatum, 259
  lydium, 52, 102, 133, 258
  murale, *see* S. album murale
  oppositifolium, *see* Umbilicus oppositifolius
  rupestre, 21, 83, 259
  sexangulare, 52, 102, 259
  spathulifolium, 47, 83, 259
  spathulifolium purpureum, 259
  spathulifolium var. capablanca, 259
  spurium, 21, 47, 83, 259
  spurium Schorbuser Blut., 47, 84, 105, 133, 259

Sedum, spurium splendens, 47, 83, 259
  spinosum, 261
  Stahlii, 261
  Winkleri, 261
Seedboxes, 300–2
Seed pans, 300–2
Seed-raising systems, 302–4
Seed saving, 306–9
Seedlings, 300, 304–6
Selliera, 261
  radicans, 26, 52, 59, 102, 103, 133, 260, 261
Sempervivum, 110, 127, 261–2
  arachnoideum, 133, 261
  arachnoideum Stansfieldii, 261
  arachnoideum tomentosum, 261
  tectorum, 133, 261, 262
  tectorum calcareum, 262
  tectorum glaucum, 262
  triste, *see* S. tectorum
Seradix 'B', 289
Serratula, 262
  nudicaulis, *see* S. Shawii
  Shawii, 25, 48, 134, 262
Shooting Stars, 186
Sikkim Cowslip, *see* Primula sikkimensis
Silene, 256, 263–4
  acualis, 263
  acaulis Elliotts Variety, 264
  acaulis exscapa, 263
  alpestris, 263
  maritima, 263
  maritima rosea, 263
  Schafta, 134, 263
Sisyrinchium, 137, 264–5
  augustifolium, 48, 264
  bellum, 48, 135, 264
  bermudianum, 48, 264
  Douglasii, 53, 264
  Douglasii album, 53, 265
  filifolium, 53, 265
  grandiflorum, *see* S. Douglasii
Slope, construction, 92
Slugs, 31, 181, 305
Small rock garden, 106–37
  building, 113–16
  Fish, 125
  Flat site, 116–17

347

Index

Small rock garden, planting, 126, 128
Small plants, 127, 129–37
  pool garden, 117–19
  rock, 109–13
  site, 108–9
  water-carved outcrop, 117–19
  water garden, 119–21, 123
  water plants, 125
  waterfall rock garden, 121–6
Snow in Summer, *see* Cerastium
Snowdrop, 167
Soft-wooded cuttings, 283–8
Soil layering, 20, 232, 279, 293
Soils, *see* Alpine soils
Solidago, 265
  brachystachys, 26, 48, 84, 134, 265
  Virgaurea, *see* S. brachystachys
Specific names, glossary, 317–33
Spider plant, *see* Sempervivum
  arachnoideum
Spiraea, *see* Astilbe
Stachys, 99, 266
  corsica, 102, 266
Sternbergia lutea, 51, 168
Stimcut, 290
Stone, 90, 91, *see also* Rock
Stonecrop, *see* Sedum acre
Sun Rose, *see* Helianthemum

Thrift, 65, *see also* Armeria
Thyme, *see* Thymus
Thyme Lawn, 99, 268
Thymus, 93, 96, 266–8
  azoricus, *see* T. caespititius
  caespititius, 267
  carnosus, 48, 266
  citriodorus, 266
  citriodorus aureus, 266
  citriodorus argenteus, 266
  citriodorus Silver Queen, 266
  Doerfleri, 84, 267
  Herba-barona, 267
  hirsutus Doerfleri, *see* T. Doerfleri
  lanuginosus, 84, 267
  lanuginosus floribundus, 84
  micans, *see* T. Herba-barona
  nitidus, 48, 266
  nummularius, 102, 268
  pseudolanuginosus floribundus, 267

Thymus, pseudolanuginosus, *see* T.
  lanuginosus
  Serpyllum, 99, 102, 267, 268
  Serpyllum albus, 102, 134, 268
  Serpyllum Annie Hall, 102, 268
  Serpyllum aureus, 102, 268
  Serpyllum carmineus, 102, 134, 268
  Serpyllum coccineus, 102, 134, 268
  Serpyllum major, 25, 52, 84, 103,
    134, 268
  Serpyllum nummularius, *see* T.
    nummularius
  Serpyllum Pink Chintz, 103, 268
  Serpyllum superbus, *see* T. Serpyl-
    lum major
  vulgaris, 266
Triteleia, 168
  uniflora, 26, 51, 168, 170
  uniflora caerulea, 168
  uniflora violacea, 51, 168
Tulipa, 167, 170
  dasystemon, *see* T. tarda
  praestans var. Tubergen, 51, 167
  tarda, 51, 167, 170
Twelve Apostles, *see* Campanula
  glomerata

Umbilicus, 269
  oppositifolius, 26, 48, 84, 134, 269

Veronica, 20, 269–72
  Allionii, 48, 271
  armena, 84, 134, 270
  Bonarota, 48, 270
  catarractae, 271
  cuppressoides, 271
  filiformis, 271
  fruticans, 271
  lutea, 48, 270
  pectinata, 84, 270
  pectinata rosea, 84, 270
  prostrata, 20, 269
  pyroliformis, 48, 134, 270
  repens, 103, 270
  rupestris, 20, 63, 84, 88, 269, 279
  rupestris alba, 270
  rupestris Mrs. Holt, 84, 134, 269
  rupestris rosea, 84, 269
  satureioides, 48, 271

Index

Veronica, saxatilis, 48, 134, 271
  spicata nana, 48, 271
  teucrinum dubia, *see* V. rupestris
Viola, 272–4
  aetolica saxatilis, *see* V. saxatilis
    aetolica
  arenaria rosea, 48, 104, 272–3
  biflora, 49, 273
  Bluestone, 272
  bosniaca, *see* V. elegantula
  Chantryland, 272
  conspersa, 274
  cornuta minor, 49, 134, 272
  elegantula, 49, 272
  hederacea, 49, 273
  hispida, *see* V. rothamgensis
  Reichenbachiana, *see* V. arenaria
    rosea
  rothamgensis, 134, 272
  saxatilis aetolica, 48, 272
  sylvestris rosea, *see* V. arenaria
    rosea
Viscaria alpina, *see* Lychnis alpina

Wahlenbergia, 275–6
  dalmatica, 49, 275

Wahlenbergia, dinarica, 49, 134, 275
  graminifolia, 49, 275
  pumilio, 49, 134, 275, 276
  serpyllifolia major, 49, 134, 275,
    276, 292
Waldsteinia, 276
  fragarioides, 60, 87, 276
  siberica, *see* W. trifolia
  tenata, *see* W. trifolia
  trifolia, 60, 276
Warley Rose, *see* Aethionema
Water, use in rock garden, *see* Small
    rock garden
Water plants, 125
Waterside, list of plants, 127, 135
Weed-killer, 17, 18, 90, 94, 95
Weeds, 16, 17, 18, 299, 300
White Rocket, *see* Arabis
Winter Aconite, *see* Eranthis hye-
    malis
Woodland Crocus, *see* Gentiana
    saxosa
Woodlice, 181

Zauschneria, 68, 276–7
  californica, 84, 135, 276–7